"This book is a road map of pathways to pursue and pitfalls to avoid in handling Scripture. D. A. Carson would be the first to agree that God himself upholds his written word, the Bible. But God uses means. In recent decades, Carson's voice has been among the most forthright, consistent, rigorous, faithful, and compelling in serving the vital divine end of testifying to Scripture's veracity. This book guides readers to the priceless destination of confidence in God's Word through refutation of its critics and commendation of its truth."

Robert W. Yarbrough, Professor of New Testament,
New Testament Department Chair, Trinity Evangelical Divinity School

"As a young theological student I wrestled with the authority and inerrancy of Scripture. No one helped me more to understand what Scripture teaches about itself than D. A. Carson. His insightful essays and incisive reviews preserved and shaped my doctrine of Scripture. I rejoice to see some of those older essays (along with some new essays and reviews) presented together in one place in this volume, for the issues of yesterday are not dramatically different from what we face today, and Carson's words continue to speak powerfully to our contemporary situation. Fidelity to Scripture and rigorous reasoning mark this volume, reminding us that the words of Scripture are the very words of God."

Thomas R. Schreiner, James Buchanan Harrison
Professor of New Testament Interpretation, The Southern Baptist Theological Seminary

"D. A. Carson is one of the most prolific and profound biblical scholars of our generation. Perhaps it is not far-fetched to predict that his *Collected Writings on Scripture* will become a classic as an evangelical defense of Holy Scripture's authority. Carson courteously but persuasively reveals the weaknesses of arguments designed by critics to discredit or render obsolete the historic teaching of the Western Christian churches, namely, biblical inerrancy. This book is a masterful 'must read' for those persons who want to understand better the nature of Scripture's authority. The volume may very well take its place as a benchmark study, side by side with *Inspiration* (1881), the influential essay penned by A. A. Hodge and B. B. Warfield."

John D. Woodbridge, Research Professor of Church History
and Christian Thought, Trinity Evangelical Divinity School

"The breadth of these essays is matched by their depth. When reading Carson's survey of the scholarly landscape, you know it's coming from a leading member of the guild; when reading his discerning counsel about how to navigate both spurious and legitimate challenges concerning the nature, authority, and interpretation of Scripture, you know it's coming from a pastoral heart. This is pure gold."

Michael Horton, J. Gresham Machen Professor of Systematic Theology
and Apologetics, Westminster Seminary California

"D. A. Carson is for this generation what B. B. Warfield was for his—the scholarly stalwart for the doctrine of Scripture, possessed of prodigious skills both as an interpreter of Scripture and as a biblical and systematic theologian, critically engaging the most significant arguments of the day and upholding the historic position of the Christian church and the Bible's own self-attestation. Everything that comes from his pen is worthy of careful attention. Given the current state of the doctrine of Scripture (in theory and practice) in evangelical academia, this is an important and timely volume. Seminarians and pastors alike need to be abreast of present trends in this vital subject. The classic essays and critical reviews in this book offer a bird's-eye view of the past thirty years of the discussion, as well as world-class scholarship and discernment in articulating rejoinders to sub-biblical theories while positively presenting a faithful view of the inspiration and authority of the Scriptures and their entailments."

Ligon Duncan, Senior Minister, First Presbyterian Church, Jackson, Mississippi;
President, Alliance of Confessing Evangelicals

"With tedious regularity, the doctrine of Scripture comes under attack again and again, and while many of the arguments used are familiar and hackneyed, each generation adds its own twists and turns to the cries of criticism. Thankfully, the church has always had eloquent defenders of the truthfulness of the Scriptures and of the God who inspired them. In our time, Don Carson is one such figure; and in this volume, the reader will find many of his most significant essays on Scripture. Scholarly, reverent, carefully argued, and generously footnoted, these pieces all make important contributions to current debates; and taken as a whole, they admirably expose the problems of the revisionism offered by certain voices within the church while pointing readers to a better way."

Carl Trueman, Academic Dean and Vice President,
Westminster Theological Seminary

"The Bible is both true and precious to the Christian, as the psalmist reminds us: 'Your commands are my delight. Your statutes are forever right' (Ps. 119:143–44). In this wide-ranging set of essays, D. A. Carson reminds us of these two most important facts. Combining remarkable erudition and keen insight with pastoral sensitivity and an emphasis on the value of Scripture for Christian living, Carson impresses upon us that the Bible is the true word of God and that it is the delight of a believer in Christ. Pastors and church leaders will benefit—both intellectually and spiritually—from digesting these essays. Read them, for your good and for the good of Christ's church."

Shawn D. Wright, Associate Professor of Church History,
The Southern Baptist Theological Seminary

"I've always admired Don Carson's ability to minister so effectively in two different worlds. On the one hand, he's one of the sharpest-thinking, best-respected minds in the realm of New Testament scholarship. On the other, he's one of the clearest, most down-to-earth preachers I've ever heard. He simply has a remarkable ability both to grasp and to communicate complex issues understandably. This collection is a classic demonstration of that ability."

Donald S. Whitney, Professor of Biblical Spirituality and Senior Associate Dean,
The Southern Baptist Theological Seminary

"I have read some of these pieces before in other formats, but they are all excellent and worthily reproduced in one easily accessible volume. The article on N. T. Wright's view of Scripture is worth the price of the whole. Carson displays eminently his characteristics of intellectual insight and graceful poise, matched with a forensic surgical skill at identifying the weaknesses of those with whom he disagrees. Coming from one of the preeminent evangelical biblical scholars of his generation, Carson's thoughts on Scripture repay study, reflection, and modeling. The church is the better for his work. Not only are our minds filled when reading this book, but our hearts are moved to worship as a God-centered approach bleeds through every page."

Josh Moody, Senior Pastor, College Church, Wheaton, Illinois;
author, *Authentic Spirituality: Finding God without Losing Your Mind*

COLLECTED WRITINGS ON
SCRIPTURE

Other Crossway books by D. A. Carson

COLLECTED WRITINGS ON
SCRIPTURE

D. A. CARSON

Compiled by Andrew David Naselli

 CROSSWAY

WHEATON, ILLINOIS

Collected Writings on Scripture
Copyright © 2010 by D. A. Carson
Published by Crossway
        1300 Crescent Street
        Wheaton, Illinois 60187

Cover design: Studio Gearbox
Cover artwork: Photos.com
Interior design and typesetting: Lakeside Design Plus
First printing 2010
Printed in the United States of America

Unless otherwise indicated, Scripture quotations are taken from the HOLY BIBLE, NEW INTERNATIONAL VERSION®. Copyright © 1973, 1978, 1984 Biblica. Used by permission of Zondervan. All rights reserved. The "NIV" and "New International Version" trademarks are registered in the United States Patent and Trademark Office by Biblica. Use of either trademark requires the permission of Biblica.

All emphases in Scripture quotations have been added by the author.

Hardcover ISBN: 978-1-4335-1441-8
PDF ISBN: 978-1-4335-2566-7
Mobipocket ISBN: 978-1-4335-2564-3
ePub ISBN: 978-1-4335-2565-0

Library of Congress Cataloging-in-Publication Data
Carson, D. A.
    Collected writings on Scripture / D. A. Carson ; compiled by Andrew David Naselli.
        p. cm.
    Includes bibliographical references and indexes.
    ISBN 978-1-4335-1441-8 (hc)
    1. Bible—Criticism, interpretation, etc. I. Naselli, Andrew David. II. Title.

BS511.3.C375 2010
220.601—dc22
                                                            2009047834
Crossway is a publishing ministry of Good News Publishers.

SH   21   20   19   18   17   16   15   14   13   12   11
14   13   12   11   10   9   8   7   6   5   4   3   2

Contents

Preface

Over the last three decades I have written a number of essays and edited two or three books dealing with the nature of Scripture. One of the effects of getting older, I suppose, is that colleagues sometimes suggest that some of what one has written earlier be gathered together in useful collections. In this case the guilty parties are primarily Mark Dever and Tom Schreiner, who independently pressed me to gather into one place some of this material on the nature of the Bible and how to interpret it. The result is this book.

The material is quite diverse. The first essay, "Approaching the Bible," was first written as the lead piece for a new edition of the *New Bible Commentary*. It does not aim to be groundbreaking or adventuresome, but to spell out for those who might use the *Commentary* how Christians ought to think about the Bible and interpret it as they study Scripture and any commentary upon it. My slant is broadly confessional, and the overview may help some who are just getting started in serious study of Scripture.

The next three essays are of a more technical nature (nevertheless the text is pretty accessible, if not the footnotes). All three appeared in either *Scripture and Truth* (1983) or in *Hermeneutics, Authority, and Canon* (1986), two volumes that John Woodbridge and I edited a quarter of a century ago. Pulling out my three contributions to those volumes is dictated by the desire to group my scribbles on this subject in one place, but I must insist that there are numerous essays in those two books that are still worth reading today, even if discussion has in some cases eclipsed them. The three essays reprinted here have very different aims. "Recent Developments in the Doctrine of Scripture" surveys trends in how Scripture was viewed and handled during the two or three decades prior to the publication of the piece in 1986, so inevitably the discussion is dated. Yet it is worth including here for two reasons: first, many younger students focus almost exclusively on recent literature and lose sight of how many discussions from earlier times ought to be taken into account; and second, not a few treatments of the nature of Scripture introduce what are boldly claimed to be new insights, when in reality they are barely touched-up echoes from earlier debates. Historical perspective is never to be despised. The essay titled "Redaction Criticism: On the Legitimacy and Illegitimacy of a Literary Tool" is less significant today than it was twenty-five years ago, because the percentage of biblical scholars who use this "tool" has greatly declined. Yet the *approach* to evaluating redaction criticism as a literary tool could usefully be duplicated with respect to more recent literary tools that hold majority attention today, including narrative criticism, reader response criticism, and so forth. The other essay, "Unity and Diversity in the New Testament: The Possibility of Systematic Theology" was, when it was written, unbelievable to those who do not think one God actually stands behind the rich diversity of biblical books, and it will be equally unbelievable to similar readers now. For those who *do* hold to historic confessionalism, however, it is important to reflect constantly on the possible relationships between exegesis and systematic constructions. There is little in that essay I would change today, but in the light of more recent developments it is the merest introduction. Introductions are still needed, of course, so I have included it here. If the Lord gives me enough birthdays, I would like to write more on this topic. Some readers may want to go on to read I. Howard Marshall, *Beyond the Bible: Moving from Scripture to Theology*, including the appended interaction by Kevin J. Vanhoozer. Further, considerable attention has been paid in recent years to "theological hermeneutics," a notoriously slippery category that deserves careful and evenhanded exploration. Meanwhile my essay may help some to establish a few basic moorings.

The fifth essay, "Is the Doctrine of *Claritas Scripturae* Still Relevant Today?" was included in the Festschrift for Gerhard Maier, *Dein Wort ist die Wahrheit—Beiträge zu einer schriftgemäßen Theologie* (1997). The impact of so-called postmodern epistemology, especially in its more extreme forms, raised questions as to whether the historic Protestant stance on the perspicuity of Scripture (*claritas scripturae*) was still defensible. My more recent book, *Christ and Culture Revisited* (2008), pursues some of the same epistemological questions a little more deeply.

The review section of this book is made up of two longish review articles, each probing three books on Scripture, plus an additional three individual reviews, treating a total of nine books. These reviews are more detailed than book reviews normally are, and the reason for including them here is that some students and others are helped by listening in on a debate. In other words, to the relatively uninitiated, a new book on a topic such as the doctrine of Scripture can sound wonderfully incisive and even prophetic, but probing reviews often put its contribution (or otherwise!) into perspective and foster critical engagement.

Discussion about the nature of Scripture continues apace. Readers interested in a recent survey of developments might find helpful an essay by Robert W. Yarbrough (in the 34, no. 1 issue of *Themelios*, published online at thegospelcoalition.org). Of the numerous books on Scripture written within the last five years, the best is that of Timothy Ward, *Words of Life: Scripture as the Living and Active Word of God* (2009). I am currently working, with about thirty-five others, on a two-volume set to be published by Eerdmans in 2012. Tentatively titled *The Scripture Project*, the set aims to work through fundamental biblical, theological, historical, and philosophical issues related to the doctrine of Scripture. I would like to think of this current collection as constituting steps along the way in this broader enterprise toward a robust confessionalism on this topic.

My profound thanks go to Andy Naselli for compiling this material into one manuscript. His intelligence, industry, and cheerfulness as he undertakes tasks that demand picky attention to countless details are beyond praise. He ensured that the spelling became consistently American and that the abbreviations of sources followed *The SBL Handbook of* Style. He is responsible too for the subject and name indexes, which always make a book of this sort more useful. The essays themselves are unchanged except for minor corrections and editing to bring uniformity to the whole on matters such as capitalization, spelling and hyphenation, reference information, and headings. The place where each chapter of this book was originally published is specified at the beginning of each piece. Because several chapters first appeared in multicontributor works, the occasional cross-reference to another author or chapter in those volumes should be understood in that light. I am grateful to the various publishers for permitting use of the material in this new collection. And finally, thanks to the folk at Crossway, and especially to Allan Fisher and Jill Carter, for the efficient and courteous way they took on this project.

Abbreviations

ARG	*Archiv für Reformationsgeschichte*
AUSS	*Andrews University Seminary Studies*
Bapt.	Augustine, *De baptismo contra Donatistas* (*Baptism*)
Ber.	*Berakot*
BETS	*Bulletin of the Evangelical Theological Society*
BJRL	*Bulletin of the John Rylands University Library of Manchester*
BSac	*Bibliotheca sacra*
BTB	*Biblical Theology Bulletin*
CBQ	*Catholic Biblical Quarterly*
CCSL	Corpus Christianorum: Series Latina
CH	*Church History*
Chm	*Churchman*
Conf.	Augustine, *Confessionum libri XIII* (*Confessions*)
CSEL	Corpus scriptorum ecclesiasticorum Latinorum
Dial.	Justin Martyr, *Dialogus cum Tryphone* (*Dialogue with Trypho*)
Doctr. chr.	Augustine, *De doctrina christiana* (*Christian Instruction*)
ETR	*Études théologiques et religieuses*
ETS	Evangelical Theological Society
EQ	*Evangelical Quarterly*
ExpTim	*Expository Times*
Fund.	Augustine, *Contra epistulam Manichaei quam vocant Fundamenti* (*Against the Letter of the Manichaeans That They Call "The Basics"*)
Haer.	Irenaeus, *Adversus haereses* (*Against Heresies*)
Institutes	John Calvin, *Institutes of the Christian Religion*

Int	*Interpretation*
JBL	*Journal of Biblical Literature*
JETS	*Journal of the Evangelical Theological Society*
JSOT	*Journal for the Study of the Old Testament*
JTS	*Journal of Theological Studies*
KD	*Kerygma und Dogma*
Marc.	Tertullian, *Adversus Marcionem* (*Against Marcion*)
MTZ	*Münchener theologische Zeitschrift*
NCB	New Century Bible
NICNT	New International Commentary on the New Testament
NIGTC	New International Greek Testament Commentary
NIV	New International Version
NovTSup	Novum Testamentum Supplements
NRTh	*La nouvelle revue théologique*
NSBT	New Studies in Biblical Theology
NT	New Testament
NTD	Das Neue Testament Deutsch
NTS	*New Testament Studies*
OT	Old Testament
PG	Patrologia Graeca
PL	Patrologia Latina
Praescr.	Tertullian, *De praescriptione haereticorum* (*Prescription against Heretics*)
Presb	*Presbyterion*
Princ.	Origen, *De principiis* (First Principles)
PSB	*Princeton Seminary Bulletin*
Pud.	Tertullian, *De pudicitia* (*Modesty*)
RB	*Revue biblique*
RSV	Revised Standard Version
SBLDS	Society of Biblical Literature Dissertation Series
SJT	*Scottish Journal of Theology*
SNTSMS	Society for New Testament Studies Monograph Series
TGl	*Theologie und Glaube*
Them	*Themelios*
ThTo	*Theology Today*
TJ	*Trinity Journal*
TLZ	*Theologische Literaturzeitung*
TynBul	*Tyndale Bulletin*

USQR	*Union Seminary Quarterly Review*
Util. cred.	Augustine, *De utilitate credendi* (*The Usefulness of Believing*)
VC	*Vigiliae christianae*
WTJ	*Westminster Theological Journal*
WUNT	Wissenschaftliche Untersuchungen zum Neuen Testament
ZKG	*Zeitschrift für Kirchengeschichte*
ZTK	*Zeitschrift für Theologie und Kirche*

PART 1

ESSAYS

1

Approaching the Bible

What the Bible Is

Revelation

Biblical theology forms an organic whole. This means not only that one can approach any part of the subject by beginning at any other point of the subject (though some vantage points are certainly more helpful than others), but that to treat some element of biblical theology as if it existed in splendid isolation seriously distorts the whole picture.

On few subjects is this more obviously true than with regard to one's doctrine of Scripture. In this skeptical age it is doubtful if an articulate and coherent understanding of the nature of Scripture and how to interpret it can long be sustained where there is not at the same time a grasp of the biblical view of God, of human beings, of sin, of redemption, and of the rush of history toward its ultimate goal.

For instance, if it is true that the Bible tells us about God, not least what kind of God he is, it is no less true that unless God really is that sort of God, it is impossible to appreciate the Bible for what it is. To approach the Bible correctly it is important to know something of the God who stands behind it.

God is both transcendent (i.e., he is "above" space and time) and personal. He is the sovereign and all-powerful Creator to whom the entire universe owes its

Reprint of D. A. Carson, "Approaching the Bible," in *New Bible Commentary: 21st Century Edition*, ed. D. A. Carson, R. T. France, J. A. Motyer, and G. J. Wenham; 4th ed. (Leicester: Inter-Varsity; Downers Grove, IL: InterVarsity, 1994), 1–19.

existence, yet he is the God who graciously condescends to interact with us human beings whom he has himself formed in his own image. Because we are locked in time and space, God meets us here; he is the personal God who interacts with other persons, persons he has made to glorify him and to enjoy him forever.

In short, God has chosen to reveal himself to us, for otherwise we would know very little about him. True, his existence and power are disclosed in the created order, even though that order has been deeply scarred by human rebellion and its consequences (Gen. 3:18; Rom. 8:19–22; see Ps. 19:1–2; Rom. 1:19–20). It is also true that rather a dim image of God's moral attributes is reflected in the human conscience (Rom. 2:14–16). But this knowledge is not sufficient to lead to salvation. Moreover, human sinfulness is so ingenious that not a little energy is devoted to explaining away even such revelation as this. But in his unmeasured grace God has actively intervened in the world he made in order to reveal himself to men and women in still more powerful ways.

This was true even before the fall. God assigned certain responsibilities to the creatures whom he made in his image (itself an act of revelation), and then met with them in the garden he had made for them. When God chose Abraham, he established a covenant with him, revealing himself as *his* God (Genesis 15; 17). When he redeemed Israel from slavery, God not only conversed with Moses but displayed himself in terrifying plagues and in the thunder and lightning of Sinai. Though the whole earth is his, he chose Israel as his covenant people and made them a kingdom of priests and a holy nation (Ex. 19:5–6). To them he disclosed himself not only in spectacular displays of power but in his Torah (lit. "instruction"), which included not only detailed prescriptions for daily life but entire structures of mandated religious observance (tabernacle/temple, sacrifices, priesthood).

Throughout the period covered by the Old Testament, God revealed himself in providence (e.g., the arrangements that brought Joseph to Egypt, Genesis 37–50; 50:19–20; sleeplessness on a certain night in the life of Xerxes, Est. 6:1ff.; the decrees of Cyrus and Darius that effected the return of some Hebrews to Jerusalem after the exile), in miraculous events (e.g., the burning bush, Exodus 3; the fire at Mount Carmel, 1 Kings 18), in prophetic words (the "word of the LORD" repeatedly "comes" to the prophets), in poetry and songs (e.g., Psalms). But even while Old Testament believers knew that God had disclosed himself to his covenant people, they were aware that he had promised more definitive revelation in the future. God promised a time when a new shoot would emerge from David's line (Isa. 11), a man who would sit on David's throne but who would, nevertheless, be called the Mighty God, the Everlasting Father, the Prince of Peace (Isa. 9). God himself would come down and usher in a new heaven and a new earth (Isaiah 65). He would pour out his Spirit (Joel 2), introduce a new covenant (Jeremiah 31; Ezekiel 36), raise the dead (Ezekiel 37), and much more.

The New Testament writers are convinced that the long-awaited self-disclosure of God and his salvation have been brought near in Jesus Christ, God's Son. In the past God had revealed himself primarily through the prophets, but now in these last days he has revealed himself supremely and climactically in the Son (Heb. 1:2). The Son is the perfect image of the Father (2 Cor. 4:4; Col. 1:15; Heb. 1:3); all God's fullness dwells in him (Col. 1:19; 2:9). He is the incarnation of God's self-expression; he is God's Word made flesh (John 1:1, 14, 18).

This Son-centered revelation is found not only in the person of Jesus but also in his deeds. Not only in his teaching, preaching, and healing, but supremely in the cross and resurrection Jesus reveals God and accomplishes the divine plan of redemption. By the Spirit whom the exalted Christ has bequeathed (John 14–16) God convicts the world (John 16:7–11), assists believers in their witness (John 15:27), and above all, manifests God to them, taking up residence in them (John 14:19–26). Thus God reveals himself by the Holy Spirit, who is the guarantee and down payment of the promised inheritance (Eph. 1:13–14). One day the ultimate self-disclosure will occur, and every knee shall bow and every tongue confess that Jesus is Lord to the glory of God the Father (Phil. 2:11; cf. Rev. 19–22).

The point to emphasize is that a genuinely Christian understanding of the Bible presupposes the God of the Bible, a God who makes himself known in a wide diversity of ways so that human beings may know the purpose for which they were made—to know and love and worship God, and so delight in that relationship that God is glorified while they receive the matchless benefit of becoming all that God wants them to be. Any genuine knowledge human beings have of God depends on God's first disclosing himself.

The Word of God

What must not be overlooked is that this God is a talking God. Doubtless he reveals himself to us in many ways, but word is not the least of them.

In English "revelation" can be understood actively or passively, i.e., as either the activity whereby God reveals himself, or the substance of that disclosure. When it refers to God's self-disclosure in speech, the active sense envisages God's making himself known in words, while the passive sense focuses on the words themselves insofar as they constitute the message God chooses to convey.

The importance of God's speech as a fundamental means of his self-disclosure cannot be overestimated. Creation itself is the product of God's speech: God speaks, and worlds leap into being (Genesis 1). Many of God's most dramatic deeds of revelation would not have been understandable apart from God's accompanying speech. Moses views the burning bush as a curiosity until the voice tells him to remove his sandals and assigns him his new responsibilities. Abraham would have had no reason to leave Ur were it not for God's revelation in words. Again and again the prophets carry the burden of "the word of the LORD" to the people. Verbal revelation is essential even in the case of the Lord Jesus: during the days of his flesh, he was, first of all, the teacher. Moreover, apart from the explanation of the significance of his death and resurrection, preserved both in the Gospels and in the letters, even these momentous events would have been unbearably and tragically obscure. So central is God's speech to his own self-disclosure that when John the Evangelist casts around for an encompassing way to refer to God's ultimate self-disclosure in his Son, he chooses to refer to him as "the Word, and the Word was with God, and the Word was God . . . . The Word became flesh" (John 1:1, 14). The horseman of Revelation 19 is called "Faithful and True . . . . He is dressed in a robe dipped in blood, and his name is the Word of God" (19:11, 13).

Of course, to establish that God is a talking God, and that his words constitute a foundational element in his gracious manifestation of himself to us, does not itself demonstrate that the Bible is the product of that active revelation, and thus itself revelation in the passive sense. Indeed, the expression "the word of God" in the Bible has a wide range of uses. All of them presuppose that God talks, that he is not simply an impersonal "ground of all being" or a mysterious "other"; but the variety of uses is noteworthy. For example, "the word of God" or "the word of the LORD" is frequently said to "come" to one of his prophets (e.g., Jer. 1:2; Ezek. 30:1; Hos. 1:1; Luke 3:2). How this "word" or "message" comes is usually not explained. Clearly, however, even these instances are sufficient to demonstrate that in the Bible itself "the word of God" is not necessarily identical with Scripture.

Some who make this observation go farther and argue that it is inappropriate to speak of Scripture as the word of God. Alternatively, they hold that if "the word of God" is used to refer to the Bible, it must be in some vague sense: the Bible's message, what God has in general terms revealed to human witnesses, or the like. It must not be used to refer to the actual words of Scripture.

But this is surely to err on the other side. Jesus can reproach his opponents for setting their tradition above "the word of God" (Mark 7:13), and what he has in mind is the Scripture that has already been given. If some messages from God are cast in the most general terms, a very substantial number are cast as oracles, utterances, from God himself. Thus the prophecy of Amos modestly begins, "The words of Amos . . . ," but oracle after oracle throughout the book is prefaced by some such expression as "This is what the LORD says" (2:6) or "This is what the Sovereign LORD says" (3:11). Jeremiah pictures God's revelation as coming in almost dictation fashion, so that when the initial manuscript is destroyed, God graciously delivers the message again (Jer. 30:2; 36:27–32). David insists that

> the words [the Heb. means "words" or "utterances," not "promises" as in the RSV]
>> of the Lord are flawless,
>> like silver refined in a furnace of clay,
>> purified seven times. (Ps. 12:6)

When we extend our inquiry into the New Testament, we find writer after writer saying that "*God* says" something that is found in one or another canonical book. While New Testament writers frequently refer to what Moses or Isaiah or someone else says (e.g., Rom. 9:29; 10:19), they can also refer to what God himself says when he addresses the writer of the Old Testament book (e.g., Rom. 9:15, 25). Moreover, they can say that "God says" or "the Holy Spirit" says even when quoting passages of Scripture where the Old Testament writer is not in fact directly addressed by God (e.g., Heb. 7:21; 10:15). Sometimes a longer formula is used, e.g., "what the Lord had said through the prophet" (Matt. 1:22); "the Holy Spirit spoke long ago through the mouth of David" (Acts 1:16).

This very brief sketch of the evidence has tried to show that God has disclosed himself in many ways, but especially in verbal revelation. We have glimpsed evidence that this is tied to Scripture itself, but we have not yet probed very far in that direction. Before proceeding, there is one related element in the biblical revelation that must be briefly mentioned.

The Word of Human Beings

Even a cursory reading of the Bible shows it is not the product of a flat divine dictation, still less something that has been handed down from heaven on golden plates. Despite its many claims to divine revelation and authority, the Bible is an astonishingly human document—or, more precisely, sixty-six astonishingly human documents. Later writers in the canon cite the earlier human authors by name, treating many of the documents as the products of well-known historical persons without for a moment hinting that this human dimension diminishes the documents' authority. Indeed, some of the allusions to Old Testament Scripture are made with surprising informality, e.g., "But there is a place where someone has testified" (Heb. 2:6). If we are to think clearly about how Christians should approach the Bible, then however much we affirm that the Scriptures constitute

God's word (a point still to be pressed) this decidedly human dimension must not be overlooked.

There are a number of important implications. The Bible did not come to us in one go, but across a period of about a millennium and a half, at the hands of many human beings, the identity of some being entirely unknown. The first implication, then, is that the Bible is deeply grounded in history. The various human authors represent concrete cultures, languages, historical events, assumptions, idioms. The obvious parallel, and one to which attention has often been drawn, is the incarnation. The eternal Son, the pre-existent Word, became incarnate. He is both God and man. The classic formulation is still the best: the eternal Son became incarnate in history, two natures, one person. Jesus Christ cannot be truly perceived and believed if either his deity or his humanity is disowned or diluted. Somewhat similarly, the Bible is both divine and human in origin. It is God's revelation, and it is a human record. The message, extending to the very words, is divine, originating with the eternal God, yet it is deeply human, written in history, one book with two natures. Of course, the analogy must not be pushed too far. Jesus Christ is himself both God and man, but no one would affirm that the Bible is itself God and man; it is never more than an instrument in the hands of a self-disclosing God. Jesus Christ is to be worshipped; the Bible itself must not be worshipped. Nevertheless, the comparison, properly restrained, is helpful if it provides us with some categories to help us understand what the Bible is, and if it encourages us to be humble as we approach the Bible. In all our probing of Scripture, we must never discard the virtue of humility—humility before the God who has so graciously accommodated himself to our needs as to disclose himself powerfully both in the Word incarnate and in the Word written.

The second implication is that the revelation preserved in the Bible is not an abstract system, whether philosophical or ethical or theological. Buddhism stands or falls as a system of thought: if it could be proved that Gautama the Buddha never lived, the religion named for him would not be jeopardized. Not so Christianity. Despite the immense literary diversity in the Bible, as a whole it tells a story, and that story takes place in time and space. Despite the best efforts of some scholars to argue that biblical faith must never be made hostage to historical research, there is a profound sense in which the nature of God's gracious self-manifestation, taking place in ordinary history (however spectacular or miraculous some elements of that revelation may be), ensures that there can be no escape from historical enquiry. If Jesus Christ never lived, Christianity is destroyed; if he never died on the cross, Christianity is destroyed; if he never rose from the dead, Christianity is destroyed. However much the ultimate object of Christian faith is God, that faith is incoherent if it affirms faith in the God of the Bible but not in the God who according to the Bible discloses himself in history that is largely accessible and testable. In short, the elements of the large-scale biblical story are essential to the integrity of the Christian message.

Third, because the Bible is so compellingly human, it includes not only God's gracious self-revelation to us, but also human witness to God. The book of Acts, for instance, relates many incidents in which the apostles boldly confronted the authorities who were trying to silence them, and the unshakable confidence of these first Christians is tied to the unassailability of their conviction that Jesus had risen from the dead. They had seen him; indeed, according to Paul, more than five hundred witnesses had seen him (1 Corinthians 15). Many of the Psalms offer moving testimony as to how those who believe in the living God react to the changing circumstances and storms of life. More broadly, many people described in Scripture or writing Scripture are deeply engaged with their contemporaries. They are not mere secretaries taking down dictation. One cannot read the passion of, say, Paul in 2 Corinthians 10–13, or the moral indignation of Amos, or the deep hurt reflected in Lamentations or Habakkuk, or the concern of Jude in the face of theological drift, or the deeply committed witness of Matthew and John, or the transparent affection of Paul in Philippians, without recognizing that the Bible depicts and was written by real people. However much they are being used to convey God's truth to later generations, they also bear witness to their deep experience of God in their own.

These three implications come together in a fourth. The human authors of the Bible, we have seen, are deeply enmeshed in history; they tell their parts of the story; they bear witness. What we discover is that the later biblical writers not only assume the historicity of the major redemptive-historical events (such as the fall, the call of Abraham and God's covenant with him, the exodus and the giving of the law, the rise of the prophets, the onset of the Davidic monarchy, the ministry, death, and resurrection of Jesus), but even the biblical reports of relatively minor historical events are assumed to be trustworthy. The Queen of the South visited Solomon (Matt. 12:42; Luke 11:31–32); David ate the consecrated bread (Mark 2:25–26), Moses lifted up the serpent in the desert (John 3:14); Abraham gave a tenth of the spoils to Melchizedek (Heb. 7:2); eight people were saved in the ark (1 Pet. 3:20); Balaam's ass spoke (2 Pet. 2:16)—to provide but a few examples. One of the most intriguing examples is found on the lips of Jesus (Matt. 22:41–46; Mark 12:35–37). Jesus cites Psalm 110, which, according to the superscription, is a psalm of David. The important thing to observe is that the validity of Jesus' argument here depends utterly on the assumption that the superscription is accurate.

If the psalm was not written by David, then David did not speak of the Messiah as his Lord, while still referring to the "my Lord" to whom "the LORD" spoke. If, say, a courtier had composed the psalm, then "my Lord" could easily be understood to refer to David himself, or to one of the monarchs who succeeded him (as many modern critics suppose). But if, with Jesus, we take the superscription to be telling the truth, some form of messianic interpretation of the psalm is almost inevitable. In short, the historical references are not only plentiful and interlocking, but whenever later Scripture refers back to earlier examples, it never breeds a suspicion that the account is misleading, ahistorical, correct only at a theological level, or the like.

Finally, granted that the Bible was written by many people over many centuries, one cannot be surprised that it comprises many literary genres. Poetry and prose, narrative and discourse, oracle and lament, parable and fable, history and theology, genealogy and apocalyptic, proverb and psalm, Gospel and letter, law and Wisdom Literature, missive and sermon, couplet and epic—the Bible is made up of all of these, and more. Covenantal patterns emerge with some likeness to Hittite treaties; tables of household duties are found with startling resemblances to codes of conduct in the Hellenistic world. And these realities, a by-product of the humanness of the Bible, necessarily affect how we must approach the Bible to interpret it aright.

Scripture and Canon

If we grant that God is a talking God, that his self-disclosure includes verbal revelation, and that he has frequently used human beings as his mouthpieces, we must ask, first, how we jump from what seems to be primarily a personal and oral process to public, written Scripture (the subject of this section); and second, how we are to conceive of the relation between what God speaks and what his human agent speaks (the subject of the next).

It is obvious that although Scripture describes God's speaking through human beings, the only access we have to such phenomena during the period of history embraced by Scripture is found in Scripture. That is presupposed, for instance, by Jesus' rhetorical question: "Have you not read what God said . . . ?" (Matt. 22:31). The resulting alternatives seem to be, then, that either Scripture is nothing more than a (fallible) witness to such divine verbal revelation, or nothing other than the product of such revelation. In the former case, the interpreter must sort out, to the best of his or her ability, what parts of Scripture constitute faithful witness to the God who reveals himself in deeds and words and what parts are unfaithful or unreliable witness—and to disclose the grounds on which such decisions are based. In the latter case, the Bible must be understood to be not only a faithful witness to God's gracious self-disclosure in words and deeds, but also the very embodiment of God's verbal revelation to humankind. These alternative visions as to what Scripture is will certainly affect the way we approach Scripture.

There ought to be little doubt about the way later Scripture refers to earlier Scripture; scores and scores of passages make it plain that for these writers, whatever Scripture says, God says. Such a formulation, of course, allows for Satan and all manner of evil persons to be recorded as speaking within Scripture; the contexts invariably make clear that the purpose of recording such utterances is to form part of a larger account in which God's perspective is implicitly or explicitly drawn. However, much care must be exercised to discern exactly what genre of literature is being deployed and exactly what message is being conveyed; the result is nothing other than God's mind on the matter.

Thus in Matthew 19:5, the words of Genesis 2:24, not attributed to God in the Genesis narrative, are nonetheless presented as what God "said." God himself spoke by the mouths of the holy prophets (e.g., Luke 1:70). If the disciples are judged foolish for failing to believe "all that the prophets have spoken" (Luke 24:25), the substance of what the disciples should have grasped, and which Jesus then expounds to them, is "what was said in all the Scriptures concerning himself" (24:27). The gospel is nothing other than what God "promised beforehand through his prophets in the Holy Scriptures regarding his Son" (Rom. 1:2–3). The words of Scripture and the words of God are so equated that Paul can personify Scripture: "For the Scripture says to Pharaoh" (Rom. 9:17); "The Scripture foresaw that God would justify the Gentiles by faith" (Gal. 3:8); "But the Scripture declares that the whole world is a prisoner of sin" (Gal. 3:22). None of these clauses makes any sense unless Paul presupposes that what Scripture says, God says. The point comes to explicit formulation in 2 Timothy 3:16: "All Scripture [*graphē*] is God-breathed and is useful. . . ." True, the reference in this context is to what we call Old Testament Scripture (note the preceding verse: Timothy had known from infancy "the holy Scriptures" [*hiera grammata*]); moreover, nothing in this passage declares the precise limits of Scripture, establishing an agreed canon. What the passage does do, however, is affirm that if a corpus of literature is included in "Scripture," it must be judged to be "God-breathed" (on which more below) and treated accordingly.

The same stance, according to the Gospel writers, is presupposed by the Lord Jesus himself. He insisted that "the Scripture cannot be broken" (John 10:35). When he refers to Moses, Jesus is thinking of what Moses wrote, i.e., of Scripture: "Your accuser is Moses [he said to some of his opponents], on whom your hopes are set. If you believed Moses, you would believe me, for he wrote about me. But since you do not believe what he wrote, how are you going to believe what I say?" (John 5:45–47). However difficult the interpretation of Matthew 5:17–20 may be, or how disputed the exact nature of the "fulfillment," surely it is clear that when Jesus says, "I tell you the truth, until heaven and earth disappear, not the smallest letter, not the least stroke of a pen, will by any means disappear from the Law until everything is accomplished" (Matt. 5:18), he assumes the truthfulness and reliability of "the Law" (which in the context refers to all of Scripture: cf. "the Law" and "the Prophets" in 5:17; 7:12) *as it is enshrined in Scripture.* The divine authority that both Jesus and his first followers assign to Scripture constitutes the power that is presupposed by the frequently repeated formula introducing many Scripture quotations: "It is written" (e.g., Matt. 4:4; Rom. 9:33), they said—and that was enough.

Only a scant part of the evidence has been introduced here, but it is enough to show that for Jesus and the New Testament writers the Scripture already in existence was not perceived as merely written witness to God's revelation; rather, such Scripture was itself simultaneously the product of human authors and the revelation of the God who talks. What Scripture said, God said. However derived its authority, what the Bible says is stamped with God's authority, for its words are God's words.

THE CANON OF SCRIPTURE

By itself, this discussion says nothing about the extent of Scripture. To agree on the nature of Scripture still leaves open the question as to what writings constitute Scripture. What makes up the canon of Scripture and how we know this to be the case is a complex subject on which much as been written. This briefest of summaries must suffice.

1. Many have argued that the Old Testament Scriptures were canonized (i.e., recognized as a closed list of writings) in three stages: first, Torah (here understood to mean what we call the Pentateuch, the first five books); second, the Prophets; third, the Writings. The last stage, it is often argued, was not reached until the end of the first century AD, at the Council of Jamnia. Increasingly, however, it has been recognized that, so far as the canon is concerned, Jamnia did nothing more than review arguments for two of the books in the Writings (Ecclesiastes and Song of Songs)—much as Luther would later review the arguments for James. In both cases, the inherited assumption was that the writings in question did indeed belong to the canon, and the point raised was whether or not this assumption could be sustained.

2. Indirect evidence concerning the status of Old Testament books is derived from the New Testament. According to Luke 24:44, Jesus himself referred to the

Scripture as "the Law of Moses, the Prophets and the Psalms"—traditional designation of the three divisions of the Hebrew canon, to which reference has just been made. More broadly, the New Testament quotes from every section and most books of the Old Testament and treats such quotations as "Scripture." Not every ancient writing was thought of as Scripture, so to treat some books as Scripture and not others presupposes that those doing the quoting are operating with a list of "Scripture" books in their minds. Thus, quotations from Cleanthes in Acts 17:28, Menander in 1 Corinthians 15:33, Epimenides in Titus 1:12, or 1 Enoch in Jude 14–15 are not introduced as Scripture. Interestingly enough, no allusion to books of the Apocrypha is treated as Scripture either. Although the copies of the Septuagint (the Greek translations of the Old Testament) that have come down to us from the fourth and fifth centuries AD include most of the apocryphal books, it is widely recognized that these manuscripts provide little evidence of what first-century Jews in Palestine thought, and may not even provide any evidence for a larger Jewish canon maintained by Jews in, say, Alexandria.

3. Obviously one cannot approach the closing of the New Testament canon, i.e., the point at which it was universally agreed there were no more books to be added to a closed list of books of authoritative Scripture, in exactly the same way, since that would entail a still later corpus to authenticate it, and so on and on in an endless regression. Even so, it is worth noting how some later documents in the New Testament refer to some earlier ones as "Scripture" (1 Tim. 5:18; 2 Pet. 3:16).

4. Most important, perhaps, are a number of passages where Christ himself is made the center of what became the New Testament canon. In particular, the opening verses of Hebrews contrast how God "spoke to our forefathers through the prophets at many times and in various ways" with the manner in which "in these last days he has spoken to us by his Son" (Heb. 1:1–2). The Son himself is the apex of revelation; to use the language of John, Jesus himself, as we have seen, is the ultimate "Word," God's self-expression, the Word incarnate. Thus, any notion of a New Testament canon immediately becomes tied to its relation to him. Certainly Jesus prepared his small band of apostles for the increased measure of understanding that would come to them in the wake of his resurrection and the descent of the Spirit (John 14:26; 16:12–15). Certainly, too, there is evidence that, although the twelve apostles and Paul could and did make mistakes (e.g., Gal. 2:11–14), they could on occasion be so conscious that what they were writing was nothing less than the Lord's command that even New Testament prophets who questioned them at that point were to be regarded as beyond the pale (1 Cor. 14:37–38).

5. Some have given the entirely false impression that the early church took an inordinately long time to recognize the authority of the New Testament documents. In fact it is vital to distinguish the recognition of the authority of these documents from a universal recognition as to the content of a closed list of New Testament documents. The New Testament books were circulating a long time before the latter happened, most of them accepted everywhere as divinely authoritative, and all of them accepted in at least large parts of the church. Most of the New Testament documents are cited as authorities very early indeed; this includes the four Gospels, Acts, the thirteen Pauline letters, 1 Peter, and 1 John. Most of the rest of the contours of the New Testament canon were well in place by the time of Eusebius, in the early fourth century.

6. The criteria by which the early church agreed that certain books were authoritative were basically three. First, the church Fathers looked for apostolicity, i.e., a document had to be written by an apostle or by someone in immediate contact with the apostles. Thus Mark was understood to have the witness of Peter behind him; Luke was connected with Paul. As soon as the Fathers discussed the possibility, they rejected any document under the suspicion of pseudonymity (written by someone other than the claimed author). Second, a basic requirement for canonicity was conformity to the "rule of faith," i.e., to basic, orthodox Christianity recognized as normative in the churches. Third, and scarcely less important, the document had to have enjoyed widespread and continuous usage by the churches. Incidentally, this criterion requires the passage of time to be useful, and helps to explain why so much time elapsed before the "closing" of the canon (i.e., before the church had almost universally agreed on the status of all twenty-seven New Testament documents). One of the reasons Hebrews was not accepted in the West as early as some letters was that it was anonymous (not pseudonymous!), and in fact it was more quickly accepted in the East where many (wrongly) thought it to have been written by Paul.

7. Perhaps the most important thing to recognize is that although there was no ecclesiastical machinery or hierarchy, akin to the medieval papacy, to enforce decisions, eventually almost all of the universal church came to recognize the same twenty-seven books. In other words, this was not so much "official" recognition as the people of God in many different places coming to recognize what other believers elsewhere had also found to be true. The point must be constantly emphasized.

The fact that substantially the whole church came to recognize the same twenty-seven books as canonical is remarkable when it is remembered that the result was not contrived. All that the several churches throughout the Empire could do was to witness to their own experience with the documents and share whatever knowledge they might have about their origin and character. When consideration is given to the diversity in cultural backgrounds and in orientation to the essentials of the Christian faith within the churches, their common agreement about which books belonged to the New Testament serves to suggest that this final decision did not originate solely at the human level. (Glenn W. Barker, William L. Lane, and J. Ramsey Michaels, *The New Testament Speaks* [New York: Harper & Row, 1969], 29)

The church, then, did not confer a certain status on documents that would otherwise have lacked it, as if the church were an institution with authority independent of the Scriptures or in tandem to the Scriptures. Rather, the New Testament documents were Scripture because of what God had revealed; the church, providentially led, came to wide recognition of what God had done in his climactic self-disclosure in his Son and in the documents that bore witness to and gathered up the strands of the Son-revelation.

Inspiration and Authority

If the Scriptures are simultaneously God's verbal revelation and the product of human hands, we must ask for at least some account of the relation between the two. For at least the past several hundred years, the term that has been most commonly used in this connection is *inspiration*. Like *Trinity*, the word *inspiration* is not a biblical word but summarizes some important facets of biblical truth. Inspiration is normally defined (at least in Protestant circles) as that supernatural work of God's Holy Spirit upon the human authors of Scripture such that what they wrote was precisely what God intended them to write in order to communicate his truth.

Some observations on this definition will clarify it, signal its usefulness, and defend it against common misinterpretations.

1. The definition speaks both of God's action, by his Spirit, in the human author and of the nature of the resulting text. This double emphasis is an attempt to capture two elements demonstrably present in the Bible's summary of what is taking place. On the one hand, we are told that "no prophecy of Scripture came about by the prophet's own interpretation" (presumably a private interpretation of the way things are); indeed, "prophecy [clearly, in context, the prophecy that constitutes Scripture] never had its origin in the will of man, but men spoke from God as they were carried along by the Holy Spirit" (2 Pet. 1:20–21). On the other hand, not only are the human authors of Scripture "carried along by the Holy Spirit," but the

resulting Scripture is "God-breathed" (2 Tim. 3:16). The Greek expression might well be rendered "breathed out by God." The striking point is that it is Scripture, the text, that is so described, not the human author. If we choose to use the word "inspired" instead of "God-breathed," then we must say (according to this passage) that it is the text that is inspired, not the human authors. Alternatively, if we attach the term "inspire" to the fact that the human authors were "carried along by the Holy Spirit," then the authors of Scripture were inspired. In any case, the wording of the definition is designed to embrace both the work of the Spirit in the human author and the resulting status of the text of Scripture.

2. There is nothing in the definition that lays down a particular mode of inspiration. Doubtless inspiration may operate through some abnormal state of the human mind, e.g., a vision, a trance-like dream, hearing voices, and much else. But there is nothing in the definition that requires such phenomena; indeed, judging by the text of Scripture, it is far from clear that all of the biblical writers were always self-consciously aware that what they were writing was canonical Scripture. Nor is there any reason to depreciate Luke's description of his work, characterized by research and careful sifting of sources (Luke 1:1–4). In fact, the term *inspiration* is not much more than a convenient label to attach to the process whereby God has brought about the existence of the Scriptures as they have been described in the previous pages: verbal revelation and historical witness, words of human beings and words of God, the truth that God chose to communicate and the particular forms of individual human authors.

3. It is important to distinguish this use of *inspiration* from two other uses. The first springs from the contemporary world of art. We speak of composers, writers, painters, sculptors, musicians, and others as being "inspired." If we stop to think about this usage at all, we might suppose that these people have been "inspired" by the Muse; the more theologically inclined might assign the "inspiration" to God's "common grace." Apart from such reflection, we do not mean very much more than that their work is excellent, the elite from the first class. In consequence we might conclude that their work is "inspiring," i.e., it makes those who gaze at it lift their horizons a little, or attempt something new, or otherwise find themselves ennobled. Such use is not normally taken to mean that the sovereign God has thereby communicated his truth in permanent form to his covenant people.

The second use of *inspiration* with which our definition must not be confused is that found in the usage of the church Fathers. It has often been noticed that "inspiration" never functions among the Fathers as a criterion for canonicity. This is not because the Fathers do not think the Scriptures are inspired, for in fact they do; rather, it is because in their usage inspiration is not something that attaches exclusively to Scripture. Thus in a sermon Eusebius attributes to Emperor Constantine (whether or not this attribution is correct), the preacher begins, "May the mighty inspiration of the Father and of his Son . . . be with me in speaking these things." In one of his letters to Jerome, Augustine goes so far as to say that Jerome writes under the dictation of the Holy Spirit. Gregory of Nyssa can use the same word translated "God-breathed" ("inspired") in 2 Timothy to refer to his brother Basil's commentary on the six days of creation. In short, a number of Fathers use a variety of expressions, including "inspiration," to lump together what many theologians today would separate into the two categories "inspiration" and "illumination." The latter acknowledges the work of the Holy Spirit in the mind of countless believers, not least preachers, Christian writers, and teachers, but denies to their thoughts and words and writings the kind of universal authority that is binding on all Christians everywhere and that is today connected with the word *inspiration*. Implicitly, of course, the Fathers make the same sort of distinction (even if their categories are different) insofar as they recognize only certain documents as canonical, i.e., a closed list of Scriptures with binding authority on the entire church.

For our purposes, then, *inspiration* will not be used as in the world of art, or as in the Fathers, but in the theological sense it has acquired during the past several centuries.

4. A number of writers attempt to weaken *inspiration* as here defined by pointing out, rightly, that a passage such as 2 Timothy 3:16–17 tells us the purpose of such God-breathed Scripture: it is "useful for teaching, rebuking, correcting and training in righteousness, so that the man of God may be thoroughly equipped for every good work." If this is its purpose, they argue, then it is futile to link inspiration with truthfulness and authority. In fact, this is an error of categories. It is important to distinguish the *mode* of revelation (dream, vision, dictation, etc.) from the *manner* of inspiration (the employment of various literary techniques and genres) from the *result* of inspiration (what Scripture says, God says) and the *purpose* of inspiration (to make us wise unto salvation).

5. Many attempt to weaken the authority of Scripture implicit in the account given here by one of several paths. Only a few can be mentioned. First, it has been argued that one must create a doctrine of Scripture not only out of passages where Scripture assesses Scripture, but out of the allegedly unyielding difficulties where Scripture actually cites Scripture in ways that on first reading are quite astonishing. Certainly the two approaches must go hand in hand. In practice, however, those who begin with the second usually do not take the first very seriously; those who begin with the first, if they are careful, usually uncover valid exegetical and

theological reasons for the peculiar phenomena themselves. A variation on this argument insists that the Bible presents such different pictures of, say, God, that it is futile to speak of "biblical" theology or "biblical Christianity." The Bible, according to this argument, embraces competing theologies and reflects different and mutually contradictory streams of Christianity. How can any book be said to be inspired and authoritative that forbids the wearing of clothes made from more than one kind of fabric (Lev. 19:19)? But such works, it must be gently said, while scoring well among popular audiences and convinced skeptics, simply do not engage with the best confessional literature. For example, the question about the different fabrics, not uncommon in the literature, is pressed forward as if no one has ever thought seriously about the ways in which covenantal stipulations of the Old Testament are to be applied to believers living under a new covenant.

Second, many argue that a necessary result of God's gracious accommodation of himself to human speech is the introduction of error. To err is human; the biblical documents are human, therefore they must prove as unreliable as human beings are. But not only does such an assessment of Scripture fly in the face of the conviction of Jesus and of the New Testament writers, it depends on a fraying logic. Doubtless it is true that this side of the fall "to err is human"; that does not mean that to be human is necessarily to err on every occasion and in every utterance. That the sovereign, transcendent God has graciously accommodated himself to human speech is a wonderful truth. But it is this accommodated speech which is then described as the word or words of God that are "flawless" (Ps. 12:6) and treated by Jesus himself as the Scripture that cannot be broken.

Third, traditional Roman Catholics, while holding to the inspiration and authority of the Bible, deny that the Bible is sufficient as a rule of faith and practice. Before the written Word came the oral tradition, and this tradition continues alongside the written Word in the magisterial office of the Roman Church. The effects are substantial; a doctrine such as the immaculate conception of Mary, not taught in Scripture, can be set forth as something that all loyal Catholics must believe. Conversely, doctrines that most non-Catholics find in the Scriptures may be set aside or trimmed on the church's authority. The issues are too complex to broach here.

Fourth, in a manner that characteristically goes beyond anything that Karl Barth, the father of neo-orthodoxy, would have espoused, some neo-orthodox theologians insist that the Bible, so far as its form is concerned, is simply one more religious book, albeit an important one, and therefore not itself immune from errors large and small. It is not truth in the sense that what it says, God says. Rather, the Bible is truth insofar as God works through it to disclose himself to individuals. It becomes the word of God whenever the Holy Spirit illumines it to the individual. Thus inspiration and illumination are again confused; or, more exactly, the former is swallowed up by the latter. Certainly neo-orthodoxy was right to protest against a dead "word" that neither transformed nor gave life to individuals. But its solution is too drastic and ends up denying what Jesus and the earliest believers understood the Scripture to be.

Fifth, various forms of classic liberalism simply deny any special status to the Scripture. In its most virulent form, this view denies the existence of a personal/ transcendent God who invades history. Supernaturalism is assumed to be impossible; God is reduced to the proportions of deism or pantheism. The religion of the Bible must be studied in the framework of discussion about any or all other religions, and in no other framework. A thoughtful response to this vision of reality would take us far beyond the scope of this article. What is clear, however, is that this vision quickly domesticates Scripture and ends up imposing some current ideas on the Bible. In the end, the dispute turns not simply on the nature of the Bible, but on the nature and character of God.

Finally, the rise of the "new hermeneutic" has encouraged many thinkers simply to sidestep the debate over the locus of revelation and authority. But since this view is integrally tied to questions about how the Bible is to be interpreted, brief discussion can await the next section.

Final Reflections

Some might object that this entire presentation is hopelessly circular. If we begin with our views of God, and from this perspective start to think our way toward the nature of the Bible, we must pause and admit that our views of God are (in the Christian perspective) drawn from the Bible. If we begin instead with, say, Jesus' assessment of the authority of Scripture, that assessment is itself drawn from Scripture. The entire project of constructing a doctrine of Scripture is deeply flawed.

This charge touches on some of the most complex questions about how we come to "know" things, and whether they are "true." Although these questions cannot be probed very effectively here, a few comments may be helpful to some.

First, there is a profound sense in which all human thought (except perhaps that which is bounded by agreed rules of logic and built on defined values, like most branches of mathematics) is circular in some sense. We are finite creatures; without the faculty of omniscience we have no absolutely certain base on which to build. The Christian's claim is that God himself, who does enjoy perfect knowledge, provides that basis for us—but that, of course, means the basis itself must be taken (so far as finite creatures are concerned) on faith. In this view, "faith" is not some subjectively constrained opinion to be put over against some other "faith," but a God-given ability to perceive at least a little of God and his truth and to trust him accordingly. This is not to deny for a moment that all kinds of arguments can be advanced to justify Christian belief, including belief about God and the Bible. Rather, it is to admit that such arguments will not prove convincing to everyone.

Second, although we admit that the argument is in some measure circular, and insist that almost all human thought is in some measure circular, that is not to suggest that the circularity is intrinsically false. We do not turn to the Bible for certain proof about the nature of the Bible; rather, we turn to it for information. If the Bible made no claims about the nature of the Bible, we would have less reason for holding to the doctrine of Scripture outlined here. To go further, informed Christians may want to argue for the utter truthfulness and reliability of Scripture, but they will not want to argue for the utter truthfulness and reliability of their doctrine of Scripture. Methodologically speaking, they proceed with the creation of a doctrine of Scripture exactly the same way they proceed with the creation of a doctrine of Christ. Both are subject to revision as more light breaks from God's gracious self-disclosure, as already given in the Scriptures.

Third, thoughtful Christians will be the first to admit that there are unknowns and difficulties in the formulation of a responsible doctrine of Scripture. But this does not daunt us; the same could be said for almost any biblical doctrine: the nature of God, the heart of the atonement, the work of the Spirit, the resurrection from the dead. This does not mean that nothing true can be said about such matters; it means, rather, that since all of them have to do with a personal/ transcendent God who cannot possibly be exhaustively known by finite and rebellious creatures, there will inevitably remain mysteries and areas of hiddenness.

Fourth, we must not underestimate the impact of sin on our ability to think through these matters clearly. A substantial element in our original fall was the unbridled lust for self-sufficiency, for independent knowledge. We wanted to be the center of the universe—and that is the heart of all idolatry. John 8:45 reports Jesus addressing his opponents in these shocking words: "Yet because I tell you the truth, you do not believe me!" If it is the truth itself that ensures our unbelief, how deep and tragic and abominable is our lostness. Small wonder, then, that God does not present himself to us in such a way that we may feel we can control him. Those who demand signs of Jesus are firmly rebuked, for he knows that to give in to such demands would be to submit to the agenda of others. He would quickly be domesticated, nothing more than a magical, spiritual genie.

For the same reason the wisdom of the world—systems of thought that provide nicely packaged explanations of everything—cannot possibly come to grips with the cross of Christ (1 Cor. 1:18–31). When God speaks from heaven, there will always be some who hear only thunder (John 12:29). In the same way, God's gracious self-disclosure in Scripture can never be adequately assessed by those who insist on being independent knowers: for God to structure his revelation to accommodate such a desire would be to foster the sin from which the gospel frees us. God in his great mercy refuses to pander to our unlimited lust to be gods. He has ensured that his own self-disclosure should be abundantly clear to those who by grace have eyes to see and ears to hear, but can never be as rigorously self-evident as a mathematical theorem where human beings control all the definitions and the rules of the relationships.

We walk by faith, and not by sight.

How to Interpret the Bible

The Changing Face of Hermeneutics

When Paul tells Timothy to strive to be someone who "correctly handles the word of truth" (2 Tim. 2:15), the assumption is that it is dangerously possible to be someone who does not correctly handle the word of truth. And that raises important questions about how to interpret the Bible. To approach the Bible wisely it is necessary to know not only what it is, but how to handle it.

Hermeneutics is the term that has traditionally been applied to the interpretation of texts. But hermeneutics itself has recently gone through such major changes that it is worth pausing to consider the ways in which the discipline of interpretation has changed. We may discern three stages (though all of them overlap toward the end).

First, hermeneutics was once understood to be the science and art of biblical interpretation: science, because there were some important rules and principles that could be applied to the task, and art, because there were many calls for mature judgment borne of experience and competence. The task of the interpreter was to understand what the text said, and it was assumed that if two interpreters of equal competence understood the rules of interpretation well enough, then in the overwhelming majority of cases their grasp of what a passage says would coincide. In this vision of hermeneutics, a great deal of attention is paid to grammar, parables, and other literary genres, principles for studying words, how to relate biblical themes, and the like.

Second, *hermeneutics* was increasingly used to refer to the deployment of an array of literary-critical "tools": source criticism, form criticism, tradition criticism, redaction criticism, and, more recently, various forms of narrative criticism. Although some gains were made by such approaches, there were also losses: much of the purpose of these techniques was to reconstruct the history and belief-structure of particular believing communities behind the text, rather than to listen to the message of the text.

Both of these approaches have largely been eclipsed in importance by a third wave, the "new hermeneutic." Here the important insight that human beings bring their own biases and limitations to the interpretative task is raised to a controlling pitch in the discussion. At one level this observation is entirely salutary. We inevitably bring our own interpretative "grids" with us; there is no such thing as a totally open mind. The new hermeneutic reminds us that the authority of Scripture must not be transferred to the authority of the interpreter, that we invariably fit new pieces of information into already established "grids" in our minds (which are mixtures of sense and nonsense), that some of what we think is true doubtless needs to be modified or corrected or abandoned, that we have more to learn, that our frameworks of understanding are separated from the human writers of Scripture by barriers of time, geography, language, and culture.

But at the same time, many proponents of the new hermeneutic overstep the mark. They argue that since each person's interpretation will differ in some measure from every other person's interpretation, we cannot legitimately speak of the meaning of the text (as if it were something objective). Meaning, they argue, resides not in the text but in the readers, the interpreters, of the text. If different interpretations are legitimate, then one cannot speak of the correct interpretation or the true interpretation; such expressions, they think, dissolve into affirmations of personal preference. If no single interpretation is right, then either all interpretations are equally meaningless (which leads to the hermeneutical nihilism known as "deconstructionism") or all are equally "right"—i.e., all are good or bad insofar as they are satisfying, or meet the needs of a particular person or community or culture, or meet certain arbitrary criteria. In this vein, these proponents of the new hermeneutic foster different "readings" of Scripture: a sub-Saharan Black African reading, a liberation theology reading, a feminist reading, a white Anglo-Saxon male Protestant reading, a "gay" reading, and so forth. Aligned with the powerful respect contemporary Western culture assigns to pluralism, this new hermeneutic rules no interpretation invalid except that one which claims it is right and that others are invalid.

The issues surrounding the new hermeneutic are so complex that they cannot satisfactorily be handled here. It is important to recognize that this approach to understanding governs much of the agenda not only in contemporary biblical interpretation but also in the disciplines of history, literature, politics, and much else besides. Despite its many valuable insights, the new hermeneutic must be challenged on many fronts. Intuitively, there is something weak about a theory that propounds the relativity of all knowledge gleaned from reading, while producing countless books that insist on the rightness of this view. To insist that all meaning lies with the knower and not with the text, and then to write texts to prove the point, is almost unimaginably self-contradictory. Worse, the theory in this form assumes that the author's intent is not reliably expressed in the text. It erects an impenetrable barrier between the author and the reader and calls it "text." The irony is that these ideas are written by authors who expect their readers to understand what they say, authors who write what they mean and hope that their readers will be persuaded by their reasoning. It is devoutly to be wished that such authors would extend the same courtesy to Moses, Isaiah, and Paul.

Even if finite human beings may not attain an exhaustive knowledge of a text (or of anything else for that matter), it is difficult to see why they cannot gain true knowledge. Moreover, the fact of our differences is easier to absorb against the background of our common heritage; all of us have been made in the image of God, who alone enjoys perfect and exhaustive knowledge. To suppose that we can attain knowledge in every way like his would be idolatrous, but that is no reason to think that we cannot gain objective knowledge at all.

Indeed, there are ways of thinking about the acquisition of understanding from a text that help us see a little of how the process works. Doubtless a reader may be largely controlled by personal biases and rigid agendas when first approaching the Scriptures (the text that concerns us here), and thus "find" in the text all kinds of things the author (and the Author) did not intend to place there; or, alternatively, he or she may not see many of the things that are in fact there. The total mental baggage of the reader, what moderns often call the reader's "horizon of understanding," may be so far removed from the horizon of understanding of the author as expressed in the text that very great distortions occur. But it is possible that the reader will read and reread the text, learn something of the language and culture of the authors, discover what elements of his or her own "baggage" must be jettisoned, and gradually "fuse" his or her horizon of understanding with that of the text (to use the current jargon). Others speak of the "hermeneutical spiral": the interpreter "spirals in" on the meaning of the text.

If the new hermeneutic is treated in this fashion, there are considerable gains that can come to the church. It reminds us that God's verbal revelation to us in the Scripture not only comes to us clothed in the language and idiom of particular historical cultures, but that to improve our understanding of the objective truth that is there disclosed it is necessary to think our way back into those cultures, so far as this is possible, to minimize the dangers of interpretative distortion. It reminds us that even if an individual interpreter gains some real, objective understanding of the text, none will understand it exhaustively, and other interpreters may bring to light content that is genuinely there in the text and that we ourselves have missed. For instance, believers in Africa might be quicker to detect Pauline metaphors for the corporate character of the church, while many in the West will find it harder to see them owing to their heritage of individualism. Christians need each other; this is as true in the hermeneutical arena as elsewhere. Provided there is a shared deep commitment to submit to the authority of God's revelation, and not the passing fads and agendas (academic and otherwise) of those who want to pass judgment on Scripture, the recognition that none of us knows it all encourages humility and willingness to listen and learn.

Indeed, properly applied, some of the insights of the new hermeneutic remind us that human beings bring enormous cultural and conceptual baggage to the Scriptures they claim to interpret, and that this fact, allied with the Bible's insistence that our sin and idolatrous self-focus drive us away from the light (e.g., John 3:19–20), may send us to our knees in the belated recognition that the interpretation of God's Word is not merely an intellectual discipline, but turns also on moral and spiritual bearings. In the Bible's view of the relation between God and his people, we need the help of God's Holy Spirit to understand the truth as much as we need his help to do the truth. However that help may be mediated to us, the aim of thoughtful Christians, after all, is not so much to become masters of Scripture, but to be mastered by it, both for God's glory and his people's good.

Some Introductory Principles of Biblical Interpretation

What follows is a selection of principles of interpretation for those who hold that a proper approach to the Bible includes not only some appreciation for what the Bible is, but some care in how to read it and understand it.

THE PRIORITY OF THE ORIGINAL LANGUAGES OF THE BIBLE

The original languages take precedence. This is a corollary of the fact that this revelation took place through specific individuals at concrete historical junctures in real and time-specific human languages. True, linguistics has amply demonstrated that anything that can be said in one language can be translated into any other language. But it has also demonstrated that not all of the meaning of the donor language can be conveyed at the same time and in the same amount of space. Moreover, all translation involves interpretation; translation is not a mechanical discipline. Thus to approach as closely as possible to the intention of the author as expressed in a text it is best to interpose as few intermediary interpretations as possible. Of course, if one does not know the original languages one will be grateful for the translations; moreover a poor interpreter who knows the original languages may make more interpretative errors than many translations, the best of which have been undertaken by competent people. But all things being equal, the point, though intuitively obvious, needs repeating.

For the busy preacher or Bible teacher, this observation has two practical implications. First, if the main point of a sermon or lesson turns on the peculiar mode of expression in just one translation, in most cases it is not the major point of the passage, and may not be justified at all. Second, the first priority in commentaries and other interpretative helps should be to reflect work in the original languages, even if the presentation (as in this one-volume commentary) is geared for readers who enjoy no technical expertise.

SOME WORDS ON WORDS

Word studies, important as they are in their own right, must be undertaken with some care, and never in isolation from larger questions about the way words are used in phrases, sentences, discourses, particular genres. Lexica (dictionaries written in English that treat the words of the original languages) can provide the range of meanings that various scholars have identified (insofar as those scholars are right!), but within certain limitations the most important factor in the determination of the meaning of a word is its use in a specific context. To plumb for a meaning associated with the word's etymology is often misleading (just as it is entirely unhelpful to recognize that *pineapple* comes from *pine* and *apple*); the only time when etymology becomes a cautious priority occurs when a word crops up so infrequently and in such ambiguous contexts that there is no other recourse. To try to build up an entire theology based on a single word and its use is a doubtful enterprise; to preach "reverse etymology," where the meaning of a word is affirmed to be something like later developments of that word or its cognates (such as the assertion that *dynamis*, "power," properly calls to mind "dynamite"—which had not been invented when the New Testament writers penned their books) is anachronistic at best, ridiculous at worst. Moreover, to try to import the word's entire semantic range into every occurrence (as in the Amplified Bible) is to fail to understand how language works.

Despite the warnings, careful exegesis will be much interested in how words are used by specific biblical authors, and in other biblical books. Just as the meaning of sentences and discourses shapes the meaning of words, so the meaning of words shapes the sentence and discourse; in language, everything holds together. It is valuable to try to find out what the underlying Hebrew and Greek words behind many words in our English Bibles mean, not least words that have traditionally borne a great deal of theological weight, e.g., *atonement, Messiah* (*Christ*), *truth, apostle, sin, head, resurrection, spirit, flesh, law*, and countless more. Even if a per-

son's study merely confirms what some secondary sources say, the discipline itself
is valuable. It not only provides a degree of familiarity with the Scripture that
cannot easily be gained otherwise, but it reminds the Christian that God himself
has chosen to disclose himself in discourse, sentences, and words.

THE IMPORTANCE OF BECOMING A GOOD READER

It is essential to develop literary sensitivity—or, to put it another way, to become
a good reader.

At the micro level, countless literary devices serve as pointers for the alert
reader. "Inclusions" begin and end a section with similar or even identical words
in order to underline the importance of certain themes. Thus the beatitudes in
Matthew 5:3–10 begin and end with the same reward ("for theirs is the kingdom
of heaven"), thereby establishing that the beatitudes are setting forth the norms
of the kingdom. The body of the Sermon on the Mount opens with the words,
"Do not think that I have come to abolish the Law or the Prophets" (Matt. 5:17),
and ends with, "So in everything, do to others what you would have them do to
you, for this sums up the Law and the Prophets" (Matt. 7:12). This "inclusion"
suggests that the Sermon on the Mount is, among other things, an exposition of
the Old Testament Scriptures ("the Law and the Prophets") in the light of Jesus'
coming and ministry, his commitment to "fulfill" them, and what this will mean
in the lives of his followers. Hebrew poetry is much less interested in rhyme and
even in rhythm than in parallelism of various sorts. In Psalm 73:21–22,

> When my heart was grieved
>   and my spirit embittered,
> I was senseless and ignorant;
>   I was a brute beast before you,

the second line repeats the content of the first, if in other words; the fourth does
the same for the third. These are instances of synonymous parallelism. Lines 3–4
take the thought on from lines 1–2; this is step parallelism. Elsewhere one finds
antithetic parallelism, as in Proverbs 14:31:

> He who oppresses the poor shows contempt for their Maker,
>   but whoever is kind to the needy honors God.

There are of course far more complex structures of parallelism. There are also
chiasms, where two or more lines work into the center and then work out again.
These can be very elementary, or complex ones such as in Matthew 13:

1 the parable of the soils (13:3b–9)

  2 interlude (13:10–23)

  (a) on understanding parables (13:10–17)

  (b) interpretation of the parable of the soils (13:18–23)

    3 the parable of the weeds (13:24–30)

      4 the parable of the mustard seed (13:31–32)

        5 the parable of the yeast (13:33)

        Pause (13:34–43)

        —parables as fulfillment of prophecy (13:34–35)

        —interpretation of the parable of the weeds (13:36–43)

        5' parable of the hidden treasure (13:44)

      4' the parable of the expensive pearl (13:45–46)

    3' the parable of the net (13:47–48)

  2' interlude (13:49–51)

  (b') interpretation of the parable of the net (13:49–50)

  (a') on understanding parables (13:51)

1' the parable of the teacher of the law (13:52)

It must be conceded that chiasms are sometimes rather more in the eye of the beholder than in the text. If the elements become too complex, or the parallels decidedly forced, one may reasonably ask whether a chiasm is really present. On the other hand, some interpreters, burned by long lists of unconvincing chiasms, dismiss too easily chiasms that are really there. It has often been shown that those who spoke Semitic languages commonly framed chiasms as part of their speech patterns, so one should not become too skeptical. Certainly, there are many borderline cases; indeed, many expositors will be unpersuaded by the example just provided. So perhaps it is worth venturing a slightly simpler example, this one based on Matthew 23:13–32:

1 First woe (23:13)—failing to recognize Jesus as the Messiah

  2 Second woe (23:15)—superficially zealous, yet doing more harm than good

    3 Third woe (23:16–22)—misguided use of Scripture

      4 Fourth woe (23:23–24)—fundamental failure to discern the thrust of Scripture

    3' Fifth woe (23:25–26)—misguided use of Scripture

  2' Sixth woe (23:27–28)—superficially zealous, yet doing more harm than good

1' Seventh woe (23:29–32)—heirs of those who failed to recognize the prophets.

What this chiasm accomplishes, of course, is to drive the reader's focus to the center—the fundamental failure to discern the thrust of Scripture, a major theme in Matthew's Gospel.

Still more important, perhaps, is the ability to understand how larger structures work, and especially the nature of literary genre. Wisdom Literature is not law; to read, say, Proverbs, as if it offered judgments in case law, is to make it ludicrous (compare Prov. 26:4 and 26:5). In the New Testament the word "parable" can refer to a proverb (Luke 4:23), a profound or obscure saying (Mark 13:35), a nonverbal image or symbol (Heb. 9:9; 11:19), an illustrative or suggestive comparison, whether without the form of a story (Matt. 15:15; 24:32) or with a story (Matt. 13:3–9—the so-called "narrative" parables). Many treatments of parables think only of narrative parables, not least because they are so plentiful in the first three Gospels, and draw up principles for the interpretation of (such) parables. Certainly all agree that in the case of narrative parables we need not ask if the story that is told really happened.

In the same way, we must ask how apocalyptic is to be understood, what a "gospel" is, how letters functioned in the first century. Jehoash told a fable (2 Kings 14:9); is the modern critic right when the book of Jonah is designated a "fable"? No, this is a mistake of literary category. A fable tells a story of animals or other nonhuman, natural life-forms in order to draw a moral; it does not intermingle with human beings. The effort of Jehoash qualifies; the book of Jonah does not. With increased information we may ask what "midrash" and other first-century literary categories meant. All Bible students will wrestle with the meaning of passages such as Galatians 4:24–31. The point is that truth is conveyed in different ways in different literary genres. The person who thinks Jeremiah is speaking literally in Jeremiah 20:14–18 will have some very difficult things to explain. It would be better to hear the particular outrage of lament.

Above all, good reading goes with the flow. Although it is always worth meditating on individual words and phrases (especially in discourse), even so, the meaning of those words is shaped by their context. Good readers will diligently strive to make sense of the flow of the argument. (The exception occurs when there are lists of, say, proverbs—but even many of these are thematically arranged.) This is no less true in narrative than in discourse. Many casual readers of the Gospels think of them as more or less disjointed accounts. Closer reading discloses themes interwoven with other themes. One might ask, for example, how Luke 10:38–11:13 is tied together. Rereading shows that these verses gather up some analysis of why there is so little prayerfulness and what is today called spirituality: a distortion of priorities and values (10:38–42); a lack of knowledge and of good models (11:1–4); and a want of assurance and persistence (11:5–13). Similarly, this entire section of Luke makes its own contribution to the larger flow of his text.

IMMEDIATE AND MORE DISTANT CONTEXTS

Generally speaking the immediate context takes precedence over both the distant context and merely formal parallels. For instance, in Matthew 6:7 Jesus warns his followers not to "keep on babbling like pagans, for they think they will be heard because of their many words"; in Luke 18:1–8 Jesus tells his disciples a parable "to show them that they should always pray and not give up." It will not do to reduce the impact of one of these passages by citing the other. The prohibition in Matthew makes good sense in its context; the saying confronts religion that is merely formal, or that thinks it can wrest advantages from God by trying harder. With his well-known interest in prayer, Luke reports far more of Jesus' prayer life, and in chapter 18 reports some of his teaching designed to trim the sails of those whose piety is neither passionate nor persistent.

Of the many interpretations of John 3:5, where Jesus tells Nicodemus he must be born "of water and the Spirit" if he is to inherit the kingdom of God, one of the most popular is achieved by bringing Titus 3:4–6 to bear, which speaks of "God our Savior" saving us "through the washing of rebirth and renewal by the Holy Spirit, whom he poured out on us generously through Jesus Christ our Savior." That there are conceptual and verbal parallels no one will deny. Still, John 3:5 was not only penned by another author, but attributed to Jesus during the days of his flesh. More importantly, in the immediate context Nicodemus is reproached for not understanding what Jesus is talking about (3:10), presumably on the grounds that, as a revered teacher of Scripture, he should have known what Scripture said. A combination of these and other factors leads many commentators, rightly, to see a reference in John 3:5 to the anticipated fulfillment of Ezekiel 36:25–27. This is in line with the expectation that Jesus would perform Spirit-baptism, a point already articulated in this Gospel (John 1:26–33).

Of course, any text is surrounded by expanding concentric circles of context. How large a context should be appealed to at any point is not easy to legislate. Certainly word studies should begin within the text (how does Mark, say, use a term, before asking how Luke, Paul, the New Testament, and ultimately the Hellenistic world use the term).

Some contextual markers are important in moving from chapter to chapter. For example, although according to Matthew the opening words of ministry ascribed to John the Baptist and to Jesus respectively are identical ("Repent, for the kingdom of heaven is near," Matt. 3:2; 4:17), their immediate contexts give the two sayings a quite different shade. The utterance of the Baptist is cast within the shadow of the words from Isaiah that show the Baptist was preparing the way for another; the words of Jesus are cast within the shadow of words from Isaiah that show Jesus was fulfilling the promise to bring light to the Gentiles. Thus John the Baptist is primarily announcing the impending arrival of the kingdom of heaven; Jesus is announcing its inauguration. That is consistent with themes throughout Matthew (and the Synoptics, for that matter). At the same time, in other cases it is helpful to link themes and technical expressions to many different spots throughout the canon—but more of this below.

THE ROLE OF THE "ANALOGY OF THE FAITH"

The appeal to the "analogy of the faith," though helpful, must be exercised with some caution. As used in Protestant theology, this appeal argues that, if any passage is ambiguous, it should be interpreted in line with the great "givens" of biblical Christianity; it should never be interpreted in such a way as to jeopardize those givens. At one level this is surely sound advice, granted that God's mind ultimately stands behind all the Scriptures. Nevertheless, there are several dangers inherent in a thoughtless application of the analogy of the faith. First, the interpreter may succumb to anachronism. God did not provide his people with all of the Bible all at once. There is a progression to his revelation, and to read the whole back into some early part may seriously distort that part, so that its true significance in the flow of redemptive history is obscured. For example, to read a full-blown Pauline doctrine of the Holy Spirit into every passage where "Spirit" occurs in, say, the Psalms, will certainly generate some interpretative blunders.

Second, the interpreter's theological grasp, his or her "systematic theology" (for all of us who read and teach Scripture develop certain syntheses, whether we call them "systematic theology" or not), may be faulty at many points, but it may be very difficult to spot the faults. The reason is that this synthesis, this systematic theology, itself becomes a controlling grid by which to interpret Scripture, under the guise of serving as the analogy of the faith.

Third, many Christians develop favorite passages of Scripture, and these become a kind of "canon within the canon" that serves as the touchstone by which to handle other passages. This inner canon becomes, for such Christians, the best summary of "the faith." This can lead, for instance, to some fairly bizarre reading of James 2:14–26 on the ground that Paul in Romans 4 and Galatians 3 apparently says something rather different, and Paul's perspective is given automatic priority.

THE VALUE OF HISTORICAL AND ARCHAEOLOGICAL BACKGROUND INFORMATION

Because there are so many historical referents in the biblical text, it is entirely proper to seek relevant background information where such information would be shared by the human author and the first readers. This, too, is a function of the fact that the Bible is historically conditioned. When Isaiah writes, "In the year that King Uzziah died . . . ," it is very helpful to find out what Kings and Chronicles say about Uzziah, for it contributes to our understanding of what Isaiah is saying— and after all the same sort of information was presumably available (if not exactly in that form) to both Isaiah and his first readers. A fair bit of nonsense has been written about the exalted Christ's words to the Laodiceans: "I know your deeds, that you are neither cold nor hot. I wish you were either one or the other!" (Rev. 3:15). Many have argued that this means God prefers people who are "spiritually cold" above those who are "spiritually lukewarm," even though his first preference is for those who are "spiritually hot." Ingenious explanations are then offered to defend the proposition that spiritual coldness is a superior state to spiritual lukewarmness.

All of this can comfortably be abandoned once responsible archaeology has made its contribution. Laodicea shared the Lycus valley with two other cities mentioned in the New Testament. Colosse was the only one that enjoyed fresh, cold, spring water; Hierapolis was known for its hot springs and became a place to which people would resort to enjoy these healing baths. By contrast, Laodicea put up with water that was neither cold and useful, nor hot and useful; it was lukewarm, loaded with chemicals, and with an international reputation for being nauseating. That brings us to Jesus' assessment of the Christians there: they were not useful in any sense, they were simply disgusting, so nauseating he would vomit them away. The interpretation would be clear enough to anyone living in the Lycus valley in the first century; it takes a bit of background information to make the point clear today. Similarly, knowledge of certain ancient social patterns can shed a great deal of light on some passages, such as the parable of the five wise and five foolish virgins (Matt. 25:1–13).

When interpreters and translators ask themselves how the first readers would have understood a passage, they are not asking a merely hypothetical question impossible to answer (since we have no access to their minds). Rather, this is simply a way of getting at a host of subsidiary questions: How would these words have been understood at the time? What issues and themes were of resounding importance? What kind of conceptual framework would the biblical text confront? To raise such questions is not to affirm that we can always find perfect answers. Sometimes we can infer responsible answers by "mirror-reading" the text itself. It is obvious, for instance, that Paul is opposing certain people in his letter to the Galatians, and some things about those opponents are reasonably clear. Sometimes the evidence is more difficult, but still worth pondering. For example, however powerfully 1 John may be applied to a modern congregation, in the first instance it was designed to offer assurance to believers at the end of the first century who were suffering various forms of doubt owing in part to the recent departure of some schismatic group (1 John 2:19). If we conclude that this group embraced some form of proto-Gnosticism (about which we know a fair bit from extrabiblical sources), a number of other things in the letter become clear.

None of this endangers the Bible's sufficiency and clarity, for the main purposes of the Bible remain unaltered by such judgments. But because the Bible was graciously given to us by God *in a lengthy series of specific historical contexts*, significant light can be shed on a passage by patiently probing some of those contexts.

THE IMPORTANCE OF ASKING APPROPRIATE QUESTIONS
It is important to ask many questions of a text, and also to learn what questions are inappropriate.

On the positive side, in narrative it is almost always worth asking the obvious elementary questions: when, where, to whom, how, why, for how long, and so forth. Above all, it is important to ask what the theme and purpose are of the unit of text on which you are working, and how the various parts of the text make their contributions to that dominant theme and point. It is often worth asking what subsidiary themes are present. Sometimes one should ask questions related to an author's use of a particular word or expression, e.g., why did Paul use this word in this context when he might have used that one?

But it is easy to ask inappropriate questions. For instance, if one asks, "What does this passage say about Christian assurance?" when it is at best remotely related to such a theme, one may "find" answers that are not really there. One of the best signs of interpretative maturity is the kind of self-critical and reflective questioning of a biblical text that so "listens" to what is being said that the questions themselves are progressively honed, discarded, sharpened, corrected. This is an extraordinarily important component in spiraling in on the meaning of a text.

FITTING THE BIBLE TOGETHER
It is important to locate a passage in its place in redemptive history. Of course, scholars who think all the biblical books should be treated separately, who do not perceive one mind behind the whole, are inclined to give this principle short

shrift. For those who approach the Bible in the manner advocated here, however, this is merely responsible reading. This means more than organizing the historical material of the Bible into its chronological sequence, though it does not mean less. It means trying to understand the theological nature of the sequence.

One of the most useful avenues of study in this regard is how later Scripture writers refer to earlier ones. For example, one of the important titles assigned to Jesus in Matthew's Gospel is "Son of God." At Jesus' baptism, the voice from heaven declares, "This is my Son . . ." (3:17). Immediately Jesus is led by the Spirit into the desert to be tempted. There he spends forty days and forty nights in a difficult fast. The first assault of the devil begins with the taunt, "If you are the Son of God . . ." (4:3). Jesus replies with words from Deuteronomy 8 that first applied to Israel. At that point it is almost impossible not to remember that as early as Exodus 4 God refers to Israel as his son. As God's son, Israel spent forty years in the desert being taught but failing to learn that "man does not live on bread alone, but on every word that comes from the mouth of God" (Deut. 8:3; Matt. 4:4); Jesus the true Son now spends forty days in the desert and demonstrates that he has learned that lesson. Indeed, the entire passage is criss-crossed with themes drawn from the period of the exodus, and throughout Jesus is presented as the "son" that Israel never was: obedient, persevering, submissive to God's word—in short, the locus of the true Israel. That becomes a major theme in Matthew's Gospel.

In a similar way, Christian readers soon notice the way Paul handles the law, Hebrews refers to the sacrificial system, and the Apocalypse constantly alludes to Daniel and Ezekiel, to name but a few of the textual connections between the books of the old covenant and the books of the new. The perspective of redemptive history must constantly be borne in mind. Thus, while treating, say, Exodus 4 fairly within its own context, the Christian teacher and preacher will feel obliged to give some indication where the theme of "Son of God" heads along the axis of God's gracious self-disclosure. Avoiding both anachronism (which reads the later material back into earlier material) and atomization (which refuses to consider canonical connections), this Christian will be eager to learn in what way, as John's Gospel insists, the Scriptures speak of Christ.

At few points is this disciplined exercise more challenging than in the interpretation of the Gospels. On their face, the Gospels describe the life, ministry, death, and resurrection of Jesus, before his ascension, the descent of the Spirit, and the formation of an international, multicultural and interracial church. On the other hand, the Gospels were clearly written several decades after those events by committed Christians concerned not only to bear witness to those events but to meet the needs and questions of their own readers. There are many ways by which the four Evangelists signal their concerns for both history and theology, for witness that avoids anachronism yet points the direction in which Jesus' teaching is taking his nascent church. In the Fourth Gospel, for example, John constantly draws attention to how much even the disciples did not understand at the time. Only after Jesus rose from the dead did some of his teachings, and their connection with Scripture, become clear (e.g., John 2:19–22). That John should draw attention to this fact reflects his concern to be true both to what actually took place and to its meaning for later believers.

Handling the Gospels sensitively means, among other things, that we cannot treat the first disciples' coming to full Christian faith exactly like the coming to faith of people today. In the case of the first disciples, for fully Christian faith they had to wait until the next major redemptive-historical event—the cross and resurrection of the Lord Jesus. Thus their steps in faith can never be exactly like ours, for we look back on those events while they had to wait for them. That means we must never teach and preach from the Gospels as if they were written simply to provide psychological profiles in discipleship, or as if they were exemplary "how-to" manuals for Christian living (though they certainly provide rich materials for such constructions). Rather, they are more like books that tell us how-we-got-from-there-to-here; above all they focus on who Jesus is, why he came, how and why he was so largely misunderstood, how his teaching and life led to the cross and resurrection, why he is worthy of all trust, the purpose of his mission, and much more. And as we focus on Jesus Christ himself, we are called to trusting and faithful discipleship.

At stake, of course, is how the Bible fits together. This is not to suggest that these are easy topics. Entire schools of interpretation have built up around various schema in which a few irreducible principles have become the fulcrum on which the rest of the evidence has been made to turn. But that fact should call us, not to despair, but to the large-hearted recognition that the inner-biblical connections are many and nuanced, and that there is still more insight to emerge from the study of God's Word.

AIMING FOR BIBLICAL BALANCE

Theological synthesis is important, but shoddy synthesis is misleading and dangerous. It has often been observed that a large part of orthodoxy resides in properly relating passage with passage, truth with truth. That observation is both a call to careful work and a warning against reductionism. Biblical balance is an important goal. For a start, we will avoid all approaches to interpretation that seize on some esoteric point from an obscure and isolated passage (e.g., 1 Cor. 15:29) to establish the basic framework out of which we interpret Scripture. If the political mood of our age favors one-issue politics, and sometimes one-issue Christianity, serious readers of the Bible must think more comprehensively. They will want to stress what Scripture stresses, and focus on the largest and more certain themes of God's gracious self-disclosure.

Nowhere are warnings against shoddy synthesis more important than when the Bible addresses themes that frankly invoke mystery. We are not going to understand everything about God; if we could we would be God, and even the assumption that we have such a right betrays our lostness, our wretched self-focus. God is more interested in our loving and trusting obedience and adoration than in our I.Q.s. Thus when we come across passages such as John 5:16–30, which powerfully articulates the relationship of Jesus the Son of God with his Father, or Romans 9, which unhesitatingly deploys strong predestinarian language, our recognizing the limitations of the evidence and the even greater limitations of our understanding of it is an important component in the interpretative task.

For the sake of simplification, little has been said about the exploration of how these themes have been handled throughout the history of the church. In fact, it is enormously important to recognize that, just as the interpreter does not approach the Scripture in a vacuum and must therefore become aware of his or her own biases, so also is it true, ironically, that one of the greatest helps in freeing us from unwitting slavery to our biases is the careful reading of the history of interpretation. Such reading must never usurp the place of the reading of Scripture; it is possible to become so expert in secondary opinions that one never ponders the text of Scripture itself. But once the warning has been noted, it is important, so far as we are able, to understand how Christians before us have wrestled with Scripture, not least the most controversial themes and passages. Such discipline will induce humility, clear our minds of unwarranted assumptions, expose faulty interpretations that have long since (and rightly) been dismissed, and remind us that responsible interpretation of Scripture must never be a solitary task.

DETERMINING THE FUNCTIONS OF BIBLICAL THEMES

Especially where biblical themes are complex and intertwined, it is important to observe the Bible's use of such themes, to determine their specific functions, and to resolve to follow such biblical patterns in our own theological reflection. For example, the Bible never infers that because he is sovereign God stands in the same way behind evil as he stands behind good, or that all human effort is irrelevant, or that fatalism is warranted. Far from it. From God's sovereignty it is inferred that grace must stand (Romans 9), that God can be trusted even when we cannot see the way ahead (Rom. 8:28), and much more. From the fact that God made us, people often infer that God is the Father of us all, and we are all "brothers and sisters"; doubtless in some sense that is true. Still, the fact remains that "Father" language applied to God in the Bible is reserved for those who have entered into covenant relationship with him; under the new covenant, "brothers" is applied to believers. If we start associating these terms with structures of thought widely at variance from their biblical usage, it will not be long before we import into Scripture things that are not there, even while we blind ourselves to things that are.

To take an example of a slightly different kind, the author of the letter to the Hebrews reminds us that "Jesus Christ is the same yesterday and today and forever" (13:8). Some zealous Christians have drawn inferences such as this: "Jesus healed all who came to him in the days of his flesh; he is the same yesterday and today and forever; therefore he will heal me if I come to him." Jesus may or may not heal today, but in any case the reasoning is bad. Why not similarly say, "Jesus walked on water in the days of his flesh; Jesus is the same yesterday, today, and forever; therefore he walks on water today"? The point is that the author of Hebrews was not uttering a principle that could be applied to every single facet of Jesus' life. The context of Hebrews 13 shows to what purpose the author was putting this truth.

THE DISTINCTION BETWEEN INTERPRETATION AND APPLICATION
While approaching the Bible reverently, we must constantly distinguish responsible interpretation of Scripture from personal or corporate application. Of course, in hortatory passages the line between the two becomes thin; or, better put, it becomes easier to move from one to the other. But unless we preserve a principled distinction we are likely to succumb to many harmful interpretations.

For instance, we may so quickly pursue "what the Bible means to me," greatly emphasizing "to me," that we completely ignore the distance between ourselves and the text, and compromise the Bible's historical specificity and thus the nature of God's graciously given verbal revelation. Worse, the morbid person given to endless introspection will glumly focus on all the passages that establish human guilt; the triumphalistic extrovert will fasten on everything that shouts of victory; the self-seeking hedonist will find passages that speak of life and joy. It is far better for all Christians to read every part of the Scripture, think it through on its own terms, discern, so far as possible, its contribution to the whole of the canon, and then ask how such truth applies to themselves, and to the church and the society of which they are a part.

THE IMPORTANCE OF GODLINESS
Because the Bible is God's word, it is vitally important to cultivate humility as we read, to foster a meditative prayerfulness as we reflect and study, to seek the help

Approaching the Bible   53

of the Holy Spirit as we try to understand and obey, to confess sin and pursue purity of heart and motive and relationships as we grow in understanding. Failure in these areas may produce scholars, but not mature Christians.

Above all, we must remember that we will one day give an account to the one who says,

> This is the one I esteem:
>> he who is humble and contrite in spirit,
>> and trembles at my word. (Isa. 66:2)

Further Reading

Carson, D. A., and J. D. Woodbridge, eds. *Hermeneutics, Authority, and Canon.* Grand Rapids: Zondervan, 1986.

———. *Scripture and Truth.* Grand Rapids: Baker, 1992.

Fee, G. D., and D. Stuart. *How to Read the Bible for All Its Worth.* Grand Rapids: Zondervan, 1981 (3d ed., 2003).

Morris, L. *I Believe in Revelation.* London: Hodder & Stoughton; Grand Rapids: Eerdmans, 1976.

Motyer, S. *Unlock the Bible.* London: Scripture Union, 1990.

Osborne, G. R. *The Hermeneutical Spiral.* Downers Grove, IL: InterVarsity, 1991 (2d ed., 2006).

2

Recent Developments in the Doctrine of Scripture

The pattern of Christian thought that emerged from the Reformation is often summed up under the three phrases: *sola gratia, sola fides,* and *sola scriptura.* When I was a boy, I sometimes wondered how logic could be preserved if there were *three* statements each claiming that something or other was "*sola*"; but in due course I learned that grace is the sole ground of salvation, faith is the sole means of salvation, and the Scriptures are the sole ultimate authority for faith and life—all set in the context of the polemics of the Reformation period.

Precisely because the Reformers' theological formulations were shaped by the controversies of their age, it is clear that the "faith and life" formula was meant to be an all-embracing rubric, not a limiting one. They claimed that the deposit of truth lies in the Bible, not in the church or in the magisterium of the church. Their concern, in other words, was to spell out the locus of authority in order to rebut their Roman Catholic opponents, not to restrict the range of the Bible's authority to religious life and thought, away from history and the natural world.[1] The modern disjunction would have seemed strange to them.

This side of the Enlightenment, debate over the Scriptures soon moved on to broader matters. Although the history of these debates has been chronicled many

---

Reprint of D. A. Carson, "Recent Developments in the Doctrine of Scripture," in *Hermeneutics, Authority, and Canon,* ed. D. A. Carson and John D. Woodbridge (Grand Rapids: Zondervan, 1986), 1–48, 363–74.

[1]Contra Jack B. Rogers and Donald K. McKim, *The Authority and Interpretation of the Bible: An Historical Approach* (San Francisco: Harper & Row, 1979), 89ff.

times,[2] a great deal of detailed work still needs to be done. But perhaps the most difficult period to comprehend, in some ways, is the most recent. We do not yet have the advantage of distance; and the twists in the debate are many and intricate. Not a few of the issues raised are so fresh or are so much a part of modern scholarly thought that evenhanded and disinterested evaluation is extraordinarily difficult.

The essays printed in this volume and in the companion volume[3] have been written in order to address the most important of these issues. We have written as evangelicals; and so far as the doctrine of Scripture is concerned, we believe we stand within the central tradition of the church and in line with the teaching of the Scriptures themselves. This ancient tradition is worth defending, examining, and rearticulating as theological fashions raise new questions. The present essay attempts to scan rather rapidly some of these recent developments, in the hope that a bird's-eye view will provide these volumes with breadth and unity that might otherwise be lacking. The aim is not to deal with denominational bodies (e.g., the Missouri Synod or the Southern Baptist Convention) or particular publications that have agonized over the issue (e.g., *Churchman*) but to focus on theological, philosophical, and historical matters that in the modern debate impinge directly on how we view the Bible.

The resurgence of interest in the doctrine of Scripture can be traced to many factors; but four deserve brief mention. The *first* is the growing strength of evangelicals. It is no longer possible to ignore them. Their churches are growing, their seminaries are bulging, their books keep pouring off the presses. In any large movement, of course, much of the momentum is kept up at the purely popular level; but evangelicalism can no longer be responsibly dismissed as an academic wasteland. While nonconservative seminaries are lowering academic standards, multiplying D.Min. tracks, and reducing Greek and Hebrew requirements in order to avoid disastrous collapse of student enrollment, seminaries within evangelicalism continue to blossom. At some Ivy League seminaries, only 30 percent of the students take any Greek; most evangelical institutions require at least one year of Greek as a prerequisite for entrance and insist on a minimum of one year of Greek beyond that. One of the results is that a disproportionate number of current doctoral candidates both in America and in Britain spring from conservative backgrounds; they are more likely to have the linguistic competence for advanced training. The rising tide of interest in the doctrine of Scripture in nonconserva-

---

[2]See especially H. D. McDonald, *Theories of Revelation: An Historical Study 1700–1960* (original titles *Ideas of Revelation* and *Theories of Revelation*, 1959 and 1963; repr., Grand Rapids: Baker, 1979); and S. L. Greenslade, ed., *The Cambridge History of the Bible: The West from the Reformation to the Present Day* (Cambridge: Cambridge University Press, 1963).

[3]Viz., D. A. Carson and John D. Woodbridge, eds., *Scripture and Truth* (Grand Rapids: Zondervan, 1983).

tive circles[4] is not a reaction against conservatives who are becoming even more conservative than the heritage from which they have emerged (as some have suggested).[5] Rather, it is at least partly a reaction to the increasing visibility of conservatives.

The *second* factor is scarcely less important: evangelicalism is becoming somewhat fragmented. Never a truly monolithic movement, evangelicalism long enjoyed a fair measure of agreement over certain central teachings; but in its contemporary guise it is pulling itself apart on several different doctrinal fronts—and one of these is the doctrine of Scripture. Some of this fragmentation is the predictable but tragic fruit of remarkable numerical growth. Whatever the reason, some of the strongest attacks on the evangelicals' traditional understanding of Scripture—even some of the least temperate criticisms—have been penned by those who today are viewed as evangelicals[6]—though it is by no means certain that the evangelicals of forty years ago, were they somehow to reappear on the scene, would recognize them as fellow travelers. Perhaps it should be mentioned that this fragmentation of evangelicals' views on Scripture is not restricted to North America—as, for instance, a comparison of the papers of the Keele and Nottingham conferences quickly proves with reference to England (with similar evidence available for other places).

---

[4]The recent literature is legion. The most important books and articles include the following: Paul J. Achtemeier, *The Inspiration of Scripture: Problems and Proposals* (Philadelphia: Westminster, 1980); M. R. Austin, "How Biblical Is 'The Inspiration of Scripture'?" *ExpTim* 93 (1981–1982): 75–79; James Barr, *The Scope and Authority of the Bible* (London: SCM, 1980; Philadelphia: Westminster, 1981); idem, *Holy Scripture: Canon, Authority, Criticism* (Oxford: Oxford University Press, 1983; David L. Bartlett, *The Shape of Scriptural Authority* (Philadelphia: Fortress, 1983); Robert Gnuse, "Authority of the Scriptures: Quest for a Norm," *BTB* 13 (1983): 59–66; Paul D. Hanson, *The Diversity of Scripture: A Theological Interpretation* (Philadelphia: Fortress, 1982); Krister Stendahl, "The Bible as a Classic and the Bible as Holy Scripture," *JBL* 103 (1984): 3–10; idem, *Meanings: The Bible as Document and as Guide* (Philadelphia: Fortress, 1984). Also, many works on the interpretation of Scripture have important things to say about the Bible's authority. The same point could be made for some works published in other languages: the debate between Gerhard Maier, *Das Ende der historisch-kritischen Methode*, 5th ed. (Wuppertal: Brockhaus, 1984), and Peter Stuhlmacher, *Schriftauslegung auf dem Wege zur biblischen Theologie* (Göttingen: Vandenhoeck & Ruprecht, 1975); or the essay by Pierre Gisel, "Pour une theologie de l'Ecriture: Réactions face à la 'Theologie du mouvement évangelique,'" *ETR* 59 (1984): 509–21. Cf. also Eckhard Schnabel, "Die neuere Diskussion um die Inspiration der Heiligen Schrift," *Bibel und Gemeinde* 84 (1984): 409–30.

[5]So, for instance, James D. G. Dunn, "The Authority of Scripture According to Scripture," *Chm* 96 (1982): 105–6. When Dunn argues that at the turn of the century the range of opinion among evangelicals ranged from Warfield to Orr, he is, of course, right; but what he fails to assess is the *distribution* of those opinions among the evangelicals. This sort of historical question receives a little more attention below.

[6]There is an enormous range of positions within this "left wing" of evangelicals, as well as an enormous range of competency—from the mature and articulate to the astonishingly ignorant. Representative recent works include: William J. Abraham, *The Divine Inspiration of Holy Scripture* (New York/Oxford: Oxford University Press, 1981); idem, *Divine Revelation and the Limits of Historical Criticism* (Oxford: Oxford University Press, 1983); G. C. Berkouwer, *Studies in Dogmatics: Holy Scripture* (Grand Rapids: Eerdmans, 1975); Donald G. Bloesch, *The Ground of Certainty: Toward an Evangelical Theology of Revelation* (Grand Rapids: Eerdmans, 1971); idem, *Essentials of Evangelical Theology*, vol. 1, *God, Authority, and Salvation* (San Francisco: Harper & Row, 1978), 51–87; Dunn, "The Authority of Scripture According to Scripture," 104–22, 201–25; I. Howard Marshall, *Biblical Inspiration* (Grand Rapids: Eerdmans, 1982); Robert M. Price, "Inerrant the Wind: The Troubled House of North American Evangelicals," *EQ* 55 (1983): 129–44; Bernard Ramm, *After Fundamentalism* (San Francisco: Harper & Row, 1983); Jack B. Rogers, "Biblical Authority and Confessional Change," *Journal of Presbyterian History* 59 (1981): 131–58; Rogers and McKim, *The Authority and Interpretation of the Bible*.

It is astonishing how much of the literature written by mainline evangelicals on the doctrine of Scripture has been penned in response to one or both of these first two trends. Conservatives have often been accused of fixating on Scripture; but careful perusal of the treatments of the last fifteen years shows that, if anything, the reverse is true: nonconservatives have taken up the theme, and conservatives have responded. That may not say much for the creativity of conservatives; but it does exonerate them from the charge of endlessly banging the drum. The creation of the ICBI (International Council on Biblical Inerrancy) was prompted by apologetic concerns; and only a few of the authors who have published under its aegis have attempted new and more profound analysis of the nature of Scripture. The majority have simply aimed to restate the traditional positions and delineate the weaknesses of their opponents. Like the works of the nonconservatives, the essays of those who have contributed to ICBI have varied from the average and the shallow to the acute and the insightful.[7] As an instance of the latter, it would be a great help to clarity of thought if no one would comment on the appropriateness or otherwise of the term *inerrancy* without reading the essay of Paul Feinberg that deals with this subject.[8]

ICBI is perhaps simultaneously too encompassing and too unrepresentative in its membership. Because it is too encompassing, it has sometimes published essays of doubtful worth along with far better pieces, but this policy, though it has encouraged the involvement of many, has set the organization up for caricature that is not itself entirely fair. Owing to the prominence of the organization, some have failed to recognize that many evangelicals in America and abroad have contributed to the debate without any organizational connection to ICBI; in that sense, ICBI is somewhat unrepresentative.[9]

In any case, it would be quite mistaken to suppose that conservatives on the doctrine of Scripture are an embattled few who can manage nothing more credible than throwing a few defensive javelins into the crowd, hurled from the safety of a stony rampart called "orthodoxy." In addition to the *magnum*

---

[7]In addition to some purely popular publications, the principal ICBI-sponsored publications are as follows: Norman L. Geisler, ed., *Inerrancy* (Grand Rapids: Zondervan, 1979); idem, *Biblical Errancy: Its Philosophical Roots* (Grand Rapids: Zondervan, 1981); Earl D. Radmacher and Robert D. Preus, eds., *Hermeneutics, Inerrancy, and the Bible* (Grand Rapids: Zondervan, 1984); John D. Hannah, ed., *Inerrancy and the Church* (Chicago: Moody, 1984); Gordon Lewis and Bruce Demarest, eds., *Challenges to Inerrancy* (Chicago: Moody, 1984).

[8]Paul D. Feinberg, "The Meaning of Inerrancy," in *Inerrancy*, ed. Norman L. Geisler (Grand Rapids: Zondervan, 1979), 267–304.

[9]Most of the contributors to this present volume and *Scripture and Truth*, including the two editors, have written nothing for ICBI. In addition, many books and articles have been published recently whose authors or editors may hold some connection with ICBI, even though the publication itself has not been sponsored by that organization: e.g., Roger R. Nicole and J. Ramsay Michaels, eds., *Inerrancy and Common Sense* (Grand Rapids: Baker, 1980); J. I. Packer, *God Has Spoken* (Downers Grove, IL: InterVarsity, 1979); Paul Ronald Wells, *James Barr and the Bible: A Critique of the New Liberalism* (Phillipsburg, NJ: Presbyterian and Reformed, 1980); Leon Morris, *I Believe in Revelation* (Grand Rapids: Eerdmans, 1976).

opus of Henry,[10] there is a plethora of studies by evangelicals—philosophical, exegetical, hermeneutical, historical, critical—that do not address directly the question of the truthfulness of Scripture, but operate within the framework of that "functional nonnegotiable"[11] and by demonstrating a certain coherence and maturity, contribute to the same end.

The fragmentation of evangelicalism, therefore, has produced mixed fruit. On one end of the spectrum, it has weakened its distinctiveness; on the other end, it has flirted with obscurantism. Yet there still remains a considerable strength; and part of the resurgence of interest in the doctrine of Scripture reflects the self-examination of the movement as it struggles with its own identity. But of this I shall say more in a few moments.

The *third* factor that has helped to raise again the subject of Scripture is the crisis of authority that stamps so much of modern Western Christianity—especially in academic circles. Children of the Enlightenment, like moths to a light we are drawn to the incandescence of the autonomy of reason. But having destroyed all the pretensions of external authority, we have discovered somewhat aghast that reason is corruptible, that one human mind does not often agree in great detail with another human mind, that reason by itself is a rather stumbling criterion of truth, beset as it is by a smorgasbord of values, theories, and predispositions shaped in remarkable independence of reason.

In the ensuing vacuum, there has arisen a muted hunger for authority. Finding all the gods dead, some people have manufactured their own: faddish gurus, unrestrained hedonism, and the pious pursuit of self-fulfillment are among the current contenders. But many wonder if the authority of Scripture should not be looked at again. Nor is this a concern of conservatives alone. The crisis of authority infects every stratum of our society; and, therefore, many people—unable to bear the sight of the epistemological abyss, yet unwilling to call in question the proposition that the human race is the final measure of all things—have come to affirm the authority of Scripture, though in some attenuated sense. The nature of such attenuation is a recurring theme in this essay; but for now it is enough to point out that the search for meaningful authority has contributed to the renascence of interest in the doctrine of Scripture.

The *fourth* factor contributing to this renascence is the theological revolution that has taken place and is taking place in the Roman Catholic Church. Pope John XXIII and Vatican II have had a profound influence on academic Roman Catholic

[10]Carl F. H. Henry, *God, Revelation and Authority*, 6 vols. (Waco, TX: Word, 1976–1983).
[11]I have defined the term in D. A. Carson, "Historical Tradition and the Fourth Gospel: After Dodd, What?" in *Gospel Perspectives*, vol. 2, ed. R. T. France and David Wenham (Sheffield: JSOT, 1981), 83–145.

theology, confirming and accelerating the more "liberal" wing of the church in its adoption of a position on Scripture that is almost indistinguishable from that of "liberal" Protestantism. By and large, this trend has not been as uncontrolled in Catholicism as in Protestantism, owing in part to the constraints of Catholicism's theology of tradition; but the changes are so far-reaching that to compare the academic publications of the Roman Catholic Church of forty or fifty years ago with those of the past two decades is to enter two entirely different worlds. The dramatic change is attested even by the successive drafts at Vatican II. The first draft schema, reflecting the longstanding tradition of the church, dealt with inerrancy as follows:

> Since divine inspiration extends to all things [in the Bible], it follows directly and necessarily that the entire Sacred Scripture is absolutely immune from error. By the ancient and constant faith of the Church we are taught that it is absolutely wrong to concede that a sacred writer has erred, since divine inspiration by its very nature excludes and rejects every error in every field, religious or profane. This necessarily follows because God, the supreme truth, can be the author of no error whatever.

However, it was the fifth draft that was actually adopted:

> Since everything which the inspired author or sacred writer asserted must be held to have been asserted by the Holy Spirit, it must equally be held that the books of Scripture teach firmly, faithfully, and without error that truth which God willed to be put down in the sacred writings for the sake of our salvation.[12]

The changes are dramatic. First the Bible is now restricted to truth "for the sake of our salvation," and, second—and more importantly—the expression "that truth which God willed to be put down in the sacred writings" not only comes short of making God's truth at least as extensive as the writings but also thereby leaves it entirely open to each reader (or to the church) to decide which parts of the sacred writings embody God's truth. Everyone from a fundamentalist to a "Christian atheist" could assent to this formulation—which is another way of saying that this final draft masks massive disagreement in the Roman Catholic Church. Creedally speaking, its fine phrases are worth less than the ink that enables us to read them.

---

[12]Walter M. Abbott, ed., *The Documents of Vatican II* (New York: Guild, 1966), 119. See discussion by someone sympathetic to the final draft in Bruce Vawter, *Biblical Inspiration* (Philadelphia: Westminster, 1972; London: Hutchinson, 1972), 144–50.

This revolution is evident not only in the content of much Roman Catholic scholarship[13] but now also in the self-conscious defense of these developments.[14] Roman Catholic scholars who adopt a conservative stance on the Scriptures continue to publish their findings;[15] but by and large they have neither advanced a well-thought-out defense of their position nor devised a mature critique of their more liberal colleagues. The few explicit attempts to accomplish the latter are too personal and insufficiently knowledgeable to carry much weight in the academic marketplace.[16]

Whatever the factors that have contributed to bringing about renewed discussion of the nature of Scripture, this essay attempts to chart some of the most important of the recent developments. The eight sections in the rest of this paper do not attempt to be comprehensive; rather, the focus is on those issues that seem to have the greatest bearing on the traditional view of the authority and truthfulness of Scripture held by the church across the centuries.[17] Among other things, this means that a disproportionate amount of space is devoted to positions that are *nearest to but somewhat divergent from* the traditional view. Moreover, issues discussed at length in one of the other articles in these two volumes are usually accorded only brief discussion in this essay, along with a note drawing attention to the more extensive treatment.

Revisionist Historiography

Summary of Recent Historiography

As late as 1975, Martin E. Marty, in an essay largely devoted to tracing the *differences* between fundamentalism and evangelicalism,[18] could nevertheless insist that so far as the doctrine of the inerrancy of Scripture is concerned

---

[13]I am referring to commentaries, journal articles, published dissertations, works of theology, and the like that approach the truthfulness of Scripture in ways that an earlier generation of Catholic scholars could scarcely imagine. These include not only the contributions of North Atlantic scholars (e.g., Eduard Schillebeeckx and Hans Kung) but many "third world" works as well (e.g., the left wing of the largely Roman Catholic theology of liberation movement).

[14]E.g., *inter alia* Raymond E. Brown, "Rome and the Freedom of Catholic Biblical Studies," in *Search the Scriptures* (Festschrift for R. T. Stamm), ed. J. M. Mvers et al. (Leiden: Brill, 1969), 129–50; idem, *The Critical Meaning of the Bible* (New York: Paulist, 1981); Vawter, *Biblical Inspiration*; Avery Dulles, *Models of Revelation* (New York: Doubleday, 1983).

[15]I am thinking of the works of such scholars as Albert Vanhoye and Ignace de la Potterie.

[16]E.g., George A. Kelly, *The New Biblical Theorists: Raymond E. Brown and Beyond* (Ann Arbor: Servant, 1983). For recent Protestant assessments, see Robert L. Saucy, "Recent Roman Catholic Theology," in *Challenges to Inerrancy: A Theological Response*, ed. Gordon Lewis and Bruce Demarest (Chicago: Moody, 1984), 215–46.

[17]The cohesiveness of this tradition I shall briefly mention below; but one caveat must be entered immediately. Differences between Protestants and Roman Catholics in the wake of the Reformation do not focus on the truthfulness of Scripture—or on its authority per se—but on the means of obtaining an authoritative interpretation of Scripture and on whether the Scripture alone is the sole locus of absolute authority in the church. Whenever the present study appeals to the cohesiveness of the tradition across the centuries regarding the Bible's authority, it allows for this sort of caveat, since the issues raised by it are of little consequence to the present discussion.

[18]Martin E. Marty, "Tensions Within Contemporary Evangelicalism: A Critical Appraisal," in *The Evangelicals*, ed. David F. Wells and John D. Woodbridge (Nashville: Abingdon, 1975), 170–88.

there was no difference between the two groups.[19] That may have been a slight exaggeration, for even in 1975 there were a few scholars who called themselves evangelicals but who expressed their displeasure with any notion of "inerrancy" as traditionally understood. But Marty's assessment highlights a point of some importance: until fairly recently, the infallibility or inerrancy of Scripture was one of the self-identifying flags of evangelicalism, recognized by friend and foe alike. In debates with nonconservatives, both sides agreed that the conservatives were in line with the historic tradition of the church. Nonconservatives simply argued that such a position was no longer tenable in any intellectually respectable climate; and conservatives sought to show that the position was not only defensible but one without which the heart of the gospel too easily slipped from one's grasp. Of course, there have been a few exceptions to this understanding. In his debates with Warfield, for instance, Charles Briggs[20] sought to show that the position he held was in line with Reformation teaching; but his argument was not taken up and developed by others. Karl Barth likewise insisted that his understanding of Scripture was but a modern restatement of historic and especially Reformation Christianity; but although in his strong defense of the Bible's authority there is considerable justification for his claim, nevertheless there are nuances in his position that remove him somewhat from the heritage to which he lays claim.[21] By and large, then, conservatives and nonconservatives alike have in the past agreed that the witness of history has favored the conservatives.

That consensus is rapidly dissipating. A new generation of historians is arguing that the modern conservative position on Scripture is something of an aberration that owes its impetus in part to scholastic theology of the post-Reformation period and in part to the Princetonians, especially Charles Hodge and Benjamin B. Warfield. Probably the best-known work to espouse this view is that of Jack Rogers and Donald McKim.[22] They seek to establish this thesis by a comprehensive outline of the way the Bible was described and treated throughout (largely Western) church history. Their conclusion is that the historic position of the church defends the Bible's authority in the areas of faith and practice (understood in a restrictive sense), not its reliable truthfulness in every area on which it chooses to speak.

Initial response was largely affirming; but it was not long before major weaknesses came to light. Owing not least to the detailed rebuttal by John D.

---

[19]Ibid., 173, 180.
[20]See especially his *Biblical Study: Its Principles, Methods and History* (New York: Scribner, 1883).
[21]See especially the essays by Geoffrey Bromiley and John Frame in this volume.
[22]Rogers and McKim, *The Authority and Interpretation of the Bible*.

Woodbridge,[23] rising numbers of scholars have pointed out the fatal flaws. While Rogers and McKim accuse conservatives of reading Warfield into Calvin and the Fathers, it soon becomes apparent that they read Barth and Berkouwer into Calvin and the Fathers. Misunderstanding some of their sources and quoting others with prejudicial selectivity, they finally succumb to a certain "ahistoricism" that neglects the church's sustained attempt to guard the form of the message as well as the message itself.[24]

The work of Rogers and McKim is based in one small part on an influential book by Ernest Sandeen,[25] who argues that belief in "the inerrancy of the Scriptures in the original documents" was innovatively raised to the level of creedal standard by Benjamin Warfield and Archibald Alexander in an 1881 essay on "Inspiration." This part of Sandeen's examination of fundamentalism's roots was woven into the larger pattern spun by Rogers and McKim. One of the benefits of their work has been a renewed interest in this and related historical questions. As a result, major essays have been written to show, *inter alia*, that primary sources (letters, magazine articles, books, and manuscripts) of the nineteenth century amply attest that the view articulated by Warfield and Hodge was popular long before 1881,[26] that the magisterial Reformers were consistent in their defense of an inerrant Scripture,[27] that Abraham Kuyper and Herman Bavinck of the "Old Amsterdam" school cannot legitimately be taken as forerunners of Barth and Berkouwer,[28] and much more. We anticipate more of these careful historical treatments in the next few years.

---

[23]John D. Woodbridge, "Biblical Authority: Towards an Evaluation of the Rogers and McKim Proposal," *TJ* 1 (1980): 165–236; idem, *Biblical Authority: A Critique of the Rogers/McKim Proposal* (Grand Rapids: Zondervan, 1982). One reviewer of Woodbridge's book rather badly missed the point by suggesting that although Rogers and McKim had been answered at the historical level, Woodbridge had failed to tackle the important hermeneutical issues that Rogers and McKim had raised. But, in fact, theirs was not a hermeneutical but a historical thesis. Another (William J. Abraham, "Redeeming the Evangelical Experiment," *Theological Students Fellowship Bulletin* 8, no. 3 [January–February 1985]: 12n5) obliquely refers to Woodbridge's work to excoriate conservative claims "about the Bible" because "they rest on arguments which are narrowly historical in nature." The lack of evenhanded rigor in such a charge is frankly astonishing; Rogers and McKim set forth a thesis based on their historical understanding, and they were refuted in the same arena. Why, then, is it the conservative arguments that are "narrowly historical in nature"?

[24]The word is chosen by Rodney L. Petersen in his review of Rogers and McKim in *PSB* 4 (1983): 61–63.

[25]Ernest R. Sandeen, *Roots of Fundamentalism: British and American Millenarianism, 1800–1930* (Chicago: University of Chicago Press, 1970; repr., Grand Rapids: Baker, 1978).

[26]See especially Randall H. Balmer, "The Old Princeton Doctrine of Inspiration in the Context of Nineteenth-Century Theology: A Reappraisal" (M.A. thesis, Trinity Evangelical Divinity School, 1981); idem, "The Princetonians and Scripture: A Reconsideration," *WTJ* 44 (1982): 352–65; John D. Woodbridge and Randall H. Balmer, "The Princetonians and Biblical Authority: An Assessment of the Ernest Sandeen Proposal," in *Scripture and Truth*, ed. Carson and Woodbridge, 245–79, 396–410.

[27]Numerous writers have recently taken up this point (though a substantial part of contemporary scholarship continues to take the opposite view): e.g., James I. Packer, "John Calvin and the Inerrancy of Holy Scripture," in *Inerrancy and the Church*, 143–88; W. Robert Godfrey, "Biblical Authority in the Sixteenth and Seventeenth Centuries: A Question of Transition," in *Scripture and Truth*, ed. Carson and Woodbridge, 225–43, 391–97; Roger R. Nicole, "John Calvin and Inerrancy," *JETS* 25 (1982): 425–42; Eugene F. Klug, "Word and Spirit in Luther Studies since World War II," *TJ* 5 (1984): 3–46.

[28]Richard B. Gaffin Jr., "Old Amsterdam and Inerrancy?" *WTJ* 44 (1982): 250–89; 45 (1983): 219–72.

Rennie's Proposal

This much of recent revisionist historiography and the responses it has called forth is common knowledge. But subtler influences are at work. In a conference held in June 1981 at the Institute for Christian Studies in Toronto, Ian Rennie delivered a paper written as a response to Rogers and McKim but containing several important and innovative proposals.[29] Rennie argues that the view expounded by Rogers and McKim has conceptual links with "plenary inspiration" as understood in Britain in the nineteenth century. Plenary inspiration, according to Rennie, was distinguished from verbal inspiration and was characterized by (1) a willingness to recognize several different modes of inspiration, (2) insistence nonetheless that all the Bible is inspired, (3) confidence that because all the Bible is authoritative it will not lead anyone aside from the truth on any subject (though it is peculiarly authoritative when it deals with the central Christian truths), and (4) greater openness to interpretive innovation than its competitor. Plenary inspiration could describe the Bible as infallible and without error. It is the view closest to the relatively unformed doctrine of Scripture held by the church until the Reformation.

By contrast, the Germanic lands in the sixteenth century began to advance the verbal inspiration view—a view that held sway in countries heavily influenced by Germany but one that made almost no impact on the Anglo-American world until the nineteenth century, when it began to be defended by Alexander Carson, Robert Haldane, J. C. Ryle, and many others. The verbal inspiration theory is painfully literalistic in its approach, and it becomes characteristic of Christianity in decline and defensiveness. The plenary view reflects a Christianity that is both orthodox and robust, and it becomes one of the vehicles of the First and Second Evangelical Awakenings. Historically, it even enabled those who opposed the slave trade to "break through the literalism that sanctioned slavery, and affirm that in such issues it was the spirit of love and redemptive freedom that validly reinterpreted texts that otherwise possessed the death-disseminating quality of the culture-bound."[30]

There are two rather substantial weaknesses with Rennie's proposal. The first is the conceptual inappropriateness of the disjunction he draws. As Rennie characterizes plenary and verbal inspiration, it appears that the differences between the two viewpoints center on competing hermeneutical systems and have almost

---

[29]Ian S. Rennie, "Mixed Metaphors, Misunderstood Models, and Puzzling Paradigms: A Contemporary Effort to Correct Some Misunderstandings Regarding the Authority and Interpretation of the Bible: An Historical Response," a mimeographed but unpublished paper delivered at the conference, "Interpreting an Authoritative Scripture," in Toronto, Ontario, Canada, on June 22–26, 1981.
[30]Ibid., 11.

nothing to do with either inspiration or the Bible's truthfulness. Thus, he affirms that the verbal inspiration view is quick to say the Bible is without error and is fully authoritative; but, of course, the plenary inspiration viewpoint would not want to disagree. According to Rennie, the verbal inspiration view sees the locus of inspiration in the words themselves and tends to develop formulations in deductivist or Aristotelian fashion. By contrast, the plenary inspiration view sees the locus of inspiration in the human authors and tends to develop its formulations from the actual phenomena of Scripture. The irony in this disjunction is that the one passage where inspiration is overtly brought up in the Bible (surely, therefore, one of the "phenomena" to be embraced) tells the reader that it is the Scripture itself that is "inspired" ("God-breathed," 2 Tim. 3:16)—not the human authors. But apart from such distinctions, about which I'll say more in a later section, the primary disjunctions Rennie draws between the two viewpoints are hermeneutical and functional: plenary inspiration is open-minded, aware of the Enlightenment and able to come to terms with it, relevant, prophetic, against slavery, while verbal inspiration is defensive, incapable of relevantly addressing the age, strong on literalism and the defense of slavery.

These observations drive us to the second substantial weakness in Rennie's analysis.[31] His argument, of course, is essentially a historical one, based on his reading of certain texts; but it is not at all certain that he has understood those texts correctly. Certainly in the nineteenth century there were some who preferred to adopt the plenary inspiration viewpoint, and others were happier to label their view verbal inspiration. On the other hand, there is little evidence that the two labels were set over against each other. Those who upheld verbal inspiration were also happy to affirm plenary inspiration;[32] and *both* sides adopted the plenary inspiration label over against the Unitarians, who opted for a much "lower" view of the Bible.[33] In other words, all evangelicals labeled their view "plenary inspiration" when they were distinguishing their position from the "limited inspiration" of the Unitarians. More telling yet, at least some of those who disparaged verbal inspiration while affirm-

---

[31]For this paragraph and the next, I am heavily indebted to Richard Riss in an unpublished paper, "A Critical Examination of Ian Rennie's Historiography of Biblical Inspiration." See also his forthcoming thesis, "Early Nineteenth Century Protestant Views of Biblical Inspiration in the English Speaking World" (M.A. thesis, Trinity Evangelical Divinity School, 1986).

[32]Riss points out that "plenary inspiration" is not distinguished from "verbal inspiration" in Ebenezer Henderson's *Divine Inspiration* (1836), in Daniel Wilson's *The Evidences of Christianity* (1852), or in such important discussions of the doctrine as John Dick's *Essay on the Inspiration of the Holy Scriptures of the Old and New Testaments* (1811) or T. F. Curtis's *The Human Element in the Inspiration of the Sacred Scriptures* (1867).

[33]Thus, William Cooke, who held to verbal inspiration, could write that his "immediate object" was "to maintain the plenary inspiration of the sacred writers, and to show that the books of the Old and New Testament are the authentic oracles of God" (*Christian Theology* [London: Hamilton, Adams, and Co., 1879], 55). Cooke is not exceptional: cf. Eleazar Lord, *The Plenary Inspiration of the Holy Scriptures* (New York: A. D. F. Randolph, 1858); John Farrar, *Biblical and Theological Dictionary*, ed. J. Robinson Gregory (London: Charles H. Kelly, 1889), 354.

ing plenary inspiration did so because they mistakenly equated the former with a theory of mechanical dictation—a theory the ablest defenders of verbal inspiration disavowed—and with such things as verbatim reportage, which rendered Gospel harmonization principially impossible.[34] Similarly, even into the first third of the twentieth century, a few British evangelicals so associated the term *inerrancy* with crude literalism, or with a failure to recognize the progressive nature of revelation, that they therefore avoided associating themselves with the term—even though, by modern usage, that is what they believed.[35] As for those who in the early part of the twentieth century adopted the view that the Scriptures contained many errors on all sorts of incidental matters (e.g., James Orr, James Denney, and Marcus Dods), not only was their view outside the classic formulations of scriptural infallibility and plenary inspiration, but it was supported by surprisingly little exegesis.

It appears, then, that Rennie's assessment needs some major qualifications. It is true that the verbal inspiration viewpoint was prominent in Germanic lands, owing in part to the struggles Protestants found themselves engaged in with Roman Catholics and Socinians; but contra Rennie, it is not true that this view-point was first introduced into Britain through the hyper-Calvinist John Gill in his *Body of Practical Divinity* (1770). For instance, forty years earlier Ridgley had argued at some length "that the inspired writers have given us a true narration of things, and consequently that the words, as well as the matter, are truly divine."[36] Indeed, his argument is shaped by the assumption that his view is shared by

---

[34]So, for instance, Henry Alford, in the sixth section of the first chapter of his preface to *The Greek Testament*. Similarly, Daniel Wilson, whom Rennie lists as a fine exponent of plenary inspiration, can emphasize that the Bible is "the unerring standard of truth" and was "universally considered as the infallible word of God" throughout the preceding sixteen or seventeen centuries (*The Evidences of Christianity*, 254–55).

[35]See the discussion by David F. Wright, "Soundings in the Doctrine of Scripture in British Evangelicalism in the First Half of the Twentieth Century," *TynBul* 31 (1980): 87–106, who fails to treat this point adequately. He goes on to suggest that "[one] reason why Britain did not experience a Fundamentalist controversy in the 1910's and 1920's akin to the bitter battle in America lay in the more widespread acceptance of biological evolution by thinking evangelicals before the beginning of the century" (92). But not only does this overlook the fact that Warfield himself was an evolutionist; it stands as an unproved judgment in need of immediate qualification by other factors. For instance, most Christians in England belonged to the state church; and a state church makes the kind of cleavage found in North America structurally almost impossible. The vast majority of institutions for theological training were either university faculties or state church theological colleges. Even so, the Baptist Union (a powerful independent denomination of evangelicals in Britain as late as 1885) shortly thereafter split over the doctrine of Scripture, largely owing to the influence of C. H. Spurgeon. Moreover, many today would argue that the relative strength of American evangelicals' institutions at the end of the twentieth century—and the consequent growth of the church—largely validates the painful and often courageous decisions to withdraw in the 1920s and 1930s from the parent organizations increasingly characterized at the time by straightforward unbelief.

[36]Thomas Ridgley, *A Body of Divinity*, vol. 1 (New York: Robert Carter and Broehters, 1855), 57. Rennie's view needs further qualification from the thesis of Henning Graf Reventlow, *Bibelautorität und Geist der Moderne: Die Bedeutung des Bibelverständnisses für die geistesgeschichtliche und politische Entwicklung in England von der Reformation bis zur Aufklärung* (Göttingen: Vandenhoeck & Ruprecht, 1980), who argues that the eighteenth-century German moves adopting increasingly skeptical biblical criticism were dependent on seventeenth-century *English* developments. Reventlow's seminal study rightly debunks the stereotypical presentation of the rise of biblical criticism by showing that its roots are much earlier than the eighteenth century and are not simply German; but I suspect his important thesis unwittingly introduces a new reductionism by failing to discuss continental (especially French and Dutch) seventeenth-century intellectual history as well as English seventeenth-century intellectual history.

the vast majority of his readers. In any case, it is not at all clear that those who held to verbal inspiration in the nineteenth century were reflections of Christianity in decline. To support this rather startling thesis, Rennie merely offers the judgment that the opposing view opened up interpretative possibilities that made antislavery and other social reform movements possible. But a staunch supporter of verbal inspiration like Edward Kirk (1802–1874), the translator of Louis Gaussen's influential *Theopneustia*, was a leader in the American Anti-Slavery Society[37] and a champion of relief for the poor.[38] Rennie's underlying thesis is, on any reading, too generalizing: Christianity given to thoughtful doctrinal precision may not be in decline but in faithful consolidation and advance. Very frequently in the history of the church the attacks of new philosophical and theological positions have proved to be the occasion for the orthodox to formulate their own positions more carefully. These are the historical circumstances that under God breed an Athanasius or a Calvin.

The "Faith and Practice" Restriction

Another example of revisionist historiography merits mention. For some time it has been popular in many circles to speak of the Bible's authority, and even its inerrancy, in the realms of "faith and practice"—but not in such realms as history and science. All sides agree that the Bible is not a textbook on, say, high-energy physics; but those who hold a high view of Scripture argue that wherever Scripture speaks, it speaks truthfully. As the essays in this pair of volumes show, appropriate allowance is made for the genre of any biblical text, generalizing language, phenomenological descriptions, the problem of the hermeneutical circle, and so forth; but there is still in this camp a reasoned defense of the view that *whatever* the Scripture says, properly interpreted, is true. The restriction offered by the opposing camp—namely, that the Bible is necessarily true only when it addresses questions of faith and practice—is sometimes now read back into the history of the church as if the restriction belonged to the mainstream of the church's understanding of the Bible. One of the more influential articulations of this perspective is the work of Bruce Vawter.[39] His argument depends in part on a certain understanding of "accommodation" about which I shall say more in a subsequent section; but more central yet to his position is his repeated insistence that the "inerrancy" or "infallibility" position he freely concedes to be in the Fathers, in the Middle Ages, and in the Reformers is restricted to matters of faith and practice.

---

[37]Cf. Edward Norris Kirk, *Speech of Rev. E. N. Kirk at the Second Anniversary of the American Anti-Slavery Society* (New York: Anti-Slavery Society, 1835).
[38]Edward Norris Kirk, *A Plea for the Poor* (Boston: Tappan and Dennet, 1843).
[39]Vawter, *Biblical Inspiration*; idem, "Creationism: Creative Misuse of the Bible," in *Is God a Creationist? The Religious Case Against Creation-Science*, ed. Roland Mushat Frye (New York: Scribner, 1983), 71–82.

This reconstruction of history does not appear to stand up very well to close scrutiny. In the third of his recent W. H. Griffith Thomas lectures, John Wood-bridge[40] has carefully documented, in a preliminary way, some of the hurdles such a reconstruction must overcome. Vawter insists that the modern inerrantist who sees in the Bible a source of knowledge instead of a source of religious experience is hopelessly ensnared by modern scientific paradigms of "knowledge" illegitimately transferred to the Scripture. Too great a dependence on a "paradigmatic" view of the development of science is one of the weaknesses in Vawter's proposal;[41] but, more important, he fails to recognize that in the Middle Ages, for instance, the Bible held the supreme place of honor as the highest source of knowledge.

> Manuscript collections were organized under three rubrics: manuscripts of Scripture standing supremely by themselves, manuscripts which helped readers understand the Scriptures, and diverse manuscripts. Archivists know of few, if any, exceptions to this organizational division for medieval manuscript collections.[42]

Moreover the heavy weather that the Copernican theory faced from Catholic, Lutheran, and Calvinist thinkers alike stemmed from the fact that they thought the Bible flatly contradicted a heliocentric view of the universe—which, of course, presupposes that they believed the Bible could address such scientific issues. When Johannes Kepler (1571–1630) sided with Copernicus, he tried to persuade his critics that the theory of Copernicus could be squared with the Bible, not that the Bible does not address such questions or that it may be in error over them.[43] In fact, Kepler went so far as to say that he would willingly abandon whatever parts of the Copernican hypotheses could be shown to be contrary to Scripture.[44] The conclusion Woodbridge documents is inescapable:

---

[40]The title of the series is "Recent Interpretations of Biblical Authority." The third lecture is subtitled, "Does the Bible Teach 'Science'?" All are currently being published *ad seriatim* in BSac. I am indebted to Professor Woodbridge for stimulating discussions and important documentation in this area. See also his essay in this volume, "Some Misconceptions of the Impact of the 'Enlightenment' on the Doctrine of Scripture."

[41]The paradigmatic approach to the history of science was put on a respectable and influential footing by Thomas S. Kuhn, *The Structure of Scientific Revolutions* (Chicago: University of Chicago Press, 1962, 1970); but the theory has suffered a rather devastating attack in Frederick Suppe, ed., *The Structure of Scientific Theories*, 2d ed. (Urbana: University of Illinois Press, 1977); Galy Gutting, ed., *Paradigms and Revolutions: Applications and Appraisals of Thomas Kuhn's Philosophy of Science* (Notre Dame: University of Notre Dame Press, 1980).

[42]John D. Woodbridge, "Does the Bible Teach 'Science'?" BSac 142 (1985): 199, referring to Wolfgang Milde.

[43]See especially Edward Rosen, "Kepler and the Lutheran Attitude Towards Copernicanism in the Context of the Struggle Between Science and Religion," in *Kepler, Four Hundred Years: Proceedings of Conferences Held in Honour of Johannes Kepler*, ed. Arthur Beer and Peter Beer (Oxford: Pergamon, 1975), 332–33.

[44]Ibid., 328.

Contrary to the interpretations found in the works of Vawter, Rogers and McKim, and Roland Mushat Frye, the choice that Christians faced until the middle of the seventeenth century was generally this: Should each passage of an infallible Bible which speaks of the natural world be interpreted literally or should some interpretive allowance be made for the fact that a number of passages are couched in the language of appearance? The choice was not between a belief in a completely infallible Bible and a Bible whose infallibility was limited to faith and practice. Parties from both sides of this debate included "science" and history within their definition of infallibility, but they interpreted passages which dealt with the natural world in differing ways. Those persons who did believe the Bible contained errors included, among others, Socinians, libertines, skeptics, deists, remonstrants like Grotius, and members of smaller radical rationalist sects.[45]

The Bible was well on its way to being uncoupled from science, at least in many intellectual circles, by the second half of the seventeenth century; but this uncoupling was normally accompanied by a shift to a theological position that no longer affirmed the infallibility of Scripture. Therefore, those who now wish to affirm the Bible's infallibility in the spheres of "faith and practice" but not in all areas on which it speaks are doubly removed from the mainstream of historical antecedents. Whatever the merits or demerits of their theological position, they cannot legitimately appeal to the sustained commitment of the church in order to bolster that position.

Common Sense Realism

Another sector of modern historiography has become extremely influential—namely, the reassessment of the role and influence of Scottish Common Sense Realism.[46] This offspring of Thomas Reid[47] is charged with so influencing

---

[45]Woodbridge, "Does the Bible Teach 'Science'?" 202.

[46]Cf. *inter alia*, Sydney E. Ahlstrom, "The Scottish Philosophy and American Theology," *CH* 24 (1955): 257–72; Theodore Dwight Bozemann, *Protestants in an Age of Science: The Baconian Ideal and Antebellum American Religious Thought* (Chapel Hill: University of North Carolina Press, 1977); George M. Marsden, *The Evangelical Mind and the New School Presbyterian Experience* (New Haven, CT: Yale University Press, 1970), 47–52; idem, *Fundamentalism and American Culture: The Shaping of Twentieth-Century Evangelicalism, 1870–1925* (New York: Oxford University Press, 1980), 55–61, 212–20; idem, "Preachers of Paradox: The Religious New Right in Historical Perspective," in *Religion in America: Spirituality in a Secular Age* (Boston: Beacon, 1982, 1983), 150–68 (esp. 163–64); Henry F. May, *The Enlightenment in America* (New York: Oxford University Press, 1976), 307–62; E. Brooks Holifield, *The Gentlemen Theologians: American Theology in Southern Culture, 1795–1860* (Durham, NC: Duke University Press, 1978), 72–154; John C. Vander Stelt, *Philosophy and Scripture: A Study in Old Princeton and Westminster Theology* (Marlton: Mack, 1978); Mark A. Noll, "Common Sense Traditions and American Evangelical Thought" (unpublished paper read at the 1984 Annual Meetings of the Evangelical Theological Society). These works are not all of a piece: the Ahlstrom essay is seminal and judicious, virtues not present in all of the others.

[47]This is, of course, a simplification. Some antecedents in Common Sense can be traced to Aquinas and Aristotle; and the title of "founder" of the movement is often assigned to Gershom Carmichael or James McCosh. But Reid is widely recognized as the "archetypical Scottish Philosopher" (the language is that of Ahlstrom, "The Scottish Philosophy," 260).

American evangelicalism that it introduced profound distortions. Common Sense traditions are said to have been influential in generating the Princetonians' doctrine of Scripture,[48] in pushing the "fundamentalist mentality" toward a commitment to "inductive rationalism"[49] in focusing too much attention on biblical "facts" and "truths" at the expense of knowing God, in developing certain approaches to systematic theology that resulted in dispensationalism, in engendering assorted Arminianisms, verbal inspiration, evidential apologetics, an overemphasis on individual conversion as over against group conversion, and much more.

The point of these essays, more frequently insinuated than enunciated, is that if evangelicalism/fundamentalism were to strip itself of the warping influence of Common Sense Realism, then these other unfortunate accretions, including the doctrine of inerrancy, would wither away, or at the very least lose a substantial part of their support. If we have taken deep draughts from the wells of Baconianism and Scottish Common Sense Realism, we are inescapably corrupted and, therefore, need to revise our views along several doctrinal fronts. In short, Common Sense is perilously close to becoming the whipping boy for certain features in the life of American evangelicalism that some church historians do not like.

It is no doubt true that Common Sense traditions had a wide impact on nineteenth-century America; and some of this influence was doubtless pernicious. But it is not at all clear that an evenhanded analysis of the extent to which Common Sense actually shaped American evangelicalism, and in particular its doctrine of Scripture, has yet been written. We have already surveyed some of the studies that show the doctrine of inerrancy not only antedates Thomas Reid but characterizes the church's view of Holy Scripture across the centuries until fairly recent times. Similar things could be said in some other doctrinal areas. For instance, it is not true to history to lay the blame for all evidentialism at the feet of Common Sense traditions (see further discussion in the section "The New Hermeneutic and Problems of Epistemology," below).

More broadly, the popularity of certain doctrines is too commonly explained in monocausational terms, especially in Marsden's work; or, to put the matter in a broader framework, simple causal relationships are often affirmed without being demonstrated. Besides being a priori methodologically suspect,[50] the approach

---

[48]See especially Rogers and McKim, *The Authority and Interpretation of the Bible*, 235–48.

[49]Marsden, "Preachers of Paradox," 163.

[50]See David Hackett Fischer, *Historians' Fallacies: Toward a Logic of Historical Thought* (New York: Harper Torchbooks, 1970), 164–86, and the piercing critique of the method in the review by Gordon S. Woods of Gary Wills, *Explaining America: The Federalist*, in *The New York Review of Books* 28 (April 2, 1981): 16–18.

fails to weigh certain important evidence. If Hodge was so hopelessly ensnared by Common Sense traditions, how was he able to rigorously critique certain points in Reid's position, as well as the positions of such supporters of Common Sense as William Hamilton and Dugald Stewart?[51] If Scottish Common Sense was so determinative in the Princetonians and in subsequent evangelicalism so far as their doctrine of Scripture was concerned, how was it that other groups equally under the spell of Common Sense did not generate such a doctrine of Scripture?[52] How many of these studies have adequately examined the book and journal trade both before and after the alleged impact of Common Sense Realism in order to determine what doctrines and concepts arose only after that impact, what ones were common both before and after that impact, and what ones were in some way modified or slightly reformulated as a result of that impact?[53] How many of the studies have adequately weighed competing explanations of the same historical phenomena?[54]

The Princetonians were extraordinarily widely read scholars. Warfield was as familiar with Augustine, Calvin, and the Westminster divines as he was with Thomas Reid. Such breadth of learning is likely to militate against a controlling dependence on any one tradition. Hodge was accused of being a slavish follower of Turretin—who had *no* connection with Common Sense. More positively, certain doctrines, including the doctrine of the Scripture's infallibility, are so widely distributed throughout the history of the church that one must conclude they are not paradigmatically determined by any single undergirding philosophy. After all, no one can write without reflecting the philosophical systems that have contributed to his or her thinking; but it does not necessarily follow that a reasonable knowledge of those systems will enable the historian to predict each doctrine the writer will hold. To the extent that the Princetonians used Common Sense categories to express themselves (a point still not adequately examined, in my view), they were thinkers of their time; but it does not necessarily follow that the categories of their time made their

---

[51]See Charles Hodge, *Systematic Theology*, 3 vols. (New York: Scribner, Armstrong, 1872–1874), 1:340–65; 2:278–309.

[52]At a generalizing level, several scholars have pointed out that Common Sense traditions had great impact on the broad sweep of American intellectual life (e.g., Ahlstrom, "The Scottish Philosophy"); but insufficient attention has been paid to particulars. Arguably, for instance, the Yale systematician Nathaniel W. Taylor, in his *Lectures on the Moral Government of God*, 2 vols. (New York: Clark, Austin, and Smith, 1859), especially in his understanding of free agency (see vol. 2, esp. chaps. 7 and 12), displays greater dependence on Common Sense categories than does any of the Princetonians.

[53]See the penetrating review of Marsden's *Fundamentalism* by Steve Martin in *TJ* 2 (1981): 94–99.

[54]Interestingly, in his most recent essay, Marsden has begun to back away from making Common Sense the general whipping boy. Impressed by the miasma of subjectivity into which certain strands of modern historiography have sunk, he now suggests we can learn from Thomas Reid—but not so far as Reid's approach to science is concerned. See George M. Marsden, "Common Sense and the Spiritual Vision of History," in *History and Historical Understanding*, ed. C. T. McIntire and Ronald A. Wells (Grand Rapids: Eerdmans, 1984), 55–68.

doctrine of Scripture innovative. Perhaps that is why one recent writer is able to argue that the Princetonians—and later Machen—used the Scottish Common Sense traditions in a self-critical way to defend and articulate the *historic* doctrine of Scripture.[55]

Frequently quoted as proof of his irremediable dependence on Scottish Common Sense are the following words from Charles Hodge: "The Bible is to the theologian what nature is to the man of science. It is his storehouse of facts; and his method of ascertaining what the Bible teaches is the same as that which the natural philosopher adopts to ascertain what nature teaches."[56] These words are commonly taken to reflect at least two unfortunate shifts: first, an uncritical dependence on induction in theology, a method taken over directly from Baconianism mediated through Scottish Common Sense; and, second, a novel view of the Bible that deemphasizes its role as a guide for life, a source for truths necessary for salvation, and a means of grace, while seeing it as a "storehouse of facts," the quarry from which systematic theology is hewn.

Probably too much is being made of this sentence. It is essential to recognize that Hodge makes his remark *in the context of his treatment of the inductive method as applied to theology*—and to nothing else. Hodge develops the thought further to show such principles as the importance of collecting, if possible, *all* that the Bible has to say on a subject before proceeding to inductive statements on the subject, undertaking the collection (like the collection of facts in science) with care, and constantly revising the induction in the light of fresh information. He does not in this section of his work seek to establish the nature of the Bible's truthfulness; his subject is prolegomena, not bibliology. When Hodge does, in fact, turn to the doctrine of Scripture, he is immensely sophisticated and balanced; but here his focus is elsewhere. The most that could be deduced from this one passage about Hodge's doctrine of Scripture are his beliefs that all the Bible is true, that its content is the stuff of systematic theology, and that its material is sufficiently interrelated to belong to the same system. It is hard to see how anyone with a truly high view of Scripture could say much less, even though much more needs to be said (much of which Hodge himself says elsewhere). Like most analogies, this one between science and theology is not perfect; for instance, the nature of experimentation in science is rather different from the trial and error of formulating systematic theology. Certainly there is a place in theology for experience, a place rather different

---

[55]Darryl G. Hart, "The Princeton Mind in the Modern World and the Common Sense of J. Gresham Machen," *WTJ* 46 (1984): 1–25.
[56]Hodge, *Systematic Theology*, 1:10.

from anything in the empirical sciences;[57] and the role of the Holy Spirit must be incorporated into the discussion. These, however, are steps that Hodge himself undertakes in other sections of his *magnum opus*. But so far as the narrow subject of induction is concerned, the analogy is not all that bad.[58] I shall say more about induction in the next section; but granted what else Hodge writes on Scripture, truth, and method, there is little warrant for reading too much into this one sentence. For exactly the same reason, the admittedly positivistic nature of nineteenth-century science cannot legitimately be held to tarnish his sophisticated epistemology.

The Significance of Recent Historiography

This rather introductory survey of recent revisionist historiography is not an attempt to establish a certain doctrine of Scripture by simple appeal to the tradition of the church. The discipline of church history cannot by itself establish the rightness or wrongness of what ought to be believed. On the other hand, evangelicals in particular, precisely because of their high view of Scripture, have often been content to know far too little about the history of the church; and efforts to overcome this common ignorance can only be commended. Thoughtful Christians who sincerely seek to base their beliefs on the Scriptures will be a little nervous if the beliefs they think are biblical form no part of the major streams of tradition throughout the history of the church; and, therefore, historical theology, though it cannot in itself justify a belief system, not only sharpens the categories and informs the debate but serves as a major checkpoint to help us prevent uncontrolled speculation, purely private theological articulation, and overly imaginative exegesis.

That is precisely why at least some of this recent historiography is rather important. If it is basically right, at the very least it shifts the burden of proof. In the past, inerrantists could comfort themselves that their position was in line with the historical position of most thoughtful Christians in most generations since the first century, even if in the modern environment their position needs fresh defense and articulation; but if now (as they are told) they must admit to being the innovators, they must contend not only with the larger part of modern biblical scholarship arrayed against them but also with the weighty witness of the history of the church. If, on the other hand, the recent historiography has embraced some fundamental misjudgments on these matters, the *perception* that the burden of

---

[57] Some of the problems involved in defining how one may legitimately go about constructing a systematic theology are discussed in the essays by Carson and by Packer in *Scripture and Truth*, ed. Carson and Woodbridge.

[58] Even Vander Stelt, *Philosophy and Scripture*, 125, points out that in 1841, Hodge was proving the Bible's divine origin by appealing to internal evidences.

proof has shifted remains. That is why so many essays in this pair of volumes have dealt with essentially historical matters.

To put the matter another way, this recent historiography has necessarily set a certain agenda. Those convinced it is right must conclude that a major redefinition of evangelicalism is called for. In one sense, this can only be applauded. There are, after all, so many theological aberrations, cultural hang-ups, and differences of opinion within evangelicalism that the movement *ought* to go back to basics again and again to examine how much of its intellectual structure is based on the Bible, its putative authority. But the redefinition envisaged by some of evangelicalism's recent historians frequently ignores, sidesteps, or downplays—on alleged historical grounds—one of the central planks that binds the diverse strands of evangelicalism together and to church history.[59] The redefinition, in other words, is in danger of destroying what it seeks to define.

What cannot escape notice is that the driving figures in this movement are historians, not exegetes or theologians. That, of course, is as it should be; they are engaged in historical theology. But quite apart from whether or not this or that historical conclusion is valid, a larger question looms: At what point do the historians who are setting a theological agenda need to interact more directly with scriptural and theological data themselves?[60] The question grows in importance if it is claimed that the observable cultural forces can be identified without making theological judgments in the process:

> While [the historian] must keep in mind certain theological criteria, he may refrain from explicit judgments on what is properly Christian while he concentrates on observable cultural forces. By identifying these forces, he provides material which individuals of various theological persuasions may use to help distinguish God's genuine work from practices that have no greater authority than the customs or ways of thinking of a particular time and place. How one judges any religious phenomenon will, however, depend more on one's theological stance than on one's identification of the historical conditions in which it arose.[61]

---

[59]This attempt at redefinition is currently appearing in articles, books, and conferences: e.g., Thomas Finger, "Evangelical Theology: Where Do We Begin?" *Theological Students Fellowship Bulletin* 8 (November–December 1984): 10–14; Clark H. Pinnock, *The Scripture Principle* (San Francisco: Harper & Row, 1984); Donald G. Bloesch, *Essentials of Evangelical Theology*, 2 vols. (San Francisco: Harper & Row, 1978–1979).

[60]That the historian often becomes the persuader can scarcely be doubted. See, for instance, at least some of the essays in George M. Marsden, ed., *Evangelicalism and Modern America* (Grand Rapids: Eerdmans, 1984), especially the essays by Joel Carpenter, Grant Wacker, Martin E. Marty, Nathan O. Hatch, and Richard V. Pierard. Or again, while many fundamentalists are claiming much more vibrant Christianity in America's early roots than the evidence allows, the response can be equally biased in the opposite direction—e.g., Mark A. Noll, Nathan O. Hatch, and George M. Marsden, *The Search for Christian America* (Westchester, IL: Crossway, 1983), and the review in *CH* 53 (1984): 539–40.

[61]Marsden, *Fundamentalism and American Culture*, 230.

The last sentence is surely largely true; but the rest of the quotation, by distancing the historian from the theological matrix where judgments are made, almost sounds as if the historian is able to provide value-free data, grist for the theological mill turned by colleagues in another department.

In short, while some of the revisionist historians have been much concerned, and rightly so, to explain more adequately the intellectual roots of fundamentalism and evangelicalism, they have not always displayed a critical awareness of the direction from which they themselves are coming.

Focus on the Phenomena of the Bible

In the exchange of views on the doctrine of Scripture between James D. G. Dunn and Roger Nicole, to which reference has already been made, there was a final exchange of open letters that attempted to delineate the substantive issues that lie between the two viewpoints.[62] Dunn argues that such qualifications to their position as the inerrantists make (e.g., precision is not the issue, not all commandments in the Old Testament are equally binding today, and so forth) are generated and demonstrated by studying Scripture itself. In his words: "*It is the recognition of what Scripture actually consists of which makes such qualifications of the inerrancy position necessary.* But once you grant this methodological principle . . . you must surely also recognize that my position emerges from an application of that same principle."[63] The difficulties in, say, synoptic relationships are such that Dunn asks the question, "Do inerrantists *take with sufficient seriousness even the most basic exegetical findings*, particularly with regard to the synoptic gospels?"[64] Exactly the same charge appears in many recent discussions. Paul Achtemeier writes:

> Faced with the overwhelming evidence which critical scholarship has uncovered concerning the way in which Scriptures have been composed of traditions that are used and reused, reinterpreted and recombined, conservative scholarship has sought to defend its precritical view of Scripture by imposing that view on Scripture as a prior principle. Unless evidence can be turned or bent to show the inerrancy of Scripture, the evidence is denied (e.g., it did not appear in the errorless autographs). . . . Critical scholarship is therefore an attempt to allow Scripture itself to tell us what it is rather than to impose upon Scripture, for whatever worthy motives, a concept of

---

[62]*Chm* 98 (1984): 208–16.
[63]Ibid., 210; emphasis original.
[64]Ibid., 211; emphasis original.

its nature which is not derived from the materials, the "phenomena," found in Scripture itself.[65]

James Barr puts the matter even more forcefully:

> My argument is simply and squarely that fundamentalist interpretation, because it insists that the Bible cannot err, not even in historical regards, has been forced to interpret the Bible wrongly; conversely, it is the critical analysis, and not the fundamentalist approach, that has taken the Bible for what it is and interpreted it accordingly. The problem of fundamentalism is that, far from being a biblical religion, an interpretation of scripture in its own terms, it has evaded the natural and literal sense of the Bible in order to imprison it within a particular tradition of human interpretation. The fact that this tradition—one drawn from older Protestant orthodoxy—assigns an extremely high place to the nature and authority of the Bible in no way alters the situation described, namely that it functions as a human tradition which obscures and imprisons the meaning of Scripture.[66]

It is important to understand the nature of this charge. Inerrantists, we are told, do not shape their doctrine of Scripture by the Scripture itself, or if they do, they—while constructing their doctrine of Scripture from a few passages that seem to justify the high view they espouse—ignore the actual *phenomena* of Scripture. Worse, once this doctrine is in place, it so distorts their approach to the text that they become the least "biblical" of all.

The issues involved turn out to be surprisingly complex: but at least the following observations are relevant:

Evangelicals' Distortion of Exegesis

Certainly evangelicals can be as guilty of distorting exegesis as non-evangelicals. The real question is whether or not that distortion is primarily the result of a high view of Scripture. Clarity of thought is not gained when one particularly notorious example (e.g., the suggestion that the difficulties in reconciling the accounts of Peter's denials can be accomplished by an additive harmonization that postulates six cock crowings)[67] is paraded about as if it were typical of evangelical scholarship. It is most emphatically not, as a quick scan of recent commentaries on the Gos-

---

[65] Achtemeier, *The Inspiration of Scripture*, 95.
[66] James Barr, "The Problem of Fundamentalism Today," in *The Scope and Authority of the Bible*, 79. I have discussed that book at some length in D. A. Carson, "Three Books on the Bible: A Critical Review," *JETS* 26 (1983): 337–67.
[67] Harold Lindsell, *The Battle for the Bible* (Grand Rapids: Zondervan, 1976), 174–76.

pels testifies.[68] Such charges do not seem much fairer than those by conservatives who point out, with some glee, that nonconservatives have sometimes adopted preposterous positions as well (e.g., what really happened at the feeding of the five thousand was that the little boy's generosity shamed everybody else into sharing the lunches they had surreptitiously hidden).

In fact, it is somewhat frustrating to be told again and again that evangelicals don't really understand the Bible, without being offered realistic test cases where responsible "scholarly consensus" is pitted against responsible consensus of evangelicals. Without hard cases, the charge against conservatives is emotive (Who, after all, wants to be told he does not understand what he reads?) but not particularly compelling. The few cases that are brought up have usually been discussed at considerable length in the literature; and there we discover that the conservative position is often defended by many scholars who would not call themselves conservatives. One thinks of a John A. T. Robinson, for instance, certainly not an "evangelical" but many of whose critical views are more conservative than those of the present writer. Even though not many scholars have agreed with him, few of his colleagues would charge him with fundamentally distorting the text. It appears, then, that it is not the individual exegetical position that critics find distasteful or obscurantist; rather, it is a configuration of positions in line with a high view of Scripture. In other words, it is not so much the exegesis that is offensive after all, as the high view of Scripture itself.

Be that as it may, evangelicals as well as others have needed for some time to articulate the exegetical procedures they follow and the reasons for choosing this or that option—and to do so in such a way that numerous hard cases are used as tests. That is part of the reasoning behind the essays by Silva and Blomberg in these two volumes.

"Qualifications" of Inerrancy

Dunn's estimate of the way "qualifications" to the doctrine of inerrancy have come about deserves further reflection. At various points, he raises three such "qualifications"—the contention that precision is not a determining factor in any estimate of the Scripture's truth content, the recognition that not all commandments in the Old Testament are perceived to be equally binding today, and the insistence that the considerable diversity of interpretations is not injurious to the doctrine—and argues that these "qualifications" have been wrung out of the conservatives by the phenomena of the Scriptures themselves. But although

---

[68]My library has many scores of evangelicals' commentaries and expositions on the Gospels, and not one adopts Lindsell's interpretation.

there is some merit in his assessment, it is injudiciously cast. Statements about the truthfulness of Scripture are not dependent upon the accuracy or uniformity with which the Scripture may be interpreted. There is an immense conceptual difference between the effort to interpret a certainly truthful text and the effort to interpret a doubtfully truthful text—regardless of the validity of the interpretative effort. Moreover, the lack of precision in many biblical statements is not the primary source of a qualification begrudgingly conceded by entrenched conservatives forced to face up to unavoidable phenomena. Far more important is the fact that the Scriptures themselves, though they lead the reader to expect the Scriptures to be true, do not lead the reader to expect the Scriptures to be *uniformly* precise. Signals as to degree of precision to be expected, like signals as to genre, are often subtle things; but a difficulty would arise only where all the signals point unambiguously to one degree of precision when a considerably lower one is present. This question has been discussed in the companion to this volume.[69] Also, no thoughtful conservative from Irenaeus or Augustine to the present has found the intricate question of the relationships between the covenants to be a threat to his doctrine of Scripture, precisely because the Scripture itself teaches that it covers salvation-historical development: there is before and after, prophecy and fulfillment, type and antitype, as well as mere command. The truthfulness of Scripture does not necessitate viewing all commands in Scripture on the same covenantal footing. What is somewhat astonishing is that this should have been perceived as a weakness in the conservative position.

Scripture's Phenomena and Truth Claims

The central question being raised, I think, may be put like this: Granted for the moment that the Scriptures *claim* to be entirely truthful (a point some critics would concede and others deny), do the hard phenomena of the Scriptures allow the claim to stand? Do the conservatives who accept the authority of the Scripture's truth claims equally accept the authority of the phenomena that must be set in juxtaposition with and perhaps in antithesis to those truth claims?

The question is extremely important. Unfortunately it is often cast in such a way as to suggest that the Bible's claims in support of its own truthfulness are slight and indirect, while the difficulties cast up by larger categories—e.g., the use of the Old Testament in the New, logical or chronological contradictions, historical impossibilities, and the like—are so pervasive that there is only one possible conclusion for a fair-minded scholar. Nothing could be farther from the

---

[69] See Wayne A. Grudem, "Scripture's Self-Attestation and the Problem of Formulating a Doctrine of Scripture," *Scripture and Truth*, ed. Carson and Woodbridge, 19–59 (esp. 51–53).

truth. The Scripture's self-attesting truth claims are extremely pervasive;[70] and the difficulties raised by the biblical phenomena are on the whole a good deal less intractable than is sometimes suggested.

Part of the problem is that many critics have come to accept as true a certain tradition of critical exegesis that not only highlights problems but sometimes discovers them where there are none. As a result, it is a certain interpretation of the phenomena of the text, not the phenomena themselves, that is being set over against the Scripture's truth claims. The careful reader does not need more than a couple of hours with, say, Bultmann's *magnum opus* on the Synoptics[71] before discovering dozens of alleged contradictions based on little more than assertion and disjunctive thinking.

Nevertheless, it must be admitted that a substantial proportion of evangelical writing has avoided the difficulties or provided facile answers. This sad state of affairs came about in part because of the decimation of evangelicalism's intellectual leadership in the wake of the fundamentalist/modernist controversies. In part (if only in part), this loss has been retrieved: now there are not only older works dealing with some of the difficult phenomena of Scripture[72] but also major commentaries[73] and technical essays on particular passages (e.g., Matt. 27:3–10[74] or Eph. 4:7–9[75]).

Behind this debate lurks an important methodological question: Granted that there are many statements about Scripture in the Bible, and granted that there are many biblical phenomena to consider when it comes to constructing a doctrine of Scripture, what should be the relation between the two kinds of data? Critics of the traditional view increasingly stress the primacy of induction from the phenomena; but this approach must be challenged. Twenty years ago Nicole, in a review of the first edition of Beegle's book on Scripture,[76] wrote the following:

> Dr. Beegle very vigorously contends that a proper approach to the doctrine of inspiration is to start with induction from what he calls "the phenomena of Scripture" rather than with deduction from certain Biblical statements about the Scripture. . . . This particular point needs to be controverted. If

---

[70]Ibid.

[71]Rudolf Bultmann, *The History of the Synoptic Tradition* (Oxford: Basil Blackwell, 1963).

[72]E.g., E. J. Young, *Thy Word Is Truth* (Grand Rapids: Eerdmans, 1957).

[73]One thinks, for instance, of William Lane, *The Gospel According to Mark* (Grand Rapids: Eerdmans, 1974), and Peter T. O'Brien, *Colossians, Philemon* (Waco, TX: Word, 1982).

[74]Douglas J. Moo, "Tradition and Old Testament in Matt 27:3–10," in *Gospel Perspectives*, vol. 3, *Studies in Midrash and Historiography*, ed. R. T. France and David Wenham (Sheffield: JSOT, 1983), 157–75.

[75]Gary V. Smith, "Paul's Use of Psalm 68:18 in Ephesians 4:8," *JETS* 15 (1975): 181–89.

[76]Dewey M. Beegle, *The Inspiration of Scripture* (Grand Rapids: Eerdmans, 1963 [*Scripture, Tradition and Infallibility*, rev. ed. (Grand Rapids: Eerdmans, 1973)]).

the Bible does make certain express statements about itself, these mani-
festly must have a priority in our attempts to formulate a doctrine of Scripture. Quite obviously, induction from Bible phenomena will also have its
due place, for it may tend to correct certain inaccuracies which might take
place in the deductive process. The statements of Scripture, however, are
always primary. To apply the method advocated by Dr. Beegle in other areas
would quite probably lead to seriously erroneous results. For instance, if we
attempted to construct our view of the relation of Christ to sin merely in
terms of the concrete data given us in the Gospels about His life, and without regard to certain express statements found in the New Testament about
His sinlessness, we might mistakenly conclude that Christ was not sinless.
... [This] is not meant to disallow induction as a legitimate factor, but it is
meant to deny it the priority in religious matters. First must come the statements of revelation, and then induction may be introduced as a legitimate
confirmation, and, in some cases, as a corrective in areas where our interpretation of these statements and their implications may be at fault.[77]

In other words, if particular texts, despite evenhanded exegetical coaxing, cannot
fit into the theological theory (for that is what a doctrine is) that has emerged
from explicit statements of Scripture on the subject, then the theory may have
to be modified, recast, reformulated—or, alternatively, the exegesis may have to
begin again. But because hard cases make not only bad law but bad theology, one
should not give *priority* to them in the articulation of doctrine, even though each
one must be thoughtfully considered.

The Relation of Deduction and Induction
Related to this debate is the broader question of the proper relation between
deduction and induction in theological inquiry. This question has both historical and methodological foci. In the historical focus, Rogers and McKim, as we
have seen, charge the scholastic Reformed theologians and the Princetonians
after them with an innovative dependence on deduction; infected by Baconianism, it is alleged, they began with a central proposition (such as "God cannot
lie") and deduced a sweeping doctrine of Scripture.[78] More recently, others (as
we saw in the last section) have charged the Princetonians in particular with
too heavy a reliance on induction. It is alleged that they treat the Bible as a

---

[77]Roger R. Nicole, "The Inspiration of Scripture: B. B. Warfield and Dr. Dewey M. Beegle," *The Gordon Review* 8
(1964–65): 106.

[78]This same argument is especially stressed by William J. Abraham, *The Divine Inspiration of Holy Scripture* (Oxford:
Oxford University Press, 1981). I have discussed that book at some length in Carson, "Three Books on the Bible."

mere sourcebook of facts from which, by the process of induction, they create their theological theories. It is doubtful if the charge of innovation is historically justifiable in either case; and, in any case, if the Princetonians are to be permitted neither induction nor deduction, it might be easier to dismiss them just because they think.

At the methodological level, the problem is much deeper. In the first place, Sproul has pointed out how distinct groups of inerrantists have defended the doctrine on quite different grounds—i.e., the doctrine is not entirely hostage to a particular form of reasoning.[79] More important, any complex theory in any field of human thought (some areas of mathematics possibly excluded) depends not only on intricate interplay between induction and deduction but on what is variously called adduction, abduction, or retroduction—which is not so much a category entirely distinct from induction and deduction as a label that incorporates these two processes while going beyond them to include the creative thought, sudden insight, and perception of links that are essential to all intellectual advance. These matters are commonplace among those who deal with theory formation and justification;[80] and it is, therefore, disconcerting to find them so consistently overlooked.

Debates over Various Terms

Packer warns us of the dangers in oversimplifications:

> I am sure that my evangelical readers have all had abundant experience of this particular evil. I am sure we have all had cause in our time to complain of over-simplifications which others have forced on us in the debate about Scripture—the facile antithesis, for instance, between revelation as propositional or as personal, when it has to be the first in order to be the second; or the false question as to whether the Bible is or becomes the Word of God, when both alternatives, rightly understood, are true; or the choice between the theory of mechanical dictation and the presence of human error in the Bible, when in fact we are not shut up to either option. I am sure we have all found how hard it is to explain the evangelical view of Scripture to persons

---

[79]R. C. Sproul, "The Case for Inerrancy: A Methodological Analysis," in *God's Inerrant Word: An International Symposium on the Trustworthiness of Scripture*, ed. John Warwick Montgomery (Minneapolis: Bethany House, 1973), 242–61; see also Paul Helm, "Faith, Evidence, and the Scriptures," in *Scripture and Truth*, ed. Carson and Woodbridge, 303–20, 411.

[80]See Arthur F. Holmes, "Ordinary Language Analysis and Theological Method," *BETS* 11 (1968): 131–38; John Warwick Montgomery, "The Theologian's Craft: A Discussion of Theory Formation and Theory Testing in Theology," in *The Suicide of Christian Theology* (Minneapolis: Bethany House, 1970), 267–313; James I. Packer, "Hermeneutics and Biblical Authority," *Them* 1 (Autumn 1975): 3–12; Feinberg, "The Meaning of Inerrancy," 265–304, 468–71; and the literature cited in these works.

whose minds have once embraced these over-simplifications as controlling concepts.[81]

These oversimplifications are in no small measure the result of defective definitions. *Truth* is one such term frequently subjected to reductionism; but as it was discussed in the first of this pair of volumes,[82] I shall largely leave it aside and make brief mention of three other terms that have become important in recent discussion. But two remarks about *truth* seem in order. First although it is sometimes suggested that conservatives reduce truth to words and propositions—and thereby ignore the centrality of Christ as truth incarnate—this failing is rare in conservatives of any stature. It is far more common for the reductionism to work the other way: the nonconservative of stature is more likely to affirm the centrality of Christ while ignoring the truth claims of the Scriptures themselves. Second, the diversity of meanings bound up in the word *true* and its cognates (and ably expounded by Nicole) does not itself jeopardize allegiance to a correspondence theory of truth, on which the doctrine of a truthful Scripture is partly based. For instance, I might say, "My wife is my true friend"—even though I do hold to a correspondence theory of truth. My sample sentence merely demonstrates that the semantic range of "true" and its cognates cannot be reduced to usages congenial to the correspondence theory of truth. Opponents would have to show either that the Hebrew and Greek words for truth never take on the correspondence meaning, or at least that they never have such force when they refer to Scripture.

Accommodation

The *first* additional term to consider is *accommodation*. If the transcendent, personal God is to communicate with us, his finite and sinful creatures, he must in some measure *accommodate* himself to and *condescend* to our capacity to receive that revelation. The point has been recognized from the earliest centuries of the church, and it received considerable attention during the Reformation. In recent discussion, however, this notion of accommodation as applied to the Scriptures is frequently assumed to entail error. Thus, Barth writes:

> If God was not ashamed of the fallibility of all the human words of the Bible, of their historical and scientific inaccuracies, their theological contradictions, the uncertainty of their tradition, and, above all, their Judaism, but adopted and made use of these expressions in all their fallibility, we do not need to be ashamed when He wills to renew it to us in all its fallibility as

---

[81] Packer, "Hermeneutics and Biblical Authority," 3.
[82] Roger R. Nicole, "The Biblical Concept of Truth," *Scripture and Truth*, ed. Carson and Woodbridge, 283–98.

witness, and it is mere self-will and disobedience to try to find some infallible elements in the Bible.[83]

Less ambiguously, Vawter writes:

> We should think of inspiration as always a positive divine and human interaction in which the principle of condescension has been taken at face value. To conceive of an absolute inerrancy as the effect of the inspiration was not really to believe that God had condescended to the human sphere but rather that He had transmuted it into something else. A human literature containing no error would indeed be a contradiction in terms, since nothing is more human than to err.[84]

Similarly, in his latest book, Clark Pinnock attempts to relate the possibility of error to the principle of accommodation:

> What we all have to deal with is a Bible with apparent errors in it whose exact status we cannot precisely know. Whether in his inspiration or in his providence, God has permitted them to exist. . . . What God aims to do through inspiration is to stir up faith in the gospel through the word of Scripture, which remains a human text beset by normal weaknesses.[85]

There are numerous other examples of the same approach, often accompanied by the assumption that this is the view of accommodation that has prevailed throughout much of church history.

The first thing that must be said by way of response is that some of these treatments are not very consistent. In the same context as the last quotation, for instance, Pinnock writes: "The Bible does not attempt to give the impression that it is flawless in historical or scientific ways. God uses writers with weaknesses and still teaches the truth of revelation through them."[86] But here there is a shift from error in certain spheres of thought (history and science) to error caused by the humanity of Scripture. One begins to suspect that the latter argument is being used to restrict the Bible's authority to purely religious matters, not to whatever subject it chooses to address. But the argument is more dangerous than Pinnock seems to think; for if the potential for error is grounded in Scripture's humanity, by

---

[83]Karl Barth, *Church Dogmatics* I, part 2, *The Doctrine of the Word of God* (Edinburgh: T&T Clark, 1956), 531. Similarly, see Ramm, *After Fundamentalism*, 103.

[84]Vawter, *Biblical Inspiration*, 169.

[85]Pinnock, *The Scripture Principle*, 97, 100.

[86]Ibid., 99–100.

what argument should that error be restricted to the fields of history and science? Why does not human fallibility also entail error in the religious and theological spheres? Or conversely, if someone wishes to argue that God has preserved the human authors from error in religion and theology, what prevents God from doing so in other areas of thought?

Second, this approach to accommodation is certainly far removed from the understanding of accommodation worked out both in the early church and in the Reformation. The most recent authority rightly insists:

> The Reformers and their scholastic followers all recognized that God in some way must condescend or accommodate himself to human ways of knowing in order to reveal himself: this *accommodatio* occurs specifically in the use of human words and concepts for the communication of the law and the gospel, but it in no way implies the loss of truth or the lessening of scriptural authority. The *accommodatio* or *condescensio* refers to the manner or mode of revelation, the gift of wisdom of infinite God in finite form, not to the quality of the revelation or to the matter revealed. A parallel idea occurs in the scholastic protestant distinction between *theologia archetype* and *theologia ectype*. Note that the sense of *accommodatio* which implies not only a divine condescension but also a use of time-bound and even erroneous statements as a medium for revelation arose in the eighteenth century in the thought of Semler and his contemporaries and has no relation either to the position of the Reformers or to that of the protestant scholastics, either Lutheran or Reformed.[87]

Third, the argument that error is essentially human ("nothing is more human than to err," writes Vawter) is extremely problematic and cries out for further analysis. Error, of course, is distinguishable from sin and can be the result of nothing more than finitude; but much human error results from the play of sin on human finitude. The question is whether it is error that is essential to humanness, or finitude. If the latter, it is difficult to see why Scripture would be any less "human" if God so superintended its writing that no error was committed. Human beings are always finite; but it does not follow they are always in error. Error does not seem to be essential to humanness. But if someone wishes to controvert the point, then to be consistent that person must also insist that between the fall and the new heaven and the new earth, not only error but *sinfulness* is essential to humanness.

---

[87]Richard A. Muller, *Dictionary of Latin and Greek Theological Terms: Drawn Principally from Protestant Scholastic Theology* (Grand Rapids: Baker, 1985), s.v. *accommodatio*, 19. See also John D. Woodbridge, "Some Misconceptions of the Impact of the 'Enlightenment' on the Doctrine of Scripture" (in this volume).

No writer of Scripture escaped the sinfulness of his fallen nature while composing what came to be recognized as Holy Writ: does this mean that the humanness of Scripture entails not only error but sinfulness? And if not, why not? Who wishes to say Scripture is sinful? This is not mere *reductio ad absurdem*: rather, it is a way of showing that human beings who in the course of their lives inevitably err and sin do not necessarily err and sin in any particular circumstance. Their humanness is not compromised when they fail to err or sin. By the same token, a God who safeguards them from error in a particular circumstance—namely, the writing of Scripture—has not thereby vitiated their humanness.

Fourth, there is an unavoidable christological connection, raised (perhaps unwittingly) by Vawter himself:

> The Fathers and the Church have always been fond of the analogy by which the Scripture as word of God in words of men may be compared with Christ the incarnate Word, the divine in human flesh. But if the incarnate Word disclaimed omniscience (Mk 13.32, etc.), it must seem singularly inappropriate to exploit the analogy as an argument for an utterly inerrant Scripture.[88]

The logic, of course, is faulty: to be a valid argument, Vawter would have had to conclude with the words: ". . . it must seem singularly inappropriate to exploit the analogy as an argument for an utterly omniscient Scripture." I'm not sure what "omniscient Scripture" would mean: presumably a Scripture that "knows" or "tells" or "records" absolutely everything. But no one claims that. However, if the Scripture/Christ analogy holds, Vawter's argument can be made to stand on its head. If error is the *inevitable* result of lack of omniscience, and if lack of omniscience is characteristic of all humanness (including that of Jesus, according to the biblical passage to which Vawter refers), then there are errors not only in Scripture but in Jesus' teaching as well.

Calvin understood the problem and, therefore, appealed to accommodation not only in his treatment of Scripture but as a function of God's gracious self-disclosure to us in many forms: in the use of language, in the use of anthropomorphism, in the doctrine of Scripture—and in the incarnation itself.[89] But it was precisely that breadth of view that enabled him to see that whatever accommodation entails, it cannot entail sin or error: the costs are too high right across the spectrum of Christian theology.

---

[88]Vawter, *Biblical Inspiration*, 152.
[89]See especially Ford Lewis Battles, "God Was Accommodating Himself to Human Capacity," *Interpretation* 31 (1977): 19–38.

Inspiration

A *second* term that is currently undergoing creative redefinition is *inspiration*. Most of the major proposals over the past fifty years or so for an appropriate meaning of the term are reasonably well known and need not be canvassed here. More recently, William J. Abraham has put forward another suggestion with some novel features.[90] He argues that during much of the church's history Christians believed the Bible was simply dictated by God. Advances in knowledge made so simple a view no longer tenable; and it was in that context that Warfield and others articulated their "concursive" theory of inspiration—i.e., that God in his sovereignty so supervised and controlled the human writers of Scripture that although what they wrote was genuinely their own, and in their own idiom, it was nevertheless the very word of God, right down to the individual words. The trouble with this view, Abraham argues, is that, for all intents and purposes, it remains indistinguishable from the older dictation theory. There are too many difficulties and contradictions in the Bible for the theory to be tenable (although he declines to enumerate any of these). What we must do is recognize that all talk about God is analogical talk; and, therefore, what we mean when we say "God inspires someone" must be determined by analogy to what we mean when we say something like "A teacher inspires his pupil." This does not mean that the pupil quotes the teacher verbatim, or even that the pupil remains entirely faithful to all that the teacher holds true. Some of what the pupil passes on will be accidental distortion of what the teacher taught; some may even be self-conscious revision of it; and some distortion may occur because of the pupil's limited capacity. But if the teacher is very "inspiring," the pupil will faithfully pass on the heart of what the teacher taught. So it is in the relationship between God and the writers of Scripture: he inspires them as a teacher does his pupils. But to claim "verbal inspiration" or inerrancy or infallibility in any strict sense would be a denial of the insights gained from an analogical approach to the way we talk about God.

Abraham's view has received adequate critique elsewhere;[91] but a few comments may be in order. First, one cannot help noting that while other historians accuse Warfield of tightening up the doctrine of Scripture (see the first section of this paper), Abraham charges him with loosening it—but not enough. The charge depends on the antecedent judgment that writers before Warfield, in particular Gaussen,[92] held to a dictation view of inspiration. Certainly such writers occasionally use the word "dictation," but it has been shown repeatedly that

---

[90]William J. Abraham, *The Divine Inspiration of Holy Scripture* (Oxford: Oxford University Press, 1981).

[91]See the review by Tony Lane in *Them* 8 (1982): 32–33; Carson, "Three Books on the Bible" (esp. 337–47).

[92]Louis Gaussen, *Theopneusty: or, The Plenary Inspiration of the Holy Scriptures*, trans. Edward Kirk (New York: John S. Taylor & Co., 1845 [French original 1841]).

many older writers use "dictation" language to refer to the *results* of inspiration, not its *mode*—i.e., the *result* was nothing less than the very words of God. As for the mode, Gaussen himself forcefully insists that the human authors of Scripture are not merely "the pens, hands, and secretaries of the Holy Ghost," for in much of Scripture we can easily discern "the individual character of the person who writes."[93] Warfield does not seem so innovative after all.

Second, Abraham attempts to formulate an entire doctrine of Scripture on the basis of his treatment of inspiration. What he never undertakes, however, is a close study of the wide-ranging ways in which Scripture speaks of itself, claims to be truthful, identifies the words of man with the words of God, and so forth—the kind of material that Grudem has put together.[94] More important yet, in the one passage in the New Testament that is closest to using our word *inspiration* (2 Tim. 3:16), it is not the human author who is "inspired" but the text: the Scripture itself is *theopneustos*. At a blow, the analogy of a teacher inspiring his pupils falls to the ground—a point the much-maligned Warfield treated with some rigor almost a century ago.[95]

What strikes the evangelical reader who contemplates Abraham's proposals is the degree of arbitrariness intrinsic to the selection of the model. The same is true about other recent proposals. The "biblical theology" movement, for instance, has often suggested that God has revealed himself through a sequence of revelatory events, to which Scripture is added as the result of the Spirit's inspiring human minds to bear witness to the revelation. The revelatory pattern as a whole is the act of God; but because the human witness may be faulty, individual steps along the line of that revelatory pattern may have to be dismissed; and, in any case, there is certainly no identification of God's words with man's words. These and many other proposals, as insightful as they are at some points, are strikingly arbitrary in that they select some model or other without dealing effectively with the Bible's account of its own nature.

Inerrancy

A *third* term that has elicited some discussion is *inerrancy*. Besides the fact that it is essentially a negative term, many have charged that the use of the term in the modern debate is not only innovative (Why move from, say, *infallibility*?) but also logically inadequate. Marshall, for instance, comments that many propositions about alleged historical phenomena can be meaningfully judged to be inerrant

---

[93]Ibid., 128.
[94]Grudem, "Scripture's Self-Attestation."
[95]Benjamin B. Warfield, "'God-Inspired Scripture,'" *Presbyterian and Reformed Review* 11 (1900): 89–130; reprinted in idem, *The Inspiration and Authority of the Bible*, ed. Samuel G. Craig (Philadelphia: Presbyterian and Reformed, 1948), 245–96.

(i.e., true); but many statements in Scripture cannot be so treated. If Jesus says, "Take away the stone" (John 11:39), his command is neither true nor false: the categories are inappropriate. What may be true or false is the biblical proposition that Jesus actually uttered this command, not the command itself. The same is true of much of the advice of Job's comforters, of fictional narratives like Jotham's fable or Jesus' parables, and of much more. As a result, Marshall prefers to adopt the language of "infallibility," understood to mean something like "entirely trustworthy for the purposes for which it is given."[96]

In one sense there is wisdom here: if evangelicals use words as frequently misunderstood and as easily mocked as this one, they may be erecting unnecessary barriers to others who are trying to understand their position. Certainly it is easy enough to articulate a comprehensive doctrine of Scripture without using that particular word,[97] even though "inerrant" and especially the longer "without error" have a notable pedigree.

On the other hand, it rather misses the point to say that *inerrant* is a term inappropriate to commands and parables. Inerrancy does not mean that every conceivable sequence of linguistic data in the Bible must be susceptible to the term *inerrant*, only that no errant assertion occurs. In any case, even if *inerrancy* were inappropriate at the merely lexical level, any one-word summary of a complex doctrine must be understood as a construct. This is true even of a word like *God*: what a writer who uses this term means cannot be established from a lexicon. Once again, Feinberg's essay on the meaning of inerrancy comes to mind.[98] More important, it is arguable that those who today defend the use of the term *inerrancy* mean no more and no less than did most of those who used the term *infallibility* forty years ago. One of the factors that has prompted the switch has been the progressive qualification of *infallibility*: Marshall wants it to mean "entirely trustworthy for the purposes for which it is given." That qualification may be entirely laudable, if the "purposes" are discovered inductively and not arbitrarily narrowed to salvific matters, as if to imply that the Bible is not trustworthy when it treats history or the external world. After all, one might suggest that the purpose of Scripture is to bring glory to God, or to explain truthfully God's nature and plan of redemption to a fallen race in order to bring many sons to glory: under such definitions of "purpose" the comprehensiveness of Scripture's truth claims cannot be so easily circumvented. In short, conservatives may in some measure be innovative in stressing one word above another as that which most accurately

---

[96] Marshall, *Biblical Inspiration* (esp. chap. 3).
[97] E.g., the so-called Ligonier Affirmation.
[98] Feinberg, "The Meaning of Inerrancy"; see also Carson, "Three Books on the Bible" (esp. 354–67).

characterizes their views; but it is not at all clear that by so doing they have succumbed to doctrinal innovation insensitive to normal linguistic usage.

Uncritical Attitudes toward Literary and Other Tools

It must be frankly admitted that evangelicals have on the whole been somewhat slow to make use of genuine advances in literary criticism. On the other hand, it must also be admitted that some scholars have deposited a naive confidence in these same tools that would be touching if it were not so harmful to accurate biblical exegesis and to profound humility before the Word of God. We are already in some peril when we use our tools in Procrustean ways to make us masters of the Word, when it is far more important to be mastered by it.

In the first of these two volumes, one essay briefly discussed the limits and usefulness of redaction criticism and of its antecedents;[99] and for that reason this section may be kept short. Four observations, however, may be of value.

The first is that literary tools almost never bring with them the control of a mechanic's "tools." The label "literary tool" is, therefore, potentially deceptive. One need only read certain structuralist treatments of Jesus' parables,[100] for instance, to observe how often the interpretation turns out to be an invitation to authentic existence or an openness to worldview reversal or the like: Jesus would have been surprised. If, in days gone by, the "orthodox" Christians were the first to impose their theology on the text, they seem to have been displaced in recent scholarly discussion by a new generation so gifted in the use of their "tools" that they can find confirmation of their theology in every text they examine. This process has been speeded up by the impact of the new hermeneutic, about which I shall say more in the sixth section of this paper ("The New Hermeneutic and Problems of Epistemology"). For the moment it is enough to remark that although literary tools offer to interpreters of Scripture a variety of devices to bring out the meaning of the text, they have sometimes become ponderous ways of saying the obvious,[101] or (which is worse) refined ways of distorting the obvious.[102]

---

[99]D. A. Carson, "Redaction Criticism: On the Legitimacy and Illegitimacy of a Literary Tool," *Scripture and Truth*, ed. Carson and Woodbridge, 115–42. [Reprinted as chapter 4 in this volume.]

[100]See, *inter alios*, Eta Linnemann, *Parables of Jesus* (London: SPCK, 1966); D. O. Via, *The Parables* (Philadelphia: Fortress, 1967); J. D. Crossan, *In Parables* (New York: Harper & Row, 1973). For surveys of the extraordinary complex questions related to the interpretation of parables, see J. G. Little, "Parable Research in the Twentieth Century," *ExpTim* 87 (1975–1976): 356–60; 88 (1976–1977): 40–44, 71–75; W. S. Kissinger, *The Parables of Jesus: A History of Interpretation and Bibliography* (Metuchen: Scarecrow, 1979); Craig L. Blomberg, "New Horizons in Parable Research," *TJ* 3 (1982): 3–17.

[101]E.g., B. Olsson, *Structure and Meaning in the Fourth Gospel: A Text-Linguistic Analysis of John 2:1–11 and 4:1–42* (Lund: C. W. K. Gleerup, 1974).

[102]E.g., Daniel Patte, *Paul's Faith and the Power of the Gospel: A Structural Introduction to the Pauline Letters* (Philadelphia: Fortress, 1983), 31ff., where the dependency on discovering certain structural opposites frequently leads to a distortion of Galatians.

Second, new literary "tools" are being developed constantly; and frequently some time must elapse before profound understanding of the tool's nature and limits can be reached. This is true not only for something fairly simple, such as audience criticism, but also for the range of techniques and procedures covered by, say, "rhetorical criticism." There is no doubt, for instance, that Culpepper's recent book on John[103] breaks new ground; but, equally, there is no doubt that by appealing to the formal characteristics of a nineteenth- and twentieth-century novel as the grid by which the Fourth Gospel should be interpreted, there is a substantial loss both in accuracy of exegesis and in the book's real authority.[104] One common feature of rhetorical criticism is the removal of the external referent in the interpretative process and (in the hands of most interpreters) *in the final assessment of the text's relation to external reality*.[105] The result seems to be a two-tier approach to history and even to truth itself—one in the external world and one in the "story," with few obvious relations between the two. What that will do to the "scandal of particularity" inherent in the revelation of a self-incarnating God can only be imagined. It is probably still too early for deep assessments; but this "literary tool" clearly marks out an area where a great deal more work needs to be done.

The confusion extends well beyond conservative circles, of course. At the 1983 meetings of *Studiorum Novi Testamenti Societas* held in Canterbury, the section on John spent many hours debating the proper relationships between rhetorical criticism and the older, more established "tools." In that sense, there is some gain; for if the evidence that serves to justify, say, source-critical division of a text can with equal or better reason serve to justify the unity of the text when read with rhetorical-critical questions in mind, one wonders what justification is left for the source criticism of the passage. It will not do to suggest that a source-critical reading of the text justifies the initial partition theory, and the rhetorical reading of the text justifies the unity imposed by the final redactor; for it is *the same evidence* to which appeal is being made. If that evidence is satisfactorily explained by rhetorical considerations, then it *cannot* serve to ground partition. It would not, of course, be fair to give the converse argument ("If that evidence is satisfactorily explained by source-critical considerations, then it *cannot* serve to ground unity.") equal weight, because we have the text as a unified whole before us. The *onus probandi* in this sort of debate always rests with the source critic. Thus, when Ackerman[106] contends that the doubling in the Joseph story has a literary purpose,

---

[103]R. Alan Culpepper, *Anatomy of the Fourth Gospel: A Study in Literary Design* (Philadelphia: Fortress, 1983).
[104]See the review in *TJ* 4 (1983): 122–26.
[105]These developments have come about in part because of the influential work of Hans W. Frei, *The Eclipse of Biblical Narrative: A Study in Eighteenth and Nineteenth Century Hermeneutics* (New Haven, CT: Yale University Press, 1974).
[106]James S. Ackerman, "Joseph, Judah, and Jacob," in *Literary Interpretations of Biblical Narratives Volume 2*, ed. Kenneth R. Gros Louis and James S. Ackerman (Nashville: Abingdon, 1982), 85–113. Of course, this does not mean

he is inevitably calling in question the view that the doubling betrays a conflation of disparate sources. At some point the student must opt for one line of argument or the other, presumably on the basis of which method offers the best fit. But we may at least be grateful that some of the new literary tools are again opening up questions that have too often been illegitimately closed.

Third, one of the more influential of the new approaches to Scripture is the application of the principles of sociological analysis to the exegesis of the text. There is much to be gained by such an approach. Just as the contemporary church can be studied using sociological categories, there is no intrinsic reason why the same categories cannot be used for groupings of people in the Scripture. Certainly social forces have real impact on individuals and groups; and sometimes those (like theologians) who prefer to focus on abstract ideas at the expense of thinking about social forces may overlook important factors that bear on the historical events described in the sacred texts. For this reason, many of these studies have considerable value.[107]

Nevertheless, we must differentiate between the numerous sociological appeals being made. Sometimes the Scripture is studied by a historian or exegete who is sensitive to sociological issues; sometimes explicitly sociological categories intrude: "class," "millenarian cult," "charismatic authority figure," and so forth. Already there are two crucial issues lurking behind the surface: (1) Are the sociological appeals presented in a reductionistic fashion that ultimately sidesteps or even deprecates questions of ultimate truth and authority? If sociology warns us against a too facile appeal to *deus ex machina*, does it also sometimes banish God altogether, or fail to see his sovereign hand over social forces? (2) Are the categories of modern sociology applied to ancient societies with requisite care? Are discontinuities as carefully observed as continuities?

But we may go further and note those studies that apply particular sociological theory to specific problems.[108] Here there are sometimes unrecognized difficulties, as Rodd[109] has pointed out. What begins as a heuristic device may end up as

---

that rhetorical criticism justifies the *historicity* of the passage in question. In one of his essays in the same volume (viz., "The Jesus Birth Stories," 273–84), Gros Louis stresses that Matthew and Luke display such different literary approaches in their respective birth narratives that it is improper to attempt conflation. More broadly, many practitioners of the new literary criticism begin with models drawn from novels—a form devoted to fiction.
[107]E.g., Gerd Thiessen, *The First Followers of Jesus: A Sociological Analysis of Earliest Christianity* (London: SCM, 1978); idem, *The Miracle Stories of the Early Christian Tradition* (Philadelphia: Fortress, 1983), especially the third part of the book; David L. Mealand, *Poverty and Expectation in the Gospels* (London: SPCK, 1979); Robert P. Carroll, *When Prophecy Failed* (London: SCM, 1979); John H. Elliott, *A Home for the Homeless* (London: SCM, 1982); E. A. Judge, *The Social Pattern of the Christian Groups in the First Century* (London: Tyndale, 1960). Cf. R. Scroggs, "The Sociological Interpretation of the New Testament: The Present State of Research," *NTS* 26 (1979–1980): 164–79; and especially the perceptive review article by Edwin Yamauchi, "Sociology, Scripture and the Supernatural," *JETS* 27 (1984): 169–92.
[108]E.g., John G. Gager, *Kingdom and Community* (Englewood Cliffs, NJ: Prentice-Hall, 1975).
[109]Cyril S. Rodd, "On Applying a Sociological Theory to Biblical Studies," *JSOT* 19 (1981): 95–106. See also Derek Tidball, *An Introduction to the Sociology of the New Testament* (Exeter: Paternoster, 1983).

a reductionistic explanation. Moreover, sociology gains in accuracy when it can study at first hand large groups of people under carefully worked out controls; and, even then, different sociologists may interpret the data rather differently. How accurate then are sociological analyses and explanations of social forces to which we have only remote and indirect access through documents two thousand and more years old? In short, at what point does dependence upon the "tool" become not only exegetically distorting but thereby also destructive not only of biblical authority but even of elementary exegesis? Marshall's judgment is balanced:

> The scholar who studies religious history from a sociological point of view may well believe that sociological considerations are largely sufficient to explain it. He may be wrong in adopting such an absolute standpoint—a Christian believer would certainly want to claim this—but nevertheless the adoption of his standpoint will probably bring to light historical facts and explanations which would have eluded the historian who ignored the insights of sociology.[110]

Finally, although it is true that conservatives have often been the slowest to adopt what is useful and fair in the so-called "literary tools," in some cases the opposite is true: evangelicals use certain tools with increasing skill, while their less conservative colleagues are engaged in depreciating the same tools. Precisely because they put such a high premium on the Word, conservatives have devoted large amounts of energy to the study of the biblical languages and to the principles of what is often called "grammatical-historical exegesis." To scan the abstracts of the 1984 meetings of the Society of Biblical Literature will convince most observers that such discipline is in decline in the larger community of biblical scholars, suspended by approaches and themes judged more current, not to say faddish. Or again, harmonization is often presented as an unscholarly capitulation to conservatism, and far too little thought has been given to its nature, proper use, and abuse. For that reason the essay by Blomberg[111] in this volume marks a step forward, even if—or indeed, precisely because—it cuts across the grain.

Sensitivity to "Propositions" and "Literary Genre"

By and large, conservatives during the past one hundred years have not been slow to focus on *words*. They have pointed out, rightly, that inspiration extends beyond revelation of mere concepts—concepts that the human authors are left to flesh

---

[110]I. Howard Marshall, *Luke: Historian and Theologian* (Exeter: Paternoster, 1970), 28.
[111]Craig L. Blomberg, "The Legitimacy and Limits of Harmonization."

out without any divine superintendence so far as the actual *words* are concerned—
to the actual *words* of the sacred text. But they have been slower to deal at length
with more substantial literary units. How are words related to propositions? How
are propositions related to any particular literary genre? How are the truth questions related to words, propositions, and literary genres? What exactly does it
mean to say that Acts 15, Matthew's genealogy of Jesus, and Jotham's fable are all
true? What is to be made of the fact that the first four books of the New Testament
are "Gospels"?

At a popular level, any reasonably conscientious and intelligent reader makes
various literary distinctions as the various parts of the Bible are encountered.
Parables may not be understood very well; but few readers take the narrative
parables to be descriptive of historical events. All will make subtle, if inarticulate,
adjustments as they pass from genealogy to discourse, from discourse to apocalyptic, from apocalyptic to psalm. Few will read Jeremiah's psalm of malediction
as a literal curse on the man who brought his father the news of Jeremiah's birth
or as a serious wish that his mother should have remained forever pregnant (Jer.
20:14–18): thoughtful reading recognizes lament rather than vindictiveness. That
intuitive "feel" for what a passage means, however, demands rigorous attention
and analytical thought. For, otherwise, we may unhappily fall into one of two
opposite errors: we may insist that Scripture is saying something it is not in fact
saying; or, alternatively, we may appeal to literary genre in a vague and undisci-
plined way that enables us to escape what Scripture is saying.

The issue was thrust upon evangelicals in North America in the painful debates
occasioned by Gundry's commentary on Matthew.[112] This is not the place to offer
a blow by blow account of the debate; but quite clearly a substantial part of the
criticism leveled against him by conservatives was ill-conceived.[113] Gundry holds
that whatever Matthew writes that is different from or in addition to Mark and Q
(which he understands to be considerably longer than the 250 or so verses normally so labeled) has no historical referent: rather, it belongs to midrash, a genre of
literature that happily expands on historical material in order to make theological
(not historical) points. Moreover, Gundry holds this while also maintaining, with
integrity, the full authority and inerrancy of Scripture. Entirely without merit is the
charge that because Gundry denies that the referent in certain passages is historical,
therefore he runs into flat contradiction with other passages that treat the same

---

[112]Robert H. Gundry, *Matthew: A Commentary on His Literary and Theological Art* (Grand Rapids: Eerdmans, 1982).
[113]See especially the unfortunate exchange: Norman L. Geisler, "Methodological Unorthodoxy," *JETS* 26 (1983): 87–94; Robert H. Gundry, "A Response to 'Methodological Unorthodoxy,'" 95–100; Norman L. Geisler, "Is There Madness in the Method? A Rejoinder to Robert H. Gundry," 101–8; Robert H. Gundry, "A Surrejoinder to Norman L. Geisler," 109–15.

referent as historical; for in each such case, Gundry has a ready-made answer. In some instances, such as the accounts in Matthew and Luke of the virginal conception of Jesus, he denies the historicity of Matthew's account (on the grounds that Matthew is writing midrash) while upholding the historicity of Luke's account (on the grounds that Luke is writing history, or theologically tinged history). In other instances he might simply argue that his opponent has not found any passage where the referent can be judged historical, *once it is agreed that the relevant passages all belong to the category of midrash*. Several of Gundry's critics fail to see that the problem lies solely at the interpretative level. A Calvinist might as easily argue that the Arminian who denies that certain texts teach the unqualified sovereignty of God is in reality denying the authority and inerrancy of Scripture. The only legitimate way to offer telling critique of Gundry's interpretation of Matthew is to combine careful assessment of some of his methods with demonstration that his handling of the literary genre "midrash" is fundamentally mistaken.[114]

To take another example, the "Gospels" have often been compared with better known and more widely distributed literary genres from the ancient world, in an attempt to define the manner in which a "Gospel" may be expected to convey truth.[115] Most such efforts result in some depreciation of the importance of "history" in a Gospel. Individual efforts to treat individual Gospels in a more conservative vein have not been entirely lacking;[116] but one of the best treatments of the problem is an essay by Aune,[117] whose work is immaculately researched and whose conclusions are nuanced. One of the more important of these is that "genre" is a category frequently without fixed boundaries; and an individual genre is often some amalgamation reshaping of antecedent genres. The result is a telling critique of reductionist approaches to the Gospels. Similar studies are required to tell us just what the "Epistles" are (here the essay by Longenecker in the first of these two volumes will be of use[118]) and just what sort of "history" is recorded in the book of Acts.[119] No less pressing is the need for further studies of such Hellenistic categories as the diatribe and of such Jewish categories as pesher.

---

[114]See D. A. Carson, "Gundry on Matthew: A Critical Review," *TJ* 3 (1982): 71–91; and the exchange: Douglas J. Moo, "Matthew and Midrash: An Evaluation of Robert H. Gundry's Approach," *JETS* 26 (1983): 31–39; Robert H. Gundry, "A Response to 'Matthew and Midrash,'" 41–56; Douglas J. Moo, "Once Again, 'Matthew and Midrash': A Rejoinder to Robert H. Gundry," 57–70; Robert H. Gundry, "A Surrejoinder to Douglas J. Moo," 71–86.

[115]E.g., C. H. Talbert, *What Is a Gospel? The Genre of the Canonical Gospels* (Philadelphia: Fortress, 1977); Philip L. Shuler, *A Genre for the Gospels: The Biographical Character of Matthew* (Philadelphia: Fortress, 1982).

[116]E.g., Marshall, *Luke: Historian and Theologian.*

[117]D. E. Aune, "The Problem of the Genre of the Gospels: A Critique of C. H. Talbert's *What Is a Gospel?*" in *Gospel Perspectives*, vol. 2, ed. France and Wenham, 9–60.

[118]Richard N. Longenecker, "On the Form, Function, and Authority of the New Testament Letters," *Scripture and Truth*, ed. Carson and Woodbridge, 97–114.

[119]The literature on this subject is voluminous and generally well known; but often overlooked is the work of Loveday C. A. Alexander, "Luke-Acts in Its Contemporary Setting with Special Reference to the Prefaces (Luke 1:1–4 and Acts 1:1)" (D.Phil. diss., Oxford University, 1977). She argues that there is a distinct break from about the third century

Comparable ambiguities surround the nature of propositions. The central questions may be introduced by quoting from a review of the first of these two volumes:

> While some of the authors distinguish between the message or truth of Scripture and the words (e.g., Bromiley), others (e.g., Gruden [*sic*]) tend to equate the human witness and the divine revelation. The latter are prone to ignore those passages that imply the discontinuity between human speech and understanding on the one hand and the Word of God on the other (cf. Ps. 71:15; 119:18, 19; 139:6; Isa. 55:8, 9; Job 42:3; Dan. 12:8; 1 Cor. 2:8, 9; 1 Pet. 1:10, 11). Instead, they concentrate on the character of Scripture itself as revelation.[120]

The criticism is in certain respects telling, as we shall see; but it also muddies the central issues a little. In the first place, the biblical passages to which references are made are not all of a piece, and in any case they do not prove what the reviewer thinks they do. For instance, Isaiah 55:8–9 does not affirm that because God's thoughts are higher than our thoughts they cannot be "reduced" to human language. The context shows that God's thoughts are "higher" than ours in the moral realm, and therefore our response must be repentance, not some kind of awareness of the ineffable. Psalm 71:15 and similar passages make it clear that the psalmist recognizes the limitations on his knowledge; but equally they show that the psalmist can utter in human language what he *does* know of God's ways. Passages such as Psalm 119:18 and 1 Corinthians 2:8–9 presuppose that the epistemological cruxes to understanding the Word of God go beyond mere analysis of language (about which a little more will be said in the next section); but they do not suggest that there is a fundamental disjunction between Scripture and truth. Second, the reviewer does not attempt interaction with the voluminous biblical evidence Grudem adduces to show that the Scriptures themselves develop the view that what Scripture says, God says. And third, the review moves unexpectedly from a possible distinction between the message or the truth of Scripture and its words to a distinction between the human *witness* and the divine *revelation*—a change in categories that prematurely closes the discussion.

BC on in the formal characteristics of the prefaces to Greek books; the "historical" tradition is increasingly differentiated from the "scientific" tradition. The former works are characterized by much greater freedom from the historical reality they describe and much more rhetorical embellishment for various dramatic purposes; the latter are characterized by much greater fidelity to the historical reality. Luke's prologues, she demonstrates, are formally and substantially in the tradition of the prefaces to the latter works.

[120]Donald G. Bloesch, "In Defense of Biblical Authority," *Reformed Journal* 34 (September 1984): 28–29.

Nevertheless, the reviewer has raised some important points. Certainly there is a formal distinction between, say, Grudem and Bromiley. But the reviewer's own suggestion is a trifle disconcerting:

We need to ask seriously whether words contain their meaning. Infallibility and inerrancy pertain to the revelatory meaning of the biblical words, but is this meaning endemic to the words themselves? Or is it given by the Holy Spirit to the eyes of faith when the words are seen in their integral relationship to God's self-revelation in Jesus Christ?[121]

The difficulty is that the infallible meaning is removed not only from the words but from the realm of the text: it is "given" by the Holy Spirit to the eyes of faith. Apart from the fact that the work of the Holy Spirit is crucial to all human knowing of things divine (see the essay by Frame in this volume),[122] the kind of transfer of the locus of authority envisaged by our reviewer cannot be made to square with the biblical evidence amassed in the Grudem essay. But may it not be that the apparent discrepancy between a Grudem and a Bromiley is merely formal? The one reflects the fact that the Bible itself treats its words as God's words; the other reflects the linguistic stance that treats words as concatenations of phonemes or orthographical conventions that are mere vehicles for meaning. The one treats words in a "popular" or "ordinary" way and is delighted to find that these very human words of Scripture are also God's words; the other treats words in the framework of modern theoretical linguistics and therefore sees a certain disjunction between naked words and meaning.[123] But our reviewer goes beyond both of these complementary positions to a new stance that locates meaning only in the Spirit-illumined knower.

The question, then, at least in part, is whether admittedly human words, when so superintended by God himself, can convey divine truth—not exhaustively, of course, but truly. I think they can, and I find insuperable difficulties with any other position[124]—though this is not the place to defend that view. But there is a second question, namely, whether the "propositions" the words make up convey

---

[121]Ibid., 29.

[122]John M. Frame, "The Spirit and the Scriptures."

[123]The failure to make this distinction between "ordinary" usage and a more "technical" usage of "word" stands behind a plethora of slightly skewed criticism—e.g., "Since the autographs of the Scriptures are collections of symbolic markings on objects suitable for the purpose, it seems odd to think of them as revealed of or by God. Any educated person can make intelligible marks on smooth, flat surfaces" (Stanley Obitts, "A Philosophical Analysis of Certain Assumptions of the Doctrine of the Inerrancy of the Bible," *JETS* 26 [1983]: 129–36).

[124]Cf. Anthony C. Thiselton, *The Two Horizons* (Grand Rapids: Eerdmans, 1980), esp. 432–38; John M. Frame, "God and Biblical Language: Transcendence and Immanence," in *God's Inerrant Word*, ed. John Warwick Montgomery (Minneapolis: Bethany Fellowship, 1974), 159–77; Brenton L. Thorwall, "Prolegomena for a Theocentric Theory of Language" (M.A. thesis, Trinity Evangelical Divinity School, 1981).

meaning or merely serve as meaning's vehicle. What quickly becomes obvious is that "proposition" is given various definitions that feed back and affect one's use of "propositional revelation" and even of "verbal inspiration."

It is here that Vanhoozer[125] is a reliable guide and makes significant advances in resolving these perplexing issues. He forces us to think through these slippery categories, and he points to ways in which we may preserve the substance of "propositional, verbal revelation" (i.e., the emphasis on verbal, cognitive communication with authority vested in the text itself) while simultaneously appreciating the ordinariness of the language of Scripture, the diversity of its literary forms, and therefore what it means to speak of Scripture's truthfulness.

The New Hermeneutic and Problems of Epistemology

Few questions are more persistent and more important in this decade than those dealing with hermeneutics. Among the most influential of the developments of this generation is that the older hermeneutical models that focused on the processes whereby the interpreter interpreted the objective text have been radically transformed into newer models that set up a "hermeneutical circle" between the text and its interpreter. Each time the interpreter asks questions of the text, the questions themselves emerge out of the limitations of the interpreter; and, therefore, the responses are skewed to fit that grid. But those responses shape the interpreter; they may radically alter one's worldview if they provide sharp surprises. Therefore, when the interpreter returns to the text, the questions he or she now asks come out of a slightly different matrix—and, therefore, the responses are correspondingly modified. Not only is the interpreter interpreting the text; the text in this model is "interpreting" the interpreter. Understanding does not depend in any important way on a grasp of the referents of words (i.e., that to which they refer) but emerges out of the heart of language itself. The text merely provides the room or the vehicle for the language-event, now understood to be the origin of all understanding.

Only recently have evangelicals contributed tellingly to the contemporary discussion.[126] Generalizations about the outcome of the debate are still premature, owing not least to the fact that not all who appeal to the new hermeneutic

---

[125]Kevin J. Vanhoozer, "The Semantics of Biblical Literature: Truth and Scripture's Diverse Literary Forms" (in this volume).

[126]The most important work is that of Thiselton, *The Two Horizons*; but cf. also Hendrik Krabbendam, "The New Hermeneutic," *Hermeneutics, Inerrancy, and the Bible*, ed. Earl D. Radmacher and Robert D. Preus (Grand Rapids: Zondervan, 1984), 533–58, and the equally important "Responses" by J. I. Packer and Royce Gruenler (559–89); J. I. Packer, "Infallible Scripture and the Role of Hermeneutics," *Scripture and Truth*, ed. Carson and Woodbridge, 321–56. Broader treatments that shed considerable light on the topic include Richard E. Palmer, *Hermeneutics* (Evanston, IL: Northwestern University Press, 1969), and Roy J. Howard, *Three Faces of Hermeneutics: An Introduction to Current Theories of Understanding* (Berkeley: University of California Press, 1982).

adopt the full range of philosophical baggage that others want to associate with the movement. What is clear is that the authority and objective truthfulness of Scripture are bound up in the debate—and this at several levels.

Different Frameworks

Achtemeier introduces one of these when he argues that conservatives have paid too little attention to the vastly different frameworks out of which interpreters in different generations approach the text:

> If Scripture is in fact free from error in the form in which it purveys divine truth, it must be free from such error not only for the time for which it was written but also for future times in which it will be read. Scripture therefore must be recognizably as free from error to the medieval scientist searching for the way to transmute base metal into gold as it must be free from error to the modern physicist seeking a field theory of physical forces, despite the widely differing presuppositions each brings to Scripture about the nature of the physical world. If truth is one, and the Bible as truth must exclude error, on whose presuppositions is that truth to be explained, the alchemist's or the modern physicist's? . . . The fact that this problem is seldom if ever addressed by conservatives points to a naive absolutizing of our current level of scientific theory and knowledge on the part of conservatives. . . . It is as though conservatives assumed that to our time and our time alone the final, unchanging truth of the universe had been revealed. . . . The need for apologetics for a particular world view and the idea of truth as unchangeable from age to age make the task of conservative apologetics for Scriptural inerrancy a uniquely unprofitable one.[127]

The telltale impact of the new hermeneutic is self-evident in this paragraph: a fundamental confusion of meaning and truth. It is possible to raise hermeneutical questions without raising truth questions—but not in the eyes of the strongest proponents of the new hermeneutic, who hold that where a different hermeneutic operates, there must also be a different theory of truth. Achtemeier does not here discuss whether or not the biblical text is thoroughly truthful; rather, he discusses whether or not the biblical text can possibly be *perceived* to be perfectly truthful by people living under different intellectual paradigms.[128] If Achtemeier's argument were pushed hard, however, it would have a painful sting in its tail. Because each human being is different from every other human being, therefore, to some

---

[127]Achtemeier, *The Inspiration of Scripture*, 96–97.
[128]We have thus returned to the theories of Thomas Kuhn, briefly discussed earlier in this study.

extent, each of us operates under antecedent knowledge and bias that are different from those of every other human being; and this suggests that the notion of
objective truth disappears forever. If that is so, one cannot help but wonder why
Achtemeier should bother to try to convince others of the soundness, the rightness, the truthfulness of his views. That the problem is endemic to the discussion
may be exemplified by a recent review of a book by Rudolf Schnackenburg, in
which the reviewer tells us that the commentary in question

> ...remains a victim of...the penchant to oppose a univocal concept of his-
> tory to the category of literature. And the very emphasis to seek the "original
> intention" of the writer or editors, frequently called the "intentional fallacy,"
> artificially restricts literary criticism and implicitly denies the existence of a
> literary universe in which texts have meanings that authors may never have
> dreamed of. This is as assured an assertion as the law of acoustics affirming
> the existence of overtones independently of a composer's intentions.[129]

Joseph Cahill skirts rather quickly around the distinction many make between
"meaning" and "significance." Moreover, he slightly distorts the "intentional fal-
lacy," which historically has not sought to deny intent to the author of a text but,
instead, warns against all interpretative procedures that seek to determine the
author's intention independently of the text. In other words, one must adopt as
a basic operating principle that the author's intention is expressed in the text.
Some authors may produce texts *designed* to be evocative, to have a certain narrative world of their own; and others may produce texts *designed* to convey certain
information or opinions—very much like Cahill's review. What is quite certain,
however, is that Cahill reflects a sizable and growing body of opinion that understands the discipline of history itself to be less concerned with what actually took
place at some point in time and space than with the creation of a theory about
what took place, based on fragmentary evidence and controlled by the historian's
biases. Exactly the same assessment is now commonly made of the discipline of
exegesis.[130]

Positivism or Subjectivity

Some of these developments are nothing more than a healthy reaction to the positivism of von Ranke. But proponents of the new history and of the new hermeneu-

---

[129]P. Joseph Cahill, in *CBQ* 46 (1984): 368, reviewing Rudolf Schnackenburg, *The Gospel According to St. John*, vol. 3, *Commentary on Chapters 13–21* (New York: Crossroad, 1982).
[130]The literature on this subject is now immense. See the bibliography of the essay by Kevin J. Vanhoozer, "The Se-
mantics of Biblical Literature," in this volume; and cf. J. G. Davies, "Subjectivity and Objectivity in Biblical Exegesis,"
BJRL 66 (1983): 44–53.

tic sometimes offer us an unhelpful disjunction: either suffer the epistemological bankruptcy of wishful historical positivism or admit the unqualified subjectivity of the historical enterprise.

Passmore offers important insight on this matter.[131] He admits that history is not a science the way many branches of physics are a science—controllable under the rigorous terms of repeatable experiments and quantifiable to many decimal places of precision. But history is as objective a "science" as, say, geology and many other "natural" sciences. Passmore examines eight criteria for objectivity and argues compellingly that if they are applied rigorously, they exclude geology as swiftly as history; and if the criteria are softened a little to allow geology into the academy of the sciences, history slips in as well. For instance, his "criterion six" reads as follows: "An inquiry is objective only if it does not select from within its material." "Criterion eight" reads: "In objective inquiries, conclusions are reached which are universally acceptable." A moment's reflection reveals how many of the natural sciences will suffer as much difficulty under a tight understanding of such criteria as will history.

Exactly the same point may be made with respect to exegesis, that is, with respect to the understanding of Scripture. The new hermeneutic has helpfully warned us of our finiteness, our ignorance, our biases, the influence of our individual worldviews. Its more sophisticated exponents have also insisted on the process of "distanciation" in the interpretative enterprise; and *distanciation presupposes an ultimate distinction between the knower (subject) and the text (object)*. The interpreter must self-consciously distance self and its worldview, its "horizon of understanding," from the worldview or "horizon of understanding" of the text. Only then can progress be made toward bringing the interpreter's horizon of understanding in line with that of the text, toward fusing the two horizons. When such fusion takes place, even if it is not perfect (let alone exhaustive) it allows the objective meaning of the text to be understood by the knower. This interpreter's understanding may not capture the meaning of the text exhaustively; but there is no compelling reason why it cannot approach asymptotically toward the ideal of capturing it truly. This is assumed by most scholars when they try to convince their colleagues and others of the rightness of their exegetical conclusions; and ironically, it is also assumed by the proponents of uncontrolled polyvalence in meaning when they write articles of considerable learning in order to persuade their readers. If it is true that there is no direct access to pristine, empirical reality,

---

[131]J. A. Passmore, "The Objectivity of History," in *Philosophical Analysis and History*, ed. W. H. Dray (New York/London: Harper & Row, 1966), 75–84. On the related questions of the nature of proof and belief in such matters, cf. George I. Mavrodes, *Belief in God: A Study in the Epistemology of Religion* (New York: Random House, 1970).

it is equally true that the person who argues there is therefore no real world out there, but that every "world" depends on value-laden constructions of reality, has opted for a self-defeating position; for we cannot espouse both value-ladenness and ontological relativity, because in that case it becomes impossible to talk meaningfully about conceptual relativity.

The issue has come to practical expression in the contemporary debate over "contextualization."[132] When books and articles offer "a feminist reading" or "a Black reading" or "an African reading" or "a liberation theology reading" of this or that text, there can be no initial, principial objection; for, after all, some of us are busy giving unwitting White, Black, Protestant, Reformed or Arminian, conservative or nonconservative readings. If the readings from a different perspective challenge us to come to grips with our own biases, if they call in question the depth of our commitment to distanciation and thereby teach us humility, they perform an invaluable service. But it cannot follow that every reading is equally valuable or valid, for some of the interpretations are mutually exclusive. The tragedy is that many modern "readings" of Scripture go beyond inadvertent bias to a self-conscious adoption of a grid fundamentally at odds with the text—all in the name of the polyvalence of the text and under the authority of the new hermeneutic. The relationship between the meaning that pops into my head under the stimulus of the text and the meaning held by the writer becomes a matter of complete indifference. Utterly ignored is the crucial role that distanciation must play. By such hermeneutical irresponsibility the text can be made to authorize literally anything. As I have discussed contextualization theory at some length elsewhere,[133] however, I do not propose to pursue it again here.

Scripture's Use of Scripture

At quite another level, the hermeneutical debate has been pushed back *into* the canon. How does Scripture treat Scripture? How can we meaningfully talk about Scripture's authority if, as is alleged, later writers of Scripture not only self-consciously violate earlier Scripture but unconsciously impose on it an interpretative grid that makes a mockery of any natural reading of the text? What is left if even the New Testament corpora reflect divergent views of the content of the Christian faith? Perhaps it is not too surprising to read in a recent work that the authority of the Bible for the modern believer does not extend beyond a minimalist affirmation: "Properly speaking, a believing reader shares with his biblical

---

[132]One of the better brief introductions to the subject is the article by D. J. Hesselgrave, "Contextualization of Theology," in *Evangelical Dictionary of Theology*, ed. Walter A. Elwell (Grand Rapids: Baker, 1984), 271–72.

[133]D. A. Carson, "Reflections on Contextualization and the Third Horizon," in *The Church in the Bible and the World: An International Study*, ed. D. A. Carson (Exeter: Paternoster, 1986), 11–29.

predecessors the God of Abraham, the God of Paul, and only coincidentally does
he hold other beliefs which make his outlook similar to theirs."[134] One wonders
how the author can be so certain that it is the same God, if what we think of him
has only coincidental overlap with the faith of Abraham or of Paul. Or again, one
wonders how much genuine authority can be salvaged when the Bible is understood to be a casebook that leaves the interpreter free to seek the cases judged
most relevant to the interpreter's situation. Thus, Kraft argues that each culture
has the right, even the responsibility, to choose those parts of the Bible it finds
most congenial and to downplay the rest—a stance that leads Kraft to suggest:

> We need to ask which of these varieties of theology branded "heretical"
> were genuinely out of bounds (measured by scriptural standards, and which
> were valid contextualizations of scriptural truth within varieties of culture
> or subculture that the party in power refused to take seriously. *It is likely that
> most of the "heresies" can validly be classed as cultural adaptations rather than
> as theological aberrations.* They, therefore, *show what ought to be done today*
> rather than what ought to be feared. The "history of traditions" becomes
> intensely relevant when studied from this perspective.[135]

The "scriptural standards" to which Kraft refers are not what the Bible as a whole
says but a range of disparate theologies each based on separate parts of the Bible,
a range that sets the limits and nature of the allowable diversity. Kraft here heavily
depends on the work of von Allmen, extensively discussed elsewhere.[136] Appeals
to a "supra-cultural core" in order to preserve at least some unity in Christianity
are far more problematic than is commonly recognized.[137] It is not clear how or
why God's macrosalvific purposes should escape the vicissitudes of paradigm
shifts or cultural expression: even as simple a statement as "Jesus is Lord" means
something quite different when transposed to a Buddhist context.[138] Finite human
beings have no culture-free access to truth, nor can they express it in culture-free
ways. Our only hope—and it is adequate—is in every instance so to work through

---

[134]Bruce D. Chilton, *A Galilean Rabbi and His Bible: Jesus' Use of the Interpreted Scripture of His Time* (Wilmington: Michael Glazier, 1984), 150.
[135]Charles H. Kraft, *Christianity in Culture: A Study in Dynamic Biblical Theologizing in Cross-Cultural Perspective* (Mary-knoll, NY: Orbis, 1980), 296; emphasis original.
[136]Daniel von Allmen, "The Birth of Theology: Contextualization as the dynamic element in the formation of New Testament theology," *International Review of Mission* 64 (1975): 37–52; reprinted in *Readings in Dynamic Indigeneity*, ed. Charles H. Kraft and Tom N. Wisbey (South Pasadena, CA: William Carey Library, 1979). This work is discussed at length in Carson, "Reflections on Contextualization and the Third Horizon."
[137]For examples of such an appeal, see Daniel von Allmen, Charles H. Kraft, and G. C. Berkouwer, *Studies in Dogmatics: Holy Scripture* (Grand Rapids: Eerdmans, 1975).
[138]A devout Buddhist would take this to mean, among other things, that Jesus is inferior to the Buddha, since something is here predicated of him.

problems of distanciation and the fusion of horizons of understanding that the meaning of the text is truly grasped. But if that is so for what I have called the macrosalvific truths, it is difficult to see why it should not be so for incidental details.[139]

Brown is only slightly oversimplifying the issue when he writes:

Prior to Bauer, the prevailing view was that Christianity, whether it was true or false, was at least a relatively well-defined and fixed body of doctrine; after Bauer, it was more often assumed that doctrine was constantly in the process of development and that "historic Christian orthodoxy," far from having been a constant for close to two thousand years, was only the theological fashion of a particular age.[140]

The related issues are so complex that four essays in this pair of volumes have been devoted to them: Moises Silva has written two of them, one dealing with the text form of the Old Testament as it is quoted by the New[141] and the other with the place of historical reconstruction in biblical exegesis;[142] Douglas Moo has discussed the way the New Testament actually cites the Old, and he ties his discussion to modern debates over *sensus plenior*;[143] and a fourth essay has attempted to point a way toward a recognition of the genuine unity in the New Testament when it is interpreted within a certain salvation-historical framework.[144]

Such inner-canonical questions inevitably raise again the question of the nature of the canon: What justification is there for treating these books and not others as the authoritative Word of God? None, some would reply.[145] Others, impressed by the canon criticism of Sanders[146] or of Childs[147] or convinced by traditional

---

[139]I have discussed this at greater length in "Reflections on Contextualization and the Third Horizon."

[140]Harold O. J. Brown, *Heresies: The Image of Christ in the Mirror of Heresy and Orthodoxy from the Apostles to the Present* (New York: Doubleday, 1984), 26.

[141]Moisés Silva, "The New Testament Use of the Old Testament: Text Form and Authority," in *Scripture and Truth*, ed. Carson and Woodbridge, 143–65.

[142]Moisés Silva, "The Place of Historical Reconstruction in New Testament Criticism" (in this volume).

[143]Douglas J. Moo, "*Sensus Plenior* and the New Testament Use of the Old" (in this volume).

[144]D. A. Carson, "Unity and Diversity in the New Testament: The Possibility of Systematic Theology," in *Scripture and Truth*, ed. Carson and Woodbridge, 61–95. [Reprinted as chapter 3 in this volume.]

[145]E.g., Helmut Koester, *Introduction to the New Testament*, 2 vols. (Philadelphia: Fortress, 1980, 1982), especially 2:1ff.

[146]Cf. James A. Sanders, *Torah and Canon* (Philadelphia: Fortress, 1972); idem, "Adaptable for Life: The Nature and Function of Canon," in *Magnalia Dei* (Festschrift for G. Ernest Wright), ed. F. M. Cross et al. (Garden City, NY: Doubleday, 1976), 531–60; idem, "Hermeneutics," *Interpreter's Dictionary of the Bible, Supplementary Volume* (Nashville: Abingdon, 1976), 404–5; idem, "Biblical Criticism and the Bible as Canon," *USQR* 32 (1977): 157–65; idem, "Text and Canon: Concept and Method," *JBL* 98 (1979): 5–29; idem, *Canon and Community: A Guide to Canonical Criticism* (Philadelphia: Fortress, 1984).

[147]Brevard S. Childs, *Biblical Theology in Crisis* (Philadelphia: Westminster, 1970); idem, "The Canonical Shape of the Book of Jonah," in *Biblical and Near Eastern Studies* (Festschrift for W. S. LaSor), ed. G. Tuttle (Grand Rapids: Eerdmans, 1978), 122–28; idem, "The Canonical Shape of the Prophetic Literature," *Int* 32 (1978): 46–55; idem, *Introduction to the Old Testament as Scripture* (Philadelphia: Fortress, 1979); idem, "Some Reflections on the Search for a Biblical

Roman Catholic arguments, adopt the general framework of the canon largely on the basis of the established tradition of the church. These issues, too, are extremely complex, and only infrequently discussed with knowledge and care by conservatives; and, therefore, David Dunbar's well-researched essay will prove particularly welcome to many.[148]

Epistemological Questions

At the deepest level, however, the questions raised by the new hermeneutic are epistemological. Some recent Reformed thought has unwittingly played into the hands of the more radical exponents of the new hermeneutic by dismissing both evidentialism and classical foundationalism and seeking to build a system on the view that belief in God is itself foundational, properly basic. If so, it is argued, Reformed epistemology and our belief in God enable us to escape the weaknesses of foundationalism and to stand above the mere amassing of bits of evidence. This line of approach is then sometimes projected back onto Calvin himself.

Quite apart from whether or not Calvin can be claimed in support for this view,[149] it seems open to the criticisms of Van Hook,[150] who, arguing primarily against Nicholas Wolterstorff and Alvin Plantinga,[151] convincingly demonstrates that this new "Reformed epistemology" may justify the *rationality* of belief in God, but it is wholly inadequate to justify any God-talk as *knowledge*.[152] Van Hook, therefore, suggests we should follow the proposals of Rorty: redefine knowledge, defining it not epistemologically but sociologically—knowledge is "what our peers let us get away with saying." That means that whether any particular datum is to be considered knowledge very largely depends on the locus of the "peers": a different set of peers may generate a different assessment as to whether or not the datum is to be classified as knowledge.[153] The parallels to the subjective and relative interpretations generated by a skeptical handling of the new hermeneutic are obvious.

Perhaps part of the problem is that we have been so frightened by the extreme claims of philosophically naive evidentialists that some of us have been catapulted

---

Theology," *Horizons in Biblical Theology* 4 (1982): 1–12; and his methods are well exemplified in idem, *The Book of Exodus: A Critical, Theological Commentary* (Philadelphia: Westminster; London: SCM, 1974).

[148]David G. Dunbar, "The Biblical Canon in Recent Study" (in this volume).

[149]For a balanced treatment (though now somewhat dated) of Calvin's appeal to evidence, see Kenneth S. Kantzer, "John Calvin's Theory of the Knowledge of God and the Word of God" (Ph.D. diss., Harvard University, 1950).

[150]Jay M. Van Hook, "Knowledge, Belief, and Reformed Epistemology," *Reformed Journal* 31, no. 7 (July 1981): 12–17.

[151]Most recently, see Alvin Plantinga and Nicholas Wolterstorff, eds., *Faith and Rationality: Reason and Belief in God* (Notre Dame: University of Notre Dame Press, 1983).

[152]Knowledge, unlike belief, is commonly defined in such a way as to make it immune to falsity. Belief may be mistaken; knowledge cannot be, or by definition it is not knowledge.

[153]Richard Rorty, *Philosophy and the Mirror of Nature* (Princeton: Princeton University Press, 1979).

into a reactionary insistence that evidences are useless.[154] One inevitable result is the depreciation of such evidence as exists, the establishment of an unbridgeable gulf between hard data and theological truth claims. Another part of the problem may be that much conservative writing has a wholly inadequate treatment of the work of the Holy Spirit.

Be that as it may, two essays in this pair of volumes have attempted to take steps to alleviate the need. Paul Helm[155] argues for a modified fideism to justify belief in the Bible as the authoritative word of God, and John Frame[156] discusses the role of the Holy Spirit both in the creation of the written Word and in bringing people to place their confidence in it. These are seminal essays in an area where a great deal more work needs to be done.

Discounting the Concursive Theory

It is safe to say that the central line of evangelical thought on the truthfulness of the Scriptures has entailed the adoption of the concursive theory: God in his sovereignty so superintended the freely composed human writings we call the Scriptures that the result was nothing less than God's words and, therefore, entirely truthful. Recently, however, the Basinger brothers,[157] in an apparent attempt to discount the concursive theory, have argued that it is illogical to defend simultaneously the concursive theory in bibliology and the free will defense (FWD) in theodicy. The former means one has accepted as true some such proposition as the following: "Human activities (such as penning a book) can be totally controlled by God without violating human freedom."[158] And that, of course, stands in contradiction to most formulations of the FWD. One must, therefore, choose between inerrancy (and the concursive theory on which it depends) and the FWD.

As the argument stands, it is valid; but perhaps it is revealing that the Basingers do not extend their argument to the major redemptive events. For instance, the death of Jesus Christ is presented as a conspiracy of leaders of Jews and Gentiles (Acts 4:27); yet those leaders "did what [God's] power and will had decided beforehand should happen" (Acts 4:28). God is not presented as a great chess

---

[154]For instance, Colin Brown, *Miracles and the Critical Mind* (Grand Rapids: Eerdmans, 1984), brilliantly surveys a vast amount of literature and concludes that miracles cannot reasonably have any evidential force. In a perceptive review article (*JETS* 27, no. 4 [December 1984]: 473–85), William Craig persuasively demonstrates that Brown forces later categories onto many of his historical sources by requiring that miracles address the radical, post-Kantian skepticism with which we have become familiar. Historically, appeals to miracles were far more likely made in the face of competing theistic claims; and here they do enjoy certain evidential force.

[155]Helm, "Faith, Evidence, and the Scriptures," 299–320.

[156]John Frame, "The Spirit and the Scriptures," in this volume.

[157]Randall Basinger and David Basinger, "Inerrancy, Dictation and the Free Will Defense," *EQ* 55 (1983): 177–80.

[158]Ibid., 176.

player who brilliantly outfoxes his opponents by anticipating and allowing for their every move: the conspirators did what God himself decided beforehand should happen. Yet the conspirators are not thereby excused: they are still regarded as guilty. Any other view will either depreciate the heinousness of the sin or render the cross a last minute arrangement by which God cleverly snatched victory out of the jaws of defeat, rather than the heart of his redemptive purposes. If some sort of concursive theory is not maintained in this instance, one wonders what is left of an orthodox doctrine of God. And if the concursive theory is required here, why may it not be permitted elsewhere? Is it possible for any true theist with any degree of consistency to believe Romans 8:28 while arguing against a concursive theory of inspiration?

The philosophical issues cannot be probed here; but it is worth mentioning that human responsibility can be grounded in something other than "free will," where free will is understood to entail absolute power to the contrary.[159] And theodicy has other options than the FWD.[160]

The Diminishing Authority of the Scriptures in the Churches

A high view of Scripture is of little value to us if we do not enthusiastically embrace the Scripture's authority. But today we multiply the means for circumventing or dissipating that authority. I am not here speaking of those who formally deny the Scripture's authority: it is only to be expected that they should avoid the hard sayings and uncomfortable truths. But those of us who uphold the thorough truthfulness of God's Word have no excuse.

The reasons for such failure are many. In part, we reflect the antiauthoritarian stance that is currently endemic to the Western world, and we forget that the Bible portrays true freedom not as absolute but as freedom from sin. This libertarianism has engendered two surprising children. The first is a new love of authoritarianism among some believers: they do not feel safe and orthodox unless some leader is telling them exactly what to say, do, and think. Inevitably this brings some power lovers to positions of religious leadership, supported sometimes by a theology that ascribes "apostleship" or some other special, charismatic enduement to them, sometimes by a theology of churchmanship that makes each pastor a pope. The authority of the Scriptures is in such instances almost always formally affirmed; but an observer may be forgiven if he or she senses that these self-promoted leaders characteristically so elevate their opin-

---

[159] Cf. C. Samuel Storms, "Jonathan Edwards on the Freedom of the Will," *TJ* 3 (1982): 131–69.

[160] John Feinberg, *Theologies and Evil* (Washington, DC: University Press of America, 1979); idem, "And the Atheist Shall Lie Down with the Calvinist: Atheism, Calvinism, and the Free Will Defense," *TJ* 1 (1980): 142–52; D. A. Carson, *Divine Sovereignty and Human Responsibility* (Atlanta: John Knox, 1981), especially the last chapter.

ions over the Scripture, often in the name of the Scripture, that the Word of God becomes muted. The church cries out for those who proclaim the Scriptures with unction and authority while simultaneously demonstrating that they stand under that authority themselves.

The second is a fairly conservative mood, a reaction to the times, that some interpret as a great blessing. But this conservative swing does not appear to be characterized by brokenness and contrition. Far from it: it is imbued with a "can do" mentality not far removed from arrogance. Many of the most respected religious leaders among us are those who project an image of total command, endless competence, glorious success, formulaic cleverness. We are experts, and we live in a generation of experts. But the cost is high: we gradually lose our sense of indebtedness to grace, we no longer cherish our complete dependence on the God of all grace, and we begin to reject themes like self-sacrifice and discipleship in favor of courses on successful living and leadership in the church. We forget that the God of the Bible declares:

> This is the one I esteem:
>> he who is humble and contrite in spirit,
>> and trembles at my word. (Isa. 66:2)

Mere conservatism must not be confused with godliness, mere discipline with discipleship, mere assent to orthodox doctrine with wholehearted delight in the truth. If Tozer were still alive, he would pronounce no improvement in the years that have elapsed since the publication of his moving lament on "The Waning Authority of Christ in the Churches."[161]

Along with the arrogance has come the exegetical and philosophical sophistication that enables us to make Scripture support almost anything we want. Henry incisively comments:

> . . . in recent years a . . . type of theft has emerged as some fellow evangelicals, along with non-evangelicals, wrest from the Bible segments that they derogate as no longer Word of God. Some now even introduce authorial intention or the cultural context of language as specious rationalizations for this crime against the Bible, much as some rapist might assure me that he is assaulting my wife for my own or for her good. They misuse Scrip-

---

[161] The article was first published posthumously in *The Alliance Witness* on May 15, 1963 and has been republished many times—most recently in *Banner of Truth* 255 (December 1984): 1–4.

ture in order to champion as biblically true what in fact does violence to Scripture.[162]

Worse, even some of us who would never dream of formally disentangling some parts of the Bible from the rest and declaring them less authoritative than other parts can by exegetical ingenuity get the Scriptures to say just about whatever we want—and this we thunder to the age as if it were a prophetic word, when it is little more than the message of the age bounced off Holy Scripture. To our shame, we have hungered to be masters of the Word much more than we have hungered to be mastered by it.

The pervasiveness of the problem erupts in the "Christian" merchant whose faith has no bearing on the integrity of his or her dealings, or in the way material possessions are assessed. It is reflected in an accelerating divorce rate in Christian homes and among the clergy themselves—with little sense of shame and no entailment in their "ministries." It is seen in its most pathetic garb when considerable exegetical skill goes into proving, say, that the Bible condemns promiscuous homosexuality but not homosexuality itself (though careful handling of the evidence overturns the thesis),[163] or that the Bible's use of "head" in passages dealing with male/female relationships follows allegedly characteristic Greek usage and, therefore, means "source" (when close scrutiny of the primary evidence fails to turn up more than a handful of disputable instances of the meaning "source" in over two thousand occurrences).[164] It finds new lease when popular evangelicals publicly abandon any mention of "sin"—allegedly on the ground that the term no longer "communicates"—without recognizing that adjacent truths (e.g., those dealing with the fall, the law of God, the nature of transgression, the wrath of God, and even the gracious atonement itself) undergo telling transformation.

While I fear that evangelicalism is heading for another severe conflict on the doctrine of Scripture, and while it is necessary to face these impending debates with humility and courage, what is far more alarming is the diminishing authority of the Scriptures in the churches. This is taking place not only among those who depreciate the consistent truthfulness of Scripture but also (if for different reasons) among those who most vociferously defend it. To some extent we are all part of the problem; and perhaps we can do most to salvage something of value

---

[162]Carl F. H. Henry, "The Bible and the Conscience of Our Age," in *Hermeneutics, Inerrancy, and the Bible*, ed. Radmacher and Preus, 917.

[163]See especially David F. Wright, "Homosexuals or Prostitutes? The Meaning of ΑΡΣΕΝΟΚΟΙΤΑΙ (1 Cor. 6:9; 1 Tim. 1:10)," *VC* 38 (1984): 125–53.

[164]See especially Wayne Grudem, "Does *kephalē* ('head') Mean 'Source' or 'Authority Over' in Greek Literature? A Survey of 2,336 Examples," *TJ* 6 (1985): 38–59.

from the growing fragmentation by pledging ourselves in repentance and faith to learning and obeying God's most holy Word. Then we shall also be reminded that the challenge to preserve and articulate a fully self-consistent and orthodox doctrine of Scripture cannot be met by intellectual powers alone, but only on our knees and by the power of God.

3

Unity and Diversity in the New Testament: The Possibility of Systematic Theology

Statement of the Problem

One might well ask, in the contemporary climate of academic theology, why a student whose prime focus of scholarly interest is the New Testament documents should meddle with questions concerning the foundations of systematic theology. The reasons are many, and few of them easy. We live in an age of increasing specialization (owing in part to the rapid expansion of knowledge), and disciplines that a priori ought to work hand in glove are being driven apart. More important, there is a growing consensus among New Testament scholars that any systematic theology that claims to summarize biblical truth is obsolete at best and perverse at worst. Any possibility of legitimate systematic theology presupposes that the discipline will look elsewhere for its norms, or begin from some center smaller than or different from the Christian canon.

It is important to grasp the proportions of the modern dilemma. At its center stand several close-knit assumptions: the New Testament is full of contradictions, it embraces many different theological perspectives that cannot be arranged into

Reprint of D. A. Carson, "Unity and Diversity in the New Testament: The Possibility of Systematic Theology," in *Scripture and Truth*, ed. D. A. Carson and John D. Woodbridge (Grand Rapids: Zondervan, 1983), 65–95, 368–75.

one system, its diversity is not only linguistic but conceptual, and it is made up of documents that come from so long a time span that major developments have rendered obsolete the theological positions of the earlier documents. The conclusion to be drawn from this cluster of propositions is that a systematic theology of the New Testament is impossible, let alone one that embraces both Testaments. In that sense, one cannot legitimately speak of "New Testament theology" but only of "New Testament theologies." The former category, "New Testament theology," may be considered an appropriate designation for the discipline of studying such theology as may be found in the New Testament, but not for referring to some supposed unified structure of theistic belief. As a result, it is not too surprising that of the ten major New Testament theologies published between 1967 and 1976, no two scholars agree on the nature, scope, purpose, or method of the discipline.[1]

It is not my purpose to trace the rise of these developments. Their roots stretch far back into the Enlightenment; and my knowledge of their growth is sufficient only to assure me that I do not possess the detailed understanding of history required to untangle them. My more modest goal is to focus on a number of representative works, first with description and then with criticism, and, following this, to offer some reflections that may be of use to the student who is persuaded that the New Testament documents are nothing less than the word of God, yet who cannot in all integrity fail to grapple with their substantial diversity. For convenience I will limit myself largely to the New Testament, although similar analysis could be extended to the Bible as a whole. I will not address directly the question of whether a transcendent/personal God can use the languages of finite men[2] nor wrestle with current developments in hermeneutics that argue for disjunction between the author's intent and the reader's understanding.[3] Such questions, though related to this inquiry, are of sufficient complexity to deserve separate treatment.

We may profitably begin with the enormously influential book by Walter Bauer, *Orthodoxy and Heresy in Earliest Christianity.*[4] The question Bauer sets himself is whether the church early embraced a clearly defined doctrinal corpus that enabled

---

[1] Cf. G. Hasel, *New Testament Theology: Basic Issues in the Current Debate* (Grand Rapids: Eerdmans, 1978), 9–10.

[2] Cf. R. L. Reymond, "Some Prolegomenous Issues Confronting the Systematic Theologian," *Presb* 4 (1978): 5–23; J. I. Packer, "The Adequacy of Human Language," in *Inerrancy*, ed. Norman L. Geisler (Grand Rapids: Zondervan, 1979), 197–226; Carl F. H. Henry, *God, Revelation and Authority*, 5 vols. (Waco, TX: Word, 1976–), vol. 1.

[3] Cf. Henry, *God, Revelation and Authority*, 4:463–66; D. A. Carson, "Hermeneutics: A Brief Assessment of Some Recent Trends," *Them* 5, no. 2 (1979–1980): 12–20; and especially A. C. Thiselton, *The Two Horizons: New Testament Hermeneutics and Philosophical Description* (Grand Rapids: Eerdmans, 1980).

[4] W. Bauer, *Rechtglaübigkeit und Ketzerei im ältesten Christentum* (Tübingen: Mohr/Siebeck, 1934). The English translation was based on the second edition (1964) and was edited by Robert A. Kraft and Gerhard Krodel (Philadelphia: Fortress, 1971).

it to reject false belief, or whether the distinction between orthodoxy and heresy is a rather late development. Methodologically, Bauer abandons the New Testament evidence because it is so disputed and conducts his readers on a whirlwind tour of second-century Christianity. He concludes that from the beginning so-called heretical and orthodox churches existed side by side, the latter frequently in the minority; and the reasons why the "orthodox" groups eventually won out have less to do with self-conscious theological incompatibility than with what we might call politics. The implication of all this is that even *first*-century Christianity was no different: highly diverse and even mutually exclusive beliefs were tolerated without embarrassment.

This reconstruction of early church history is very popular among New Testament scholars today. It wielded enormous influence on Bultmann and his disciples, but to one degree or another its impact was also felt in much wider circles. In an appendix to the 1964 edition of Bauer's book, G. Strecker developed the argument further and concluded that Jewish Christianity in the first century not only was diverse but was, by later "orthodox" standards, itself heretical.[5] A similar point of view is developed in Elaine Pagels's recent book, where it is argued that the theological options of the first two centuries, finally judged heretical, were not so lightly esteemed in their own time and should therefore be explored afresh as valid options for us today.[6] E. P. Sanders presupposes that at some point divisions between the "heretical" and the "orthodox" began to take place, but that this "shift in the consciousness of the Christian community" did not occur until the second and third centuries.[7] Stephen S. Smalley examines the Gospel and epistles of John and concludes that even there great diversity exists, so much so that this corpus "can hardly be regarded as consciously orthodox or heretical; it is neither one nor the other."[8]

In short, Bauer's work has established a new critical orthodoxy on this point, and recent studies tend to follow this direction.[9] From such a perspective, it is not difficult to exclude the possibility of a systematic theology based on the New Testament documents. One writer tells us that "the Bible is not a unified writing but a composite body of literature";[10] at some level this disjunction is surely false. Another tells us that "the New Testament is a repository of many *kerygmas*,

---

[5]Bauer, *Orthodoxy and Heresy*, 241–85.
[6]Elaine Pagels, *The Gnostic Gospels* (New York: Random, 1979).
[7]E. P. Sanders, ed., *Jewish and Christian Self-Definition*, vol. 1, *The Shaping of Christianity in the Second and Third Centuries* (Philadelphia: Fortress, 1980), ix.
[8]Stephen S. Smalley, "Diversity and Development in John," *NTS* 17 (1970–1971): 276–92, esp. 279.
[9]E.g., R. A. Kraft, "The Development of the Concept of 'Orthodoxy' in Early Christianity," in *Current Issues in Biblical and Patristic Interpretation*, ed. G. F. Hawthorne (Grand Rapids: Eerdmans, 1975), 47–59.
[10]James Barr, *The Bible in the Modern World* (New York: Harper & Row, 1973), 157.

not one,"[11] while a third rejoices that there are many contradictions in Scripture because they constitute "an aid in establishing chronology and in discerning the use of sources or the development of traditions, and through this an aid to historical reconstruction in general."[12]

This critical reconstruction of early church history, coupled with other developments that equally depreciate the truthfulness of the New Testament, has generated a host of writings exploring the nature of New Testament theology. Lost confidence in the unity of the New Testament stretches back a long way,[13] but the results are much with us. Scholars now ask if a New Testament theology is possible;[14] or they develop esoteric, narrow, and extrabiblical criteria for what such theology might include;[15] or, in the case of Roman Catholics, they frankly appeal to the authority of the Catholic Church as the only way out of the dilemma.[16]

The solution to the post-Enlightenment epistemological crisis that Gabler proposes—viz., to distinguish sharply between systematic and biblical theology, the latter alone being recognized as a historical discipline[17]—has largely petered out. The biblical-theology movement enjoyed its heyday from roughly 1930 to 1960; but its decline has been chronicled.[18] Even those who plaintively insist that the death notice is premature[19] do not provide any solid solutions, for in reality the movement has always lacked unity. It was useful in encouraging nuanced study of the various corpora that make up Scripture, but it was largely incapable of forging a consensus regarding what should be preached in the churches. Its proponents could not even agree that *theology* was a proper term, since it implies a coherent system, at least within each corpus.

The malaise is profound. Sensitive Bible scholars have come to recognize that the loss of confidence in the unity of the New Testament entails some kind of

---

[11]M. J. Suggs, "The Christian Two Way Tradition: Its Antiquity, Form, and Function," in *Studies in New Testament and Early Christian Literature*, ed. D. E. Aune, NovTSup 33 (Leiden: Brill, 1972), 62–74.

[12]Nils A. Dahl, *Studies in Paul* (Minneapolis: Augsburg, 1977), 159.

[13]Cf. the collection of essays edited by G. Strecker, *Das Problem der Theologie des Neuen Testaments* (Darmstadt: Wissenschaftliche Buchgesellschaft, 1975).

[14]E.g., W. Lohff, "Zur Einführung: Über die Mögligkeit, Theologie im Überblick, darzustellen," *Wissenschaftliche Theologie im Überblick*, ed. W. Lohff and F. Hahn (Göttingen: Vandenhoeck & Ruprecht, 1974), 5–12.

[15]E.g., D. Tracy, *Blessed Rage for Order: The New Pluralism in Theology* (New York: Seabury, 1975); R. T. Voelkel, *The Shape of the Theological Task* (Philadelphia: Westminster, 1968). Cf. also R. Morgan, *The Nature of New Testament Theology* (London: SCM, 1973), esp. 1–67.

[16]E.g., A. Ziegenhaus, "Die Bildung des Schriftkanons als Formprinzip der Theologie," *MTZ* 29 (1978): 264–83.

[17]J. Gabler, *De justo discrimine theologiae biblicae et dogmaticae regundisque recte utriusque finibus* ("On the proper distinction between biblical and dogmatic theology and the correct delimitation of their boundaries"). First delivered in 1787, this essay is available in a German translation in D. Merk, *Biblische Theologie des Neuen Testaments in ihrer Anfangszeit* (Marburg: Elwert, 1972), 273–84, and in G. Strecker, *Problem*, 32–44. Cf. the sensitive treatment of Gabler in Hendrikus Boers, *What Is New Testament Theology?* (Philadelphia: Fortress, 1979), 23–38.

[18]In particular, cf. Brevard Childs, *Biblical Theology in Crisis* (Philadelphia: Westminster, 1970).

[19]E.g., James D. Smart, *The Past, Present, and Future of Biblical Theology* (Philadelphia: Westminster, 1979). Others besides Smart are optimistic; e.g., Klaus Haacker et al., *Biblische Theologie heute* (Neukirchen-Vluyn: Neukirchener Verlag, 1977).

pick-and-choose method when it comes to preaching; and very often it is preaching that reveals our deepest theology. Ernst Käsemann advocates a "canon within the canon,"[20] but there is no possibility of establishing broadly agreed criteria for delineating such a mini-canon. As radical as he is, Käsemann is troubled by the loss of control and comments elsewhere, in an oft-repeated quote: "The main virtue of the historian and the beginning of all meaningful hermeneutic is for me the practice of hearing, which begins simply by letting what is historically foreign maintain its validity and does not regard rape as the basic form of engagement."[21] The problem is that Käsemann continues to practice rape as, if not the basic, then at least a primary, form of engagement. A fairly conservative critic like Peter Stuhlmacher wants to be open to "the possibility of transcendence" and to every method and every truth, but he cannot bring himself to accept everything the New Testament says because it includes (he argues) numerous contradictions— like that between Paul and James.[22] The net result of such hesitations is a deeply disturbing subjectivity, a subjectivity that among at least some New Testament scholars has a frankly atheistic structure.[23] At the end of the day the only kind of authority the New Testament can enjoy in this climate is some kind of latitudinarian "functional" authority.[24]

It should not be thought that there have been no positive voices. Ronald A. Ward insists that the New Testament presents a unified plan of salvation.[25] The New Testament theology written by Ladd has received wide circulation,[26] but though Ladd handles admirably the vast literature and competently traces out the main themes in each corpus, he does not attempt the promised unification of the results of his theology. Hasel's survey of problems relative to New Testament theology is extraordinarily useful,[27] but when it comes to delineating the unity of the New Testament, he is surprisingly hesitant.[28] The center of the New

---

[20]Ernst Käsemann, "Begrundet der neutestamentliche Kanon die Einheit der Kirche?" in *Das Neue Testament als Kanon*, ed. Ernst Käsemann (Göttingen: Vandenhoeck & Ruprecht, 1970), 124–33. Käsemann does want more scriptural control than some of his contributors, but he draws no clear lines.

[21]Ernst Käsemann, "Zum Thema der urchristlichen Apokalyptik," *ZTK* 59 (1962): 259.

[22]Cf. Peter Stuhlmacher, *Schriftauslegung auf dem Wege zur biblischen Theologie* (Göttingen: Vandenhoeck & Ruprecht, 1975). Part of this work has been recorded in English as *Historical Criticism and Theological Interpretation of Scripture*, trans. Roy A. Harrisville (Philadelphia: Fortress, 1977). Idem, *Vom Verstehen des Neuen Testaments: Eine Hermeneutik* (Göttingen: Vandenhoeck & Ruprecht, 1979).

[23]Cf. E. Rudolph, "Die atheistische Struktur der neuzeitlichen Subjektivität," *Neue Zeitschrift für systematische Theologie und Religionsphilosophie* 21 (1979): 119–38.

[24]Cf. especially David H. Kelsey, *The Uses of Scripture in Recent Theology* (Philadelphia: Fortress, 1975). Such authority rests not in what Scripture says (i.e., its content) but in its patterns. Which pattern or selection of patterns is chosen is entirely incidental. See the discussion in Henry, *God, Revelation and Authority*, 4:470–75.

[25]Ronald A. Ward, *The Pattern of Our Salvation: A Study of New Testament Unity* (Waco, TX: Word, 1978).

[26]George E. Ladd, *A Theology of the New Testament* (Grand Rapids: Eerdmans, 1974).

[27]Hasel, *New Testament Theology*.

[28]Ibid., 217–19.

Testament, he says, is simply Jesus himself;[29] this statement is true but it scarcely
tackles the problem before us. R. P. Martin, in a recent essay, surveys the field
and opts to use "Paul and his disciples" as the central touchstone (by this rubric
he manages to include the entire Pauline corpus while denying Pauline authorship to some of the epistles ascribed to him);[30] but when one inquires on what
basis Paul is selected, the answer is, "Paul towers over the terrain of the apostolic
community—in so far as we can judge from the surviving documents—as the
great champion of the divine initiative in salvation."[31] The theme to pursue is
reconciliation, "found principally in Paul but embracing all stages of the trajectory
that runs from pre-Pauline Christianity by way of the apostle himself to his disciples in the post-Pauline period."[32] One cannot help but wonder on what basis
such choices are made. No exegetical or theological defense is proffered. Why not
a completely different theme?

This chapter is designed to outline the seriousness of the problem and does
not give consideration to other influential contributors to the debate, such as
William Wrede, Adolf Schlatter, and Rudolf Bultmann. Nor have I traced the rise
of canon criticism since, unless I am greatly mistaken, it suffers at the moment,
in its various forms, from the same epistemological problems afflicting much of
the biblical-theology movement.

By far the most influential recent work on the topic of this chapter is the latest
book by J. D. G. Dunn, *Unity and Diversity in the New Testament: An Inquiry into
the Character of Earliest Christianity*.[33] Far longer and more sophisticated than its
near contemporary, J. L. Houlden's *Patterns of Faith: A Study in the Relationship
between the New Testament and Christian Doctrine*,[34] Dunn's book deserves special
treatment: not least because it comes from the pen of one who aligns himself with
so conservative a professional association as the Tyndale Fellowship for Biblical
Research.

Working Definitions

Before I enter into specific criticisms of Dunn's book and offer constructive suggestions, however, it is necessary to pause momentarily and define some terms
that are variously treated by different authors. I am referring to *biblical theology*
and *systematic theology*.

---

[29]Ibid., 216. Cf. also H. Riesenfeld, "Zur Frage nach der Einheit des Neuen Testaments," *Erbe und Auftrag* 53 (1977):
32–45.
[30]R. P. Martin, "New Testament Theology: Impasse and Exit," *ExpTim* 91 (1979–1980): 264–69.
[31]Ibid., 267.
[32]Ibid., 268.
[33]London: SCM, 1977.
[34]London: SCM, 1977.

The vagueness of the categories is in part responsible for the high degree of uncertainty regarding what these disciplines are or should be. Warfield pointed out a long time ago that at one level "systematic theology" is "an impertinent tautology."[35] Surely any theology worthy of the name is in some sense systematic. If the study is merely confusingly impressionistic or thoroughly incoherent, it can scarcely be classified as "theology" at all; and if it is theology, it must perforce be in some sense systematic. "Biblical theology" does not fare much better, for what systematician would like to think that his work is *un*biblical?

In the light of such ambiguities, some have argued that "biblical theology" should be used to refer to any theology that seeks to be true to the Bible and to relate the parts fairly and honestly with one another, using biblical categories.[36] By contrast, "systematic theology" emerges from the study of Scripture when alien philosophical frameworks are utilized,[37] or, alternatively, when pure biblical theology is applied to some later culture and its problems and questions.[38] Some prefer to eliminate the "systematic theology" category entirely and to use "biblical theology" to refer to all of the above save the theology that imparts an alien philosophical framework, for the latter is considered illegitimate.[39] Others are comfortable with "systematic theology" but would like to displace "biblical theology" with "history of special revelation" or the like.[40]

My own use of these labels may be briefly stated. First, although *theology* can relate to the entire scope of religious studies,[41] I use the term more narrowly to refer to the study of what the Scriptures say. This includes exegesis and historical criticism, the requisite analysis of method and epistemology, and the presentation of the biblical data in orderly fashion. I therefore exclude apologetics and ethics, except insofar as such topics are treated in Scripture.[42] By *biblical theology*

---

[35]B. B. Warfield, "The Idea of Systematic Theology," *Presbyterian and Reformed Review* 7 (1896): 243; reprinted in *The Necessity of Systematic Theology*, ed. John Jefferson Davis (Washington, DC: University Press of America, 1978), 99. All further quotes are from the latter.

[36]So, among others, Elmer A. Martens, "Tackling Old Testament Theology," *JETS* 20 (1977): 123–32; Gerhard F. Hasel, "The Future of Biblical Theology," *Perspectives on Evangelical Theology*, ed. Kenneth S. Kantzer and Stanley N. Gundry (Grand Rapids: Baker, 1979), 179–94.

[37]Ibid.

[38]This appears to be the working assumption of Hasel, *New Testament Theology*.

[39]R. B. Gaffin, "Systematic Theology and Biblical Theology," *WTJ* 38 (1975–1976): 281–99; also printed in *The New Testament Student and Theology*, ed. J. Skilton (Nutley, NJ: Presbyterian and Reformed, 1976), 32–50.

[40]G. Vos, *Biblical Theology: Old and New Testaments* (Grand Rapids: Eerdmans, 1948), 23; John Murray, "Systematic Theology," *WTJ* 26 (1963–1964): 33–46; reprinted in *The New Testament Student and Theology*, ed. J. Skilton, 18–31, esp. 18.

[41]Such an assumption stands behind the sophisticated treatment of Bernard Lonergan, especially in his book, *Method in Theology* (New York: Herder and Herder, 1972). Cf. the brief exposition by William Mathews, "Theology as Collaborative Wonder: A Portrait of the Work of Bernard Lonergan, S. J.," *ExpTim* 91 (1979–1980): 172–76. Despite the value of Lonergan's work, he does not attempt to answer unambiguously the precise nature of the authority Scripture has for him and how or to what extent it circumscribes all his endeavor.

[42]Of course, "theology" may also have a narrower sense, as in "theology proper"—what the Scriptures teach concerning God. But the usage does not interest us here.

I refer to that branch of theology whose concern it is to study each corpus of the Scripture in its own right, especially with respect to its place in the history of God's unfolding revelation. The emphasis is on history and on the individual corpus. By *systematic theology* I refer to the branch of theology that seeks to elaborate the whole and the parts of Scripture,[43] demonstrating their logical (rather than their merely historical) connections and taking full cognizance of the history of doctrine and the contemporary intellectual climate and categories and queries while finding its sole ultimate authority in the Scriptures themselves, rightly interpreted. Systematic theology deals with the Bible as a finished product.

These definitions do not avoid overlap: biblical theology must be systematic, even if it focuses on the historical place and significance of each corpus; and systematic theology, if it turns on fair exegesis, must perforce rely on historical considerations. But the distinctions I have drawn are clear enough and are not novel.[44] Warfield offers an analogy that, despite its limits, is worth repeating:

> The immediate work of exegesis may be compared to the work of a recruiting officer: it draws out from the mass of mankind the men who are to constitute the army. Biblical Theology organizes these men into companies and regiments and corps, arranged in marching order and accoutered for service. Systematic Theology combines these companies and regiments and corps into an army—a single and unitary whole, determined by its own all-pervasive principle. It, too, is composed of men—the same men who were recruited by the Exegetics; but it is composed of these men, not as individuals merely, but in their due relations to the other men of their companies and regiments and corps. The simile is far from a perfect one; but it may illustrate the mutual relations of the disciplines, and also, perhaps, suggest the historical element that attaches to Biblical Theology, and the element of all-inclusive systematization that is inseparable from Systematic Theology.[45]

The "simile" is indeed weak at several points. All the recruits get taken up into the army; and the army qua people is not more than the sum of the recruits. By contrast, not every exegetical scrap goes into systematic theology; yet, as we will see,

---

[43]By relating systematic theology to the Scripture, I mean to exclude vague definitions. For instance, Stephen Sykes, *The Integrity of Anglicanism* (London: Mowbrays, 1978), laments the fact that systematic theology has been ignored in British universities and defines such theology as "that constructive discipline which presents the substance of the Christian faith with a claim on the minds of men" (ix). Superficially, I have no quarrel with the definition, but I wonder on what basis the "substance of the Christian faith" is to be determined.

[44]See, for instance, the similar recent treatment by Roger R. Nicole, "The Relationship Between Biblical Theology and Systematic Theology," *Evangelical Roots*, ed. Kenneth S. Kantzer (Nashville: Nelson, 1978), 185–94.

[45]Warfield, "The Idea of Systematic Theology," 114.

systematic theology may at certain points be more than the sum of the exegetical data. Numerous other distinctions spring to mind, but if the analogy, like any analogy, has its limits, it also helps to clarify the distinction between biblical theology and systematic theology.

It follows, then, that questions concerning the unity and diversity of the New Testament affect both biblical theology and systematic theology. For example, if it is argued that a particular writer or book is inconsistent, owing to oversight, later redaction, the incorporation of incompatible sources, or the like, then it is impossible to develop a biblical theology for that corpus. At most one could practice the *discipline* of biblical theology and demonstrate thereby that the corpus in question embraces divergent biblical theolog*ies*. Similarly, the possibility of developing a systematic theology turns on finding that none of the books of the New Testament are inconsistent (whether such consistency is hammered out in logical, historical, functional, or other categories). If there is insurmountable inconsistency, then the *discipline* of systematic theology may remain, but no single systematic theology qua end product would be possible. The individual systematician would become free to pick and choose whatever elements of the biblical data he preferred. The resulting system would not in any primal sense be dictated by the Scriptures themselves but would be definitively shaped by outside considerations, using the biblical data as nothing more than disparate building blocks.

Granted the internal coherence of each corpus, it is theoretically possible to develop a biblical theology for each corpus, yet fail to find the consensus needed for systematic theology. If, however, a unified systematic theology is possible, biblical theology itself achieves new dignity, for one entailment of the systematic theology would be the certainty that the contributing corpuses are coherent if rightly organized in the historical framework of biblical theology.

If the definitions and relationships I have sketched in are permitted to stand, it follows that the legitimacy of pursuing a systematic theology depends on the unity of the New Testament. Such wide diversity as there is must not involve logical or historical contradiction. Conversely, if New Testament diversity is as sweeping as is often alleged, we ought forthwith to abandon the pursuit of a systematic theology, and those who write theology ought to tell us by what criteria they choose to include this or that dictum or make this or that value judgment.

Critique

What remains to be done is both negative and positive. Negatively, I propose to survey rapidly a few of the more telling responses to Walter Bauer and to interact in some detail with the recent work by J. D. G. Dunn. Positively, I propose in the next section to set forth some reflections in defense of preserving the unity of the New Testament while recognizing its diversity.

When Bauer's *Orthodoxy and Heresy in Earliest Christianity* appeared,[46] most reviews were overwhelmingly positive. There were thoughtful caveats and hesitations, but few frontal assaults.[47] This changed when A. M. Hunter published *The Unity of the New Testament*.[48] Hunter argued in considerable detail that whatever diversity the New Testament embraces, its writers exhibit a basic unity in their commitment to one Lord, one church, and one salvation.

More important yet was H. E. W. Turner's 1954 Bampton Lectures.[49] Turner examined Bauer's work in ruthless detail and exposed its repeated arguments from silence, its sustained misjudgments concerning the theological positions of such figures as Ignatius and Polycarp, and its incautious exaggerations on many fronts. Turner demonstrated that the church's understanding of its theology antedates the attempt to work the Scriptures into a religious whole: "Christians lived Trinitarily long before the evolution of Nicene orthodoxy."[50]

Various brief essays have been penned more recently. I. H. Marshall demonstrates that in virtually all of the New Testament documents, early or late, there is unambiguous recognition of the fact that certain beliefs are incompatible with the truth, and even damning.[51] This does not prove that all such stances can be made to fit together, but it does demonstrate that Bauer's central thesis—that the very concepts of orthodoxy and heresy are late developments and motivated by less than religious concerns—are false. J. F. McCue argues persuasively that Bauer's understanding of the Valentinian Gnostics is seriously deficient.[52] The Valentinians did *not* develop as an independent branch of Christianity but set themselves over against the orthodox. Moreover, early Valentinians use the books of the orthodox New Testament in a way that suggests they emerged from within an orthodox matrix.

Such considerations as these make Bauer's case untenable; yet his influence is broadly felt to this day—not least in the recent book by J. D. G. Dunn.[53] Dunn stakes out his territory for exploration on the assumption that Bauer is basically correct. "Bauer has shown," he says,

---

[46]Cf. n. 4, *supra*.

[47]A convenient collection of these is found in an appendix to the English translation (cf. n. 4, *supra*).

[48]London: SCM, 1943.

[49]H. E. W. Turner, *The Pattern of Christian Truth: A Study in the Relations Between Orthodoxy and Heresy in the Early Church* (London: Mowbray, 1954).

[50]Ibid., 28.

[51]I. H. Marshall, "Orthodoxy and Heresy in Earlier Christianity," *Them* 2, no. 1 (1976–1977): 5–14. The comparative "earlier" in Marshall's title is in reaction to Bauer who "had the effrontery to label the second century as '*earliest* Christianity'" (6).

[52]J. F. McCue, "Orthodoxy and Heresy: Walter Bauer and the Valentinians," *VC* 33 (1979): 118–30.

[53]Dunn, *Unity and Diversity*; see n. 33, *supra*.

that second-century Christianity was a very mixed bag. There was no "pure" form of Christianity that existed in the beginning which can properly be called "orthodoxy." In fact there was no uniform concept of orthodoxy at all—only different forms of Christianity competing for the loyalty of believers.[54]

It may be doubted whether Bauer is correct in any of his main theses, but Dunn, building on this foundation, now attempts to push the inquiry back into the first century, and more or less along the same lines.

Dunn gives the first two-thirds of his book over to a discussion of diversity in the New Testament. In successive chapters he treats the kerygma ("Kerygma or Kerygmata?"), the primitive confessional formulae, the role of tradition, the use of the Old Testament, concepts of ministry, patterns of worship, the sacraments, the place of the Spirit and experience, and Christ and christology. In each chapter he is concerned to demonstrate the diversity surrounding these themes in the pages of the New Testament. The final third of the book reverses procedures and searches for whatever unity may be found among such diverse groupings as Jewish Christianity, Hellenistic Christianity, Apocalyptic Christianity, and early Catholicism.

The final chapter summarizes Dunn's findings and raises some questions about the function of the canon. Dunn concludes that the diversity of first-century Christianity is very pronounced, indeed that "there was no single normative form of Christianity in the first century."[55] By this, Dunn does not mean to say only that there were various complementary theological insights and diverse ecclesiastical structures (although he affirms both of these things), but that there were mutually incompatible theologies and no consciousness of a fundamental orthodoxy/heterodoxy tension. The primary unifying feature, according to Dunn, is the common acknowledgment of the unity between Jesus the man and Jesus the exalted one. Dunn tends to trumpet this finding as if it were a major breakthrough, a glorious discovery; but the value of even this minimal confession is rather mitigated by his observation that the mode of the unity between Jesus the man and Jesus the exalted one is rather disputed and uncertain.

The crucial question arising from all this concerns the canon. What authority can the New Testament documents exercise if Dunn's reconstruction is correct? Dunn denies that the New Testament writings "are canonical because they were *more inspired* than other and later Christian writings" (emphasis his).[56] The

---

[54]Ibid., 3.
[55]Ibid., 373.
[56]Ibid., 386.

evidence, he argues, shows rather that early Christian communities functioned, in effect, each with its own "canon within the canon," and therefore what the New Testament does is establish the validity of diversity. "To affirm the canon of the NT," Dunn states, "is to affirm the diversity of Christianity."[57] The New Testament may also establish the *limits* of legitimate diversity; but what Dunn self-confessedly wants to do is to serve as a sort of broker between liberalism and conservatism, challenging each side to recognize the legitimacy of the other. With this end in view he attempts to formulate the essential, the irreducible, Christian message:

> Christianity begins from and finally depends on the conviction that in Jesus we still have a paradigm for man's relation to God and man's relation to man, that in Jesus' life, death, and life out of death we see the clearest and fullest embodiment of divine grace, of creative wisdom and power, that ever achieved historical actuality, that the Christian is accepted by God and enabled to love God and his neighbour by that same grace which we now recognize to have the character of that same Jesus. This conviction (whether in these or in alternative words) would appear to be the irreducible minimum without which "Christianity" loses any distinctive definition and becomes an empty pot into which men pour whatever meaning they choose. But to require some particular elaboration of it as the norm, to insist that some further assertion or a particular form of words is also fundamental, would be to move beyond the unifying canon within the canon, to erect a canon on only one or two strands within the NT and no longer on the broad consensus of the NT writings as a whole. It would be divisive rather than unifying. It would draw the circumference of acceptable diversity far more tightly than the canonical writings themselves justify.[58]

I confess I do not recognize much of the Christian gospel in this summary. Instead of perceiving complementary truths in various parts of the canon, Dunn hunts for the lowest common denominator. The result is a "gospel" that makes no mention of sin, gives no thought to the incarnation or the atonement, presents Jesus primarily as a paradigm instead of a Savior (Why can't we have both?), and has no more authority behind it than what can be salvaged from Dunn's reconstruction of history—all of which prompts me to wonder why his reconstruction

---

[57]Ibid., 377.
[58]Ibid., 376.

should be thought any more compelling than that of any other scholar whose predisposition is to dismiss most of the evidence.

This is not to say that Dunn's book does not have any admirable features. Dunn displays an enviable breadth of learning, a massive knowledge of the secondary literature, and an admirable clarity and felicity of expression. Unfortunately, however, the sweep of material that impresses the reader with its breadth is simultaneously a distorting compression that, as Dunn's most perceptive review has noted, "results both in indigestion and in apparently cavalier generalizations and one-sided treatments."[59] To cite but one of scores of examples: Dunn concludes, after a mere three-page discussion, that Jesus was not, in his own teaching, the object of faith—a conclusion attained by ignoring most of the evidence in the Gospels and dismissing the rest as anachronistic.

Many of the reviewers highlight not only the strengths but also the recurrent weaknesses of Dunn's book,[60] and they need not be repeated here. What might be more useful in this essay is to focus briefly on one chapter as a sample of Dunn's argument and to offer some suggestions as to possible lines of rebuttal. Rigorous detail cannot be provided in the brief compass of this section, but the shape of the confrontation can be nicely delineated.

In chapter 2, titled "Kerygma or Kerygmata?" Dunn attempts to show the diversity of kerygmata in the New Testament. The method Dunn adopts is to "make an aerial survey of the most important proclamations of the Gospel in the NT, concentrating on picking out the characteristic features of each kerygma [Doesn't such phraseology already prejudge the issue?] rather than attempting a fully balanced treatment of the whole."[61] Dunn begins with the kerygma of Jesus. He excludes the evidence in the Fourth Gospel on the grounds that it does not use the word κηρύσσω, κήρυγμα, εὐαγγελίζομαι, or εὐαγγέλιον,[62] and thereby he eliminates a substantial part of the evidence. The kerygma of Jesus, according to the Synoptic Gospels, then, is summed up in several statements. First of all, Jesus proclaimed the imminent kingdom of God but was mistaken in that his own expectations failed to materialize. Second, Jesus called for repentance and faith (in God, not in himself) "in face of the end-time power and claim of God."[63] Third, Jesus offered forgiveness and participation in the messianic feast of the new age, and on this built the ethical corollary of love.

---

[59]R. T. France, in *Them* 5 (1979–1980): 30–31.

[60]In addition to the review by France (cf. n. 59), cf. in particular the reviews in the following journals: *Theology* 81 (1978): 452–55; *ThTo* 36 (1979): 116–21; *CBQ* 49 (1978): 629–31; *JBL* 98 (1979): 135–37; *AUSS* 18 (1980): 111–13.

[61]Dunn, *Unity and Diversity*, 13.

[62]Ibid., 390n4.

[63]Ibid., 16.

I am sure critical orthodoxy will be pleased, but the effrontery is astounding nonetheless. Dunn does not here discuss the parables with their repeated emphasis on grace (e.g., servants hired at various hours) and their picture of delay before the parousia (e.g., wheat and tares). He is silent regarding the Lord's Supper and its forward-looking stance to his death and the community's continued memory (before the parousia: "till I come"!) of that death, specific sayings rich in pregnant significance (e.g., Mark 10:45, the so-called ransom saying), the acceptance of obeisance, the utter lack of any consciousness of sin coupled with the willingness and ability to forgive sin, the specific references to his church in Matthew and the dozens of passages where the community is presumed to continue, and much more. Dunn treats many of these things elsewhere but he does not treat them as if they have any reference to an understanding of Jesus' kerygma. By eliminating much evidence as anachronistic and parceling up sections of the Synoptic Gospels into mutually exclusive categories, Dunn arrives at his minimalistic conclusion. Nor does he explore Jesus' place in salvation history or the consequences such exploration might have in the way Jesus expresses himself.

Dunn then goes on to consider the kerygma in Acts. Positively, Dunn states, the kerygma in Acts proclaims the resurrection of Jesus and the need for a response characterized by repentance and faith in Jesus, issuing in the promise of forgiveness, salvation, and the Spirit. Negatively, Acts is characterized by the absence of any theology of the death of Jesus and of the tension between fulfillment and consummation ("completely lacking," Dunn says),[64] and by a subordinationist christology. To encourage faith in Jesus rather than in God is already a shift from Jesus' preaching, Dunn insists; but as we have seen, he has eliminated the relevant evidence in the Gospels. True, there is *more* emphasis on faith in Jesus in Acts than in the Gospels, but this is largely due to the new perspective brought about by the cross, resurrection, and exaltation: the stance in salvation history is now a little further advanced, and it is clearer than before just who Jesus is. In fact, Acts reveals a *growing* awareness of the implications of Jesus' death and resurrection, implications progressively developed through the earliest preaching, the ministry of Stephen, the admission of Samaritans and then of Gentiles, the developing consciousness of a new relation to Old Testament law, and so forth; but such major salvation history perspectives Dunn does not consider at this point. The Spirit is promised the believer, he says, but he does not consider how this blessed gift is climactically poured out at Pentecost and how at least some further manifestations have to do with validation of the newly converted community before the

---

[64]Ibid., 18.

Jerusalem church. How may one legitimately treat the kerygma in Acts *without* considering such things?

And is it true that Luke has no theology of the death of Christ? Dunn notes the places where Jesus' death is referred to but always finds some other explanation. Even 20:28 is dismissed because it "remains more than a little puzzling and obscure."[65] The treatment of this subject by W. J. Larkin, who gives some indication of the atonement theology presupposed in Luke-Acts, is much to be preferred.[66] And if Larkin and others are right, then 20:28 can be dropped into the text casually and without comment precisely because it was an accepted item of belief. Dunn repeatedly warns us against reading all of Galatians and Romans into passages in Acts (e.g., Acts 5:30 and 10:39), and his warning is to the point. But he pushes this warning so hard that he adopts a methodologically indefensible stance. Must everything be said about every doctrine on every occasion? Must silence or de-emphasis signify ignorance or disagreement? From the point of view of credible historical methodology, might it not be argued that allusive references to a doctrine explicitly expounded elsewhere presuppose such a doctrine as easily as deny such a doctrine? Could it be that Luke focuses more attention on the resurrection than on the atonement precisely because he is so interested in his witness theme and the part that it played in the earliest preaching? (The apostles could witness the death of Christ and the resurrected Christ but not in the deepest sense, the atonement of Christ.) Is there no significance to the fact that the Luke who penned Acts also wrote Luke 21:28; 24:21?[67] Does not this fact prompt suspicions that some, at least, of the relative silence regarding the atonement in Acts springs *not* from ignorance or disavowal but from other considerations? And why is there not so much as a mention of Leon Morris's substantial and responsible treatment of this subject from a perspective very different from that of Dunn?[68]

In the area of christology, Dunn fares no better. It is true that there is a substantial "subordinationist" strand in the christology of Acts, but Dunn's conclusions are not entailed by this fact. Equal subordinationism can be found in the Fourth Gospel,[69] a document that also embraces the highest christology. One might legitimately conclude, therefore, that some early Christians, at least, saw

---

[65]Ibid.

[66]W. J. Larkin, "Luke's Use of the Old Testament as a Key to His Soteriology," *JETS* 20 (1977): 325–35. Cf. also A. George, "Le sens de la mort de Jésus pour Luc," *RB* 80 (1973): 186–217; R. Glöckner, *Die Verkündigung des Heils beim Evangelisten Lukas* (Mainz: Matthias Grünwald, 1975), 155–95; F. Schütz, *Der beidende Christus* (Stuttgart: Kohlhammer, 1969), 93–94; and G. Voss, *Die Christologie des luckanischen Schriften* (Stuttgart: Kohlhammer, 1972), section 7.

[67]Cf. I. H. Marshall, "The Development of the Concept of Redemption in the New Testament," *Reconciliation and Hope*, ed. R. Banks (Exeter: Paternoster, 1974), 153–69.

[68]Leon Morris, *The Cross in the New Testament* (Grand Rapids: Eerdmans, 1965), esp. 63–143.

[69]Cf. especially C. K. Barrett, "'The Father Is Greater than I' (Jo 14, 28): Subordinationist Christology in the New Testament," in *Neues Testament und Kirche*, ed. J. B. Gnilka (Freiburg: Herder, 1974), 144–59.

no necessary incompatibility between the two strands. What is needed therefore is an analysis of the way these true strands complement each other.[70] Moreover it is surely illegitimate to treat the christology of Acts without again considering the flow of salvation history and the church's rising understanding of the Christ event. The question is whether or not such doctrinal development introduced categories that annulled their earlier understanding. If not, there is development but not contradiction; growth in comprehension and theological awareness, but no clashing confessions or kerygmata. At least some attempts to analyze the earliest developments in christology have proceeded along these lines,[71] but Dunn does not interact with them or show where they are in error. Why not?

The limitations of space prevent me from embarking on even a cursory response to Dunn's treatment of the kerygma in Paul and in John. The same problems abound there, coupled with two or three magnificent non sequiturs, the best of which is the following (italicized for emphasis in Dunn): "Where the very concept of and claim to apostleship was the subject of controversy, what meaning can we give to the phrase 'the apostolic faith'?"[72]

Dunn is a very competent scholar, and I have no doubt he could defend his position a little better if he tackled in depth any of the areas he treats in this book. Of course, I must not criticize him for not writing a book he did not intend to write, but in all fairness it must be said that this book could win only those who have already bought into the critical orthodoxy of the age without pausing to consider the alternative options that cry out to be heard on almost every page of Dunn's work. There is an important place for superficial books, but it is sad to see a superficial book claiming to present a profound argument.

Positive Reflections

I do not propose to *demonstrate* the unity of the New Testament except incidentally. To do so would require several books and far more time and skill than I have at my disposal. I propose instead to attempt something much more modest. I will simultaneously assume a high view of Scripture (based not least on Scripture's self-attestation)[73] and that the diversity of the New Testament documents is to be taken seriously. Beginning with these twin assumptions, I will offer a number of reflections relative to the possibility of establishing a systematic theology on

---

[70]I have attempted this for the christology of the Fourth Gospel in one chapter of my *Divine Sovereignty and Human Responsibility: Some Aspects of Johannine Theology against Jewish Background* (London: Marshall, Morgan and Scott; Nashville: John Knox, 1980).

[71]See in particular I. H. Marshall, "The Development of Christology in the Early Church," *TynBul* 18 (1967), 77–93; cf. also C. F. D. Moule, *The Origin of Christology* (Cambridge: Cambridge University Press, 1977).

[72]Dunn, *Unity and Diversity*, 24.

[73]Cf. chapter 1 by W. Grudem in this book.

the basis of such diverse documents. These reflections are neither original nor profound but they may help provide an introductory framework both for the evangelical who is attempting to establish his theology on the Scriptures and for the non-evangelical who seeks to understand why evangelicals continue to hold that a systematic theology grounded on the Bible is important.

1. *First, it is important to recognize that virtually every person not an atheist adopts some kind of systematic theology.*

This is not to say that every systematic theology is good, useful, balanced, wise, or biblical; it is to say nothing more than that most people adopt *some* kind of systematic theology.

Consider, for example, the person who says that he doesn't believe the Bible is the word of God, that it is full of errors and contradictions, and that many of its teachings are at best obsolete. If he is not an atheist, he nevertheless believes *something* about God (or gods, but for convenience we will assume he is monotheistic). In his own mind he adopts a number of beliefs that he holds to be consistent. Even a dialectician thinks his beliefs are *ultimately* reconcilable.

It may be, of course, that some of his beliefs are not consistent with other components of his belief system. But no one will consciously adopt such logical inconsistencies, except perhaps in the sense that he might temporarily hold several in tension while he tries to sort them out. He may maintain a core belief system about which he entertains few doubts and a wider circle of beliefs about which he is less certain, but unless he is insane, he will press for maximum logical consistency. This is true even when he springs from a culture in which people like to think in pictures rather than in abstract propositions, for it is a universal apperception that behind the pictures stand realities, however dimly perceived. If someone presents a structure of theology that conflicts sharply with his own system, then even if that structure is presented in pictures, it will evoke a negative reaction.

What this means is that it ill suits anyone to scoff at systematic theology or to minimize its importance, for the scoffer inevitably embraces some kind of systematic theology of his own. Relevant discussion therefore does not call into question the legitimacy of systematic theology per se, but the data base on which it is built; the methods admitted to its construction; the principles that pronounce exclusion of certain information; the language and felicity in which it is phrased; and the consistency, cogency, and precision of the results.

Consider, first, the data base. What propositions about God—his nature, characteristics, functions, relationships—do we admit into our system? Where do we find them? Which ones do we exclude? How do we verify them? What place does revelation have in providing data? Is revelation merely personal, merely propositional, or is it both personal and propositional? If merely personal, how closely do human descriptions of that personal revelation correspond with the reality?

I am not suggesting that everyone thinks through his personal theology by asking himself these questions but rather that these questions lurk unrecognized behind every systematic theology. That is why sophisticated treatments like those of, say, Hodge, Litton, and Henry devote a considerable amount of attention to introductory questions of method.[74]

If these reflections are valid, then a J. D. G. Dunn, for instance, has his own systematic theology. He has admitted as much in that he has attempted to determine the common core of the New Testament. He may believe other things in the New Testament and adopt them into his reconstructed core, but he cannot adopt all that the New Testament has to say, because he is convinced the full set of New Testament data is inconsistent and will not cohere historically or logically. But Dunn has his own systematic theology nevertheless. The crucial question in Dunn's attempt to write Christian theology is the basis on which he selects his data. Why do some New Testament truths, and not others, become central for him? On what basis are some traditional Christian beliefs rejected?

The point I am trying to make is that it is not the validity of systematic theology qua discipline that is called into question, but the cogency of one's critical tools. *Christian* systematic theology cannot be done without reference to the Bible, but what role should the Bible play? And should all of it play a role?

The data base of systematic theology is not the only consideration. Systematic theology, to be coherent to its contemporary culture, must use contemporary language and at least *some* of the paradigms of that culture (or offer astute reasons for rejecting them). Finite and sinful as every human being is, there will no doubt be some diversity in the theologies of the various systematicians. But nothing is as important as the data basis that is permitted, for this is a question of authority and legitimation, not of hermeneutics. It follows that everyone who presents a case for this or that systematizing of theology owes it to his followers to explain as unambiguously as possible what he will and will not admit into his system. He may of course go much further and justify his data base, but he must at least identify it.

---

[74]Charles Hodge, *Systematic Theology*, 3 vols. (New York: Scribner, Armstrong, 1872–74), esp. 1:1–188; Edward Arthur Litton, *Introduction to Dogmatic Theology*, ed. Philip E. Hughes (London: James Clarke, 1960), esp. 1–40; Henry, *God, Revelation and Authority*.

Dunn's work, at least in part, is an attempt to justify his extremely limited data base. Unfortunately, it is precisely at this point that his book is so weak. Dunn adopts many current, critical shibboleths, but he does not take the time to subject them to rigorous scrutiny, or even to consider whether his approach to the canon, his literary tests, his historical reconstructions, and his failure to wrestle with the alternative options offered even by those who use the same tools may not unwittingly exclude all kinds of data that should be admitted.

2. *The data base to be urged upon systematic theologians is the entire Bible, the canonical sixty-six books; and the validity of this choice depends on the adoption of four positions.*

The *first* position is that all of Scripture is trustworthy, and this of course presupposes that Scripture is truthful. If certain parts are not trustworthy, then they should not be used as data for the systematic theology.

What is objectionable about Dunn's approach is not so much that he detects errors here or there, as false (in my judgment) as his detection is, but that apart from a minimalistic common denominator he is prepared to baptize as Christian some structures of thought that in his view are mutually contradictory. This preserves, he argues, the validity of diverse theologies. But which, if any, is *true*—that is, which corresponds to historical and spiritual reality? Which, if any, is *trustworthy*? If they are mutually contradictory on any point, not more than one, and perhaps none, is true. Defending the validity of diversity in christology, for instance, may be helpful if the various christologies are mutually complementary; but if they are mutually contradictory, a defense of the diverse reduces to a defense of diverse error and untrustworthiness.

This first position, that all of Scripture is trustworthy, can be competently defended on wide grounds: the Scriptures' self-attestation, the approach of Christ to the Scriptures, the amazing reliability the Bible manifests where it is historically testable, and so forth. Some of these grounds are produced elsewhere in this volume. My concern at the moment is simply to set forth in brief form positions on which a systematic theology of the canonical Scriptures must be based and, implicitly, to show how opposing systematic theologies need to clarify their own approaches.

The *second* position presupposed by my approach to systematic theology is that the basic laws of logic—such as the law of noncontradiction or the law of the excluded middle—are not *inventions* of Aristotle or formulations of some other *savant*, but *discoveries* to do with the nature of reality and of communication. They do no more than affirm that certain relationships obtain if communication is possible and coherent, and if any truth whatsoever may be known. If anyone denies this, I reply that the true import of his denial is the opposite of what he says; and I cannot possibly be *logically* (if I may be forgiven for using the word) refuted. The substratum of *any* communication, whether between two individuals or two ages, is simple logic, regardless of the literary genre in which the communication is embedded. The "inner logic of divine revelation," to which some have appealed as a substitute, sounds devout, but either it is a way of saying that the relationships among divinely given truths in the Scripture must be established by Scripture (in which case it is difficult to see how this is opposed to logic) or else it is a way of appealing to fideism of the irrational variety.

It will not do to respond by citing Isaiah 55:8–9:

> "For my thoughts are not your thoughts,
>   neither are your ways my ways,"
>   declares the LORD.
> "As the heavens are higher than the earth,
>   so are my ways higher than your ways
>   and my thoughts than your thoughts."

The context makes it evident that the categories do not concern competing logic systems or the like; rather, they are essentially moral. The preceding verse exhorts,

> Let the wicked forsake his way
>   and the evil man his thoughts. (55:7)

Man's thoughts are to be brought into conformity with God's thoughts not by abandoning logic but by repentance.

Similarly, it is no real objection to this point to spread out the Bible's use of paradox, hyperbole, parable, and other literary forms and devices. None of these things endangers logic in the slightest, but they do caution us as to how logic is to be applied.

Logic can produce a false answer if, for instance, the premises are wrong, or if insufficient data are considered, or if a paradox is not recognized for what it is. But such failures do not threaten logic itself so much as faulty conclusions grounded in poor premises. To pit Scripture against logic is simply incoherent. Rogers and McKim thoroughly misrepresent Calvin on this matter when they say:

Calvin knew the value of logic as one of the human sciences. . . . But the law of noncontradiction, which dialectics taught, did not, for Calvin, have precedence over the teachings of Scripture. The power of truth to persuade us through faith was a greater value for Calvin with his humanist background. He commented, for example, on Matthew 27:43, "He trusts in God, let God deliver him now. . . ." He condemned as "Satan's logic" any interpretation that applied logic to God's providence and then concluded that God does not love us because we suffer. Calvin accepted that God had given logic along with physics, mathematics, and other worldly disciplines "that we may be helped . . . by the work and ministry of the ungodly." But if logic was used to drive persons away from faith in the truths of Scripture, then it was to be categorically rejected.[75]

Rogers and McKim use the phrase "Satan's logic" as if to suggest that Calvin presents logic as if it were in the peculiar domain of Satan. In fact, Calvin says that Satan attempts to drive us to despair by "this logic," that is, "this logical argument," viz., that since God watches over the safety of his people, it appears he does not love those whom he does not assist. Calvin calls Satan's ruse "this logic" because it has the form of logical argument, but he then goes on to argue that Satan's argument is false, *not on the grounds that logic must take a back seat to Scripture*, but on the grounds that the premises are inadequate. God's love cannot be reduced to the present instant, Calvin says, and God may demonstrate his love in the long haul. Moreover, God often uses adversity to train his people in obedience. In short, Calvin argues that Satan uses a prejudicial selection of the data in constructing his argument. Rogers and McKim are mistaken when they say Calvin rejected "any interpretation *that applied logic* to God's providence and then concluded that God does not love us because we suffer."[76] On the contrary, the cogency of Calvin's response depends entirely on the logic that he himself applies to the same problem, using a broader selection of data. There is not the slightest suggestion, either in his commentaries or in the *Institutes*, that Calvin ever considered logic itself as something that could, in and of itself, "drive persons away from faith in the truths of Scripture" and was therefore "to be categorically rejected."[77] The real problem is that Rogers and McKim characteristically read historical evidence

---

[75]Jack B. Rogers and Donald K. McKim, *The Authority and Interpretation of the Bible: An Historical Approach* (New York: Harper & Row, 1979), 90–91, citing *Commentary on Matthew* at 27:43 (Calvin Translation Society edition) and *Institutes* 2.2.16.

[76]Rogers and McKim, *Authority and Interpretation*, 91.

[77]Ibid.

through the spectacles of their own reconstruction of history and thereby treat it anachronistically.[78]

These two positions bring us to a *third*. If the Scriptures are trustworthy, and if the basic laws of logic are not inventions of dubious worth but discoveries of the basic relationships that make both coherent communication and knowledge of truth possible, then for systematic theology to be based on the Bible also requires that the documents that constitute the Bible deal with the same general topic. For instance, a written analysis of Elizabethan English and a text on the quantum behavior of quarks may conceivably be equally trustworthy, but it would be extremely difficult to develop a consistent synthesis from these two literary pieces. By the same token, a systematic theology based on the Bible requires that the biblical books be close enough in subject matter to cohere.

It is important to observe carefully the limits of this position. I am not saying that the Bible is like a jigsaw puzzle of five thousand pieces and that all the five thousand pieces are provided, so that with time and thought the entire picture may be completed. Rather, I am suggesting that the Bible is like a jigsaw puzzle that provides five thousand pieces along with the assurance that these pieces all belong to the same puzzle, even though ninety-five thousand pieces (the relative figures are unimportant for my analogy) are missing. Most of the pieces that are provided, the instructions insist, fit together rather nicely; but there are a lot of gaping holes, a lot of edges that cry out to be completed, and some clusters of pieces that seem to be on their own. Nevertheless, the assurance that all of the pieces do belong to one puzzle is helpful, for that makes it possible to develop the systematic theology, even though the systematic theology is not going to be completed until we receive more pieces from the One who made it. And meanwhile, even some systematicians who believe that all the pieces belong to the same puzzle are not very adept puzzle players but sometimes force pieces into slots where they don't really belong. The picture gets distorted somewhat, but it remains basically recognizable.

---

[78]This is not a harsh or unfounded charge: see the detailed review article by John Woodbridge, *TJ* n.s. 1 (1980): 165–236. Moreover, Rogers and McKim constantly try to give the impression that distinctions re contradictions appear relatively late in the history of the church. In fact, it is not difficult to find passages like this one, where Justin rebukes Trypho for responding with a passage that almost suggests a contradiction: "If you spoke these words, Trypho, and then kept silence in simplicity and with no ill intent . . . you must be forgiven; but if [you have done so] because you imagined that you could throw doubt on the passage, in order that I might say the Scriptures contradicted each other, you have erred. But I shall not venture to suppose or to say such a thing; and if a Scripture which appears to be of such a kind be brought forward, and if there be a pretext [for saying] that it is contrary [to some other], since I am entirely convinced that no Scripture contradicts another, I shall admit rather that I do not understand what is recorded, and shall strive to persuade those who imagine that the Scriptures are contradictory, rather to be of the same opinion as myself" (*Dial.* 65). Justin then goes on to give his own explanation of the troubling passage.

Finally, although good systematic theology must be phrased in the language of the present and interact with and speak to contemporary concerns,[79] it must be controlled by the biblical data. "Any number of supposedly biblical theologies in our day are so heavily infected with contemporary personalist, existential, or historical thinking as to render their biblical basis highly suspect," comments one critic;[80] and the remark is even more relevant to current systematic theology. That the control should run in this direction is an epistemological requirement that depends on the revelatory status of the Bible.[81] If this were not so, the kind of systematic theology being advocated here would be impossible, and the attempt to develop such should forthwith be abandoned.

In short, I am concerned to show the positions implicitly adopted when an evangelical maintains that the proper data base for systematic theologians is the Bible, the canonical sixty-six books, and to offer some brief comments on their reasonableness. From now on, by "systematic theology" I will refer only to systematic theology based on the canon, unless I explicitly state otherwise. It is in this narrow sense of the designation that the subtitle of this chapter is to be taken: "The Possibility of Systematic Theology."

My focus from this point on will be the New Testament rather than the entire canon, for no other reason than that the immensity of the problems and the literature requires that I reduce the field a little. The substantial questions concerning the *diversity* of the New Testament documents I have not yet directly addressed. To compare systematic theology with a jigsaw puzzle with many pieces not present begs a host of methodological questions, and to these we must now turn.

3. *Progressive revelation must be treated with all seriousness, but appeal to progressive revelation in order to exclude inconvenient components along that revelation's alleged trajectory is illegitimate.*

The term "progressive revelation" is a slippery one. Coined first in liberal circles to describe an evolutionary approach to understanding the Bible,[82] it has subsequently often been taken over and given another meaning, the meaning I wish to adopt. By "progressive revelation" I refer to the fact that God progressively revealed himself in event and in Scripture, climaxing the events with the death-

---

[79]"Evangelical theology is heretical if it is only creative and unworthy if it is only repetitious," comments Henry, *God, Revelation and Authority*, 1:9.

[80]A. Dulles, "Response to Krister Stendahl's 'Method in the Study of Biblical Theology,'" *The Bible in Modern Theology*, ed. J. P. Hyatt (Nashville: Abingdon, 1965), 210–16, esp. 214. Cf. also the warnings offered by K. Lehmann, "Über das Verhältnis der Exegese als historisch-kritischer Wissenschaft zum dogmatischen Verstehen," in *Jesus und der Menschensohn*, ed. R. Pesch and R. Schnackenburg (Freiburg: Herder, 1975), 421–34.

[81]Cf. among others, Henry, *God, Revelation and Authority*, 1:213–72.

[82]On the development of "progressive revelation," cf. J. I. Packer, "An Evangelical View of Progressive Revelation," in *Evangelical Roots*, ed. Kenneth S. Kantzer (Nashville: Nelson, 1978), 143–58.

resurrection-exaltation of Christ and climaxing the Scriptures with the closing of the canon. The result is that God's ways and purposes were progressively fulfilled not only in redemption events but also in inscripturated explanation. The earlier revelation prepares for the later; the later carries further and in some way explicates the earlier.

The most dramatic canonical shift is the shift from Old Testament to New.[83] Yet even within the New, the amount of development is astounding. Chronologically, it covers less than a century, but it moves from Judaism and the slaughter of the innocents under Herod the Great, through the preaching of John the Baptist, the public ministry of Jesus (characterized by Jesus' personal submission to Old Testament law [though he often broke with tradition], along with a host of his sayings that could adequately be comprehended only after his death and resurrection),[84] the early Jerusalem church, the progressive self-consciousness within the church that recognized the obsolescence of the temple and, because of the gift of the Spirit, the admission of believing Gentiles into a common fellowship with a shared Savior and God, the rapid evangelization of the Mediterranean world, and the growing rift between Judaism and Christianity.

Of the various models used to describe this development, the organic one (seed leads to plant) is no doubt the best analogy.[85] We are dealing with the growth of a single specimen, not transmutation into new species. It follows that systematic theology is possible, in the same way that the botanical description of a tree is possible. That there is growth and development in revealed truth within the canon requires, not the abolition of systematic theology, but treatment that is sensitive to the nature of the object being studied.

Even so, there are certain characteristics of the diversity in the New Testament that have to be borne in mind. Just as certain parts of the seed are not taken up in the plant it produces, so certain parts of the old covenant under which Jesus lived are not continued under the new covenant he inaugurated (e.g., Mark 7:19; much of Hebrews). Any systematic theology cannot escape such historical considerations. Inasmuch as it is the systematician's concern to synthesize in *contemporary* terms the truth of Scripture, he must summarize not only what God has required in the past, but especially what he requires in the present. In that sense the sys-

---

[83]Cf. especially Oscar Cullmann, *Salvation in History* (New York: Harper & Row, 1967).

[84]This is particularly clear in John's Gospel; cf. D. A. Carson, "Understanding Misunderstandings in the Fourth Gospel," *TynBul* 33 (1982): 59–91.

[85]See, for instance, C. F. D. Moule, *Christology*; R. N. Longenecker, "On the Concept of Development in Pauline Thought," in *Perspectives on Evangelical Theology*, ed. Kenneth S. Kantzer and Stanley N. Gundry (Grand Rapids: Baker, 1979), 195–207.

tematician must take special pains to discover how the earlier revelation relates to its later fulfillment and applies to himself and his contemporaries.[86]

A second characteristic of New Testament diversity lies in the fact that even after the Spirit-age begins at Pentecost, the full implications of this new age take some time to be understood (as Jesus himself suggested they would; cf. John 16:12–15),[87] and this understanding comes only in degrees, unevenly, haltingly, cautiously. The significance of the descent of the Spirit on Cornelius and his household (Acts 10–11), both to Peter and to Luke, is that the charismatic phenomena accompanying this baptism validated the reality of Gentile salvation to the Jerusalem church. But this does not prevent the circumcision crisis from precipitating the Jerusalem Council (Acts 15). According to Paul, both Peter and Barnabas failed on one occasion to live up to their own confessed understanding of the gospel (Galatians 2). Such events tend to support notions of human fallibility and sinful inconsistency, rather than the notion that there were highly diverse parties in the church with major doctrinal differences. It is not only in the present that people sometimes fail to live up to their best insights or refuse to see the entailments of their professed positions.

Can there be development within the writings of one particular author? One must distinguish between the development of a writer's subject matter, which he records and interprets (e.g., Luke-Acts), and the development of the thought of the writer himself.[88] The best test case of the latter is Paul. Most writers follow in the line of an influential pair of essays by C. H. Dodd[89] and affirm unhesitatingly that they can trace development in Paul's thought. The most careful of them, however, confess that there are formidable hurdles to overcome if any real objectivity is to be attained.[90] Quite apart from questions of authenticity, it is not easy to date all of the Pauline correspondence with certainty. Many of the epistles' different emphases stem from diverse pastoral concerns (a point to which I will return). Moreover, it is important to recognize that Paul had been a believer for a solid fifteen years or more before he penned the first letter recognized as canonical, and that is time enough to develop some pretty stable beliefs. All of Paul's canonical writing took place in a single span of fifteen years, long after he had become a mature teacher, and that is not a lengthy period in which to develop major new theological shifts.

---

[86]This has been marked out in painstaking detail for the Sabbath/Sunday issue; cf. D. A. Carson, ed., *From Sabbath to Lord's Day: A Biblical, Historical and Theological Investigation* (Grand Rapids: Zondervan, 1982).

[87]Carson, "Understanding Misunderstandings."

[88]This distinction is overlooked by Longenecker, "Development in Pauline Thought," 200–201.

[89]C. H. Dodd, "The Mind of Paul: Change and Development," *BJRL* 18 (1934): 69–110; idem, "The Mind of Paul: A Psychological Approach," *BJRL* 17 (1933): 91–105.

[90]E.g., Longenecker, "Development in Pauline Thought."

There is little reason to doubt that Paul sees himself growing in understanding and maturity, including theological maturity (cf. 1 Cor. 13:8–12; Phil. 3:12–16). But there is not the slightest evidence that Paul perceived himself to be abandoning any position he had formerly maintained in his writings.[91] It remains important that we interpret Paul by Paul,[92] not only for the sake of systematic theology but also for the sake of understanding Paul.

What must be avoided are the simplistic reconstructions of earliest church history that manufacture straight-line developments everywhere and then force the only primary data we have, the New Testament documents themselves, into some Procrustean bed. Attempts are made, for instance, to show how Paul moved from a futurist eschatology to a realized eschatology,[93] despite the fact it has been repeatedly shown that both elements are there from the beginning.[94] It is still common to argue that Acts must be late because Luke so nicely exemplifies *Frühkatholizismus*, even though it has been convincingly argued that Luke-Acts betrays *both* "early catholicism" and "enthusiasm."[95] Theology, like life, is complex. Most of us have learned to live with the "already/not yet" tension in the New Testament; why, then, do we find it so difficult to accept the "early catholicism/enthusiasm" tension? If Acts is taken seriously, there is order and discipline, not to mention recognized elders, from the earliest years of the church.

The problem for the evangelical systematician is already difficult enough when he confronts the diversity of the New Testament without having to face the dogmatic reorganization of the evidence along the lines of critical orthodoxy. While various critics are accusing him of constructing a rigid systematic theology that forces him to distort his exegesis, he may perhaps be forgiven if he finds that his critics are reconstructing church history and developing what I have elsewhere called "histmatics,"[96] thereby distorting their exegesis far more seriously.

---

[91] This, of course, is disputed, especially by those who attempt to find major dislocations in the texts. See, for instance, J. C. Hurd, *The Origin of 1 Corinthians* (New York: Seabury, 1965), on which I will say more in the next reflection.

[92] Cf. C. F. D. Moule, "Interpreting Paul by Paul: An Essay in the Comparative Study of Pauline Thought," *New Testament Christianity for Africa and the World*, ed. Mark E. Glasswell and Edward W. Fasholé-Luke (London: SPCK, 1974), 78–90.

[93] Charles Buck and G. Taylor, *Saint Paul: A Study of the Development of His Thought* (New York: Scribner, 1969).

[94] Most recently by John W. Drane, "Theological Diversity in the Letters of St. Paul," *TynBul* 26 (1976): 3–26.

[95] So Dunn, *Unity and Diversity*, 356–58, even though he uses the same contrast elsewhere; A. Sand, "Überlegungen zur gegenwärtigen Diskussion über den 'Frühkatholizismus,'" *Catholica* 33 (1979): 49–62; and I. H. Marshall, "'Early Catholicism' in the New Testament," in *New Dimensions in New Testament Study*, ed. R. N. Longenecker and Merrill C. Tenney (Grand Rapids: Zondervan, 1974), 217–31. Cf. E. Earle Ellis, "Dating the New Testament," *NTS* 26 (1979–1980): 487–502, esp. 499–500. Ellis insists that the thesis/antithesis/synthesis model is equally inappropriate in the modern reconstruction apocalypticism/delay of the parousia/salvation history. Probably all three positions developed at the same time.

[96] D. A. Carson, "Historical Tradition and the Fourth Gospel: After Dodd, What?" in *Gospel Perspectives*, vol. 2, ed. R. T. France and David Wenham (Sheffield: JSOT, 1981), 85–145.

More difficult to assess is the kind of development in Paul suggested by Murray J. Harris in his published works.[97] Harris thinks 2 Corinthians 5:1–10 is a watershed in Paul's theology, reflecting change in his eschatological thinking because of a brush with death in Asia (cf. 2 Cor. 1:8–11). He now thinks of the resurrection no longer in terms of a corporate phenomenon experienced by all deceased Christians at the parousia, but in terms of a personal transformation of each Christian at death so as to receive a "spiritual body" comparable to Christ's at that time.

This, of course, is very different from what Paul has expressed in 1 Corinthians 15 and 1 Thessalonians 4. With some hesitation, I would argue that it is an inadmissible example of "development" in Paul. Considerations that bear on my judgment include the following: (1) The New Testament presupposes a real continuity between Jesus' pre-passion body and his postresurrection body. Otherwise why the stigmata, and where did the dead body go? Inasmuch as Jesus' resurrection is the firstfruits of the harvest, how different from Jesus' resurrection may the harvest be? (2) Was the Asian experience as traumatic as all that? Second Corinthians 11 makes it clear how often Paul faced suffering and death. Is it likely therefore that one more such experience could effect so major a change in the thinking of a mature and seasoned theologian? (3) Surely the "not . . . but" construction in 2 Corinthians 5:1–10 is a Semitic way of expressing fundamental preference rather than absolute antithesis. (4) Is it possible that the crucial verses, 2 Corinthians 5:3–5, are included by Paul to cover himself against the Corinthian errorists, already confronted in 1 Corinthians 15, who might still be prone to think of verse 2 in immaterial terms? (5) If we grant that 2 Corinthians 10–13 was written after 2 Corinthians 5, then there is evidence that Paul still held to an anthropology that could conceive of human existence apart from the body (2 Cor. 12:1–10), even if it was not the ultimate mode of existence. (6) The exegetical evidence in 2 Corinthians 5:1–10 makes Harris's view possible; it by no means requires it. (7) But Harris's view faces not only the above challenges, but a question from the vantage of systematic theology. The progress of revelation in this instance is interpreted by Harris to involve so massive a change of view that Paul's earlier teaching (esp. in 1 Thessalonians 4) was *wrong*. That earlier teaching did

---

[97]Murray J. Harris, "2 Corinthians 5:1–10: Watershed in Paul's Eschatology?" *TynBul* 22 (1971): 32–57; idem, "Paul's View of Death in 2 Corinthians 5:1–10," *New Dimensions in New Testament Study*, ed. R. N. Longenecker and Merrill C. Tenney (Grand Rapids: Zondervan, 1974), 317–28. The restriction to published works is necessary, because in a private communication dated August 27, 1981, Dr. Harris told me that he no longer holds that Paul moved *from* believing that the spiritual body is received at the parousia *to* the belief that the receipt occurs at death, nor does Harris now hold that Paul *substitutes* the notion of communion with Christ after death for the notion of sleep in the grave. In that sense, he can no longer speak of 2 Corinthians 5 as a "watershed" in Paul's eschatology. These changes will be thoroughly discussed in his forthcoming book *Raised Immortal*.

not simply point forward, serve as a shadow pointing proleptically to the reality in another covenant, or constitute a part of the truth now being fully developed; rather, it was in error. For all these reasons, I am reluctant to side with Harris without seeing much more exegetical warrant.[98]

I have tried to show how the systematic theologian must be aware of questions concerning progressive revelation, and I have suggested a few things that might serve as helpful limits. One fairly common application of progressive revelation I confess I reject. This is exemplified by David Kelsey.[99] It attempts to plot the development in theology reflected in Scripture (usually on the basis of a doubtful critical orthodoxy) and then uses the *patterns thus developed*, not the Scripture itself, as normative. In fact, the events of Scripture are inseparable from their interpretation,[100] and the "patterns" Kelsey and others detect are so subjectively grounded that it is difficult to imagine how they could achieve normative status as anything more than interesting paradigms.[101] Progressive revelation must be taken in all seriousness, but appeal to progressive revelation in order to exclude inconvenient components along that revelation's alleged trajectory is illegitimate.

4. *The diversity in the New Testament very often reflects diverse pastoral concerns, with no implications whatsoever of a different creedal structure.*

It is easy to find *formal* inconsistencies and contradictions in the New Testament. "Carry each other's burdens," Paul says to the Galatians, and "in this way you will fulfill the law of Christ" (Gal. 6:2). This does not prevent him from advising them, a few verses farther on, that "each one should carry his own load" (Gal. 6:5). Most commentators have no trouble explaining how these verses could come from the pen of one man within one paragraph, and what they mean.[102]

When we move to two different epistles by the same author, however, the situation is rather different. There is still, for instance, a tendency to pit Galatians against 1 Corinthians. In two of the more recent treatments, those by Drane and Richardson,[103] much more allowance is made for the distinctive pastoral problems Paul is facing in the two cities; but even so, Drane in particular is still inclined,

---

[98]Harris himself does not admit to a change in Paul's view such that Paul's earlier belief was in error; cf. Harris's treatment of this question in his chapter "Paul's View of Death in 2 Corinthians 5:1–10," in *New Dimensions in New Testament Study*, ed. R. N. Longenecker and M. C. Tenney (Grand Rapids: Zondervan, 1974), 317–28, esp. 322–23. But I am not convinced that he has successfully overcome the problem.

[99]David H. Kelsey, *The Uses of Scripture in Recent Theology* (Philadelphia: Fortress, 1975).

[100]On this most debated of themes, cf. most recently Donald Nicholl, "Historical Understanding," *The Downside Review* 97 (1979): 99–113.

[101]Cf. the trenchant critique in Henry, *God, Revelation and Authority*, 4:470–75.

[102]Even J. C. O'Neill (*The Recovery of Paul's Letter to the Galatians* [London: SPCK, 1972]), though he denies that these verses come from Paul, is not interested in denying that they come from one particular (and unknown) glossator.

[103]John W. Drane, *Paul: Libertine or Legalist?* (London: SPCK, 1975); and Peter Richardson, "Pauline Inconsistency: 1 Corinthians 9:19–23 and Galatians 2:11–14," *NTS* 26 (1979–1980): 347–62. On Drane's work, see especially the reviews by R. N. Longenecker, *JBL* 96 (1977): 461–62 and by M. Silva, *WTJ* 40 (1977–1978): 176–80.

in my judgment, to see rather more of a change in Paul's thinking than the evidence allows. Drane sees an early Galatians denouncing attempts to impose law-keeping on Gentile believers. Unfortunately, Drane suggests, some of Paul's converts developed this theme too far, and in the permissive city of Corinth they sank into licentiousness and immorality based on a crude antinomianism. This, according to Drane, prompted Paul to write 1 Corinthians, which imposes far more rules than the Paul of Galatians could have envisaged. In fact, Paul was in danger of overreaction. Later, however, Paul penned 2 Corinthians and Romans and found the right balance.

This analysis presupposes that Galatians and 1 Corinthians are unbalanced and cannot be taken to reflect Paul's mature thought. From a methodological point of view, I would be curious to know how Drane would support his structure over against one that explains the differences in terms of the pastoral problem confronting Paul. This is not to deny that Paul's personal understanding of the dangers might not have improved with experience; but it is to deny that Paul would later have withdrawn any word from Galatians or 1 Corinthians if he had had to face those same problems again. The clues Drane finds to distinguish between the two paradigms (e.g., he argues that the Corinthians had read the epistle to the Galatians) I do not find entirely convincing.

Unfortunately, there is not space to probe this question in detail, but it is important to remember that, as one writer puts it, the epistles "are occasional documents of the first century, written out of the context of the recipients."[104] F. F. Bruce has traced a number of tensions in Paul's letters,[105] and although his synthesis is not convincing in every case, he approaches the diversity with methodological sensitivity.[106]

Part of the problem, I suspect, is that Paul, like Jesus before him, tends to absolutize the language used in addressing the current problem. Granted that Matthew 6 and Luke 18 retain authentic material, it is intriguing to note that in the former passage Jesus seems to be arguing for brief prayers that avoid both pomp and repetition, while in the latter passage he tells a parable with the express purpose of showing his disciples "that they should always pray and not give up" (Luke 18:1). Formally, the two stand in mutual contradiction. In reality, the Matthean

---

[104]Gordon D. Fee, "Hermeneutics and Common Sense," *Inerrancy and Common Sense*, ed. Roger R. Nicole and J. Ramsey Michaels (Grand Rapids: Baker, 1980), 167.

[105]F. F. Bruce, "'All Things to All Men': Diversity in Unity and Other Pauline Tensions," in *Unity and Diversity in New Testament Theology*, ed. R. Guelich (Grand Rapids: Eerdmans, 1978), 82–99.

[106]Compare E. P. Sanders, *Paul and Palestinian Judaism* (Philadelphia: Fortress, 1977), 433, 518–23, who holds that though Paul is not a systematic thinker, he is a coherent thinker. I am not entirely happy with the distinction, since I am unsure how much the unsystematic (but not incoherent) factor finds its genesis less in Paul qua thinker than in the occasional nature of his writings. But even if Paul's thoughts are believed to "cohere," that is an adequate position from the viewpoint of this chapter.

passage addresses itself to those whose prayers are merely for show, and to those who think that by their much speaking they can manipulate God. By contrast, the Lukan passage addresses itself to the sins of the doubting and the apathetic. There is no real contradiction whatsoever once the circumstances being addressed are properly understood. Jesus, preacher that he is, regularly uses strong, antithetical language to tackle *each* side of a complex question.[107] One of the values of systematic theology, therefore, is that Jesus' or Paul's approach to a host of issues is likely to receive more balanced scrutiny than by the reductionist methods of those who pit Jesus against Jesus and Paul against Paul.

The question of the diverse circumstances that call forth New Testament writings becomes more controversial yet when author is compared with author—Paul with James, for instance, or John with Paul. Not all New Testament diversity can be accounted for by appealing to diverse circumstances; but a surprising amount of it is surely influenced by such considerations. If the "faith of Abraham" is used by Paul to teach that people are justified by grace through faith and by James to teach that faith without works is dead, it does not necessarily follow that the two authors are ignorant of the other's work or in disagreement with it.[108] In the areas of eschatology and christology, C. F. D. Moule has cogently argued that varied circumstances have prompted much of the New Testament diversity.[109] His work, though widely cited, is still far too infrequently used and treated with the seriousness it deserves.[110] What we need, as E. E. Lemcio has put it, only half-facetiously, is the rise of a new sensitivity to "Circumstantionsgeschichte."[111]

Even confessional formulae must be inspected in this light. In 1 Corinthians 12:3 Paul can affirm that "no one can say, 'Jesus is Lord,' except by the Holy Spirit." In 1 John 4:2–3 John insists, "Every spirit that acknowledges that Jesus Christ has come in the flesh [or, as I would prefer, "that Jesus is Christ come in the flesh"] is from God, but every spirit that does not acknowledge Jesus is not from God." The two confessions are not mutually exclusive, nor do they reflect divergent groups of Christians whose christological statements have developed along rather different and perhaps mutually exclusive paths. Rather, in the Corinthian situation with its claims from many lords, the Pauline formulation was both necessary and sufficient. In John's historical context, in which docetists were attempting to divide Jesus

---

[107] I have pointed this out at length in *The Sermon on the Mount: An Evangelical Exposition of Matthew 5–7* (Grand Rapids: Baker, 1978).

[108] Cf. especially Richard N. Longenecker, "The 'Faith of Abraham' Theme in Paul, James and Hebrews: A Study in the Circumstantial Nature of New Testament Teaching," *JETS* 20 (1977): 203–12.

[109] C. F. D. Moule, "The Influence of Circumstances on the Use of Christological Terms," *JTS* 10 (1959): 247–63; idem, "The Influence of Circumstances on the Use of Eschatological Terms," *JTS* 15 (1964): 1–15.

[110] E.g., Dunn, *Unity and Diversity*, 25 and n. 12.

[111] In private conversation.

from Christ, the Johannine formulation is both necessary and sufficient. But Paul's formulation is inadequate to exclude heretics in John's situation, and John's formulation is inadequate to exclude heretics in Paul's situation. Both formulations—and a number of others, for that matter—are *necessary*; but it does not follow that anyone of them is *sufficient* in *every* context (notwithstanding the simplistic use of the confession "Jesus is Lord" by some elements of the WCC!).

W. L. Lane argues that such diversity (he does not use this particular example) reflects a changing theological expression based on a given creedal structure.[112] There is a sense in which he is right, even though I am unhappy with his terminology. But one must go beyond that observation to note that our *only* access to the assumed creedal structure of the earliest church is the New Testament documents. Because this is so, and also because those documents are themselves inspired, it will not do to try to recover the early creedal structure while ignoring that structure's specific and diverse exemplifications. Rather, it is precisely at this point that systematic theology is necessary, not only for an adequate exposition of the Christian faith in contemporary terms but also as the only adequate tool to handle the confessional diversity in a responsible way and thereby sketch in the creedal structure.[113]

The alternative is ironic. From all sides New Testament scholars are warned against trying to find a systematic theology in the New Testament. In fact, what these critics are doing is establishing a large number of systematic theologies in the New Testament and then pitting them against each other. A confession is isolated from the historical setting that limits its *sufficiency* (but not its *necessity*) in other settings and is built into a large structure that is set over against some other manufactured structure. Part of this procedure depends on dubious historical reconstructions, something I have already briefly discussed in this chapter, but part of it turns on an irresponsible approach to historical data, an approach that, while decrying systematic theology, is busily systematizing the diversity it finds instead of being sensitive to the mutually complementary nature of the occasional documents that constitute the New Testament.[114]

---

[112]W. L. Lane, "Creed and Theology: Reflections on Colossians," *JETS* 21 (1978): 213–20. Cf. also Dunn, *Unity and Diversity*, 359–60.

[113]One may wonder if R. P. Martin, "New Testament Theology," 266, takes these considerations into account adequately when he writes, "The use of the NT as a manual of systematic theology or a book of ecclesiastical rubric is no longer viable. 'Concepts of doctrine' (*Lehrbegriffe*) are not what the NT documents contain, though it is certainly a different question when we ask if we can in fact extrapolate Christian beliefs from what they comprise." In one sense, of course, the New Testament is *not* a manual of systematic theology. It does not come to us in that form; and systematic theology is therefore a derivative discipline. But it is not fair to the evidence to go so far as to say that the New Testament does not contain "concepts of doctrine." Quite the contrary: it contains not only a rich profusion of doctrines, but even sweeping "concepts of doctrine." What it does *not* contain is a very systematic treatment of these things.

[114]J. C. Hurd (*The Origin of First Corinthians* [Naperville, IL: Allenson, 1965]) offers a fine example of a really radical historical reconstruction in the service of demonstrating Pauline inconsistency. He uses 1 Corinthians to explore Paul's

5. *The diversity in the New Testament documents very often reflects the diverse personal interests and idiosyncratic styles of the individual writers.*

No one of any theological sophistication argues that the Holy Spirit's work in inspiring the Scriptures imposed a literary sameness on all the parts. John still sounds like John, Matthew like Matthew, and so forth.

The same phenomena afford us another view of the unity and diversity problem. The language, style, and interests of the individual writers are all to some extent idiosyncratic; and one must therefore be very careful about arguing that such and such a New Testament writer does not believe this or that simply because he does not mention it or perhaps emphasize it. This is especially important when we remember what New Testament scholars have been telling us all along, viz., that the New Testament writers are not attempting to write systematic theology. Would we attempt to delineate the entire theological structure of some modern religious thinker on the basis of two or three occasional monographs called forth in part by his own focused interests and in part by some pressing pastoral concern?

Terminology may differ from writer to writer. As is well known, Matthew uses "call" to refer to a general invitation to the lost, whereas Paul uses "call" to refer to an effectual action by God; but whereas the terminology differs, this does not itself constitute evidence that Paul denies that God invites the lost or that Matthew disbelieves in election.

---

earlier dealings with the church in Corinth and concludes that the Corinthians had remained closer to the original Pauline gospel than Paul himself had done. According to Hurd, when Paul first came to Corinth, he maintained that a man should not touch a woman (1 Cor. 7:1). He encouraged celibacy and insisted that all things were lawful (10:23) and there was no harm in eating food offered to idols. Because believers all have knowledge (8:1), Paul behaved like one outside the law (9:21). He taught that baptism and the Lord's Supper hold death in check and would continue to do so until the end, expected very shortly. He said nothing of the resurrection from the dead, and he permitted women to go without veils. Then, according to Hurd, Paul changed his mind on a number of points, and these changes were reflected in the "previous letter" (cf. 5:9). It was written to enforce the Apostolic Decree (Acts 15:29; 21:15), which now forbade eating meat offered to idols. Paul now required veils and urged separation from immorality. He recommended marriage as a safeguard against fornication and for the first time urged caution in the matter of speaking in tongues. Small wonder, argues Hurd, that the poor Corinthians were confused! Paul, therefore, wrote 1 Corinthians, a balanced missive that tried to sort it all out. Hurd says it is good to have this balance, but it would be nice to have the earlier enthusiasm as well. This entire reconstruction is thoroughly implausible. It supposes that Paul, after more than fifteen years of extensive ministry, was still sorting out the most elementary aspects of the faith and in fact reversed himself over a period of perhaps two years. Paul makes no mention of the Jerusalem Council. Moreover, it is difficult to believe that a man as pastorally sensitive as Paul would (even supposing so substantial a shift in his own thinking) impose those changes on new converts by a letter that could only have been confusing. Methodologically, Hurd has built his entire case on his reading of 1 Corinthians; and there are far more believable ways to explain the diversity found there, not least the one that pictures Paul as not only dealing with a host of issues brought up to him but also carefully handling the disunity and divergent opinions about all these matters found within the Corinthian church. Paul is therefore pastorally concerned not only to provide answers but to do so in such a way that he heals the breaches caused by the polarized opinions. This is not only a solid explanation for the kind of argumentation found in the epistle, but a further piece of evidence to confirm the pastoral (rather than merely theoretical) concerns that often prompted the apostle Paul to write. Moreover, many of the particular problems behind 1 Corinthians can be plausibly related to an overrealized eschatology and the entailed "enthusiasm"; cf. A. C. Thiselton, "Realized Eschatology at Corinth," *NTS* 24 (1977–1978): 510–26.

Brice Martin has compared Matthew and Paul with respect to the relationship between Christ and the law.[115] His major conclusion is that Matthew and Paul are utilizing two quite different sets of categories and that they therefore constitute noncontradictory, noncomplementary, but compatible, perspectives. His exegesis is not always convincing, and he underplays the importance of other considerations (such as the role of salvation history). Worse, it is difficult to see exactly what "noncomplementary but compatible perspectives" means. If both are dealing with the same God and the relationships of men with that God, their perspectives must be complementary in some ways. Martin has imposed alien philosophical categories on the material. Yet, once stripped of such antithetical language and softened by other considerations, his argument still has a point: different New Testament writers may focus on different aspects of truth and from quite different perspectives, whether for apologetic or personal reasons, and such diversity must be taken into account.

Part of the contemporary dilemma lies in the fact that many New Testament scholars who decry systematic theology are busy *over*-theologizing (if this barbarism may be forgiven) the New Testament. Every utterance, every epistle, every literary scrap, must be prompted by explicit *theological* concerns. These concerns (it is alleged) override historical considerations and personal interests. A New Testament writer is always engaged in refuting some theological opponent. Few allow for the possibility that one of the reasons why a particular pericope is admitted may be because the writer found the story interesting. It is with a sigh of relief that we turn to Morna Hooker's cheeky article, "Were There False Teachers in Colossae?"[116]

I do not mean to argue that the New Testament writers are but seldom refuting false notions or that the inclusion of this or that list of material is to be accounted for purely on the grounds of idiosyncratic preference. I mean, rather, to point out that the rich diversity of the New Testament—diversity in genre, style, confession, perhaps liturgy, even content and focus[117]—must not be interpreted solely in the categories of antithetical *theological* formulations. The evidence itself cries against it. But when such evidence is taken into account, it is difficult to see why a deep underlying theological unity is impossible, or even unlikely.

---

[115]Brice L. Martin, "Matthew and Paul on Christ and the Law: Compatible or Incompatible Theologies?" (Ph.D. diss., McMaster University, 1976); idem, "Some reflections on the unity of the New Testament," *Studies in Religion/Sciences Religieuses* 8 (1979): 143–52.

[116]Morna D. Hooker, "Were There False Teachers in Colossae?" *Christ and Spirit in the New Testament*, ed. B. Lindars and Stephen S. Smalley (Cambridge: Cambridge University Press, 1973), 315–31.

[117]Cf. R. P. Martin, "Approaches to New Testament Exegesis," in *New Testament Interpretation*, ed. I. H. Marshall (Exeter: Paternoster, 1977), 220–51.

6. On the basis of these reflections it must be insisted that there is no intrinsic disgrace to theological harmonization, which is of the essence of systematic theology.

In fact, one might even argue that there is disgrace attached to the failure to make the attempt. Are the assumptions of critical orthodoxy all that unshakable? There was more communication in the ancient world than we sometimes recognize and much more fundamental agreement among the apostles and apostolic writers than is often allowed. The modern notion of well-nigh hermetically sealed communities doing their own theology and touching up their own traditions in splendid isolation, all to produce some New Testament document by multiple authors, is gross exaggeration; and to the extent it reflects any truth at all, we must frankly admit, with Hengel,[118] that we know virtually nothing of such communities. On the positive side, there is evidence that a beginning New Testament canon was recognized very early, during the fifties, when many eyewitnesses were still alive.[119] This suggests greater agreement and harmony among the early Christians than is commonly affirmed.

Critics of systematic theology, of course, are afraid that these arguments will force the New Testament documents into an artificial conformity. That danger is certainly present. But in one sense the approach I have been following encourages theological exploration that, far from being rigid and narrow, encourages work not otherwise possible. "There is . . . a sense in which every New Testament writer communicates to Christians today more than he knew he was communicating, simply because Christians can now read his work as part of the completed New Testament canon."[120] This is not an appeal to *sensus plenior*, at least in any traditional sense. Rather, it is an acknowledgment that with greater numbers of pieces of the jigsaw puzzle provided, the individual pieces and clusters of pieces are seen in new relationships not visible before.

What, then, is the proper place for the *analogia fidei*, the "analogy of the faith"? Can we safeguard our exegesis from an untoward usage of systematic theology? The answer, I fear, is, "Not entirely." It would be convenient if we could operate exclusively along the direction shown in figure 1.

Fig. 1

Exegesis → Biblical Theology → [Historical Theology] → Systematic Theology

---

[118]Martin Hengel, *Acts and the History of the Earliest Christianity* (London: SCM, 1979).
[119]Cf. the important article by J. Carmignac, "II Corinthians iii. 6, 14 et le Début de la Formation du Nouveau Testament," *NTS* 24 (1977–1978): 383–86.
[120]James I. Packer, "Preaching as Biblical Interpretation," in *Inerrancy and Common Sense*, ed. Roger R. Nicole and J. Ramsey Michaels (Grand Rapids: Baker, 1980), 198.

(The brackets around the third element are meant to suggest that in this paradigm historical theology makes a direct contribution to the development from biblical theology to systematic theology but is not itself a part of that line.) In fact, this paradigm, though neat, is naïve. No exegesis is ever done in a vacuum. If every theist is in some sense a systematician, then he is a systematician *before* he begins his exegesis. Are we, then, locked into a hermeneutical circle, as in figure 2?

Fig. 2

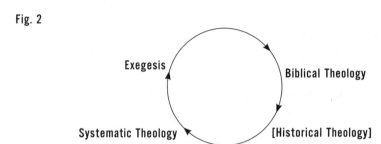

No, there is a better way. It might be diagrammed as in figure 3.

Fig. 3

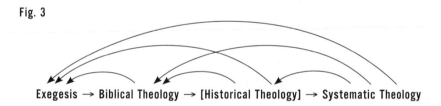

That is to say, there are feedback lines (and more lines going forward, for that matter). It is absurd to deny that one's systematic theology affects one's exegesis. Nevertheless the line of final control is the straight one from exegesis right through biblical and historical theology to systematic theology. The final authority is the Scriptures, and the Scriptures alone. For this reason exegesis, though affected by systematic theology, is not to be shackled by it. Packer is right when he argues:

> The maxim that exegesis and biblical interpretation are for the sake of an adequate systematic theology is true, yet if one stops there one has told only half the story. The other half, the complementary truth which alone can ward off the baleful misunderstanding that a particular rational orthodoxy is all that matters, is that the main reason for seeking an adequate

systematic theology is for the sake of better and more profound biblical interpretation.[121]

Even so, it is important, first, to recognize that the final control is in the Bible, and the Bible alone, and, second, to be self-consciously aware what kind of appeal is being made at each stage of the enterprise, in order not to confuse the lines of control.

If anyone objects that this is giving far too significant a place to systematic theology, I insist that in one sense my strongest opponent is doing the same thing, and perhaps less self-critically than I, for he has adopted his own kind of "systematic theology" in adopting various notions about how the New Testament can or cannot fit together. Often, in fact, such a critic will be particularly vulnerable to his own structured thought precisely because he doesn't believe it influences him unduly. My model is valid only if Scripture is trustworthy, but for various reasons I believe that it is. My concern, then, is to legitimate the harmonization implicit in systematic theology and show that such harmonization, properly handled, enriches biblical interpretation without distorting it.

There are one or two specific dangers in appealing to the *analogia fidei* that should be mentioned. Quite apart from the question of the ultimate line of control, one must beware of handling the *analogia fidei* anachronistically. This does not mean that for every revelatory text one should develop an *analogia fidei* based exclusively on *earlier* revelatory material[122] (although such a method has its own usefulness in tackling certain problems), for that would mean no really new revelation could ever be admitted. It means, rather, that the *analogia fidei* should be used cautiously as an outer limit and as a final consideration,[123] rather than as the determining device.

A second illicit procedure is that exemplified by P. K. Jewett in his book *Man as Male and Female*.[124] As Jewett develops his appeal to *analogia fidei*, it becomes clear he is in fact operating with a "canon within the canon." He isolates (at least to his own satisfaction) the central teachings of the Scriptures on his chosen subject and on that basis excludes Paul's argument in 1 Timothy 2:11–15 on the ground

---

[121]Ibid., 188. Further on the *analogia fidei*, cf. R. C. Sproul, "Biblical Interpretation and the Analogy of the Faith," in *Inerrancy and Common Sense*, ed. Roger R. Nicole and J. Ramsey Michaels (Grand Rapids: Baker, 1980), 119–35; and in its connections with biblical theology, cf. Daniel P. Fuller, "Biblical Theology and the Analogy of Faith," in *Unity and Diversity in New Testament Theology*, ed. Robert A. Guelich (Grand Rapids: Eerdmans, 1978), 195–213.

[122]Contra W. C. Kaiser Jr., *Toward an Old Testament Theology* (Grand Rapids: Zondervan, 1978), 16, 18, 19, 190, 196, 219, 267. Kaiser prefers to speak of the analogy of antecedent Scripture.

[123]Cf., among others, Robert L. Thomas, "A Hermeneutical Ambiguity of Eschatology: The Analogy of Faith," *JETS* 23 (1980): 45–53.

[124]P. K. Jewett, *Man as Male and Female: A Study in Sexual Relationships from a Theological Point of View* (Grand Rapids: Eerdmans, 1975).

that it does not cohere with the *analogia fidei* he has constructed *on the basis of his now-limited canon*. This is a novel appeal to *analogia fidei* indeed, one that is methodologically indistinguishable from the approach of Ernst Käsemann or anyone else who chooses to go with a restricted canon.[125] If Jewett wishes to follow that line of argument, that is his business; but it is illicit to christen it with the *analogia fidei* argument, which traditionally assumes that the canon is the given. In fact, one of the methodological advantages of working with systematic theology is that, rightly executed, it eliminates the pick-and-choose kind of theologizing that enables the theologian to say pretty much what he wants to say. Systematic theology carefully handled can help ensure us that we still hear the Word of God, and not just the preselected answers to carefully limited questions.

In short, with care, there is no disgrace to the theological harmonization that is of the essence of systematic theology, but there are numerous pitfalls to be avoided.

7. Systematic theologians should be careful to note how various truths and arguments function in Scripture, and they should be very cautious about stepping outside those functions with new ones.

"When considering apparently divergent passages, it is important to look at the purpose of the wording before pronouncing on the details of the language."[126] That advice is sound not only in exegesis but also in systematic theology.

Two or three rapid examples will flesh out the force of this reflection. It is as illicit to conclude from the fact that women were last at the cross and first at the tomb that therefore they should be ordained as elders as it is to conclude from the fact that all of the Twelve were men that therefore women should not be ordained as elders. Again, although the New Testament confesses that Jesus Christ is simultaneously God and man and that God cannot be tempted, it does not necessarily follow that Jesus Christ cannot be tempted.

There are two reasons why we need to be extraordinarily hesitant about stepping outside the example of Scripture in such matters. First, to ascribe certain functions to various truths or events in Scripture even though Scripture does not make use of those same truths and events to develop such functions may involve us in a prejudicial selection of data from the data base. We may fail to learn how certain truths function at a *pastoral* level, or we may unwittingly draw a conclusion that contradicts some of the primary data.

---

[125]E.g., in the area of New Testament ethics, cf. E. Schweizer, "Traditional Ethical Patterns in the Pauline and Post-Pauline Letters and Their Development (Lists of Vices and House-tables)," in *Text and Interpretation*, ed. Ernest Best and R. McL. Wilson (Cambridge: Cambridge University Press, 1979), 195–209.

[126]C. F. D. Moule, *The Epistles to the Colossians and to Philemon* (Cambridge: Cambridge University Press, 1957), 60.

The second reason lies in the fact that a number of fundamental Christian beliefs involve huge areas of unknowns. Take, for instance, the incarnation, or the Trinity, or the relationship between God's sovereignty and man's responsibility. In each of these areas, it is possible to demonstrate that there is no necessary logical contradiction; but it does not seem possible at the moment to provide an exhaustive account of how these fundamentals of the faith cohere. We are dealing with the suprarational[127] (but certainly not with the irrational or the illogical), with a painful shortage of information at crucial points. But it is surely worth observing, for instance, that God's sovereignty functions in Scripture to engender confidence in his people (e.g., Rom. 8:28) and to ensure final judgment, but it never functions to reduce man to the status of an irresponsible robot. Similarly, man is encouraged to believe, choose, obey, repent, and so forth, but his responsibilities in these areas never function in the Scriptures (as they sometimes do in other Jewish literature) to make God fundamentally contingent.[128]

These cautions, I hasten to add, do not call into question the value of logic. Rather, they highlight the complexity of the data and the fact that certain data we might desire are not to be found in Scripture. To limit oneself primarily to copying the functions found in Scripture is to adopt a methodological control that will ensure that one's systematic theology is a little more biblical than might otherwise be the case.

Conclusion

The one thing I am here to say to you is this: that it is worse than useless for Christians to talk about the importance of Christian morality, unless they are prepared to take their stand upon the fundamentals of Christian theology. It is a lie to say that dogma does not matter; it matters enormously. It is fatal to let people suppose that Christianity is only a mode of feeling; it is virtually necessary to insist that it is first and foremost a rational explanation of the universe. It is hopeless to offer Christianity as a vaguely idealistic aspiration of a simple and consoling kind; it is, on the contrary, a hard, tough, exacting, and complex doctrine, steeped in a drastic and uncompromising

---

[127] Cf. Donald G. Bloesch, *Essentials of Evangelical Theology*, 2 vols. (New York: Harper & Row, 1978–1979), 1:18: "At the same time the truth of faith cannot be translated into a finalized, coherent system which denies the mystery and paradox in faith. This is because the truth is suprarational as well as rational. Our human system must always be one that is open to revision in the light of new insights into the Word of God and the human situation. It can never be a closed, airtight, logically consistent, perfected system of truth." I can live with this judgment, provided "logically consistent" is being applied to a "perfected" and "airtight" system that presupposes, implicitly or explicitly, that God has revealed all there is to know—i.e., that we have all the pieces to the puzzle. In that case, our use of logic will fall under the fact that we labor under a false premise and correspondingly distort the evidence, trying to force pieces from the puzzle into slots where they don't properly fit. I reject the statement if it is written in defense of a logically inconsistent system.

[128] I have dealt with this problem at length in *Divine Sovereignty and Human Responsibility*.

realism. And it is fatal to imagine that everybody knows quite well what Christianity is and needs only a little encouragement to practice it. The brutal fact is that in this Christian country not one person in a hundred has the faintest notion about what the church teaches about God or man or society or the person of Jesus Christ.[129]

So writes Dorothy Sayers, and I think she is basically right. This chapter has dealt with technical articles and critical judgments, but in the final analysis what is at stake is not some purely academic dispute, but what we preach.

I am not persuaded, either by Bauer or by Dunn, that the early church was characterized by such tepid toleration and unconcern for truth that it would have put up with basic theological liberalism. As I read the evidence, I perceive great diversity in emphasis, formulation, application, genre of literature, and forms of ecclesiastical administration. But I also perceive that there is a unity of teaching that makes systematic theology not only possible but necessary, and that modern theology at variance with this stance is both methodologically and doctrinally deficient. It is difficult to conceive how systematic theology of the sort defended in this chapter is possible unless the New Testament documents (and the Old Testament documents as well, for that matter) are true and trustworthy; and it is difficult to conceive how the same documents can be true and trustworthy without finding systematic theology both possible and necessary.

There are many questions surrounding the unity and diversity of the New Testament that I have not broached here, not least the relationship of the New Testament to the Old; but if the main lines of the argument are sound, then evangelicals have every reason to ignore the demurrals and get on with writing systematic theology and training systematic theologians. And perhaps such highly desirable goals constitute sufficient reason for a student of the New Testament to step outside the area of his relative expertise.

---

[129]Dorothy L. Sayers, "Creed or Chaos?" in *The Necessity of Systematic Theology*, ed. Davis, 15–32.

4

Redaction Criticism: On the Legitimacy and Illegitimacy of a Literary Tool

A British journal recently published a short series of articles under the general title "Slippery Words."[1] Contributors treated such terms as *myth*, *eschatology*, and the like. No doubt the editor could have enlarged the list of entries had he chosen to do so; but for whatever reason, he did not. One expression that could lay large claim to consideration in any expanded list is "redaction criticism."

The ambiguity is partly denotative and partly connotative. At the denotative level, "redaction criticism" can refer to a surprising range of literary activity. It can refer to the study of how an author who depends on an earlier document has used that document—e.g., changing order, editing, polishing, transforming emphases. Elsewhere, when the source document is no longer available, "redaction criticism" can serve as a comprehensive category that includes source criticism and tradition criticism, since it is very difficult to say much about redaction until one has some idea of what is being redacted. Others use the expression in a much weaker sense to refer to the study of an author's particular emphases and tendencies.

The connotative ambiguities are not less diverse. To scholars with antisupernatural presuppositions, the practice of redaction criticism both confirms those

---

Reprint of D. A. Carson, "Redaction Criticism: On the Legitimacy and Illegitimacy of a Literary Tool," in *Scripture and Truth*, ed. D. A. Carson and John D. Woodbridge (Grand Rapids: Zondervan, 1983), 115–42, 376–81.
[1]*ExpTim* 89–90 (June–October 1978).

presuppositions and serves as a tool for expressing them.[2] On the other hand, more than one conservative evangelical has expressed strong (not to say, heated) reservations about the legitimacy of *any* use of redaction criticism.[3]

Before I can say anything useful about the legitimacy and illegitimacy of this literary tool, therefore, I will have to sketch in a little background. Having done this, I will offer a number of criticisms of the most common kinds of redaction criticism and provide a couple of examples. None of this material is original or comprehensive, but it forms the necessary backdrop to the final section, in which I will suggest some guidelines for the use of redaction criticism by those who have a high view of Scripture. In other words, at that point I will offer some pro-grammatic suggestions aimed both at advancing the debate among evangelicals a little further and at demonstrating to non-evangelicals that the reservations we maintain concerning redaction criticism are reasonable and that our use of the tool is not necessarily perversely idiosyncratic and inconsistent.

But first, something must be said about the development of the tool.

The Development of Redaction Criticism

The synoptic problem was widely recognized in the early church. The first known systematic attempt at harmonization is that of Tatian (c. 110–172); but for our purposes the fact that he made the attempt is more important than his solutions, for it is evidence of an awareness of some of the problems.

The synoptic problem, however conceived, involves some literary depen-dence; that is, some New Testament authors are using literary sources. That should not surprise us. Luke (1:1–4) tells us as much, and there is solid evidence of literary dependence elsewhere (e.g., 2 Peter/Jude). Assured that there were literary sources, modern critics of the past one hundred years or so have expended enormous amounts of energy on retrieving literary sources whose independent existence is not attested anywhere. Source criticism became one of the dominant interests of many New Testament critics at the turn of the century; and this, cou-pled with the prevailing rationalism, prompted many to date the Gospels (espe-cially Matthew and Luke) rather late and to assess their historical trustworthiness as minimal (by conservative standards).

---

[2]See, e.g., W. H. Kelber, "Redaction Criticism: On the Nature and Exposition of the Gospels," *Perspectives on Religious Studies* 6 (1979): 4–16.

[3]E.g., John Warwick Montgomery, "Why Has God Incarnate Suddenly Become Mythical?" in *Perspectives on Evangelical Theology*, ed. Kenneth S. Kantzer and Stanley N. Gundry (Grand Rapids: Baker, 1979), 57–65. At the meeting at which Montgomery read his paper (a slightly more trenchant version of his chapter), advocating that we not make use of redaction criticism at all, another conservative rose to his feet in the ensuing discussion and gently warned him about the danger of throwing out the baby with the bathwater. Montgomery replied, "Look, _____, you and I disagree. You think there's a baby in the bathwater, and I think it's all dirty bathwater."

How, then, could very much be said about the historical Jesus? Once having removed the general reliability of the Gospels, scholars could not easily locate the historical Jesus. Based in part on source criticism and in part on a complete restructuring of first-century history, their studies produced highly diverse models of Jesus. Von Harnack constructed the classic liberal Jesus;[4] and many scholars accepted this Jesus as indeed historical, retrieved from the Gospels by judicious source criticism and post-Enlightenment insight. Schweitzer, however, demonstrated how subjective this historical reconstruction really was. The quest for the historical Jesus was leading down blind alleys. Yet Schweitzer's own reconstruction depended heavily on another selective ordering of the evidence: he thought the historical Jesus was an apocalyptic but misguided itinerant Palestinian preacher.[5] It all depended on the "sources" retrieved and the nature of the history that had been worked up by the scholar. The general effect of Schweitzer's work on radical criticism was nothing less than the tolling of the death-knell over the quest for the historical Jesus. The quest, hitherto judged difficult, was now deemed impossible.

In this environment, form criticism appeared and began to flourish. Developed in a systematic way by Hermann Gunkel for use in history-of-religions research into the Old Testament,[6] form criticism was rapidly and rigorously applied to the New Testament, in particular to the Gospels, by K. L. Schmidt,[7] M. Dibelius,[8] and Rudolf Bultmann.[9] Form criticism was a way of getting behind the written materials to the oral sources. Using the studies of folklorists and anthropologists concerned with the passing on of oral tradition in primitive cultures, the form critics theorized that various kinds of story, each with its technical name ("miracle story," "apophthegm," or whatever),[10] necessarily tended to assume a certain shape or form in the course of being passed on from hearer to hearer. It was thought that if the form of any particular pericope in the Gospel is identical with the ideal form, that is solid evidence for a stable transmission of the story. If it breaks form, there have probably been a number of additions by later transmitters of the tradition or by the final redactor, who was no doubt motivated by theological concerns.

---

[4]Adolf von Harnack, especially in his *What Is Christianity?* trans. Thomas B. Saunders (New York: Putnam, 1902).
[5]Albert Schweitzer's now-famous book was originally entitled *Von Riemarus zu Wrede* (1906) and later *Geschichte der Leben-Jesu-Forschung.* The English title is *The Quest of the Historical Jesus* (London: A. and C. Black, 1910).
[6]Cf., among others, Hermann Gunkel, *The Psalms: A Form-Critical Introduction,* trans. T. M. Horner (Philadelphia: Fortress, 1967); idem, *Genesis* (Göttingen: Vandenhoeck & Ruprecht, 1917).
[7]K. L. Schmidt, *Der Rahmen der Geschichte Jesu* (Berlin: Töpelmann, 1919).
[8]M. Dibelius, *Die Formgeschichte des Evangeliums* (Tübingen: Mohr, 1919; later editions to 1959); ET, *From Tradition to Gospel,* trans. B. L. Woolf, ed. W. Barclay (London: James Clarke, 1971).
[9]The English translation is *History of the Synoptic Tradition,* trans. John Marsh (Oxford: Blackwell, 1963).
[10]The technical designations vary somewhat from form critic to form critic.

The early form critics went further, especially in two respects. First, they theorized regarding what situations in the early church (i.e., what "life-settings" or *Sitze
im Leben*) would *generate* such stories. The church, then, does not merely pass on
stories about Jesus; it *creates* them to meet various theological needs. Second, in
the case of Bultmann in particular, his handling of form criticism was so tied up
with his general historical reconstructions regarding pre-Christian Gnosticism
and his presuppositional antisupernaturalism that the net effect of his studies was
the conclusion that one could know almost nothing about the historical Jesus.

If such form-critical understanding of the formation of the Gospels is even
approximately correct, then the Evangelists (i.e., those who put the four Gospels
into their present form) were little more than compilers of discrete stories. Careful study of the Gospels, in this view, discovers very little about Jesus and a great
deal about the life-settings of the church—or, more precisely, of various churches,
since the churches behind the diverse Gospel pericopae were not thought to be
much concerned with mutual conformity and consistency. The effect of this theory on Bultmann's two-volume *Theology* is a mere thirty pages devoted to Jesus
(and those thirty pages say little that is positive) as compared with one hundred
pages devoted to the beliefs of the Hellenistic communities. Many scholars abandoned the quest for the historical Jesus.

If several Gospels preserve the same story, but with changes in emphasis and
form, then it becomes theoretically possible to plot the changes in the tradition
as the story gets passed along. By this means one can chart a *trajectory* of the form
and its changing content. As is well known, the German word *Formgeschichte* is
poorly rendered by "form criticism." It might better be translated "form history"
or "history of form." Because of adopted convention, I will continue to use the
term *form criticism*, but the German term opens a window onto what is entailed
when this literary tool is used.

In time, it came to be noticed that the Evangelists (i.e., the final compilers)
were not simply collectors of nice stories. Coupling form criticism with literary
dependence, it was argued that the Evangelists shaped the traditions that came to
them; that is, they omitted things; added details; and changed emphases, specific
utterances, and locale. They were *redactors*; that is, they edited this inherited material to express their own theology and their own view of the materials they were
passing on. They were creative theologians in their own right.

Of course, this view of the Evangelists' task introduces a new problem. One
must now distinguish between what is redactional and what is traditional—that
is, between what the Evangelist has received in the tradition that has come to him
and what he has added or changed himself. Discovering this distinction is the task

of redaction criticism. Traditionally, if redaction criticism determines that some word or phrase is redactional, then even if it is ascribed to Jesus in the text, it cannot possibly be authentic; that is, it cannot possibly derive from the historical Jesus in the days of his flesh. If, on the other hand, redaction criticism determines that some word or phrase is traditional, then at least it stretches back beyond the redactor. This does not guarantee its authenticity; it simply makes authenticity a live option. This slender distinction between redaction and tradition sparked off a new round of interest in the historical Jesus. The resulting pictures were still pretty minimalistic, but they offered more than Bultmann did.

The task of the redaction critic is to distinguish between what is redactional and what is traditional. To do this he establishes a number of criteria (some of which I will briefly consider in the next section). Hence, the validity of this initial distinction turns entirely on the validity of his chosen criteria, and redaction criticism itself turns in part on the validity of form criticism. Moreover, the expression "redaction criticism" came quickly to be used not only in the study of those places in the Synoptic Gospels where there are literary parallels, but also in parts of the Gospels where there are no parallels, and in other kinds of documents (e.g., the letters of Paul). At that point redaction criticism is implicitly involved in source criticism and form criticism, because until something is known about the alleged source, not very much can be said about the way it is being redacted. In practice, source criticism, form criticism, and redaction criticism collapse methodologically into one procedure, and the procedure is still called "redaction criticism." But it needs to be pointed out that such redaction criticism is rather different from that practiced on passages that boast close literary parallels.[11]

This rather potted history of the rise of redaction criticism is fairly well known and is detailed with rigor elsewhere.[12] The only detail I must add is that in the present discussion the expression "redaction criticism" is being used in much broader

---

[11]The distinction is clearly seen in recent discussions on the Fourth Gospel. Recent commentators practice "redaction criticism" of the sort that separates out sources, distinguishes redaction from tradition, comments on the trajectory of the tradition, and expounds the significance of the retrieved redaction all in one step. By contrast, R. T. Fortna, in his *Gospel of Signs* (Cambridge: Cambridge University Press, 1970), restricts himself to *source* criticism to isolate the principal source he thinks the Evangelist used, and then in later articles he proceeds to redaction criticism by analyzing the changes that have taken place in the (alleged) move from his (reconstructed) source to the Gospel as we have it. Cf. his "Source and Redaction in the Fourth Gospel's Portrayal of Jesus' Signs," *JBL* 89 (1970): 156–65; idem, "From Christology to Soteriology," *Int* 27 (1973): 31–47. On recent source-critical approaches to the Gospel of John, cf. E. Ruckstuhl, "Johannine Language and Style," *L'Evangile de Jean*, ed. M. de Jonge (Leuven: Leuven University Press, 1977), 125–47; D. A. Carson, "Current Source Criticism of the Fourth Gospel: Some Methodological Questions," *JBL* 97 (1978): 411–29.

[12]In addition to the standard introductions to the New Testament, cf. in particular the relevant sections of W. G. Kümmel, *The New Testament: The History of the Investigation of Its Problems*, trans. S. McLean Gilmour and Howard C. Kee (Nashville: Abingdon, 1972); Stephen Neill, *The Interpretation of the New Testament, 1861–1961* (Oxford: Oxford University Press, 1966); Norman Perrin, *What Is Redaction Criticism?* (Philadelphia: Fortress, 1970); G. E. Ladd, *The New Testament and Criticism* (Grand Rapids: Eerdmans, 1967); Stephen S. Smalley, "Redaction Criticism," *New Testament Interpretation*, ed. I. H. Marshall (Exeter: Paternoster, 1977), 181–95.

ways that are rather divorced from these methodological and philosophical roots. The expression is often taken to refer to the study of the particular emphases of the Evangelist (or other author) in question. For example, Mark characteristically uses εὐθύς and εὐθέως, whereas John uses κόσμος; how much do these linguistic distinctives reflect not *Jesus'* usage but the respective *Evangelists' usage*? How does the topical ordering of material and the selection of *this* pericope over *that* affect the thrust of each Evangelist's message? Such questions begin to do justice to the contribution made by each Evangelist without necessarily bringing along the radical skepticism of the pioneering form critics and redaction critics. Moreover, methodologically the attempt to wrestle with such concerns was already well demonstrated in the careful and thought-provoking work of Ned B. Stonehouse.[13] Although he never used the expression "redaction criticism," he pioneered in developing what is in fact a rather conservative redaction criticism.

What should be clear at this point is that to comment on the legitimacy and illegitimacy of this particular literary tool raises a host of problems of definition. Osborne, for instance, aware of these problems, wants to use redaction criticism to distinguish between "tradition" and "redaction," but in his use of the terms, the question of historicity does not arise. Both redactional material and traditional material are authentic, but the former refers to what the Evangelist added or changed or reworded, whereas the latter refers to the form of the tradition he received.[14] The distinction that Osborne maintains assists him in detecting peculiar emphases and interests on the part of the Evangelists; but Osborne, especially in his most recent essay, attempts to distance himself from using redaction criticism to determine authenticity.

Between this conservative use of redaction criticism and the radical one, which developed the tool, stand a number of middle-of-the-road positions.[15] Whatever their individual merits or demerits, one cannot escape two facts: redaction criticism is here to stay, and it means different things to different people. Especially the latter fact must be borne in mind when we attempt to synthesize an evangelical position.

Common Criticisms Leveled against Redaction Criticism

Before attempting to synthesize an evangelical position, I will note some of the charges against various kinds of redaction criticism. This list is neither exhaustive

---

[13]Cf. especially Stonehouse's book *The Witness of the Synoptic Gospels to Christ* (Grand Rapids: Baker, reprint 1979 of two volumes, *The Witness of Matthew and Mark to Christ* and *The Witness of Luke to Christ*); idem, *Origins of the Synoptic Gospels: Some Basic Questions* (Grand Rapids: Eerdmans, 1963). Cf. also the perceptive pair of essays by M. Silva, "Ned B. Stonehouse and Redaction Criticism, Part I: The Witness of the Synoptic Evangelists to Christ," and "Part II: The Historicity of the Synoptic Tradition," *WTJ* 40 (1977–1978): 77–78, 281–303.

[14]G. R. Osborne, "The Evangelical and Redaction Criticism," *JETS* 22 (1979): esp. 311–12.

[15]Cf. especially R. H. Lightfoot, *History and Interpretation in the Gospels* (London: Hodder & Stoughton, 1935), who, though dependent on the German form critics, actually anticipated the German redaction critics. See also many of the writings of Vincent Taylor, C. H. Dodd, and others.

nor, for the most part, original; and the entries are not in any particular order. But if we are to assess the legitimacy and illegitimacy of this literary tool, we must take rapid note of some of its widely acknowledged weaknesses.

1. A majority of New Testament scholars still hold that the most likely solution to the synoptic problem is the two-source hypothesis. If it is correct, then one may legitimately speak of the ways in which Matthew has changed, added to, or omitted something from Mark. With increasing frequency, however, the old Griesbach hypothesis has been dusted off and set up as an alternative option.[16] For those who hold it to be the correct solution, it is illegitimate to speak of Matthew changing Mark; one must speak of Mark changing Matthew. In my view, both solutions are too simple: there is more probably a certain amount of *inter*dependency. Perhaps Mark relied on an early (Aramaic?) Matthew, and Matthew relied on a finished Mark; I am uncertain. But certain parallel accounts can be more readily accounted for by assuming Mark borrowed from Matthew than vice versa (e.g., the parable of the sower),[17] even if, taken as a whole, the two-source hypothesis is more believable. If the situation is complex, one may legitimately speak of the differences and emphases peculiar to Matthew, Mark, or some other Evangelist; but only with some hesitation may one speak of one Evangelist changing or modifying the work of another.

2. It is common knowledge that the comparative studies of oral tradition (e.g., on the Maori civilization) deal with periods of three hundred years or longer. By contrast, the Gospels were written within at most sixty years of the events they purport to describe. The effects of this restriction have not been adequately considered. Some dates offered for the Gospels are improbably late; but early or late, the Gospels stand in relation to the life of Christ more or less as we stand in

---

[16]The many who have either moved toward the Griesbach hypothesis or else at the very least called into grave question the adequacy of the two-source hypothesis include E. P. Sanders, *The Tendencies of the Synoptic Tradition*, SNTSMS 9 (Cambridge: Cambridge University Press, 1969); W. R. Farmer, *The Synoptic Problem: A Critical Analysis* (Dillsboro, NC: Western North Carolina Press, 1976); idem, "Modern Developments of Griesbach's Hypothesis," *NTS* 23 (1977): 275–95; T. R. W. Longstaff, *Evidence of Conflation in Mark? A Study of the Synoptic Problem*, SBLDS 28 (Missoula: Scholars, 1977); Bernard Orchard, *Matthew, Luke and Mark* (Manchester: Koinonia, 1976); idem, "J. A. T. Robinson and the Synoptic Problem," *NTS* 22 (1975–1976): 346–52; J. B. Tyson, "Sequential Parallelism in the Synoptic Gospels," *NTS* 22 (1975–1976): 276–305; F. Neirynck, ed., *The Minor Agreements of Matthew and Luke against Mark* (Leuven: Leuven University Press, 1974); F. Neirynck, "Minor Agreements Matthew-Luke in the Transfiguration Story," in *Orientierung an Jesus* (Festschrift for J. Schmid; Freiburg: Herder, 1973), 253–66; Roland Mushat Frye, "The Synoptic Problems and Analogies in Other Literatures," in *The Relationships among the Gospels: An Interdisciplinary Dialogue*, ed. William O. Walker Jr. (San Antonio: Trinity University Press, 1978), 261–302. Cf. also the discussions and diverse perspectives presented by B. Orchard and T. L. W. Longstaff, eds., *J. J. Griesbach: Synoptic and Text-Critical Studies, 1776–1976*, SNTSMS 34 (Cambridge: Cambridge University Press, 1978). Note, too, that far more complex theories have been advanced: e.g., Tim Schramm, *Der Markus-Stoff bei Lukas*, SNTSMS 14 (Cambridge: Cambridge University Press, 1971) argues that Luke appears to rely on some otherwise unknown source in some passages (e.g., Luke 21). Whether or not this suggestion is correct, Schramm shares the dissatisfaction of others with respect to the simple two-source hypothesis.

[17]Cf. especially D. Wenham, "The Synoptic Problem Revisited: Some New Suggestions about the Composition of Mark 4:1–34," *TynBul* 23 (1972): 3–38; idem, "The Interpretation of the Parable of the Sower," *NTS* 20 (1974): 299–319.

relation to World War II or the Great Depression—*not* as we stand in relation to, say, the Restoration in Britain, the flourishing of the *coureurs de bois* in Canada, or the settling of New Amsterdam. There were *witnesses* still alive when the New Testament documents were written; but the way many form critics write one would think that all witnesses to the life, death, and resurrection of Christ had been mysteriously snatched away the moment after the Ascension, and a new group had to begin all over again.[18]

3. Gerhardsson and Riesenfeld have argued for a stability in the tradition owing to memory patterns in instruction shared by Jesus and the rabbis.[19] Even if they overstate the case, their most eloquent critic concedes there is something to it.[20]

4. Recent research has argued for *written* records that go back to Jesus' ministry.[21] Patterns in *oral* tradition have no parallel in *written* tradition. The form-critical hypotheses are beginning to appear increasingly dubious.

5. A good case can still be made for Matthean authorship of the Gospel of Matthew.[22] If that were once conceded, even as a possibility, then the first Evangelist, even if he relied on Mark (and why shouldn't he?), was also an eyewitness. The wedge between redaction and tradition would become worthless as far as questions of authenticity are concerned.

6. Radical form criticism assumes we have a much greater knowledge of the life-settings of the church than we do. All we think we know of such settings is derived from speculation based on form-critical theories and fertile imaginations. Of course, such speculations *may* be sound, but they are *at best* nothing more than speculations.[23] As Humphrey Palmer has rather trenchantly remarked, whether

---

[18]Cf. F. F. Bruce, "Are the New Testament Documents Still Reliable?" in *Evangelical Roots*, ed. Kenneth S. Kantzer (Nashville: Nelson, 1978), 55. Cf. the celebrated remark of Vincent Taylor (quoted also by Bruce) to the effect that if certain proponents of form criticism were right, "the disciples must have been translated to heaven immediately after the Resurrection" in his book *The Formation of the Gospel Tradition* (London: Macmillan, 1933), 41.

[19]B. Gerhardsson, *Memory and Manuscript*, trans. Eric J. Sharpe (Uppsala: Gleerup, 1964); idem, "Tradition and Transmission in Early Christianity," *Coniectanea Neotestamentica* 20 (1964); H. Riesenfeld, "The Gospel Tradition and Its Beginnings: A Study in the Limits of 'Formgeschichte,'" most readily accessible in *The Gospel Tradition* (Philadelphia: Fortress, 1970), 1–29. Cf. also the more recent work by B. Gerhardsson, *The Origins of the Gospel Traditions* (Philadelphia: Fortress, 1979).

[20]Viz., W. D. Davies, *The Setting of the Sermon on the Mount* (Cambridge: Cambridge University Press, 1966), app. XV, 464–80, esp. 480: "[Gerhardsson and Riesenfeld] have made it far more historically probable and reasonably credible, over against the skepticism of much form-criticism, that in the gospels we are within hearing of the authentic voice and within sight of the authentic activity of Jesus of Nazareth, however much muffled and obscured these may be by the process of transmission." Cf. also Peter H. Davids, "The Gospels and Jewish Tradition: Twenty Years after Gerhardsson," *Gospel Perspectives*, vol. 1, ed. R. T. France and David Wenham (Sheffield: JSOT, 1980), 75–99.

[21]Cf. especially H. Schürmann, "Die vorösterlichen Anfänge der Logientradition," in *Der historische Jesu und der kerygmatische Christus*, ed. H. Ristow and K. Matthiae (Berlin: Evangelische Verlagsanstalt, 1961), 342–70; Robert H. Gundry, *The Use of the Old Testament in St. Matthew's Gospel*, NovTSup 18 (Leiden Brill, 1967); E. Earle Ellis, "New Directions in Form Criticism," in *Jesus Christus in Historie und Theologie*, ed. G. Strecker (Tübingen: Mohr, 1975), 299–315; cf. Rainer Riesner, "Jüdische Elementarbildung und Evangelienüberlieferung,'" in *Gospel Perspectives*, vol. 1, ed. France and Wenham, 209–23; and now his dissertation, *Jesus als Lehrer* (Tübingen: J. C. B. Mohr, 1981).

[22]Cf. especially Stonehouse, *Origins*, 43–47.

[23]Cf. among others, Humphrey Palmer, *The Logic of Gospel Criticism* (New York: St. Martin's, 1968), 193; Morna D. Hooker, "On Using the Wrong Tool," *Theology* 75 (1972): 570–81; C. S. Lewis, *Fern-seed and Elephants* (Glasgow:

or not the early church was adept at thinking up stories about Jesus to fit church settings, the form critics have certainly been adept at thinking up church settings to fit the stories about Jesus.[24]

7. The radical reconstruction postulates postresurrection believers who cleverly think up a lot of profound sayings and then ascribe them all to Jesus. This is psychologically unconvincing. Worse, it tilts against the evidence, for the Gospel writers claim to be able to distinguish between what Jesus says before the cross and what the disciples understand after that event (e.g., John 2:20–22).[25]

8. The criteria that have been established to distinguish between redaction and tradition are for the most part so imprecise as to be not much more than silly. The criterion of dissimilarity is the worst of these; that is, an authentic teaching of Jesus (it is argued) is one that can be paralleled neither in the early church nor in surrounding Judaism. This criterion has been ruthlessly shredded in several essays,[26] but it is still defended in some circles. At *best* it might produce what is idiosyncratic about Jesus' teaching, but it cannot possibly produce what is characteristic about it. Is any method more than silly that requires that a historical person say nothing like what is said around him, and that, granted he is the most influential person of all time, so little influence his followers that no thought of theirs may legitimately be traced to him—even when those same followers deliberately make the connection?

To respond by saying that the criterion of dissimilarity at least has the advantage of affording the critic bedrock certainty regarding the authenticity of a few sayings out of the total complex of difficult material is nevertheless to agree with my point: the criterion is hopelessly inadequate for the task assigned it. Worse, there is an irresistible temptation to reconstruct the teaching of Jesus on the basis of this select material, and the result cannot possibly be other than a massive distortion.

9. The criterion of dissimilarity is doubly ridiculous when placed alongside the criterion of coherence. Unbounded subjectivity must be the result.[27] Moreover, the other criteria for distinguishing redaction from tradition do not fare much better.[28]

Collins, 1975), 113–17.

[24]Palmer, *Logic*, p.185.

[25]Cf. Hooker, "Wrong Tool," 576; D. A. Carson, "Understanding Misunderstandings in the Fourth Gospel," *TynBul* 33 (1982): 29–61.

[26]In addition to the essays by Hooker, "Wrong Tool," and Ellis, "Form Criticism," cited above, cf. especially R. T. France, "The Authenticity of the Sayings of Jesus," *History, Criticism and Faith*, ed. Colin Brown (Leicester: Inter-Varsity, 1976), esp. 110–14; David L. Mealand, "The Dissimilarity Test," *SJT* 31 (1978): 41–50 (though Mealand gives the test high marks for affirming the trustworthiness of the irreducible minimum).

[27]Cf. Hooker, "Wrong Tool," 577.

[28]Cf., in addition to the major introductions, n. 26 and the literature cited there.

10. Redaction criticism hangs far too much theological significance on every changed καί and δέ. Literature is not written that way. In any case, even if we suppose that Matthew used Mark as a source and effected his changes for various reasons, it is illegitimate to conclude (1) that only the changes reflect what Matthew believed, for if he used a source and left it unaltered, then surely he did so because it expressed what he wanted to say, and therefore one may legitimately deduce what Matthew believed only from his entire work, and not merely from the changes, and (2) that all changes are necessarily prompted by theological interests rather than an entire range of concerns. Redaction critics far too often see the knots on the trees; only occasionally do they see the trees. Rarely indeed do they perceive the forest.[29]

11. We speak of redaction criticism as a *tool*, a word that somehow conjures up images of scientific precision. In fact, a glance at the available redaction critical works on any Gospel reveals how terribly subjective these literary tools usually are. "Of course," Hooker comments, "NT scholars recognize the inadequacy of their tools; when different people look at one passage, and all get different answers, the inadequacy is obvious, even to NT scholars! But they do not draw the logical deduction from this fact"[30]—viz., that the tools are incapable of providing an entirely neutral and agreed judgment as to what is authentic.

12. It is methodologically irresponsible to pit history against theology as if the two could not be compatible.[31] Moreover, the oft-repeated claim that faith is independent of history is reasonable *only if* Christianity is reduced to purely existential categories. If, however, Christianity is grounded in what God in Christ did *in history*, and if faith is related in some way to propositions about God's acts *in history*, then even if historical recital or historical evidence is not *sufficient* to call faith to life, yet nevertheless faith under such premises is so bound up with

---

[29]For a fine example, cf. H. Conzelmann's redaction critical study, *Die Mitte der Zeit* (Tübingen: Mohr, 1964). On this, cf. Neill, *Interpretation*, 264–65.

[30]Hooker, "Wrong Tool," 578.

[31]Cf. Morna D. Hooker, "In His Own Image?" in *What About the New Testament?* ed. Morna Hooker and Colin Hickling (London: SPCK, 1975), 28–44, esp. 36–37, where she criticizes Perrin (see n. 12 above) for pitting history against theology. She charges Perrin with "a revealing comment" that he "makes on a study in Marcan theology written by Ernest Best, which he describes as 'a strange book in that the author combines redaction criticism with the assumption "that Mark believes that the incidents he uses actually happened"!' Now this is really an extraordinary statement. Why should the fact that Mark is a 'theologian' preclude him from writing about events which he thought had happened? Can a 'theologian' write only about imaginary events? This is obviously sheer nonsense. Against Perrin, we must quote Perrin himself: 'Mark has the right to be read on his own terms.' And what is the most obvious thing about Mark's method of writing? It is that he presented his theology in a form which 'misled' generations of scholars into believing that he was writing an historical account! This, says Perrin, 'is mute testimony to the skill of Mark as an author.' Mark may well be more skillful than has sometimes been allowed—but not if he succeeded only in concealing his purpose until the twentieth-century critic uncovered it! Was he perhaps using his skill to do precisely what he seems to be doing? He certainly gives the impression that he is writing *Heilsgeschichte*, and that theology and history are for him inextricably bound together. Is it not unlikely that he has chosen 'to introduce his particular theology of the cross' in narrative form because it is an exposition of what he understands to have actually happened?"

historical events that ahistorical faith is both nonsensical and heterodox. Paul certainly thought so (see 1 Cor. 15:1–11).

13. It is too often forgotten that whatever else Jesus was, he was an itinerant preacher. As anyone who has done much itinerant preaching knows, minor variations of the same messages or rearrangements of them come out again and again. Form and redaction critics have developed no methodology for distinguishing between, on the one hand, similar sayings in separate Gospels that do reflect a trajectory of interpretation and, on the other, similar sayings in separate Gospels that are actually *both* authentic.[32]

14. It is illegitimate to reject a priori as unhistorical all that is abnormal, the more so if the context has prompted the reader to expect the abnormal.[33]

15. Individuals, not communities, write books (or chapters of books) and think creatively. No doubt the community is *one* of the factors that help to shape an individual, but that is not what the radical critics are saying. If it were, they would need to distinguish between what the hypothetical community believed and what the writer thought and make suggestions as to the methodological problem involved in distinguishing how much of the writer's content springs from community influence and how much from other sources of influence.

16. Radical form criticism arbitrarily limits the genuine teaching of Jesus to basic simple sentences. The most influential mind in the history of the world was, as France nicely puts it, "apparently incapable of any complexity of thought or care in composition, any word of explanation or development of a theme, all of which are freely credited to his followers."[34]

17. Form and redaction criticism have not established adequate criteria for distinguishing between elements of a story that break with the theoretical standard form because they are late additions and elements of a story that break with the theoretical standard form because they are *early reminiscences* that have not yet been whipped out of the account by the process of oral transmission. A careful reading of any twenty pages of Bultmann's *History of the Synoptic Tradition* brings to light numerous examples in which the learned Marburger proceeds by way of arbitrary declaration on this point, rather than by way of explanation. But if the distinction is incapable of rigorous justification, the plotting of entire trajectories is nothing more than arbitrary.

18. Similarly, inadequate thought has been given to criteria that might distinguish in the church between a *Sitz im Leben* that *creates* a story and one that

---

[32]Cf. D. A. Carson, *The Sermon on the Mount: An Evangelical Exposition of Matthew 5–7* (Grand Rapids: Baker, 1978), 145–47.

[33]Cf. especially France, "Authenticity," 106–7.

[34]Ibid., 117–18 and n. 45.

preserves an authentic story. Unless unambiguous criteria are established to make this distinction, the results are arbitrary.

19. In any case, the suggestion that one can jump from a form to a particular creative setting in the church has been shown to be false.

> Judgments about the Sitz im Leben of a pericope have often differed considerably.... Recent research into oral tradition points to a ... flexible situation. Almost every "form" of oral tradition may be used in a wide variety of ways. Similarly, any given situation can utilize very different forms.[35]

20. Current interest in literary criticism and structuralism is calling into question the validity of any approach that focuses so narrowly on a pericope, a phrase, or a word that the broad literary unit, the Gospel itself, is overlooked. These new critics are far more interested in how each phrase or word or symbol in, say, Mark functions within the context of the entire Gospel of Mark.[36] In his recent study of this Gospel, D. H. Juel adopts just such an approach and notes in passing that if we begin to treat Mark as a piece of literature, it is very difficult to distinguish between tradition and redaction.[37] The point seems pretty obvious, but it is regularly overlooked by the redaction critics. This is not to say that these new literary critics are concerned to maintain the historicity of the Gospels. Quite the contrary: the most influential of them suspect that the redaction critics are finding more bedrock history than is really there.[38] But it is to say that other approaches that treat the Gospels in a more unified fashion are available; and they call into question the piecemeal approach of mainstream redaction criticism.

These are some—by no means all—of the criticisms that have been raised against redaction criticism and its necessary progenitor, form criticism. It must not be thought, however, that redaction criticism has been used solely in the service of skepticism. Evangelicals have recently written two massive commentaries that owe much of their volume to a mild form of redaction criticism.[39] Other scholars have used the tool to one degree or another to distinguish peculiar emphases in

---

[35]Ibid., 118.

[36]Graham Stanton, "Form Criticism Revisited," in *What About the New Testament?* ed. Morna Hooker and Colin Hickling (London: SPCK, 1975), 23.

[37]D. H. Juel, *Messiah and Temple: The Trial of Jesus in the Gospel of Mark*, SBLDS 31 (Missoula: Scholars, 1977). Cf. also J. Delorme, "L'intégration des petits unités littéraires dans l'Evangile de Marc du point de vue de la sémiotique structural," *NTS* 25 (1979): 469–91.

[38]Cf. especially Erhardt Güttgemanns, *Candid Questions Concerning Gospel Form Criticism: A Methodological Sketch of the Fundamental Problematics of Form and Redaction Criticism*, trans. William G. Doty (Pittsburgh: Pickwick, 1979).

[39]Viz., William L. Lane, *Commentary on the Gospel of Mark*, NICNT (Grand Rapids: Eerdmans, 1974); I. Howard Marshall, *Commentary on Luke*, NIGTC (Grand Rapids: Eerdmans, 1978).

the individual passion narratives,[40] to argue for the essential unity of the Matthean birth narratives,[41] and much more.

What, then, may be said in a programmatic or methodological way concerning the legitimacy and illegitimacy of redaction criticism? Before turning to such considerations, I would like to illustrate what has been written so far by examining two New Testament passages.

Two Examples

I propose to offer a few observations (not thorough redactional studies) on two passages from Matthew. The first wrestles with questions of authenticity, and the second with questions of harmonization and emphasis. I will make no attempt to present in detail the meaning and/or history of the passages. Instead, my focus is exclusively on the italicized words, phrases, and clauses.

Matthew 5:17–20

[17]*Do not think* that I have come to abolish the Law *or the Prophets*; I have not come to abolish them but to fulfill them. [18]*I tell you the truth*, until heaven and earth disappear, not the smallest letter, not the least stroke of a pen, will by any means disappear from the Law until everything is accomplished. [19]Anyone who breaks one of the least of these commandments and teaches others to do the same will be called least in the kingdom of heaven, but whoever practices and teaches these commands will be called great in the kingdom of heaven. [20]*For* I tell you that *unless* your *righteousness surpasses* that of the Pharisees and the teachers of the law, you will certainly not enter the *kingdom of heaven*.

I propose to comment briefly on a select few of the redaction critical judgments currently in vogue.

1. Some see the separate verses as originally four discrete sayings that have been put together by the Evangelist.[42] This does not seem compelling. Did Jesus speak only in one-liners? Despite the contention of Banks,[43] the connecting words like γάρ and οὖν constitute no proof that the sayings were once separate; in fact if they had been joined together, would there not have been a need for connecting particles? What criteria can be offered to distinguish the one case from the other?

---

[40]G. R. Osborne, "Redactional Trajectories in the Crucifixion Narrative," *EQ* 51 (1979): 80–96.

[41]M. J. Down, "The Matthean Birth Narratives: Matthew 1[18]–2[23]," *ExpTim* 90 (1978–1979): 51–52.

[42]E.g., J. Schniewind, *Das Evangelium nach Matthäus*, NTD (Göttingen: Vandenhoeck & Ruprecht, 1937), 53; R. Banks, "Matthew's Understanding of the Law: Authenticity and Interpretation in Matthew 5:17–20," *JBL* 93 (1974): 226–42.

[43]Ibid., 233, 238.

2. Some hold that the words "Do not think that" are a late rhetorical device that does not go back to Jesus (so also in a structurally similar verse, Matt. 10:34).[44] What external evidence is there that this is a *late* rhetorical device? How does one explain that both here and in 10:34 Matthew ascribes these words to Jesus? *If* it is a late rhetorical device, and Jesus does not say precisely these words (in Aramaic or Greek), how does one methodologically distinguish between the possibility that Matthew made this part up and the possibility that even if the expression is Matthean the essential truth content is to be traced to Jesus?

3. Several see the words "or the prophets" as a Matthean addition, since the disjunctive "or" occurs in thirteen other instances in this Gospel; and of these, nine are probably due to Matthew's redactional activity. Moreover, it is agreed that eight of these betray a similar construction, viz., a conjunction followed by a noun.[45] However, it must be noted that (1) this is not a rare construction in the New Testament; (2) the nine *probable* redactional instances of "or" are not entirely indisputable; (3) "nine out of thirteen" provides a statistical basis with a massive margin for error (or, otherwise put, the ratio is not demonstrably significant); and (4) *even* if Matthew added the term to his tradition (What tradition, precisely, if he was an eyewitness?), the joint expression may mean no more than the simpler expression, since "law" *can* refer to the entire Old Testament Scriptures (e.g., John 12:34; 15:25; 1 Cor. 14:21).

4. The words "I tell you the truth" are rejected as unauthentic by some[46] on several grounds: (1) In the parallel saying in Luke 16:17, this clause is missing; (2) the clause might well have arisen in Greek-speaking Judaism, and (3) Matthew is the only New Testament writer to use this particular formula with γάρ (ἀμὴν γὰρ λέγω ὑμῖν). But in response we may well ask: (1) Does Luke's parallel seem to come from the same occasion? Is it certain the utterance was unattached in the tradition and nailed down in one place by Matthew and in another by Luke? How can this hypothesis be distinguished from the more plausible one—that an itinerant preacher says similar things on many occasions? And *if* the two accounts have the same source, how may we know Matthew added it, rather than supposing Luke dropped it? (2) *Perhaps* the clause arose in Greek-speaking Judaism, but *perhaps* not. Note the transliterated word ἀμήν. "What does that suggest? And if the expression arose in such circles, perhaps Jesus was trilingual and invented it. And perhaps not. What *methodological* control is there to enable one to respond to any of these questions? (3) If Matthew is the only one to associate γάρ with the

---

[44]S. Légasse, "Jésus: Juif ou non?" *NRTh* 86 (1964): 692; W. Trilling, *Das wahre Israel* (Münich: Kösel-Verlag, 1964), 171.

[45]Banks, "Matthew's Understanding," 228.

[46]Ibid., 232–33. Cf. also E. Schweizer, *The Good News according to Matthew* (Atlanta: John Knox, 1975), 104.

clause, might this not just as easily mean that only γάρ was added as that the entire clause is redactional? Is it not remarkable that only Jesus in the New Testament uses ἀμήν at the *beginning* of clauses—would this not argue for authenticity? In any case, though it is true that Matthew is the only New Testament writer to use γάρ with this expression, he does so in only four of thirty-two occurrences. That means he uses the expression without γάρ twenty-eight times, but Mark uses the expression (without γάρ) only thirteen times, and Luke a mere six. Perhaps, it may be argued, if Mark or Luke had used the expression more, they too would have slipped in the odd γάρ. In any case, since I am not worried about the *ipsissima verba* of Jesus (i.e., Jesus' own words) but only about his *ipsissima vox* (i.e., Jesus' own voice), might it be that where γάρ does appear, there is simply a Matthean connection that reveals a connection that Jesus himself made, whether by contextual implication, logic, explicit statement (in Aramaic?), or some other means? How does one methodologically *eliminate* such possibilities?

5. Banks argues that the italicized words *for, unless, righteousness, surpasses,* and *kingdom of heaven* are probably all unauthentic and that the verse as a whole, though traditional, is probably not authentic. However, he insists that Matthew is nevertheless not imposing something essentially alien to Jesus' intention but is simply drawing out some practical implications from the attitude Jesus maintains.[47] My problem with this approach is in part akin to my hesitations in all the other passages; but I will press on and ask a broader question. Did Matthew (according to Banks) simply make deductions about Jesus' general *attitude* without ever hearing Jesus deal with this subject? If he *did* hear Jesus deal with it, might he not be giving the gist of what Jesus said (*ipsissima vox*)? And how, methodologically speaking, can Banks (or anyone else) distinguish between these two cases?

I must hasten to add that these reflections in no way *prove* the authenticity of this snippet or that. I am at the moment concerned only with the methodological problems inherent in redaction criticism; and I am trying to demonstrate that at least in this passage redaction criticism is *intrinsically incapable* of dealing believably with questions of authenticity. It is not really a "tool" in any precise sense: it is freighted with subjective judgments; it is based on too many implausible assumptions; and, worst of all, in each judgment it makes it ignores numerous questions that not only are relevant but expose its fundamental weakness.

It is also fairly clear, in this example at least, that the distinction between redaction and tradition is often not only unhelpful but misleading when it comes to weighing probabilities of authenticity. "Redactional" comments *may* be prompted

---

[47]Banks, "Matthew's Understanding."

by purely theological considerations, but equally they *may* be prompted by stylistic concerns or even by additional information springing from further research (Luke 1:1–4). This fundamental point is disappointingly overlooked in Jeremias's last book on Luke.[48] Despite the formal rigor of the work, not only is there some *methodological* weakness in the attempt to distinguish tradition from redaction, but, far worse, Jeremias maintains the *theoretical* distinction between the two, maintaining that Luke is heard only in the redaction and that authenticity is possible only in the tradition. Such bifurcation is without methodological justification.

Matthew 19:16–21 and Parallels

This is the first part of the parable of the rich fool. It is a particularly difficult example of somewhat divergent synoptic accounts of the same incident (see fig. 4).

Fig. 4.

Matthew 19:16–21	Mark 10:17–21	Luke 18:18–22
[16] Now a *man* came up to Jesus and asked, "Teacher, *what good thing* must I do to get eternal life?"	[17] As Jesus started on his way, *a man ran up to him and fell on his knees before him.* "*Good teacher,*" he asked, "what must I do to inherit eternal life?"	[18] *A certain ruler* asked him, "*Good teacher,* what must I do to inherit eternal life?"
[17] "Why do you *ask me about what is good?*" Jesus replied. "There is only One who is good. If you want to enter life, obey the commandments."	[18] "Why do you *call me good?*" Jesus answered. "No one is good—except God alone.	[19] "Why do you *call me good?*" Jesus answered. "No one is good—except God alone.
[18] "Which ones?" the man inquired. Jesus replied, "'Do not murder, do not commit adultery, do not steal, do not give false testimony, [19] honor your father and your mother,' and 'love your neighbor as yourself.'"	[19] You know the commandments: 'Do not murder, do not commit adultery, do not steal, do not give false testimony, do not defraud, honor your father and mother.'"	[20] You know the commandments: 'Do not commit adultery, do not murder, do not steal, do not give false testimony, honor your father and mother.'"
[20] "*All these I have kept,*" the *young man* said. "*What do I still lack?*"	[20] "*Teacher,*" he declared, "*all these I have kept since I was a boy.*"	[21] "*All these I have kept since I was a boy,*" he said.
[21] Jesus answered, "If you want to be perfect, go, sell your possessions and give to the poor, and you will have treasure in heaven. Then come, follow me."	[21] Jesus looked at him and loved him. "*One thing you lack,*" he said. "Go, sell everything you have and give to the poor, and you will have treasure in heaven. Then come, follow me."	[22] When Jesus heard this, he said to him, "*You still lack one thing.* Sell everything you have and give to the poor, and you will have treasure in heaven. Then come, follow me."

---

[48] J. Jeremias, *Die Sprache des Lukasevangeliums: Redaktion und Tradition im Nicht-Markusstoff des dritten Evangeliums*, Meyers Kritisch-exegetischer Kommentar, Sonderband; Göttingen: Vandenhoeck & Ruprecht, 1980).

The account of the rich young ruler according to the three Synoptic Gospels plays a central role in the history of Gospel criticism. It is often taken as one of the few stories in which doctrinal development is unambiguous, and therefore it functions in much critical thought as a central justification for very elaborate schemes.

The questions raised are too complex for exhaustive treatment here; but the following observations bear directly on the concerns of this chapter:

1. The parallels cited above are from a much larger pericope: Matthew 19:16–30; Mark 10:17–31; and Luke 18:18–30. Mark's account, with 279 words, is longer than the other two: Luke's has 202, and Matthew's, 270. The last figure is reduced to 225 if we eliminate Matthew 19:28, which has no parallel in the others. These figures are interesting insofar as they suggest that, given Markan priority, Matthew and Luke are not simply gratuitously *expanding* a simple account.

2. There are numerous minor variations from account to account. Only Matthew has ἰδού ("behold"; or, in the NIV, "Now . . ."). Matthew refers to the questioner as "one" (εἷς), but later tells us he was young (19:20). Mark likewise calls him "one" (εἷς; NIV, "a man"); but though he says nothing about this "one's" age, he provides a little detail regarding the encounter: it was *while Jesus was setting out on his way* that a man *ran up* to him and *knelt before him.* Luke, like Matthew, provides neither of these details, but he mentions that the questioner was "a certain ruler" (τις ἄρχων). Mark and Luke have the questioner reply, "All these I have kept since I was a boy"; but in Matthew the statement is briefer: "All these I have kept." The reference to youth is preserved only in the fact that the man himself is described as "young." In Mark and Luke, it is Jesus who says, "One thing you lack" (with some variation in the words—Mark: ἕν σε ὑστερεῖ; Luke: ἔτι ἕν σοι λείπει). But Matthew puts these words as a question on the young man's lips: "What do I still lack?" Farther on (beyond what I have cited), in the resulting interchange with his disciples, Jesus speaks of the one who gives up family and goods "for me and the gospel" (Mark 10:29), or "for my sake" (Matt. 19:29), or "for the sake of the kingdom of God" (Luke 18:29). There are other less significant minor changes in grammar, word order, and the like.

It is difficult to see how some of these changes are anything other than stylistic. There is not much difference between ἕν σε ὑστερεῖ (Mark) and ἔτι ἕν σοι λείπει (Luke). The force of ἰδού in Hellenistic Greek is so weakened that its presence changes nothing of substance. It *may* give an impression (in Matthew) that this story happens hard on the heels of the previous one; but this is doubtful. In short, some of these changes are of minimal significance.

Other changes clearly add something or take something away. Mark's statement "ran up to him and fell on his knees before him" has disappeared in Matthew and Luke; but with their shorter accounts, it appears that they are trimming and condensing a little. They certainly are not concerned to *deny* that the questioner ran up to Jesus and fell to his knees before him. Luke's added information that the questioner was "a certain ruler" does not derive from Matthew or Luke. If we may assume the two-source hypothesis, then these words are certainly redactional. However, three points must be noted: (1) Luke himself assures his readers (1:1–4) that his research has included many written and oral sources, including eyewitnesses. It is therefore entirely gratuitous to leap to the conclusion that because the words are redactional, they must not refer to what is historically true. Even the suggestion that Luke guesses the man was a ruler because he knows that he was rich is rather simple-minded. Were all synagogue rulers (or members of the Sanhedrin—the expression could mean either) rich? Were they the only ones who were rich? In the light of Luke's description of his approach to writing the Third Gospel, it is far more probable that Luke is relying on additional information for this redactional addition. (2) It is very difficult to detect theological significance in the change. It is historiographically responsible to read the three accounts and conclude that the questioner was a young, rich ruler. However, even if Luke had made something of the fact that he was a ruler, it would not necessarily follow that the additional information was not historically based. It might only mean that Matthew and Mark did not know this point, or that if they did, they chose not to make any capital out of it. What *methodological* way is there for distinguishing these options from one another? (3) It can hardly be overlooked that we have detected this redactional addition solely on the basis of the comparative passages and the assumption of the reliability of the two-source hypothesis. If at this point only Luke had preserved the narrative, there would have been no way to detect that ἄρχων was redactional; for the usual method, based on determining what words are particularly Lukan, yields false results in this case: Matthew uses the word thirteen times; Mark, twenty-eight; and Luke, thirty-one (which is proportionately fewer than Mark's usage).

The other minor variations from Gospel to Gospel are no more difficult than these, provided we remember that the Evangelists do not purport to give verbatim quotes, that they do summarize, and that they use their own language to provide an accurate impression of the historical substance. It is difficult to justify radical criticism on the basis of the variations "for my sake," "for me and the gospel," and "for the sake of the kingdom of God," since all of the Synoptists tie together Jesus, the gospel, and the kingdom as the ultimates for which a person must give up everything. Luke's "for the sake of the kingdom of God" (18:29) *may* be a conscious assimilation to 18:25 in order to promote literary unity in the narrative; and Matthew's brief "for my sake" *may* reflect the abbreviating of Mark's account characteristic of several other verses. Whether the young man asks, "What do I still lack?" (Matthew), or Jesus says, "One thing you lack," is scarcely a problem at all. It is possible that both the question and the answer were uttered: but if not, it is entirely within the range of reliable reporting to understand that the young man *in fact* was asking this question (with or without the words) by coming to Jesus with his dilemma and subsequent self-justification. He quite clearly thought of himself as perfectly obedient to the law, yet knew he was lacking something. No eyewitness would fail to perceive that he was in fact asking just this question, "What do I still lack?" whether he phrased it this way or not. Similar remarks could be made about Jesus' response. It is difficult to see how any of the three accounts says anything at this point that is not implicit in the other two.

The final minor variation I have mentioned in this section is the contrast between "All these I have kept since I was a *boy*" (νεότης, Mark and Luke), and Matthew's "All these I have kept," followed by the notice, "the young man [νεανίσκος] said." Schweizer says this is a "recasting"[49] of Mark's account. To what end, he does not suggest. Historically, the questioner would no doubt have put himself under the law in a formal way when he was twelve years old, when Jewish boys assumed the yoke of the commandments and were held responsible for them (Ber. 2:2; cf. Luke 2:42). This is necessary background behind all three synoptic accounts; so it is difficult to perceive any theological reason why it should be omitted, unless Matthew thought either that it was not particularly interesting or relevant, or that it was already well known. It is puzzling that Matthew should add ὁ νεανίσκος *only if we assume* that he had no information of the event other than what he could glean from Mark. If on the other hand we allow for the likelihood that he had other information and for the possibility that he was himself an eyewitness, there is no reason to suppose that his information is not true.

3. Up to this point, I have dealt with the minor variations and avoided the pair of major variations. I must now turn to the latter. In Mark and Luke, the questioner asks, "Good teacher, what must I do to inherit eternal life?" Jesus responds, "Why do you call me good? No one is good—except God alone." In Matthew, however,

---

[49]E. Schweizer, *The Good News according to Matthew*, trans. David E. Green (Atlanta: John Knox, 1975), 388.

the questioner opens the exchange with "Teacher, what good thing must I do to inherit eternal life?" Jesus responds, "Why do you ask me about what is good? There is only One who is good." It is commonly taken for granted that Matthew introduces a change in Mark's wording because he represents a later stage in the development of the church's doctrine when the church could no longer tolerate even the suggestion that Jesus might be sinful.[50]

The differences between Mark/Luke and Matthew at this point are indeed quite remarkable; but once acknowledged, this christological explanation for the differences must nevertheless not be adopted too hastily. Even if Matthew avoids the suggestion that Jesus was not "good," he nevertheless preserves the saying, "There is only One who is good"—an obvious reference to God. The alteration therefore "implies nothing about Jesus' status in relation to God," as David Hill has put it.[51] Stonehouse has argued at length, and convincingly, that christological concerns are not in this instance at the heart of any of the synoptic accounts.[52] Rather, in the way the story develops in the ensuing discussion with the disciples, there is a move in all three Synoptic Gospels toward recognizing "the indispensability of the sovereign action of divine grace for discipleship as one of the most foundational elements in this story."[53] More telling yet, becoming perfect and *following* Jesus (not God) are seen as one act (Matt. 19:21); and farther on, the eschatological blessing is promised to those who have left all for Jesus' sake (Matt. 19:29). And it is Matthew alone who describes the session of the Son of Man (19:28). When to these salient points is added the fact that in all of the Synoptics Jesus most frequently is concerned with God's glory, God's kingdom, God's truth, God's will, and God's judgment and presents himself as the Lord's anointed, then perhaps there is good reason for thinking that the alteration in wording is not motivated by christological concerns. Jesus in the days of his flesh manifested himself progressively, allowing those around him to perceive only gradually who he really was, speaking in terms and categories that unveiled his splendor best in the hindsight gleaned after the cross and the resurrection.[54] It is a mark of the fidelity of the Synoptists (Matthew included) to the historical situation that they have preserved this intrinsically more ambiguous self-revelation.

---

[50]E.g., Hugh Anderson, *The Gospel of Mark*, NCB (Greenwood, SC: Attic, 1976), 248–49; G. M. Styler, "Stages in Christology in the Synoptic Gospels," *NTS* 10 (1963–1964): 398–409; R. Pesch, *Das Markusevangelium*, 2 vols. (Freiburg: Herder, 1977), 2:138.

[51]David Hill, *The Gospel of Matthew*, NCB (Greenwood, SC: Attic, 1972), 64. Cf. his entire discussion, 64–65.

[52]Stonehouse, *Origins*, 93–112.

[53]Ibid., 103.

[54]Ibid., 105, and 176–92 for an excellent discussion. I take this to have been necessary because of the exigencies of the salvation-historical setting.

It must also be pointed out that the christological explanation for Matthew's alteration depends on a historical reconstruction that, however popular, takes constant liberties with the only text we have. Fair treatment of the New Testament documents does not support the view that a high christology was invented rather late.[55] The question is too large to be explored here; but it is surely a point for pause to note that Luke, apparently written *after* Matthew, does not detect any christological difficulty in Mark. Why then must we be so certain that Matthew's alteration is due to anything more than whatever prompted the change that placed the words "What do I still lack?" on the lips of the young man?

In point of fact, several different suggestions for the alteration have been offered.[56] Harmonization by mere addition (*"Good* master, what *good* thing . . . ?"* followed by Jesus giving *both* answers), though logically possible, is not very convincing as a historical reconstruction—not least because of the kinds of changes the Evangelists have made elsewhere in the narrative. Pedantic precision and verbatim quotation do not seem to be their goals. Yet those same changes warn us against facile accusations that the writers are introducing errors of fact or substance. Just as a modern writer might condense a lengthy discussion and tell of it in his own idiom and in a fraction of the total number of words actually spoken, without being charged with lies, inventiveness, distortion, or deceit, so the Gospel writers must be allowed the same freedom. This is the nature of reportage, even reportage designed to make theological and historical points.

The question, then, is whether there is a likely reconstruction of the historical event that could have generated *both* Mark/Luke and Matthew on this point. To phrase the problem in this way presupposes that Matthew had access to knowledge regarding the event other than that gleaned from Mark; but I believe that is (to say the least) highly probable. If this assumption is correct, it is historiographically irresponsible *not* to attempt a reconstruction.

Suppose, then, as one possible reconstruction among several that I can think of, that the original question was something like this: "Good teacher, what must I do to inherit eternal life?" Such a way of addressing a teacher was (as far as we can tell) extraordinary, but both the form of address and the question itself reveal the young ruler had no proper understanding of what absolute goodness, God's

---

[55]Cf. among others, H. D. McDonald, *Jesus—Human and Divine* (Grand Rapids: Zondervan, 1968); C. F. D. Moule, *The Origin of Christology* (Cambridge: Cambridge University Press, 1977); I. Howard Marshall, *The Origins of New Testament Christology* (Downers Grove, IL: InterVarsity, 1976).

[56]Cf. especially Vincent Taylor, *The Gospel according to St. Mark* (London: Macmillan, 1953), 424–27. Taylor himself proposes a different solution to the one adopted here.

goodness, really involved, nor of the need for divine initiative in order for a person to gain eternal life. If this were the opening remark, the idea of the *good* action or *good* deed is not spelled out, but is certainly bound up with the question as it stands; it is inconceivable that the ruler was asking about what *neutral* thing or *wicked* thing he would have to do to gain eternal life!

Suppose, further, that Jesus' answer was something like this: "Why do you ask *me* [with *me* emphatic] questions regarding the good? There is only One who is good, namely God." Such a statement, like many of Jesus' aphorisms, could purposely be a trifle ambiguous, precisely because it bears on the ruler's question in several complementary ways. It recognizes that the ruler's concern is what good thing he must do, even though he has not thought about absolute goodness; and it recognizes that the man is addressing Jesus as good, equally without giving thought to the absolute nature of God's goodness (cf. 1 Chron. 16:34; 2 Chron. 5:13; Pss. 106:1; 118:1, 29). The fact that the man did not in any ultimate sense wish to ascribe goodness to Jesus is revealed rather pathetically by the fact that he did not wish to obey him; and the same evidence shows his unconcern for ultimately good deeds. The root of the problem in all three Synoptic Gospels is not christological, but an abysmal failure on the part of the ruler to recognize what kind of goodness is required in order to inherit eternal life. Jesus would not allow the fuzzy categories to stand.

If this reconstruction has any plausibility, then the alteration by Matthew is no more theologically significant than the other alterations he offers in this pericope. There is in Matthew a bit more emphasis against the merit theology presupposed by the ruler's question as recorded in *all* the Synoptics, but the general thrust of the account remains the same in each Gospel. I am not arguing that this must have been what happened, still less that we should preach theoretical reconstructions (my own or anyone else's). We must preach the Scriptures as they stand, for they, and not my reconstructions, constitute the word of God written. On the other hand, I am certainly arguing that redaction criticism, which might legitimately find some small change of emphasis from Gospel to Gospel in this account, cannot be thought to have unearthed a major christological development. Such a theory requires the implausible notion that Matthew had no source other than Mark. Even if we accept such an unlikely suggestion, the exegesis of Matthew as the text stands does not encourage this kind of christological explanation, given the specific theological concerns Matthew preserves.

Christians, of course, might detect in Jesus' response, recorded in Mark and Luke, a tacit identification of Jesus with God. But this is to go beyond what the texts actually say.[57] I think the response may be part of a pattern of replies by Jesus that betray his own self-consciousness of his true identity; but in relatively few instances do such christological self-affirmations spring unambiguously from Jesus' lips. The subject is in any case too large to broach here; but it must be admitted that while radical critics have sometimes moved way beyond what the Synoptics actually say in this pericope, conservatives have sometimes done the same, if in an opposite direction.

The point of this lengthy section and its two Matthean examples is that redaction criticism is simply an inadequate tool for establishing authenticity; and although it is adequate for making a contribution to the study of an author's particular interests, even there it is not a neutral tool. It is used in connection with a broad range of reconstructions, theories, and exegetical decisions. But these observations bring me to the central question of this chapter.

Suggested Guidelines for the Use of Redaction Criticism

How legitimate, or illegitimate, is redaction criticism as a literary tool?

If its application to questions of authenticity depends on its roots in radical form criticism, the answer must surely be that redaction criticism is well-nigh useless. It can pick out eccentric bits here and there; but even then the distorted picture of Jesus thus drawn varies enormously from scholar to scholar. Redaction criticism that ignores the brevity of time between Jesus and the Evangelists, that utilizes comparative studies of oral tradition over centuries when it is dealing with a combination of written and oral tradition over decades at most, that disallows any firm connection between Jesus and Judaism or Jesus and the church, that depends on dogmatic certainties regarding the synoptic problem, and that disallows the *ipsissima vox* just because the idiom is that of the Evangelist is methodologically bankrupt and should be abandoned forthwith by all.

More recently, however, there have been efforts by some, notably Osborne and Stein,[58] to use the criteria of redaction criticism not so much to disallow the authenticity of certain sayings as to establish the authenticity of at least some of Jesus' sayings. Stein's important essay allows four of the eleven criteria he suggests to function negatively; the rest, he argues, may legitimately function only positively. This means that when a particular saying is not demonstrably authentic according to the criteria Stein lists, it still does not follow that the saying is *not*

---

[57]Marshall, *Commentary*, 684. Moreover, I have not here mentioned the text-critical problems.
[58]G. R. Osborne, "The Evangelical and Traditionsgeschichte," *JETS* 21 (1978): 117–30; Robert H. Stein, "The 'Criteria' for Authenticity," *Gospel Perspectives*, vol. 1, ed. France and Wenham, 225–63.

authentic, because the positive criteria are simply incapable, methodologically speaking, of making a negative judgment. Stein's negative criteria *could* disallow the authenticity of some saying; but in my view, the application of those negative criteria is fraught with extra difficulties he does not discuss (and which, unfortunately, I cannot detail here).

The entire approach of Stein (and other conservatives who operate this way even if they do not spell out their method as clearly as Stein) has much more to be said for it than the radical redaction criticism to which we have become accustomed. Nevertheless, two important cautions must be adopted rather urgently. The first is that even Stein's positive criteria are based, to a rather alarming extent, on a view of the descent of the tradition that still embraces critical orthodoxy but may well be called into question at point after point. If this criticism is basically sound—and my primary motive for including the earlier sections of this chapter was to demonstrate its reasonableness, at least in a preliminary way—then the conservative use of redaction criticism advocated by Stein and practiced by others must tread very cautiously lest it discover to its chagrin and danger that it has a tiger by the tail.

The second caution springs from the first. If conservative evangelical scholars adopt redaction criticism of the conservative variety and, believing that it is an objective tool, ignore the doubtful historical assumptions that make up at least part of its pedigree, they are likely to find themselves in an intensely embarrassing position. Suppose, for instance, that in the defense of a high view of Scripture they use redaction criticism apologetically to establish the authenticity of this saying or that. What happens when they come to some saying where there are inadequate grounds to claim authenticity (on the grounds of this conservative redaction criticism) and perhaps some grounds, following Stein's negative criteria, to plead *un*authenticity? There are but three options:

(1) He may abandon the traditional conservative position. When that happens, the scholar should clearly admit it and not play games with the creeds to which he has hitherto affixed his signature. In my view, he is following current critical orthodoxy on very weak grounds, methodologically speaking; but I respect his integrity if he tells us frankly where he is going. (2) He may call into question his understanding of the power of redaction criticism and become more a critic of the tool than a practitioner—at least as far as the tool's application to questions of authenticity is concerned. (3) He may wind up using redaction criticism only when it supports his high view of Scripture and appeal to other arguments when it seems to go against him. This leaves him open to the trenchant attack of James

Barr,[59] who claims evangelicals do this regularly and thereby demonstrate a serious want of scholarly integrity. Barr has a point, unless the scholar who is pursuing this option does so for purely apologetic reasons (in which case he has retreated to the second position). However, as long as a scholar feels that the results of redaction criticism are sure and reliable, he does not have the right to discount them because of his other beliefs. He must reconcile his disparate beliefs, abandoning those that engender contradiction,[60] or else he is open to the charge that he is not playing the redaction critical game with integrity. Embarrassing as it may be, Barr's charge is often valid.

Part of the problem is that redaction criticism has so much come to the fore in questions of authenticity that older methods are ignored or even cursorily dismissed as out of date. The kind of argument developed by Grudem in chapter 1 of this volume is by and large unwelcome in the scholarly world; but it is important nevertheless. The approach that tests an author against outside sources—e.g., archaeology, knowledge of the times, historical details—wherever possible and, finding that author reliable in the testable areas, concludes he is reliable elsewhere is largely passed by in silence. Harmonization of parallel accounts (by which I do *not* necessarily mean the simple addition of both accounts!)[61] is deprecated with the adjective *easy*. But surely only *glib* harmonizations ought to be dismissed; easy harmonizations ought to be given the most serious consideration. To adopt glib harmonizations is historiographically irresponsible, but refusal to adopt easy harmonizations is equally irresponsible.[62] Of course, when someone dismisses a harmonization as "easy," what he means is that it is glib. Nevertheless, my objection is more than semantic; for the underlying historiographical question—viz., when are harmonizations permissible, or even mandated?—gets buried under the euphemism "easy," so that somehow harmonization is rejected as a cop-out, something that scholars who recognize how *difficult* (as opposed to *easy*) the material is will eschew.

Why have these and other tools, for many scholars, become out of date? They are certainly no weaker than radical redaction criticism; indeed, I would judge them much stronger. Like any literary and historical tool, they can be abused; but to fail to use them and give them grades at least as high as redaction

---

[59]James Barr, *Fundamentalism* (London: SCM, 1977), esp. 120–59.
[60]Cf. the excellent discussion by George I. Mavrodes, *Belief in God: A Study in the Epistemology of Religion* (New York: Random, 1970), esp. 97–114.
[61]Exemplified in an embarrassing way by Harold Lindsell, *The Battle for the Bible* (Grand Rapids: Zondervan, 1976), 175–76.
[62]I cannot here raise other questions that affect authenticity, such as the literary genre of any book or pericope or the position that posits that the church received words from the resurrected Christ through Christian prophets and read them back into the historical Jesus—a view that questions the authenticity not of the sayings but of the settings. Nor may I here lay out the epistemological base on which I would build a high view of Scripture.

criticism betrays a sort of contemporaneity chauvinism. To use a multiplicity of methods, to adopt several competing literary tools, is a necessary safeguard. Part of the problem with redaction criticism rests on the sad fact that, as often used, it disqualifies results from older methods as if those methods were invalid. The use of many tools is cumbersome; but the more qualified and nuanced results that emerge protect the scholar from Barr's charges that the grounds for depending or not depending on redaction criticism are shifting and subjective. Far from it. Our reasons for adopting this or that conclusion turn on a multiplicity of methods and tools that are mutually limiting, and therefore there is *methodological* reason for doubting the results of one of these many tools at some particular point.

The one place where redaction criticism may offer considerably more help, and where it may function with some legitimacy, is in aiding us to discern more closely the Evangelists' individual concerns and emphases. In one sense, of course, interpreters have always been interested in such questions. In the broadest sense, therefore, redaction criticism is nothing new. But if the examples in the last section of this chapter are typical, then even here redaction criticism must tread softly. The distinction between what is traditional and what is redactional is not a happy one; it is too fraught with overtones of "authentic" and "unauthentic." And even when some snippet is demonstrably redactional, it does not follow that any particular alteration owes its existence to theological concerns. Moreover, if the method presupposes the entire package of radical form criticism and a simplistic adoption of the two-source hypothesis, then the results will inevitably prove not only slanted but ephemeral: a new scholarly fad is bound to shake one or both of these theories in years to come, jeopardizing a vast amount of current work.

It seems best, then, if redaction criticism as applied to discerning distinctive emphases is to produce work of lasting importance, that it should not take its pedigree too seriously and it should not speak too dogmatically, for instance, of Matthew's change of Mark but rather of the variations between the two.

A brief example may be helpful. A comparison of Matthew 8:18 with Mark 4:35 shows that Matthew departs from Markan sequence: in Mark, the crowd in question surrounds Jesus after his *second* period of ministry in Capernaum, but in Matthew this is still Jesus' *first* period. Matthew does not explicitly rule out Mark's sequence, but one could not possibly reconstruct it simply by reading Mark. Why, then, does Matthew follow the order he does in chapter 8? The reasons are many, and the literary dependences complex, but one quite certain conclusion is that Matthew at this point is interested in developing the theme of Jesus' authority.

Jesus' authoritative teaching is stressed in 7:28–29, and the second of the two healings at the beginning of Matthew 8 lays some emphasis on Jesus' authority as a healer (8:9). Such authority extends to many diseases and to exorcism of demons and stands in fulfillment of the Scriptures (8:16–17). There is personal lowliness attached to Jesus' authority, yet at the same time it brooks no half-hearted followers (8:18–22). It is so embracing that it extends to the realm of nature (8:23–27), the spirit world (8:28–34), the last judgment (8:29), and even the forgiveness of sins (9:2–8)—a prerogative belonging to God alone. There are other themes holding these pericopae together, but it is clear that Matthew's topical arrangement of his material forges certain themes that some other arrangement would not so explicitly reveal. Redaction criticism devoted to such study can be of genuine service to the interpretation of the Scriptures, provided the reservations already expressed are not ignored.

If redaction criticism is applied with these kinds of reservations to the study of the Gospels, it will certainly help us discern more precisely the distinctive witness of each Evangelist to Jesus Christ and may legitimately take its place alongside other literary tools. But precisely because "redaction criticism" is in the category of slippery words, qualifications and reservations are needed to keep us from worshipping before a shrine that has decidedly mixed credentials.

Appended Note

Like so many other problems in the study of Christianity (or any other topic, for that matter), the role of redaction criticism is bound up with epistemology. Epistemological questions are addressed directly elsewhere in this volume, but perhaps the connection with redaction criticism should be briefly explored here.

At a learned society meeting some months ago, a young and gifted evangelical scholar told me that he uses redaction criticism as a neutral tool and that when he uses it, he does not assume the inerrancy of Scripture. Up to that point, he asserted, he had discovered nothing that called his traditional belief into question. My reservations regarding the reliability of redaction criticism have already been expressed; I need not repeat them. But the next question to ask is how many times this scholar needs to find his beliefs taught or reinforced before he can treat them as functional nonnegotiables.[63] Everyone develops such nonnegotiables. Would he remain similarly "neutral" regarding certain points in christology or any and every other basic creedal point? Surely not. Then why this one?

---

[63]I have developed these categories in "Historical Tradition and the Fourth Gospel—After Dodd, What?" *Gospel Perspectives*, vol. 2, ed. R. T. France and David Wenham (Sheffield: JSOT, 1981).

Everyone, I have said, develops functional nonnegotiables of various strengths. For finite persons this is both desirable and unavoidable. These nonnegotiables can be overthrown (or else no one could ever change his "position" on anything), but such an overthrow is not easy. Our finiteness and our sinfulness combine to guarantee that our knowledge is always partial and frequently faulty, and therefore we need to walk humbly. But it is as reprehensible not to adopt certain nonnegotiables that are apparently taught again and again as it is to refrain from overthrowing nonnegotiables that do not stand up under close scrutiny.

In the traditional view, the knowledge that God is omniscient and without sin encourages us to believe that what he has revealed, though not exhaustively true, is nevertheless completely true. The person who holds this view thereby establishes an epistemological base of some strength. But how does he come to know this?

I hold (but cannot here defend my view) that such knowledge derives from a mixture of evidence, training, predisposition, and the secret work of the Spirit of God. The last ingredient should not be taken as being necessarily *apart* from the others, since the Spirit may use any or all of them. The problem as I see it is partly paralleled by the well-known tension between Cornelius Van Til and Francis Schaeffer. The former establishes an essentially biblical epistemology but then wrongly demands a presuppositionalist apologetic. The latter often uses a modified evidentialist apologetic, but then comes perilously close (especially in *He Is There and He Is Not Silent*)[64] to an evidentialist epistemology and unwittingly falls into Lessing's ditch. There is no necessary connection between epistemology and apologetics, for the evidences are surely things that the God of all truth uses to change predispositions. Such evidences *by themselves* do not guarantee that any particular individual will come to the truth, but this does not foreclose on our responsibility to appeal to evidences (as witness the apostles in Acts, or Paul in 1 Corinthians 15). So also with respect to the doctrine of Scripture (or any other doctrine): the evidences per se (and there are many) guarantee nothing, just as a well-witnessed resurrection from the dead will not convince everyone of who Jesus is. Nevertheless the display of evidences is important, and the cool analysis of counterarguments not less so. The traditional view of Holy Scripture, which in my view is correct, can withstand the roughest scrutiny; but even so, it must be remembered that this view holds that the Bible is the infallible word of God, not that our doctrine of the infallibility of the Word of God is infallible.[65]

---

[64]London: Hodder & Stoughton, 1972.

[65]I would like to record my gratitude to Dr. David Wenham for offering helpful suggestions while I was preparing this chapter.

5

Is the Doctrine of *Claritas Scripturae* Still Relevant Today?

The question raised by the title assigned to this essay is of enormous importance, for both a general and a particular reason. The general reason is perennially pressing: one can talk endlessly about the centrality of Scripture, the authority of Scripture, the truthfulness of Scripture, and so forth, but none of this has more than theoretical interest unless some form of responsible doctrine of *claritas scripturae*—what the English-speaking world often refers to as the perspicuity of Scripture—can be sustained. The particular reason why the titular question is pressing is that current doubts are in large measure generated by postmodern epistemology, and that is something the magisterial Reformers neither combated nor foresaw.

I propose to give the briefest thumbnail sketch of the doctrine of *claritas scripturae* in Western thought, pausing especially with Luther and Calvin, before turning to the relatively few contemporary discussions of the doctrine, along with a description and an assessment of the relevance of postmodernism to the question. I shall then sketch in the beginnings of a confessional response, with some tentative suggestions regarding the shape that *claritas scripturae* might take today.

Reprint of D. A. Carson, "Is the Doctrine of *Claritas Scripturae* Still Relevant Today?" in *Dein Wort ist die Wahrheit—Beiträge zu einer schriftgemäßen Theologie* (Festschrift for Gerhard Maier) ed. Eberhard Hahn, Rolf Hille, and Heinz-Werner Neudorfer (Wuppertal: Brockhaus Verlag, 1997), 97–111.

Historical Summary

Scripture Summary

Here a detailed treatment would multiply the length of this essay many times. Yet it is important to remind ourselves that the issue of clarity is raised by Scripture itself.[1] Deuteronomy 29:29 presupposes that what God has revealed is both intelligible and accessible; the next chapter insists on the perspicuity of the Deuteronomic covenant (Deut. 30:11–14). Paul can affirm the perspicuity of δικαιοσύνη faith (Rom. 10:6–10); elsewhere he insists that he does not write anything but what his readers can read and understand (2 Cor. 1:13). Certainly the repeated calls to hear or read or obey what is written presuppose that what is written is intelligible (e.g., Deut. 4:1–2; cf. 6:4–9; 31:9–13; Ps. 19:7–11; Rom. 4:22–25; 15:4; 1 Cor. 10:1–11; Col. 3:16; 1 Tim. 4:13; 2 Tim. 3:14–17; 1 Pet. 1:22–2:3). Passages that deploy the metaphor of a light or lamp to refer to Scripture (e.g., Ps. 119:105, 130; 2 Pet. 1:19—which suggests that clarity and certainty are tied together) assume that Scripture is understandable. There are plenty of examples where Scripture is understood (e.g., Acts 17:10–12; 2 Tim. 3:14–17). Where there is lack of understanding (תבונה) in Israel, the problem is not so much the intrinsic incomprehensibility of Scripture as the refusal to abide by it. Idol makers, for example, know (ידע) nothing, they understand (בין) nothing, for the noetic effects of sin cripple their understanding (Isa. 44:18): the problem is not with the material itself. Even when Jesus or some other person portrayed in Scripture consciously chooses to present something in a veiled way (e.g., the parables, Mark 4:10–12), there are moral reasons for the restraint, as the quotation from Isaiah 6 makes clear. When the Ethiopian eunuch asks how he can understand the passage he is reading unless someone explains it to him (Acts 8:31), it is a confession of personal inadequacy to be remedied by someone with better grasp of Scripture's content, not an assertion of the essential obscurity of the subject matter. If according to Paul the Spirit must work to take away the profound incapacity of the "natural man" (1 Cor. 2:14 KJV), at root that incapacity is moral, and betrays the human condition without diminishing Scripture. When 2 Peter 3:16 acknowledges that some things in Paul's letters are "hard to understand" (δυσνόητα), at least we are not told that they are beyond understanding (ἀνόητα).

From the Fathers to the Magisterial Reformation

The reason for pausing here for a while is that it is still necessary to counter the suggestion that *claritas scripturae* was a novel concept introduced by Luther and

---

[1]On this point, Gregg R. Allison, "The Protestant Doctrine of the Perspicuity of Scripture: A Reformulation on the Basis of Biblical Teaching" (Ph.D. diss., Trinity Evangelical Divinity School, 1995), esp. chaps. 5–7, is useful.

other Reformers in their polemical attempts to detach the authority of Scripture from the Roman Magisterium. Quite apart from what Scripture says about itself in this regard, Mark Thompson has shown that the Fathers widely appealed to the intelligibility of Scripture.[2] True, there were conditions to this perspicuity. When Justin Martyr insists to Trypho that unconverted Jews do not understand their own Scriptures, their lack of comprehension springs from their failure to grasp Scripture's christological focus, and this is at heart a moral failure rather than an intellectual one.[3] Similarly, in the early church's struggles against Gnosticism, the charge that the heretics misunderstood and distorted Scripture is repeatedly ascribed to deceit, moral perversity, willful blindness, rather than to intrinsic difficulty within the Scriptures themselves.[4] *Claritas scripturae* as a property of Scripture itself is either presupposed or enthusiastically defended.

But the seeds of change were already being sown, owing to at least two factors. (1) Many of the perceived difficulties in Scripture were resolved by appealing to allegory. Not least was this the case with the urgent task of interpreting the Old Testament in a Christian fashion. Justification was found in such passages as 2 Corinthians 3:6 and Galatians 4:21–31 (though arguably those passages were not well served in such appeals). Doubtless Clement of Alexandria and his successor Origen in the Catechetical School spurred on these developments, until Origen could speak frankly of the obscurity ($\dot{\alpha}\sigma\alpha\phi\epsilon\acute{\iota}\alpha$) of some scriptural passages that are impossible ($\dot{\alpha}\delta\upsilon\nu\alpha\tau\acute{o}\varsigma$) and meaningless ($\ddot{\alpha}\lambda o\gamma o\varsigma$) when interpreted according to the literal sense ($\tau\grave{o}$ $\dot{\rho}\eta\tau\acute{o}\nu$).[5] Even the modified Alexandrianism of Augustine, whose influence over the later church is undisputed, did not entirely escape the problem. While justifying a theory of multiple senses of Scripture, Augustine insists that figurative interpretations of a passage must not say anything other than what is plainly taught elsewhere in Scripture.[6] That solves much of the problem for the perspicuity of Scripture as a whole, though it may sanction innumerable instances of obscurity in discrete passages. But Augustine saw this as a God-given advantage. If a passage is "obscure," i.e., if its literal meaning is nonsense, this is a God-given invitation to probe more deeply into what God has disclosed. This provision simultaneously keeps us humble and challenges our epistemic corrup-

---

[2]See Mark S. Thompson, "The Relation of Authority and Interpretive Method in Luther's Approach to Scripture" (D.Phil. diss., Oxford, forthcoming). I am grateful to Mr. Thompson for showing me his stimulating work before it is completed, and I am indebted to him at several points in this subsection.

[3]*Dial.* 29 (PG 6.537). Justin is not alone in this charge: cf. Jaroslav Pelikan, *The Emergence of the Catholic Tradition*, vol. 1 of *The Christian Tradition: A History of the Development of Doctrine* (Chicago: University of Chicago Press, 1971), 15: "Virtually every major Christian writer of the first five centuries either composed a treatise in opposition to Judaism or made this issue a dominant theme in a treatise devoted to some other."

[4]E.g., Irenaeus, *Haer.* 1.3.6; 1.8.1 (PG 7.477, 521); Tertullian, *Marc.* 4.19.6 (CCSL 1.592); *Pud.* 16.24 (CCSL 2.1314–15).

[5]*Princ.* 4 (PG 11.341).

[6]*Util. cred.* 3.5 (CSEL 25.7–8).

tions, the fruit of the fall.[7] (2) It was early argued that the church, and not the Jews or the gnostic heretics, constitutes the true preserver and interpreter of Holy Scripture.[8] So much should Scripture be denied to outsiders that on occasion the Fathers could argue that in seeking to persuade heretics one should not appeal to the Scriptures that heretics, after all, reject or badly interpret, but to the analogy of faith (*regula fidei*), i.e., the body of apostolic traditions preserved and taught by the church, in particular by the orthodox episcopate. This does not mean that any of the Fathers put the authority of the episcopacy above the Scriptures. When Augustine insists he would not have believed the gospel if the authority of the catholic church had not roused him to action,[9] he does not mean that Scripture was weak, variable, lacking in authority, or unclear. After all, elsewhere Augustine insists that even universal councils err and may be refuted or corrected by later councils; Scripture alone is qualitatively above contradiction and correction.[10] He means, rather, that the church is the guardian and preserver of Scripture, and that in his case it was Ambrose, representing the church, who brought the Scriptures to life for him.[11]

But what were tendencies and nuanced positions in the patristic period tended to harden in the Middle Ages into stances that in some circles at least increasingly denied much substantive meaning to *claritas scripturae*.[12] The commitment to multiple levels of meaning became systematic, and as the full apparatus of patristic and medieval scholarship was applied, and vernacular Latin was gradually dissipated, the accessibility and thus the perspicuity of Scripture faded a little farther into the distance. Such a summary is desperately simplistic, of course, as there were remarkable exceptions: Hugh of Saint Victor, for instance, argued that the search for allegory was actually preventing a proper understanding of Scripture.[13] Doubtless there were differences of opinion on the place of the hierarchy in articulating the tradition, and the role of its authority in relation to the authority of Scripture, but the diversity of those differences of opinion cannot mask the shift, in comparison with the patristic period, that placed the center of discussion farther away from the authority and perspicuity of Scripture than it had once been.[14]

---

[7]E.g., Augustine, *Doctr. chr.* 2.6 (CCSL 32.36); *Conf.* 11.2 (CCSL 37.195).

[8]E.g., Irenaeus, *Haer.* 4.33.8; 5.20.2 (PG 7.1077, 1177–78): Tertullian, *Praescr.* 8.9; 15.3–4 (CCSL 1.193, 199).

[9]*Fund.* 1.5 (PL 42.176).

[10]*Bapt.* 2.3 (CSEL 51.178).

[11]*Conf.* 6.4 (CCSL 27.77).

[12]On this period, see especially Beryl Smalley, *The Study of the Bible in the Middle Ages*, 3d ed. (Oxford: Blackwell, 1983); Gillian R. Evans, *The Language and Logic of the Bible: The Earlier Middle Ages* (Cambridge: Cambridge University Press, 1984); idem, *The Language and Logic of the Bible: The Road to Reformation* (Cambridge: Cambridge University Press, 1985).

[13]In *Salomonis Ecclesiastes, praef* (PL 175.114–15); I am indebted to Mark Thompson, *Relation*, for this reference.

[14]In particular, Heiko Oberman, *The Harvest of Medieval Theology: Gabriel Biel and Late Medieval Nominalism* (Cambridge, MA: Harvard University Press, 1963), esp. 370–75, argues that the tradition was considered faithful because

Further, if the earlier Middle Ages were dominated by the Platonic-Augustinian tradition, which tended to emphasize the darkness of the human mind, the later Middle Ages rediscovered the Aristotelian tradition, paving the way for the Reformation's reaffirmation of *claritas scripturae*.

The Magisterial Reformation

Here the wealth of studies available could easily swamp this essay and turn it aside from its proper interest. One must therefore resist any treatment of Zwingli, whose views on the perspicuity of Scripture were rather distinctive and fluid, and of such Anabaptist greats as Balthasar Hubmeier. It is enough to remember that the essays and books of the last few decades devoted to a study of the views of Luther and Calvin on this subject invariably concur, however nuanced the articulation, on the importance of *claritas scripturae* for these fountainheads of the Protestant Reformation.

Treatments in this generation of Luther's views on the perspicuity of Scripture emphasize the important contribution this doctrine made not only to the Reformer's exegesis but, no less importantly, to his willingness and ability to confront the teachings and practices of the sixteenth-century Roman Catholic Church.[15] "There is not on earth a book more lucidly written than the Holy Scripture. Compared with all other books, it is as the sun compared with all other lights."[16] There are numerous treatments of his dispute with Erasmus on this subject, especially Luther's *De servo arbitrio*.[17] "Those who deny that the Scriptures are quite clear and plain," writes Luther, "leave us nothing but darkness. . . . In opposition to you [Erasmus], I say with respect to the whole Scripture, I will not have any part of it

---

the fathers and doctors of the church were regarded as faithful interpreters of the Bible. By contrast, the majority view argues that in practice canon law invested ecclesiastical tradition with the same authority as the Bible. See, for example, the critique of Oberman in Alister E. McGrath, *The Intellectual Origins of the European Reformation* (Oxford: Blackwell, 1987), 140–58. McGrath argues (151) that Luther's *sola scriptura* was not formally innovative (it was commonplace in the medieval period) but was substantively innovative, since the formal principle had been emasculated in practice.

[15]See, *inter alia*, Friedrich Beisser, *Claritas Scripturae bei Martin Luther* (Göttingen: Vandenhoeck & Ruprecht, 1966); Ernst-W. Kohls, "Luthers Aussagen über die Mitte, Klarheit und Selbsttätigkeit der Heiligen Schrift," *Lutherjahrbuch* 41 (1973): 46–75. More broadly, on the Catholic/Protestant controversy in this respect, see the sources in Wilbirgis Klaiber, *Katholische Kontroverstheologen und Reformer des 16. Jahrhunderts: Ein Werkverzeichnis* (Münster: Aschendorff, 1978); Louis Desgraves, *Repertoire des ouvrages de controverse entre Catholiques et Protestants en France (1598–1685)*, 2 vols. (Geneva: Droz, 1984).

[16]Commentary on Psalm 37; cited in A. Skevington Wood, *Luther's Principles of Biblical Interpretation* (London: Tyndale, 1960), esp. 17–21.

[17]E.g., Rudolf Hermann, *Von der Klarheit der heiligen Schrift: Untersuchungen und Erörterungen über Luthers Lehre von der Schrift De Servo arbitrio* (Berlin, Evangelische Verlagsanstalt, 1958); E. Wolff, "Über Klarhelt der Heiligen Schrift nach Luthers 'De servo arbitrio,'" *TLZ* 92 (1967): 721–30; C. Augustin, "Hyperaspistes I: La doctrine d'rasme et de Luther sur la 'Claritas Scripturae,'" in *Colloquia Erasmiana Turonensia*, ed. J.-C. Margolin (Toronto: University of Toronto Press, 1972), 737–38; Otto Kuss, "Über die Klarheit der Schrift: Historische und hermeneutische Überlegungen zu der Kontroverse des Erasmus und des Luther über den freien oder versklavten Willen," first appeared in *TGl* 60 (1970): 273–321; reprinted in *Schriftauslegung: Beiträge zur Hermeneutik des Neuen Testamentes und im Neuen Testament*, ed. Josef Ernst (München: F. Schöningh, 1972), 89–149.

called obscure."[18] Recently Mark Thompson, in the dissertation to which I have made reference, has been studying *claritas scripturae* in Luther's eucharistic writings. Here Luther found himself embroiled not only in controversy with Rome, but with other Reformers. Various nuances are easily discernible. For example, Luther recognizes that promises given early in the history of redemption were in fact relatively obscure, but God in his grace did not permit such obscurity to continue: the promises were enlarged, clarified, elucidated, fulfilled. Scholars have also long recognized that Luther repeatedly turns to what he judges to be the clearest elements in the gospel, and views them as the nonnegotiables that exercise certain hermeneutical control. For instance, Runia is right to comment, "No one can understand [Luther's] hermeneutics properly unless he sees that this hermeneutics [*sic*] is determined by the dialectical bipolarity of law and gospel."[19] Again, Luther's *theologia crucis* warmly influences his reading of Scripture (as his theology is shaped by Scripture) and becomes a kind of *hermeneutica crucis*.[20] It is also commonly observed that under the influence of Luther, in high German Lutheran orthodoxy the primacy of the "literal" meaning prevailed.[21] Nor would it be fair to assert that Luther advocated so direct an appeal to a perspicuous Scripture that he felt all knowledge of earlier exegesis was either vacuous or a waste of time. Far from it: he constantly appealed to the Fathers. Luther "attacked an authoritarian and self-serving appeal to tradition as a means of forcing scripture to speak with a certain voice. But he did not seek to substitute individual opinion for tradition in a way akin to the mood of post-Enlightenment rationalism."[22]

Treatments of Calvin tend to focus a little less on *claritas scripturae* per se, and a little more on the structure and practice of his exegesis and commentary writing. Yet here too the perspicuity of Scripture is repeatedly either assumed or defended, and correlated with other elements in Calvin's thought. It is true to say that in some respects Calvin was a disciple of Luther on these matters[23]—and indeed the Genevan Reformer also diligently studied the interpretive methods of Melanchthon, Bucer, Zwingli, Oecolampadius, and others.[24] At the same time, he was a superior systematician and constantly attempted to correlate the diverse elements he found in the Christian faith.

---

[18]*Luther's Works* 33.94.

[19]Klaas Runia, "The Hermeneutics of the Reformers," *Calvin Theological Journal* 19 (1984): 127.

[20]See Patricia Maxwell Hayden-Roy, "Hermeneutica gloriae vs hermeneutica crucis: Sebastian Franck and Martin Luther on the Clarity of Scripture," *ARG* 81 (1990): 50–68.

[21]E.g., Peter Stuhlmacher, *Vom Verstehen des Neuen Testaments: Eine Hermeneutik* (Göttingen: Vandenhoeck & Ruprecht, 1979), 109–11.

[22]Anthony C. Thiselton, *New Horizons in Hermeneutics* (London: HarperCollins, 1992), 182.

[23]So, rightly, Stuhlmacher, *Verstehen*, 98; Runia, "Hermeneutics," 141–42.

[24]For a brief summary of the evidence, see Hans-Joachim Kraus, "Calvin's exegetische Prinzipien," *ZKG* 79 (1968): 329–41; ET *Int* 31 (1977): 8–18.

For instance, Calvin recognizes that all of God's self-disclosure in the Bible necessarily involves some element of divine accommodation. For the transcendent God to disclose himself in the time- and culture-bound limitations of his image-bearers unavoidably drives us toward some view of accommodation.[25] But such a view of accommodation is germane to *claritas scripturae,* for it reflects the divine determination to communicate in such a way as to be understood. God does not disclose himself in esoterica that human beings cannot understand apart from some mediating interpreter. Further, Calvin is constantly concerned with the effectiveness of Scripture. Demosthenes and Cicero may move and enchant, but the Bible, Calvin insists, "will so affect you, so pierce your heart, so work its way into your very marrow, that in comparison of the impression so produced, that of orator and philosopher will almost disappear, making it manifest that there is a truth divine."[26] Elsewhere, Calvin explicitly embraces clarity and brevity.[27] Certainly he is prepared to use the entire panoply of knowledge and tools in his efforts at interpreting Scripture: he writes, "If we believe that the Spirit of God is the only fountain of truth, we shall neither reject nor despise the truth itself, wherever it shall appear, unless we wish to insult the Spirit of God; for the gifts of the Spirit cannot be undervalued without offering contempt and reproach to the Spirit himself."[28] Yet nevertheless he repeatedly argues for *brevitas et facilitas* as priorities in commentary writing, over against anything that is too complicated or difficult to understand, for in the latter case the plain meaning of Scripture is obscured[29]—which argument, of course, presupposes *claritas scripturae.* Indeed, Parker and Torrance[30] rightly point out that Calvin is influenced by Cicero in regarding perspicuity as a rhetorical concept: the interpreter of Scripture allows the text to become perspicuous, in the sense that careful and honest interpretation permits the intentions of the author to flow from the text like living speech. That is why Calvin is even more suspicious of allegorical interpretations than is Luther. Calvin also manages to overturn, hermeneutically, not a few of the structures of medieval epistemology. As Torrance sums up:

---

[25] See especially Ford Lewis Battles, "God Was Accommodating Himself to Human Capacity," *Int* 31 (1977): 19–38—though note the warnings of John D. Woodbridge, "The Impact of the 'Enlightenment' on Scripture," in *Hermeneutics, Authority, and Canon,* ed. D. A. Carson and John D. Woodbridge (Grand Rapids: Zondervan, 1986), esp. 265, to the effect that more recent discussions that appeal to Calvin's view of accommodation often go well beyond anything Calvin himself would have acknowledged.

[26] *Institutes* 1.8.1.

[27] *Corpus Reformatorum* 38.403.

[28] *Institutes* 2.2.15.

[29] See especially Richard C. Gamble, "*Brevitas et facilitas:* Toward an Understanding of Calvin's Hermeneutic," *WTJ* 47 (1985): 1–17. More broadly, see T. H. L. Parker, *Calvin's New Testament Commentaries* (Grand Rapids: Eerdmans, 1971).

[30] Parker, *Calvin's New Testament Commentaries,* 51: T. F. Torrance, *The Hermeneutics of John Calvin* (Edinburgh: Scottish Academic Press 1988), 111.

We do not think ideas as such nor propositions that intervene between our cognising and the realities we cognise. We think things and realities and employ ideas and propositions in our thought and speech about them. Thus by claiming that we do have intuitive knowledge of God Calvin laid the axe to the root of the whole conception of theology as the systematic correlation of representative ideas, i.e., as the science of abstractive theology. We do not operate in knowledge of God with "ideas in the middle," so to speak, communicated and creditive ideas that come between us and the divine Reality and from which we infer knowledge of God or deduce truths about him. While the Word of God does certainly involve the communication of truths and statements, in and through these God speaks to us directly and confronts us with the majesty and dignity of his Truth.[31]

That is why Calvin can write, "First, then, we ought to believe that Christ cannot be properly known in any other way than from the Scriptures; and if it be so, it follows that we ought to read the Scriptures with the express design of finding Christ in them."[32] Similarly, Calvin's understanding of the testimony of the Spirit is intimately bound up with the Spirit's operation through the Word.[33] The Spirit's task is not to make clear what is intrinsically obscure, but to bring home what we because of our sinful natures intrinsically reject. *Claritas scripturae*, far from being diminished, is thereby defended.

The Contemporary Challenge

But is *claritas scripturae* still defensible?

The reason I have taken so much space to summarize the dominant emphases of the doctrine as it was formulated during the Reformation is that the question posed by the title of this essay cannot responsibly be addressed unless we agree on the shape of that doctrine in its best-known and most mature form, as well as on the degree to which contemporary culture has so changed the questions that on first appearance the answers must also change rather dramatically. It is to the latter that I now briefly turn.

As I have recently described and documented at some length the nature and rise of postmodernism,[34] I may be brief here and refer readers to that publication. Although "postmodernism" is now being applied to many areas of Western culture, at heart it pertains to epistemology. The rise of the Enlightenment, con-

---

[31]Torrance, *Hermeneutics of John Calvin*, 93.

[32]Commentary on John 5:39.

[33]For a convenient summary, see Runia, "Hermeneutics," 145–46.

[34]D. A. Carson, *The Gagging of God* (Grand Rapids: Zondervan, 1996).

nected as it is with Cartesian thought, assured most Western intellectuals during the last three and a half centuries that objective truth could be discovered by unfettered human reason, that the best approach to doing so was bound up with foundationalism and rigorous method, that such truth was ahistorical and acultural, and that despite enormous difficulties and acknowledged differences of opinion, the discovery and articulation of such trans-cultural truth was the *summum bonum* of all rational and scientific enterprise. Over the centuries, cracks developed in this structure, but in large measure the structure held in most circles of Western higher education until a couple of decades ago. Gradually the Western world became more empirically pluralistic, lost many of its moorings in the foundational cultural presuppositions of Judaeo-Christian faith, became more secularistic (which permits lots of scope for religion so long as it is privatized and of little influence in the public discourse), and, in this century, increasingly committed itself to philosophical naturalism.

But now there has come about a shift in epistemology. In Germany this developed from the late 1930s to the 1960s, when the new hermeneutic became instrumental in moving the locus of meaning from the author to the text to the reader, and the model that describes the interpretive process became a hermeneutical circle. In France, inferences drawn from the fledgling discipline of linguistics developed by Ferdinand de Saussure came to be labeled deconstruction, with its various shadings (Derrida, Foucault, de Man, Lyotard) and its profound suspicion of "totalization." In America, these developments developed into "radical hermeneutics" and were not only applied to central problems in theology but often shifted from the individual interpreter to the autonomy of the interpretive community.

The net effect of these developments is profound. In law, history, literature, theology, the philosophy of science, and much else besides, many of the leading younger scholars (and some not quite so young) are profoundly committed to the view that there is no such thing as public, objective, culture-transcending truth. All interpretations are necessarily constrained by the individual and/or the interpretive community to which he or she belongs. Texts are "open"; they do not convey one truth, but many truths, polyvalent meanings; the only heresy is the view that there is such a thing as heresy. Moreover, these developments, though not universal (history is always messy), have now reached through the media into the public marketplace. Millions who have never heard any form of the word *postmodern* are nevertheless postmodern in their epistemological approaches, because of the influences of the media. Many a scientist and technician, epistemologically still modernist in their own disciplines, are postmodernist in just about every other domain.

What we must see is the revolutionary nature, epistemologically speaking, of these proposals. By and large, children of the Enlightenment, i.e., epistemological modernists, found little reason to challenge *claritas scripturae*. So great was their confidence in reason, so deep their commitment to public and universal truth, that it was easier to doubt Scripture's authority, inspiration, truthfulness, effectiveness, and power than it was to doubt its essential perspicuity. Reason could always find out what it truly meant. But that perspective is rapidly changing. If texts have no univocal meaning, still less their author's meaning, it is far from clear what *claritas scripturae* might mean. In the epistemological universe of Luther and Calvin (and of the Middle Ages too, for that matter), the God of the Bible knows everything, and has revealed some things. Human beings come to know some small part of what God truly and exhaustively knows through the revelation that he has given. The question at issue is whether that revelation is "clear" or needs some special illumination or magisterium to comprehend it and make it known. In the episte-mological universe of modernism, God may or may not exist, but so confident is the scholar of reason and intellectual effort and so assured is the view that there is public truth to pursue, that there is little sense in doubting *claritas scripturae*. But in the epistemological world of postmodernism, where reason is a culturally constrained phenomenon, where interpreters are culture-bound, where texts are polyvalent, where claims to universal interpretations are viewed as intrinsically manipulative and therefore evil, where language is perceived to be not something we use ("logocentrism") but something into which we are born, it is far from clear that *claritas scripturae* is even a coherent concept, let alone a defensible one.

That is why there is no recent writing, of which I am aware, that simultaneously defends *claritas scripturae* quite specifically while showing itself to be aware of the onset of postmodernism. Pannenberg, sitting on the fence between the two worlds, self-consciously modifies Luther by seeking to ground *claritas scripturae* not in Scripture, which he thinks to be an assignment that is now impossible, but in the events behind the texts and in the traditions mediating the biblical events rather than in the texts themselves.[35] A thoroughgoing postmodernist would find little difficulty rejecting this new locus for *claritas scripturae*; a conservative response simply retreats to Luther.[36] More recently, conservative scholars have begun to perceive the danger, yet have advocated highly questionable "solutions." Sandin, for example, holds that "some recent approaches to Biblical hermeneutics

---

[35]Wolfhart Pannenberg, *Basic Questions in Theology* (Philadelphia: Fortress, 1970), 1–14.
[36]So U. Duchrow, "Die Klarheit der Schrift und die Vernunft," *KD* 15 (1969): 1–17.

(as inspired by the writings of Dilthey, Heidegger, Bultmann and Gadamer) are in fundamental conflict with the historic Protestant principles of sola scriptura and *claritas scripturae*," and argues for "interpretation without preunderstanding"[37]— as if that were possible. Again, Burrows asks,

> How are we to undertake the task of biblical exegesis in a world which defines itself as "postmodern," an age in which exegesis of all sorts seems besieged with conflicting voices, and one in which, to recall the thrust of George Steiner's penetrating cultural analysis, the modes of "hermeneutic encounter" have been reduced to barren "archaeologies"?[38]

Still more recently, an entire dissertation devoted to the subject of the perspicuity of Scripture manages fairly sophisticated discussion of the issues within a biblicist heritage (along with the assumption of Enlightenment epistemology), without ever engaging the vast postmodernist literature that calls the entire enterprise into question.[39]

A Preliminary Response

What follows is not much more than a pump-priming exercise. The epistemological issues I have discussed at some length in *Gagging*, to which reference has already been made. The specific points below that deal with *claritas scripturae* merely sketch the kind of issues that would have to be taken on board and greatly expanded if a thoroughgoing articulation of the doctrine were to be attempted in our postmodern world.

1. One must begin by acknowledging that there is considerable truth in postmodern epistemology (if speaking of "truth" in this context is not an oxymoron!). It will aid no one if, alarmed by the sheer relativism that the most consistent forms of postmodernism open up, we retreat into modernism as if it were a sanctuary for the gospel. We may applaud modernism's passion for truth, while doubting that its confidence in the neutrality, power, and supremacy of reason, and its reliance on appropriate methods, were unmitigated blessings. Similarly, we may applaud postmodernism's recognition that we inevitably interpret texts (and everything else) out of a framework, that there is no escape from pre-understanding, while

---

[37]Robert T. Sandin, "The Clarity of Scripture," in *The Living and Active Word of God* (Festschrift for Samuel J. Schultz), ed. Morris Inch and Ronald Youngblood (Winona Lake, IN: Eisenbrauns, 1983), 236, 252.

[38]Mark Burrows, "John Gerson on the 'Traditional Sense' of Scripture as an Argument for an Ecclesial Hermeneutic," in *Biblical Hermeneutics in Historical Perspective* (Festschrift for Karlfried Froehlich), ed. Mark S. Burrows and Paul Rorem (Grand Rapids: Eerdmans, 1991), 171. The reference is to George Steiner, *Real Presences* (Chicago: University of Chicago Press, 1989), 230–31.

[39]Allison, "The Protestant Doctrine of the Perspicuity of Scripture."

doubting its insistence that no knowledge of objective truth is possible. Even some correlative insights from postmodernism, such as the importance of the interpretive community, should be recognized for their value, even if they are pushed too hard. The New Testament certainly emphasizes the role of the local church as an "interpretive community" that helps to establish new converts in the faith: this is something to be cherished and utilized. Yet again, postmodern critics go too far: the models advanced by, say, Stanley Fish, give the impression that recognizing the importance of interpretive communities and our legitimate dependencies on them obviates any question of culture-transcending truth, and locates meaning only in the community or in the individual belonging to a community. But in offering a telling critique of this stance, it is important not to reject its genuine insights.

2. One of the most common devices in the postmodernist's arsenal is the absolute antithesis: either we may know something absolutely and exhaustively, or our vaunted knowledge is necessarily relative and personal. Once that antithesis is established, it is so terribly easy to demonstrate that we do not and cannot have absolute and exhaustive knowledge about anything—after all, we are not God, and omniscience is an incommunicable attribute of God—that the alternative pole of the antithesis must be true. But in fact, the antithesis is false. It is easy enough to demonstrate the wide range of things we may know truly without knowing them exhaustively. When we speak of "certainty" or "confident knowledge," we are not claiming what can properly belong only to omniscience.[40] The falsity of the antithesis underlying so much of postmodernist theory must constantly be exposed.

3. Various useful models have been developed to conceive how understanding of a text, however partial, is achieved: e.g., distanciation (*Horizontsentfremdung*) and the fusion of two horizons (*Horizontsverschmelzung*), in which the aim is not perfect and exhaustive language but such a competent "fusion" that an excellent transfer of information from one horizon to the next is possible; the hermeneutical spiral—differing from the hermeneutical circle in this respect, that the radius is becoming smaller and smaller as one approaches the absolute, rather than remaining constant; and the asymptotic approach. This latter approach, developed by Karl Popper with respect to the philosophy of science, has been adapted to discuss more broadly based epistemological issues. An asymptote is a curved line that approaches ever more closely the straight line of an axis but never touches it.

---

[40]Even after the parousia this gap will never be closed, for to close it would mean we have become God. First Corinthians 13:10–12 does not promise that we shall know exhaustively and absolutely with the knowledge of omniscience, but that we shall then know in an unmediated way, "face to face."

So also human knowledge may approach, in some area, the absolute knowledge of God, but we will never touch the axis, for then we would be omniscient—in short, we would be God. There is inadequate space to flesh out these models here. But they must constantly be set over against the reductionism intrinsic in much postmodernist thought.

4. The bearing of these initial points on *claritas scripturae* should be obvious. *Claritas scripturae* is possible not because it claims that any Scripture or all of Scripture is so perfectly perspicuous that all readers may understand absolutely everything about the text. The kinds of caveats the Reformers themselves introduced need to be repeated and restated, while we add to them the strong insistence that what is being claimed is not an exhaustive knowledge of what a text means, but a true knowledge (however partial) of what it means.

5. Modernist epistemology, springing from the foundationalism of Descartes, attempted to provide a secure basis of human knowing without reference to an absolute. The God-centered epistemology of the Middle Ages and of the Reformation era was displaced with a finite "I": "I think, therefore I am (*Cogito, ergo sum.*)." It was only a matter of time before the limitations of this "I" became apparent: different "I"s think different things, and eventually the subject-object tension, so pervasive a problem in Western epistemology, generated postmodern epistemology. But this latest turn of the epistemological wheel is profoundly challenged if there is a transcendent and omniscient God, a talking God, who chooses to disclose himself in words and linguistic structures that his image-bearers can understand, i.e., can understand truly even if not exhaustively.

What is at issue is a worldview clash of fundamental importance. If you buy into a postmodern worldview, then even if there is an omniscient talking God, you cannot possibly know it in any objective sense. But the talking God of the Bible not only communicates, but establishes a quite different metanarrative. A metanarrative is nothing more than a narrative that establishes the meaning of all other narratives. Postmodernism loves narratives, precisely because they are texts that tend to be more "open" than, say, discourse; but it hates metanarratives with a passion, seeing in them oppressive claims of totalization that manipulate people and control the open-endedness of the postmodern world. But the God of the Bible so discloses himself that he provides us with a metanarrative: the movement from creation, through fall, Abrahamic covenant, giving of the law, rise of the kingdom, exile, etc., climaxing in the life and death and resurrection of Jesus of Nazareth, and ultimately in the parousia and the onset of the new heaven and the new earth. This metanarrative is given in words; it explains and controls the interpretation of other narratives. To claim this is "totalization" and therefore to be rejected as oppressive exploitation is a useful category only if the metanarrative is untrue; if in fact it is true, to accuse it of totalization is nothing other than the resurfacing of human hubris, the shaking of one's puny fist in the face of God, the apex of sinful rebellion.

In short, we are dealing with a worldview clash of cosmic proportions. If Christianity simply plays by the rules of postmodernists, it loses; biblically faithful Christianity must establish an alternative worldview, which overlaps with both the postmodern world and the modern world at various points, but is separate from both, critiques both, and succumbs to neither.[41]

Again, the implications for *claritas scripturae* are striking. At issue is not whether this doctrine is defensible within a worldview that makes it indefensible, but whether it can be reestablished within a worldview of biblical theology that thoughtfully confronts and challenges an age that is departing from the Judaeo-Christian heritage with increasing speed. In other words, *claritas scripturae* is certainly still defensible, but only if set within a biblical-theological view of God and the Bible's metanarrative, deployed in a contrastive matter with the philosophical postmodernism on offer. Otherwise, it would have to be redefined into unacceptable subjectivism.[42]

6. Even this introductory sketch immediately raises numerous other issues with respect to *claritas scripturae*. I can do no more than list four of them. First, the Christian worldview I have lightly sketched presupposes coherence in the Christian revelation, because there is finally one God behind it. It has often been pointed out that the Reformation emphasis on *claritas scripturae*, with its insistence that some parts of Scripture are clearer than others and can usefully be used as a help and a guide in the less clear parts, depends on the *analogia fidei*—and the *analogia fidei* itself depends utterly on the coherence of Scripture.[43] Thus the credibility of the doctrine of *claritas scripturae* continues to depend on critical biblical-theological and historical-critical work of a confessional sort, for the coherence of Scripture, even apart from postmodern interpretations of it, is no longer widely espoused in academic circles. Second, the wrestling with the role of the Holy Spirit in coming to understand what Scripture says, important to both

---

[41]In the same way, Brian Ingraffia, *Postmodern Theory and Biblical Theology* (Cambridge: Cambridge University Press, 1995), is entirely right to argue that much of modernism's and postmodernism's critique of God has not been against the God of the Bible within the framework of a genuine and responsible biblical-theological worldview, but against the God of what he calls "ontotheology," the theology that was vaguely the illegitimate offspring of Christian theology but was in fact decisively shaped by philosophical underpinnings that rejected that worldview.

[42]E.g., a postmodernist might redefine *claritas scripturae* in terms of the "clarity" of Scripture for the meaning the individual or interpretive community "finds" there, while strongly denying that there is any culture-transcending truth that is "clear" within the text itself.

[43]E.g., Henri Blocher, "The 'Analogy of Faith' in the Study of Scripture," *Scottish Bulletin of Evangelical Theology* 5 (1987): 32.

Luther and Calvin (especially the latter), demands careful rearticulation today. This must now include thoughtful examination of the Spirit's role in conversion where conversion entails a massive shift in worldview—as when, for instance, a devout Hindu becomes a Christian and abandons one worldview for another. For in our rapidly changing Western world, Christian conversion increasingly entails a similarly massive change in worldview, and worldviews decisively shape how we understand things. Third, the peculiar promises of the new covenant to the effect that those who adhere to it will no longer need mediating teachers (e.g., Jer. 31:34; 1 John 2:26–27—which passages surely again raise questions about the relative roles of Scripture and the Spirit in *claritas scripturae*), urgently call for study and reflection in the light of the postmodern challenge.[44] Finally, the Reformation doctrine of accommodation needs rearticulation in a postmodern world. The result will enable us to insist that culture-transcending truth can be known by people locked within particular cultures, but that such truth cannot be communicated in a culture-transcendent way. It must be communicated in and through the channels of culture. Within such a framework, *claritas scripturae* is not only defensible, but honors the God who is above culture and yet who has disclosed himself within the real history of time and space.

However preliminary these reflections on *claritas scripturae* may be, they are respectfully offered to Gerhard Maier on the occasion of his sixtieth birthday, with gratitude to God for his concern for the gospel and confessional faithfulness.

---

[44] I have attempted something of the sort in my forthcoming commentary on the epistles of John in the NIGTC series.

PART 2

REVIEWS

6

Three Books on the Bible: A Critical Review

William J. Abraham. *The Divine Inspiration of Holy Scripture.* Oxford: Oxford University Press, 1981. 126 pp.

James Barr. *The Scope and Authority of the Bible.* Philadelphia: Westminster, 1980; London: SCM, 1980. 150 pp.

I. Howard Marshall. *Biblical Inspiration.* London: Hodder, 1982; Grand Rapids: Eerdmans, 1983. 125 pp.

Although all three of these books deal with what older writers used to call bibliology or the doctrine of Scripture, the aims and conclusions of each work are substantially different from those of the other two. For that reason a critical review of them may help to clarify a considerable part of the current state of play on this perennially important subject.

William J. Abraham, *The Divine Inspiration of Holy Scripture*

Content

The first book, badly overpriced, was written by an Irish Methodist minister who now teaches theology and philosophy of religion at Seattle Pacific University.

Reprint of D. A. Carson, "Three Books on the Bible: A Critical Review," *JETS* 26 (1983): 337–67. William J. Abraham is now the Albert Cook Outler Professor of Wesley Studies at Perkins School of Theology at Southern Methodist University. James Barr (d. 2006) was Oriel Professor of the Interpretation of Holy Scripture and, later, Regius Professor of Hebrew at Oxford. I. Howard Marshall is professor emeritus of New Testament exegesis and honorary research professor at the University of Aberdeen.

Abraham writes from within the evangelical camp, broadly conceived. His aim is to introduce a new concept of inspiration, one he judges to be more compatible with the biblical texts and with modern scholarship than that espoused by, say, ETS members.

In the first chapter Abraham sets forth his criticism of what he calls the "conservative evangelical" view. One of its root problems, he argues, is that it is far too dependent on Packer and Warfield. Warfield was the great deductivist—i.e., he "approached the issue of inspiration deductively" (p. 16). He began with firm ideas about inspiration and deduced "by normal rules of inference what this entailed for the content and character of the Bible" (p. 16), forcing the hard data of Scripture to be squeezed into this logical mold. But the idea of inspiration with which Warfield worked was faulty, and therefore his inferences were groundless. Abraham believes that Warfield depended more than he realized on Louis Gaussen's famous *Theopneustia*,[1] which (he alleges) espoused a dictation theory of inspiration. But as scholarship discovered difficulties, various modifications and qualifications had to be introduced. For instance, the significance of errors was sometimes simply played down, as in Charles Hodge's famous "specks on the Parthenon" passage (though Abraham, p. 19, does not point out that Hodge's next lines show that he himself did not admit that there are any such specks, but only that if there are, they cannot be seen as a threat to the entire structure of Christian revelation). The root problem with Gaussen's view is that "the claim to inerrancy rests on theological doctrine and not on inductive empirical evidence" (p. 20). Warfield, discerning some of the empirical difficulties but not the dilemma in the kind of logic being used, introduced modifications. Here Abraham follows Sandeen.[2] Warfield, it is argued, innovatively distanced himself from the dictation theory, spoke rather of the concursive action of the Spirit, and restricted strict inerrancy to the autographs. But although Abraham considers it self-evidently true that if God speaks, what he says must be entirely true, this connection can be maintained for the Scriptures only under a divine dictation theory. Abandon the dictation theory, Abraham insists, and one is left with a choice: either one is surreptitiously using dictation categories under the guise of some ill-defined concursive action of the Spirit, or one must abandon the support for inerrancy grounded on divine speaking. Abraham judges that "conservative evangelicals" have done the former. Although they deny it, their doctrine of verbal inspiration is tantamount to the formally rejected dictation theory. The result is that evan-

---

[1] L. Gaussen, "*Theopneustia*": *The Plenary Inspiration of the Holy Scripture* (London: Passmore and Alabaster, 1888 [French original 1841]).
[2] E. R. Sandeen, *The Origins of Fundamentalism* (Philadelphia: Fortress, 1968).

gelicals utilize a loaded hermeneutical system, employing the standard critical tools only in ways that do not threaten their doctrine of inerrancy. To talk about doing history in the conservatives' environment "is talking about a special kind of history practiced only by those who believe in inerrancy" (p. 27).

The second chapter bears the title "The Inductive Approach," by which Abraham refers to the attempt to formulate a doctrine of Scripture on the basis of an inductive study of the actual phenomena of Scripture. Here Abraham proceeds by analyzing the work of three or four scholars. William Sanday,[3] whom Barr judges the one to be primarily responsible for persuading the Anglican Church to abandon the theory of verbal inspiration,[4] is here praised for his openness but criticized for depending too much on the confusion of divine inspiration with divine speaking. R. P. C. Hanson[5] believes that the only plausible meaning to be attached to inspiration is the classic one (which he associates with Origen) but that this view is no longer tenable. Abraham responds that although the classic doctrine cannot be salvaged, he himself has a better model to suggest. The third writer Abraham assesses is H. Wheeler Robinson,[6] who a generation ago argued that the inspiration of the Bible "is best understood as akin to aesthetic or intellectual inspiration" (p. 48). Abraham criticizes this view of inspiration for trading on an unsubstantiated view of revelation. "Generally it asserts that God is revealing himself more or less to the same degree in all history and creation. Unfortunately not everyone is aware of this. What is needed, therefore, is a highly sensitive religious mind that is sufficiently endowed with insight to bring to light what God is always and everywhere revealing himself" (p. 50). Abraham reveals what evangelical credentials he has by dissenting radically from Robinson, largely on the grounds that Robinson has surrendered to naturalistic metaphysics, sacrificed all elements of special, divine activity in the inspiration of Scripture, and overlooked how dependent we are on God's revelation of himself if we are to know anything about him. The fourth and final scholar Abraham discusses is James Barr.[7] Barr holds that inspiration "expresses the belief... that in some way the Bible comes from God, that he has in some sense a part in its origin."[8] But he insists that whatever inspiration means as predicated of the people who wrote Scripture, it means the same thing when predicated of believers today. On this view it becomes difficult to see why Scripture should be granted any normative

---

[3]W. Sanday, *Inspiration* (London: Longmans, Green, 1903).
[4]J. Barr, *Fundamentalism* (London: SCM, 1977), 348n33.
[5]R. P. C. Hanson, *The Attractiveness of God: Essays in Christian Doctrine* (London: SPCK, 1973).
[6]H. W. Robinson, *Inspiration and Revelation in the Old Testament* (Oxford: Clarendon, 1946).
[7]Especially in *Old and New in Interpretation* (London: SCM, 1966) and *The Bible in the Modern World* (London: SCM, 1973).
[8]Barr, *Bible in the Modern World*, 17.

status whatever. And, as Abraham points out, Barr's understanding of inspiration is in any case unacceptably vague.

The heart of Abraham's book is his third chapter, where his own proposals for the meaning of "inspiration" are finally introduced and explained. Abraham begins from the fundamental conception "that God is a transcendent, personal agent" (p. 58). Indeed, insists Abraham, "without the fundamental category of agency we have ceased to be theists, for theism by definition is belief in a personal God who is analogous in crucial respects to human agents" (p. 59). "Analogy" thus becomes a crucial factor. When we are told that God speaks to the Old Testament prophets, we cannot understand this to mean that God speaks exactly as men do—complete with vibrating vocal cords—but in a way analogous to our speech. Abraham follows Basil Mitchell, who states that "a word should be presumed to carry with it as many of the original entailments as the new context allows, and this is determined by the other descriptions which there is reason to believe also apply to God."[9] Indeed, elsewhere Abraham vigorously defends the view that some parts of the Bible do record God's speaking to men.[10] What the analogical principle means in practice is that we must determine the semantic range of a word in the context of human agency before we can meaningfully grasp how far and in what ways it may be used of God as an agent.

Applied to the verb *inspire*, this procedure enables Abraham to select the model of a teacher who inspires his students. This removes the notion of inspiration from any necessary connection with divine speaking. Abraham claims he is doing exactly what all of us do when we think through what it means to say God loves or knows or forgives: he begins with what these terms mean in human relationships and then extrapolates analogically to God.

The idea of a teacher who inspires his students is a polymorphous concept: it involves many elements and cannot be reduced to a single, narrowly defined mode. Moreover, students will be inspired by a teacher in varying degrees according to their ability, temperament, and interests. No student is entirely passive when he is thus inspired, and such inspiration does not preclude the possibility of other inspiring influences. The work such students produce will doubtless owe something to the thought of the teacher (how much so will depend in large part on the student) but will also reflect in some measure the student's own mind and not that of his teacher.

---

[9] B. Mitchell, *The Justification of Religious Belief* (London: Macmillan, 1973), 19.
[10] See his more recent book, *Divine Revelation and the Limits of Historical Criticism* (Oxford: Oxford University Press, 1982).

Abraham recognizes that all analogies have their limitations. And this one may be too "intellectualist" (p. 65) and does not sufficiently allow for the fact that God's inspiring is intentional (p. 67—though I wonder why it should not be said that in some measure a teacher intends to inspire). Nevertheless Abraham leans on his analogy enough to suggest that although God acts and sometimes speaks, he inspires the writers of Scripture in various degrees according to their capacity. Biblical inspiration is a polymorphous concept embracing many different divine activities, and the resulting work of those whom God has inspired will embrace a mixture of God's mind and the human mind as the degree of inspiration varies. "We cannot tell in advance what parts are reliable and to what degree; historical study will have a genuine role to play in our assurance about reliability" (p. 69). Because this model avoids any necessary connection with divine speaking, it removes the awkwardness associated with the inerrancy position. This is not of course a rejection of the possibility of divine propositional revelation but a denial that the whole Bible is constituted of propositional revelation. And the result, Abraham assures us, is that we are able to achieve peace between inspiration and historical criticism.

The fourth chapter finds Abraham defending the notion of divine speaking—a foretaste of his later book, to which reference has already been made.[11] He ably criticizes and interacts with John Hick and with the earlier biblical-theology movement as manifest in such writers as G. Ernest Wright, and he refuses to collapse revelation into providence or expand it into all of history. The result, for Abraham, is a Bible that is inspired by God (in the sense just explained) and that contains some passages of divine speaking, but also a number of errors. Abraham thus maintains, as it were, that God did actually speak to the prophets. But he does not wrestle at length with language that suggests he spoke through the prophets on some occasions when he was not speaking to them (a point to which I shall return). Nevertheless Abraham concludes that because God's spoken word, together with reports of God's action, is recorded and enshrined in the Bible, regardless of what errors are also there, "we have secure warrants for treating the Bible as canon in the life of the Church today" (p. 90).

In his fifth chapter Abraham turns to exegetical considerations. Most of this book is irenic in tone, though frequently condescending. But here a trace of mockery creeps in. Warfield spoke of an "avalanche" of evidence to support his view, but Abraham responds: "This is, of course, ridiculous and gross exaggeration. There is no such avalanche at all. There are in fact three general groups of texts" (p. 93). The first is the classic prooftexts of 2 Timothy 3:16 and 2 Peter 1:21; the

---

[11]Ibid.

second is made up of texts that show Jesus' attitude to the Old Testament; and the third embraces texts where "little distinction is made between what God says and what Scripture says" (p. 93).

On the first, Abraham points out that 2 Timothy 3:16 deals primarily with the function of Scripture, not its inerrancy, and that it says nothing about the autographa. Second Peter 1:21 says nothing more than that the Holy Spirit moved certain men to prophesy. Turning to Jesus' view of the Old Testament, Abraham begins by saying that Jesus emerges from the matrix of first-century Judaism, which held what we call the Old Testament to be of paramount religious significance but no theory of inspiration. Indeed Abraham draws attention to "the momentous silence about inspiration on the part of Jesus in the Gospels" (p. 97). John 10:35 is an *ad hominem* argument whose primary purpose "is not to articulate a position on inspiration but to defend the relation that exists between Jesus and the Father" (p. 98). Matthew 5:17–18 says no more than that Jesus fully expresses the "inner intention and purpose" of the Old Testament, and we should remember that Jesus himself effectively abolishes some laws and finds one part more binding than another (p. 101). As for the New Testament passages that say God speaks when some Old Testament passage is cited even though that passage does not purport to be a direct quotation from God, Abraham says that the "key point to be made is that if we do rely on them they support not a theory of divine inspiration but a theory of divine dictation. They support the view that the content of the Bible was spoken by God rather than that it was inspired by God" (p. 105)—and, allowing no intermediate concursive theory, Abraham feels he has already adequately refuted this view. The conclusion, then, must be this: "The best way to construe these passages is to see them as expressing traditional Jewish respect for the content of the Old Testament canon. We should not read any more into them than this" (p. 106). Justification for this approach is now sought in the way Jews at the time reverenced the Scriptures—even though, as we have seen, Abraham tries to distance himself from this conclusion when he is dealing with Jesus' background.

The final postscript (misnumbered chap. 7) repeats many of the earlier arguments and attempts to justify Abraham's place within evangelicalism by arguing that such figures as John Wesley did not hold to inerrancy in quite the way moderns do.

Critique

Doubtless Abraham would be disappointed if he did not receive a thoughtful critique of his position from several quite different theological quarters. I would summarize my own reservations about his work as follows.

First, Abraham's criticism of Warfield depends in part on a misunderstanding of Gaussen. It is true of course that Gaussen used "dictation" language. But when he came to treat the role of the human authors of Scripture, he forcefully insisted that they were not merely "the pens, hands, and secretaries of the Holy Ghost," for in much of Scripture we can easily discern "the individual character of the person who writes."[12] It has been repeatedly shown that many older writers used "dictation" language to refer to the results of inspiration, not its mode—i.e., the result was nothing less than the words God intended to be written, but this does not mean that God resorted to dictation as his mode of producing the text. This use of language is apparent in Calvin, Whitaker, Turretin, and many others. The only reason why Abraham has missed this in Gaussen is because he has unfairly abstracted Gaussen's "dictation" language from the broader matrix of his thought.

Second, it follows therefore that Warfield was not as innovative in this area as Abraham suggests. Warfield more explicitly develops the concursive theory of inspiration and more explicitly denies that dictation is the mode of inspiration, but in doing so he was in line with many previous theologians who had never taught that dictation was the mode of inspiration. In exactly the same way Warfield's ascription of infallibility to the autographa was not innovative, for a pervasive line of reasoning stretching back at least as far as Augustine had acknowledged errors in the extant manuscripts and assigned them to copyists. In this area, too, Warfield was more explicit than his theological forbears, owing to advances in textual criticism, but he was demonstrably not innovative in this respect.

There is a sad yet amusing irony in Abraham's revisionist historiography, for it clashes a little with quite a different attempt at revisionist historiography, even though both rely on the work of Ernest Sandeen.[13] The other attempt, by Rogers and McKim,[14] focuses on the question of the authority of Scripture and argues that the church before A. A. Hodge and B. B. Warfield with few exceptions held that Scripture was authoritative in matters of Christian faith and practice but not in matters of science, history, and the like. Rogers and McKim have been decisively refuted from the historical sources themselves by John D. Woodbridge.[15] Now Abraham, focusing not on the authority of Scripture but on the mode of its inspiration, argues that the church before Hodge and Warfield held to a now discredited mode of inspiration, and that is equally false. The effects of the two works, however, are rather different. Rogers and McKim accuse Hodge and War-

---

[12]Gaussen, "*Theopneustia*," 128.

[13]See n. 2.

[14]J. B. Rogers and D. K. McKim, *The Authority and Interpretation of the Bible: An Historical Approach* (New York: Harper, 1979).

[15]J. D. Woodbridge, "Biblical Authority: Towards an Evaluation of the Rogers and McKim Proposal," *TJ* 1 (1980): 165–236; idem *Biblical Authority: A Critique of the Rogers/McKim Proposal* (Grand Rapids: Zondervan, 1982).

field of tightening up the doctrine of Scripture that had come down to them, whereas Abraham accuses Warfield of trying to loosen the inherited tradition in the light of scientific advances but of failing to do so adequately. The study on which both depend is Sandeen's, but in this respect Sandeen's work is demonstrably deficient,[16] even though it has wielded enormous influence on some other historians who have not adequately tested his results.[17] Hodge and Warfield were among the most gifted and sophisticated exponents of the traditional doctrine of Scripture in their day, but they were certainly not the innovators they are accused of being.

This means that if Abraham criticizes the concursive theory of inspiration defended by Warfield, he is not taking on a late, last-ditch attempt to salvage a modified form of the dictation theory of inspiration. Rather, he is taking on a central tradition of the Christian church. Of course its historic centrality does not make it right or wrong, but it may shift perceptions a little about what is being attempted.

Third, Abraham's disjunction between the deductive and the inductive in formulating a doctrine of Scripture is indefensible, even though such a disjunction is frequently found. For a start, it has been shown that there are distinct groups of inerrantists, each constructing its doctrine of Scripture rather differently from the others.[18] Abraham's lumping of all inerrantists into one camp simply is not true to the facts. More important, any complex theory in virtually any field (some branches of mathematics might be excluded) is built up by a mixture of deduction and induction—indeed, by more than these two, but by what is variously called retroduction, abduction, or adduction.[19] The method is found in the natural sciences as well as in the humanities and constitutes a major part of theory formation and justification. In the views of most theorists, adduction (as I shall call it) is not so much separate from deduction and induction as a category that retains both while going beyond them to describe the creative thought, the sudden links and the establishment of paradigms that account for the evidence as accumulated

---

[16]See especially J. D. Woodbridge and R. Balmer, "The Princetonians and Biblical Authority: An Assessment of the Ernest Sandeen Proposal," in *Scripture and Truth*, ed. D. A. Carson and J. D. Woodbridge (Grand Rapids: Zondervan, 1983), 251–79, 396–410.

[17]E.g., G. Marsden, *Fundamentalism and American Culture: The Shaping of Twentieth Century Evangelicalism 1870–1925* (New York: Oxford University, 1980). See especially Woodbridge, *Biblical Authority*, 219n88.

[18]E.g., R. C. Sproul, "The Case for Inerrancy: A Methodological Analysis," in *God's Inerrant Word: An International Symposium on the Trustworthiness of Scripture*, ed. J. W. Montgomery (Minneapolis: Bethany Fellowship, 1973), 242–61; P. Helm, "Faith, Evidence, and the Scriptures," in *Scripture and Truth*, ed. Carson and Woodbridge, 303–20, 411.

[19]Cf. A. F. Holmes, "Ordinary Language Analysis and Theological Method," *BETS* 11 (1968): 131–38; J. W. Montgomery, "The Theologian's Craft: A Discussion of Theory Formation and Theory Testing in Theology," in *The Suicide of Christian Theology* (Minneapolis: Bethany, 1970), 267–313; J. I. Packer, "Hermeneutics and Biblical Authority," *Them* 1, no. 1 (Autumn 1975), 3–12; especially P. D. Feinberg, "The Meaning of Inerrancy," in *Inerrancy*, ed. N. L. Geisler (Grand Rapids: Zondervan, 1979), 265–304, 468–71; and the much larger literature on theory formation and justification.

and understood to that point. I dare not turn this article into an extended outline of theory formation, but there are many implications of adduction as applied to the formulation of any theological doctrine, not least a doctrine of Scripture. Some of these implications are nicely spelled out by Feinberg.[20] Unfortunately Abraham's book betrays no knowledge of such matters, let alone sensitivity to them, and the result is that his most triumphant attacks on the position he seeks to overthrow are frequently aimed in the wrong direction—viz., at straw men he himself has erected. It is simply not true that the inerrantist relies exclusively on deductivist logic.

Fourth, Abraham's mishandling of deduction and induction shows up in another way. He repeatedly insists that the inerrantist depends for his argument on an a priori definition of inspiration and mocks Warfield's claim to an avalanche of evidence. In fact, Warfield was right. The best recent survey of this avalanche, complete with classification of the many different kinds of biblical evidence (very little of it dependent on a definition of "inspiration," a priori or otherwise) is that by Grudem[21] (written after Abraham's work). But because of Abraham's reductionistic handling of the inerrantist literature in this regard, he fails to wrestle with the fact that a substantial number of arguments advanced by the traditional view depend on evidence that the Bible is God's word in the sense that what the Bible says, God says. Abraham seeks to condemn this view by saying that it cannot distinguish itself from the dictation theory it formally rejects. But it does, as we have seen, distinguish itself from the dictation theory in terms of the mode of inspiration. The classic view, in other words, attempts to integrate more of the evidence than Abraham admits into the discussion. If Abraham were to respond that the resulting theory of the mode of inspiration, labeled concursive, is suspiciously vague, inerrantists might reply (1) that it is no more vague than confessional statements about the unity of deity and humanity in Jesus Christ, statements with which Abraham himself would apparently agree, and (2) that in any case it better accounts for the hard evidence that we actually have. It certainly does not help the debate to write off substantial parts of that evidence in advance.

Conceivably Abraham could advance the argument by asking, in effect, "But what about such-and-such a bit of evidence?"—pointing to some well-known apparent discrepancy. The remarkable fact is that Abraham in his book demurs from mentioning a single such example, restricting himself to generalizations of this sort: "I would maintain that any responsible historical criticism, whether

---

[20]Feinberg, "Meaning," esp. 275–76.

[21]W. Grudem, "Scripture's Self-Attestation and the Problem of Formulating a Doctrine of Scripture," in *Scripture and Truth*, ed. Carson and Woodbridge, 15–59, 359–68.

professing to be Christian or not, must admit that the discrepancies that exist in the Gospels and elsewhere are genuine" (p. 26). Without hard examples it is difficult to know exactly what Abraham has in mind. But the traditional evangelical is likely to respond along these lines: (1) Exegetically there are often a greater number of responsible alternatives than cursory study will allow. In every case these must be carefully explored. (2) The problem of formulating a doctrine of Scripture must not be set up by beginning with all the difficulties. Difficulties cannot responsibly be ignored, but hard cases make bad theology as well as bad law. (3) The amassing of gross quantities of evidence, which is proper, will sympathetically attempt to consider and correlate both Warfield's "avalanche" and the commonly cited difficulties. (4) When this is done, whatever crucial words are used in the formulation of the doctrine—e.g., *true, infallible, sufficient, inerrant* or whatever—will have to be carefully qualified and defined, for no complex doctrine in any field ever escapes such restrictions. (5) If the evidence that demands some such formulation as "what Scripture says, God says" is very substantial and the anomalies relatively few, then either the apparent anomalies will have to be fitted into it rather than the other way around or else we will have to conclude that no coherent doctrine of Scripture is possible. (6) All such evidence considered, the traditional view claims that its interpretation is the best "fit." If in a few cases it is prepared to suspend judgment because of difficult pieces of evidence, it does not see this as admission of defeat any more than a theory in science admits defeat at that point. The theory must be rejected or modified only if there is unambiguous counter-evidence, or a clear counter-example, or if there arises another theory with a better "fit." But where none of these is the case, it ill behooves opponents of the view to list (or in Abraham's case, to refrain from listing and merely allude to) the difficulties without thoughtfully working through the strengths of the theory and its supporting evidence. Interestingly, a well-known evangelical theologian once challenged a section of the American Academy of Religion to produce the best five counter-examples they could, and there were no takers. (7) In any case, any responsible doctrine of the infallibility of Scripture does not see itself as infallible and therefore is not open to the charge of being an all-or-nothing position that some of its more zealous but less well-informed proponents suggest.

Fifth, Abraham's own handling of inspiration is disappointing. (1) He attempts to formulate an entire doctrine of Scripture from this one concept without seriously considering such biblical themes as the word of God (to mention but one), except to dismiss them occasionally as dangerously close to an indefensible dictation theory. Why inspiration should be made so determinative when it crops up only once in all of Scripture (2 Tim. 3:16) is nowhere established. When Abraham observes "the momentous silence about inspiration on the part of Jesus in the Gospels" (p. 97), one might have expected him to question the centrality of his chosen category. But instead he somehow takes this as evidence against the concursive understanding of inspiration rather than looking around for broader evidence to see just what Jesus' view of the Old Testament Scriptures really was. (2) Abraham greatly depends on an appeal to human analogy to determine what might be meant by the clause "God inspires X." This is not in itself illegitimate, though I believe it has more dangers than Abraham perceives. But the argument is singularly weak in this instance for three reasons. First, it is not evenhanded. If Abraham had applied the same method to the many (not just one) passages that speak of earlier Scripture being the words of God or having been spoken by God (even though the passages in question are not ascribed directly to God), then he would have had to adopt some form of divine speaking theory himself. Second, he nowhere asks what the Greek term *theopneustos* means—an exegetical step where the much-maligned Warfield was considerably more rigorous. And third, he fails to observe that the one New Testament passage that speaks directly of inspiration (2 Tim. 3:16) refers to an inspired text, not to inspired authors. This is so much a part of the literature on the subject that the oversight is surprising. But more important, it rules out the validity of Abraham's chosen analogy—viz., a teacher inspiring his students. If his theory of inspiration does not square with Greek usage, if the analogy on which it depends positively conflicts with the one passage where inspiration is explicitly mentioned, and if the analogical principle on which Abraham relies is not applied to the plethora of evidence about divine speaking, it is hard for even the most sympathetic reviewer to salvage much of the thesis.

Sixth, the chapter on exegetical considerations is painfully weak. I have already drawn attention to the failure to deal with the mass of evidence accumulated by (*inter alios*) Grudem and to Abraham's failure to discuss *theopneustos* even when he is considering the meaning of 2 Timothy 3:16. I have elsewhere dealt at length with Matthew 5:17–18[22] and shall refrain from repeating myself here, except to say that as Abraham earlier confused results and mode of inspiration, he here and in John 10:35 confuses mode and purpose of inspiration. Elsewhere Abraham cites 1 Corinthians 7:10, 12, 25 as evidence that Paul sometimes gave instruction that was merely "his own opinion" that "cannot be construed as being given word for word by God" (p. 103). But the view Abraham is opposing nowhere claims that every bit of Scripture was given word for word by God, if that expression suggests the mode of inspiration. And in this case Paul is almost certainly dis-

---

[22]See my "Matthew," *Expositor's Bible Commentary*, vol. 8 (Grand Rapids: Zondervan, forthcoming).

tinguishing not between levels of authority in the resulting text but between his own teaching (which has divine authority) and that of the earthly Jesus (which has divine authority). And when Abraham does briefly discuss the New Testament passages where God is said to be speaking in Old Testament Scriptures not directly attributed to his propositional dictation, Abraham, still reacting against what he perceives to be a form of the dictation theory, evacuates the texts of their meaning by reducing them to traditional Jewish expressions of respect for the Scriptures and no more.

Seventh, Abraham's attempt to make Wesley a proponent of some kind of limited errancy is not very well conceived. True, Wesley is open "to inductive considerations" (p. 116), but so are Calvin, Gaussen, Warfield, and Packer. Contra Abraham, however, it is not at all clear that Wesley and the Methodist commentator Adam Clarke are "prepared to admit that errors exist" (p. 116) in the Scriptures. Abraham refers to their treatment of Matthew 1:1 as a case in point. But in fact Clarke[23] does not call the omission of names in the genealogy an error at all but part of the Jewish way of compressing and organizing such records ("a sort of technical method of summing up generations"),[24] which Matthew faithfully preserves. I do not know of any serious conservative commentator, inerrantist or not, who fails to make similar observations. How this makes Wesley anything less than an inerrantist is beyond comprehension—especially since Wesley himself criticized another author who insisted the biblical authors "made some mistakes": Responds Wesley, "Nay, if there be any mistakes in the Bible, there may as well be a thousand. If there be one falsehood in that book, it did not come from the God of truth."[25]

We must be thankful to Abraham for compelling us to think through these issues afresh. It is perhaps regrettable that he attempts to cast himself as a centerstream evangelical while relegating his opponents to the "conservative evangelical" stream. I would be prepared to argue that if numbers and history are relevant to such assessments, perhaps his opponents might continue to use the "evan-

---

[23]A. Clarke, *Commentary* (London: Thomas Tegg, 1837), 5.36–37.
[24]Ibid., 39. Abraham does not provide the reference to his source for Wesley, and I was not able in a brief search to locate it. A later compilation of exegetical and expository remarks of "John Wesley, Adam Clarke, Matthew Henry and others," compiled as *The Methodist Commentary on the New Testament* (London: Charles H. Kelley, 1893) and recently reprinted as *One Volume New Testament Commentary* (Grand Rapids: Baker, 1957), avoids charging the Evangelist with error by pursuing another kind of argument: Matthew was simply following the public records, which were adequate to prove Jesus' lineage, and it would have provoked more controversy than it was worth if there had been any attempt to "correct the mistakes, if there were any." In other words, the Evangelist is praised for faithfully passing on the public records that may or may not have been dubious in incidental points, even though he himself knew better—so far does this compilation stretch in trying to spare him from any taint. In other words, the faithfulness and truthfulness of the Evangelist is here located in the way he passes on what the public records preserved, not in whether those records were faultless. But this is worded to make this case become analogous to, say, a Luke who faithfully passes on the doubtful wisdom of a Gamaliel.
[25]J. Wesley, *Journal*, 6.117. See also the discussion and bibliography in Woodbridge, *Biblical Authority* 213–14n39.

gelical" label for themselves after all, and without feeling threatened or defensive. Whatever the labels, it must be emphatically stressed that if he wins few of his opponents to his position, it is less because of their truculence, obscurantism, and ignorance than because he not only has failed to engage with the best of their literature but has presented a case that is historically, methodologically, and exegetically weak.

James Barr, *The Scope and Authority of the Bible*

The second book, by Barr, is in certain respects the best of the three if thoughtful interaction with the literature, cogent presentations, and clarity of thought are anything to go by. This does not mean I am persuaded by all he has written: in broad theological terms, of the three authors Barr stands farthest removed from my own position.

In some ways this is a difficult book to assess because it is not a sustained thesis or critique but a reprinting of seven papers or lectures delivered or published elsewhere. Most of Barr's published work belongs rather more to demolition than to innovation, but that is true of only two or three chapters in this collection.

Content and Critique of Chapter 1

In the first chapter, "Story and History in Biblical Theology," Barr argues that the narrative complex of the Bible is better designated "story" than "history." He does not deny that history in some sense is basic to biblical faith, but the history of which this is true cannot be identified with the story told by the biblical texts. A great deal of this assessment depends, of course, on the definition of "history" and "story." Is creation "history"? If by this we mean that the creation happened, then creation is in my view historical; but if we mean that a human being was present to record whatever happened, then creation is not historical. And even if creation is "historical" in the first sense, it is still necessary to reflect on the relation of the biblical text to the "happenedness" of the reality. Barr assesses, e.g., Noah and the flood as nonhistorical a little too quickly: What interventions of God, if any, would Barr allow to be "historical"? That sort of question he does not seriously address. That biblical narratives move "back and forth, quite without embarrassment, between human causation and divine causation" (p. 7) is taken as evidence that the Bible is not primarily historical, but again we would have been helped if Barr had defined history a little more clearly. Does he mean "that which happens," "that which happens in the space-time continuum," "that which happens in the space-time continuum and is accessible to methods that allow no supernatural discontinuities (even if such occur)," that such discontinuities cannot occur, or something else? What part, if any, does literary genre play in his determinations? Again, Barr sees it as an integral part of history that there is "critical evaluation of sources and reports" (p. 8). I would have thought that under this criterion as good a case could be made for the Chronicler or for Luke as for Herodotus.

Barr's purpose is to distinguish the biblical "story" from both (in the case of the Old Testament) the history of the period in Israel as it is reconstructed by historians and archaeologists and the history of tradition that ultimately produced the biblical texts. There is certain justification for the distinction: no one would seriously argue that the Old Testament sets out to provide a history of the Jews and nothing more, or that other sources may not flesh out our understanding of what went on under, say, a certain king, sources that reconstruct a broader "history" that is less concerned to give a theological interpretation of restricted events. But Barr's categories are so loose that almost any form of uncontrolled historical reconstruction, not to say speculation, could nestle comfortably under his umbrella without adequately subjecting its methods to rigorous criticism.

Content and Critique of Chapter 2

The second essay, Barr's Inaugural Lecture as Oriel Professor of the Interpretation of Holy Scripture at Oxford University, answers the question, "Does Biblical Study Still Belong to Theology?" Barr's discussion is relevant primarily to the situation in Britain. He notes that there has been an increase in the percentage of students who pursue some aspect or other of biblical study but who do not contemplate ordination or church ministry, and this makes the question of the chapter critical. He distinguishes between statements of the type "God is x," or "We believe God is x," or "We ought to affirm God is x," from those with the form "This or that biblical writer said, or thought, that God is x." The second type of statement, Barr reasons, represents the kind of study that anyone can pursue, and it belongs in the university; the former represents what belongs to the believer, and it stands a little more closely attached to the theological college. Barr says that although he knows personally most of the Old Testament scholars of this generation, he knows very little of their personal theological beliefs, and this confirms him in the view that there is no necessary relation between biblical studies and theology. The university approach limits such biblical study in important ways, but this cannot be helped. Barr concludes with some telling insights into the roles of empathy and presupposition in such study.

My own assessment of the situation is a little different. (1) The common university approach, at least in my experience of study in Great Britain, usually avoids profound questions of truth and ultimate loyalty. If a university scholar comes to the conclusion that what Paul writes in, say, Romans 3:20–26 is true—i.e., it is not only true that Paul wrote it but that what Paul says accurately portrays how the God who actually exists justifies the ungodly while maintaining his own justice—it is not clear how he can legitimately maintain the stance of neutrality. I am not simply saying that advocacy does not necessarily destroy credibility or objectivity (and if it did, we should rigorously fire university scholars from every position of advocacy—e.g., all Marxist historians) but that the nature of biblical Christianity demands unqualified allegiance to divine revelation. If a believing scholar raises his intellectual judgments above the demand for unqualified allegiance and total discipleship, what damage is he doing to the very structure of the revelation in which he professes to believe? Of course this danger is not restricted to university scholars. Far from it: the essence of the modern trend toward secularization is the removal of the normative power of Christianity from the central areas of life—research, science, commerce, politics, economics, judicial decisions, etc.—thereby restricting it to the purely private and personal, and this trend affects much more than universities. But the danger is perhaps particularly acute there, since in no other arena is so much emphasis placed on the distance the thinker must maintain from his chosen field. (2) But the worst danger may be to the students. It is hard to avoid magnifying intellectual attainment at the expense of such things as, say, prayer, love for neighbors, wholehearted obedience to the gospel, childlike faith, corporate worship, and sensitive evangelism. I am not saying that Christians cannot develop mature and well-balanced Christianity in the university setting but only that it is extraordinarily difficult. Nor am I saying that frankly unbelieving biblical scholars have made no genuine advances. But I am saying that the cost to the spiritual poise and maturity of the following generations of church leaders has been very high. I am thinking not only of the destruction of faith in some but of its distortion and domestication in many others, as the cutting edge of Christian discipleship is displaced by the pleasant thrill of intellectual discovery. Again, I am not in the slightest consigning such pleasure to the pit. Rather, I am suggesting that the university setting often tames the gospel and the Scriptures while unduly elevating scholarly achievement, and if that is not the essence of idolatry, I do not know what is. (3) Nevertheless I am certainly not advocating that Christians should withdraw from the university setting of biblical studies—especially in the British context. Believers need to stand in the vanguard of intellectual turmoil and deal with the world as it is. That is surely part of loving God with the mind as well as with heart and soul and strength. But they must do so with eyes wide open to the dangers. Our very failure to articulate the dangers is an index of the gravity of the problem.

Content and Critique of Chapter 3
Barr's third chapter bears the title "Historical Reading and the Theological Interpretation of Scripture." He is concerned to ask whether historical study of the

Scriptures is essentially a secular approach without justification from within theology itself, or amenable to theological justification. "Christianity is a historical religion," we might all agree. But what does this mean? Barr lists six different options. He begins to sift them in the light of recent discussion and offers some suggestions in answer to the problem he has set himself.

But before turning to his suggestions it is important to understand what Barr means by "the historical-critical method," whose role in biblical exegesis he is analyzing. By "historical" he means "a reading which aims at the reconstruction of spatial-temporal events in the past: it asks what was the actual sequence of the events to which the text refers, or what was the sequence of events by which the text came into existence" (p. 30). By "critical" he means that such a reading "accepts the possibility that events were not in fact as they are described in the text. . . . No operation is genuinely historical if it does not accept this critical component: in other words, being 'critical' is analytically involved in being historical" (pp. 30–31). I raise two questions: (1) Granted that the pursuit of the spatial-temporal aspect of events described in Scripture is one important component of exegesis, to what extent and by what means may such pursuit, important as it is, safeguard itself against a methodological inability to perceive intervention in the spatial-temporal continuum from beyond that dimension? In other words, how does it protect itself against the a priori exclusion of revelation, against succumbing to philosophical materialism? Can any genuinely Christian historian be entirely content with an understanding of history derived from Troeltsch? (2) More important, how does Barr's definition of "critical" allow for a historian to be anything other than an agnostic and a skeptic about everything he or she studies? I would have thought that "critical" should be used of the justification of methods, opinions, findings, conclusions. A "critical" opinion in this sense is one that offers justification for itself. It is opposed to the subjective opinion or the purely personal opinion. By contrast Barr's approach, demanding that the historian constantly allow for the "possibility that events were not in fact as they are described in the text," at very least needs clarification. If a historian approaches any text with such commendable open-mindedness, that is one thing. But if after sustained study he comes to the conclusion that within the genres and self-imposed limitations of the text the events there recorded are as they are described, then it seems rather curt to deny such a historian's work the adjective "critical," reserving it for his more skeptical colleagues. Barr's footnote is revealing: he is attempting by definition to eliminate conservative scholarship not only from the "critical" class but from the "responsible analytic historian" class. Unfortunately, to achieve this he has unwittingly adopted a definition that is as Procrustean and obscurantist as anything his most despised fundamentalist might dream up.

Barr's broader answer to the question he has set himself in this chapter is roughly threefold: (1) Historical analysis of the Bible shows how far the description in the text stands from the actuality and therefore prepares us to hear Scripture better as story than as history; (2) for the same reason it destroys all docetic views of revelation that evade revelation's historicalness and make it history *sui generis*, and thus it contributes to the Reformation principle *sola fide*; (3) but above all, the "legitimation of historical and critical reading lies in the relation between scripture, tradition and the church" (p. 59)—i.e., historical-critical reading of Scripture makes it more clearly the reading of tradition and thus prepares us for a deeper understanding of the proper theological role of Scripture in the history and contemporary life of the church. Along the way Barr offers preliminary critique of Brevard Childs's form of canon criticism, a critique more recently developed at greater length.[26]

At almost every point I would like to put things a little differently. Arguably, for instance, *sola fide* as understood by the magisterial Reformers has very little to do with Ebeling's use of the term, dependent as it is on an existentialist hermeneutic interested in reducing the object of faith cherished by the Reformers. In this connection it is astonishing that Barr does not consider the possibility that historical study of Scripture may find some theological justification in the substantial verification of history-claims in Scripture and thus contribute to faith. One might go so far as to suggest that appeal to the Reformation principle as Ebeling and Barr handle it, common as it is, is irresponsible from the historical-critical point of view. I wonder too if the haste with which historical particularity in revelation is labeled docetic (though historical docetism is light years removed from this problem) is in reality a failure to face up to the scandal of a self-incarnating God. And in exactly what sense does Scripture function as canon when the highly diverse reconstructions of what really happened become the most valuable source of insight into the way Scripture shapes ecclesiastical traditions?

Content and Critique of Chapter 4

The fourth chapter is more of a popular lecture and provocatively raises the question, "Has the Bible Any Authority?" Barr begins "with a vigorous 'Yes'" (p. 52). Why does the Bible have authority? "The answer, I think, is as follows: the Bible has authority because its authority, in some form or other, is built into

---

[26]See the lengthy appendix to J. Barr, *Holy Scripture: Canon, Authority, Criticism* (Oxford: Oxford University Press, 1983).

the structure of Christian faith and the Christian religion" (p. 52). This less than totally perspicuous answer is then teased out through the following pages. What quickly becomes apparent is that the Bible is not in any sense a normative authority. Otherwise put, Barr uses "authority" in a greatly attenuated sense. Thus the Bible's theism may be suitably modified or transformed by nonbiblical philosophical theism. The Bible helps in calling people to faith by asking questions ("The Bible is more a battleground than a book of true facts" [p. 53]—a rather unnecessary disjunction). The Bible is less interested in presenting the shape of the past than in pointing to the future—i.e., it is more eschatological than historical. These and other themes are of course common throughout Barr's work and are here merely summarized in convenient form.

One of the most interesting points that Barr raises (and the one that has become central in his latest book)[27] is that "the men of the Bible had no Bible: there was no Bible in the biblical period" (p. 56). When Abraham believed God, he did so without resort to a Bible. On this point Barr in this essay rests two principles: (1) The traditional order God → revelation → Scripture → church should be replaced by God → people → tradition → Scripture; and (2) faith's relationship to God is more fundamental than the Bible itself, and thus in principle it is "perfectly possible, not only to question the scientific or the historical accuracy of various biblical passages, but also to question the adequacy of the picture of God which they represent" (p. 56).

Like so much of Barr's work, his extrapolation from a corner of the truth masks difficulties he might have avoided. I mention but two: (1) Although it is true that no biblical person enjoyed a complete Bible, many of them enjoyed substantial parts of the Bible—and I would have thought it imperative in any discussion of biblical authority to raise questions about how the later people of the biblical period saw the authority of the Bible they already enjoyed and how they related their faith to it. More broadly, the alternative schematics are too disjunctive. (2) Even if we return to a man like Abraham who had no part of the Bible to hand, his faith is predicated on the basis of a God who supernaturally and propositionally revealed himself to the man. The basis of his faith is therefore not exactly the same as Barr's (unless Barr is claiming he has recently received supernatural and propositional revelation from God). Something similar could be said for the mixture of reverence for and transmutation of the Old Testament in the light of the coming of Christ: it depends on the arrival of new, supernatural revelation. Moreover Barr does not here wrestle with the move from eyewitnesses to ear-witnesses to written-witness. To deal with the temporal priority of an event in Scripture over

---

[27]Ibid.

the recording of it in Scripture as if there were enormous existential implications for the proper basis of contemporary faith, without wrestling with the nature of revelation, truth, and witness, is remarkably reductionistic. Some of these lacunae are addressed in Barr's later work, though perhaps not always satisfactorily.

Content and Critique of Chapter 5

By far the longest chapter, and the one etched in the highest concentration of acid, is the fifth: "The Problem of Fundamentalism Today." The essay offers a condensation of some of the main points in Barr's most famous book[28] and some "afterthoughts" following the responses to that larger publication. If a person of conservative Christian persuasion (whatever the label) has a sense of humor, this is an immensely enjoyable and profitable piece. "If we could see ourselves as others see us . . ."

Barr ties fundamentalism not to those who hold in general terms to the authority of Scripture but to those who say "that the doctrinal and practical authority of Scripture is necessarily tied to its infallibility and in particular to its historical inerrancy" (p. 65). This definition could be interpreted in more than one way. For instance, I do not myself think that it is necessary to hold an inerrantist view for a person to bow to the lordship of Christ and experience grace and forgiveness, only that if the inerrantist position is properly defined and delimited, it is not only the most consistent view but also the one that best squares with the hard evidence and the sustained central tradition of the church. Would Barr consider me a fundamentalist or not? I am not sure, but presumably most if not all ETS members would in Barr's view fall under his rubric. I should add that "fundamentalism" has slightly different semantic overtones in America than in Barr's homeland, but here I shall retain Barr's usage.

Fundamentalism as a movement has some learned scholars, Barr concedes, but no "first-rate theological thinkers" (p. 66). It is essentially a conservative ideology "endowed with religious sanction and made into the kernel of the message of Scripture," and as such it "becomes demonic" (p. 68). Fundamentalism is characterized not so much by emotionalism and bigotry as by rationalistic intellectualism that strangely marries intellectual self-deception with a fervent hunger for intellectual recognition (regrettably, Barr is more than half-right on this point). Those conservative scholars who rise above the crowd often espouse views their followers neither understand nor accept, and when they enter into debate with their intellectual peers, they do so on the terms and in the categories of the broader scholarly community (though arguably Paul does the same thing in Acts 17).

---

[28]Viz., *Fundamentalism* (see n. 4, *supra*).

Barr takes many telling jabs. His criticism, for instance, of the crass dependence many fundamentalists have on their leaders is a case in point. Biting overstatement can be useful in helping us see our faults. Yet sometimes his analysis is in my view less than evenhanded. I mention but three of many examples: (1) It appears that if evangelical scholars do not make use of, say, the new hermeneutic, they are throwbacks and obscurantists; and if they do, they are not really evangelicals (or fundamentalists). There seems to be no place for a judicious balance—in this case, an exploration of the field by evangelicals who honestly try to see what may be learned from each development and to assess what changes in their tradition are thereby mandated or advisable. (2) Barr shifts back and forth between criticizing fundamentalism as a movement and fundamentalism's scholarship. Thus he laments the biblical ignorance of many fundamentalist laymen and their consequent dependence on their leaders, but I venture to say that the biblical illiteracy of the masses of fundamentalism (as Barr understands the term) is considerably less than that among the masses in his own ecclesiastical and ideological circles. (3) Conservatives are repeatedly lambasted for holding up their view of Scripture as a line that can be used to develop an in/out mentality: some are in, others are out. But has not Barr himself developed a similarly restricting line? Those who insist there are manifold errors in Scripture are eligible to become first-rate theological thinkers and may be admitted to the fraternity of true scholars, while those who do not are not. By this shall we discern true and false scholars. "If we could see ourselves as others see us . . ."

Perhaps the most disappointing—indeed, astonishing—part of the essay reads as follows:

No one is going to be inspired or spiritually enriched by learning from a conservative commentary that St. Paul did after all write the letters to Timothy and Titus. No one is going to go forth to evangelize the world simply on the ground that a fundamentalist scholar has proved to his satisfaction that the Paul of Acts is in absolute agreement with the Paul of the Epistles. In fact nothing is more stodgy, dull, uninspiring and lacking in fervour than the fundamentalist scholarship of our time. For spirituality von Rad and Bultmann lie far ahead at every point. What conservative scholarship supplies, and what it is valued for, is not inspiration or spirituality, it is the rehearsal and reinforcement of the ideology of *conservatism*. (p. 87)

In part, the problem here is once more the lack of evenhandedness. If no one is uplifted or inspired by learning that Paul wrote the letter to Titus, no one is likely to be inspired or uplifted by learning that Paul did not write the letter to Titus. But instead of setting the obvious antithesis against the conservative conclusion, Barr sets the sweeping work of von Rad and Bultmann. I have learned much from both men. But at the risk of mockery, I think it likely that few are spiritually uplifted in any distinctively Christian sense by being assured by Bultmann that angels, miracles, resurrection, and a self-incarnating God are all impossible, that these and other New Testament terms must be invested with new and exclusively naturalistic meaning, that faith has no object other than an empty *dass*, that the incarnation, resurrection, and ascension of Jesus are all properly collapsed into the existential moment of encounter with the kerygma—an encounter in which our bright hope is to emerge into authentic existence, and a kerygma that has no content but the kerygma itself. If it is wrong to read conservative ideology into Scripture, it seems no less wrong to read Heidegger into Scripture. Meanwhile I know many Christians who have been inspired and uplifted by, say, J. I. Packer's *Knowing God*. And as for evangelizing the world, I wonder if Barr has recently checked the figures regarding which groups are sending out most missionaries to all kinds of church planting and relief work.

I am first to admit that much conservative scholarship is indeed stodgy and dull. May God help us to do better, and may he forgive us our frequent self-satisfaction, our own conformity to privatized religion and compromised holiness. Yet in all fairness, if I want to understand what, say, Mark actually says, as opposed to the latest speculations regarding how some pericope may conceivably have been composed, I find Cranfield and Lane far more helpful than Pesch. What I fear (though I hesitate to write it, since it sounds like a devastating charge indeed) is that in some measure Barr has not discerned any difference between, on the one hand, inspiration and spirituality, and on the other, the thrill of intellectual innovation and formulation. The latter has an important place: I would be disappointed if a physicist, geneticist, archivist, or theologian did not enjoy scholarly advance and discovery. But to confuse that with inspiration and spirituality may betray Barr's captivity to the modern *Zeitgeist* that refuses to bow to anything more elevated than the lordship of fallen and finite intellect.

Content of Chapters 6–7

Time and space considerations forbid that I interact with Barr's final two chapters: I do no more than state his focus of interest in each case. In chapter 6, under the title "The Bible as Political Document" (first published in *BJRL*), Barr surveys a variety of social and political organizations that have professed to base themselves on the authority of some part or other of the Bible (usually the Old Testament) and considers to what extent the alleged dependency is justified as measured "against the actual intentions of that particular stratum of the Bible" (p. 91). And finally, in his last chapter, Barr considers "The Bible as a Document of Believing Communities."

I. Howard Marshall, *Biblical Inspiration*

The third book comes from the prolific pen of the professor of New Testament exegesis at the University of Aberdeen. It is an expanded form of two lectures first delivered at Wycliffe Hall, an Anglican ministerial training college in Oxford. It is neither a narrowly focused study of the meaning of "inspiration" nor a collection of loosely related articles on the Bible, but a sweeping survey of what might be called the doctrine of the Bible—i.e., the nature of biblical revelation, the extent and significance of the Bible's truth claims, the appropriateness of categories like "inerrancy," some of the hermeneutical problems associated with its interpretation and application, and reflections on the nature of its authority. The style is chatty and winsome, designed for the reader with little technical background. With one exception, the book breaks no new ground but serves as a useful introduction to the author's interpretation of the current debate. It is by far the most conservative of the three books reviewed in this article.

Content of Chapter 1
Marshall winningly points out that books on this topic are inflammatory:

> Should I so much as deviate to the left and suggest that not all that Scripture says is true in the strictest sense of that term, I shall come under strong criticism and possibly even excommunication from the right, not simply for saying so, but for saying so as a confessed evangelical; and should I throw in my lot unreservedly with my colleagues on the right, I shall undoubtedly suffer at the hands of my colleagues on the left, who will doubt not only any claim I dare make to be a biblical scholar but also my sanity. (p. 7)

But he presses on valiantly anyway—and after a brief "Introduction" that raises questions in the same order by which the chapters of the book will answer them, he begins his first chapter under the question, "What does the Bible say about itself?" These few pages provide a broad survey, drawing attention to instances of divine dictation, the high status ascribed to the Old Testament by Jesus and by New Testament writers, brief treatment of crucial passages such as 2 Timothy 3:16 and 2 Peter 1:20–21, mention of the self-conscious authority of the New Testament writers, the problem of the canon, and the like. But it leaves out an enormous amount of material from consideration.[29] Some of the omissions, as we shall see, turn out to be significant.

Content and Critique of Chapter 2

The second chapter answers the question, "What do we mean by 'inspiration'?" Marshall briefly surveys and criticizes several inadequate theories: that inspiration entails simple dictation; that it means no more than that the biblical writers eloquently expressed their own religious insight; that it means the Bible is nothing but witness to revelation whose locus is exclusively event; and the varied models developed by Karl Barth, Paul Achtemeier, and William Abraham (in the first book reviewed in this article). In each case discussion is never more than a few paragraphs long and rarely mentions any of the major literature in the field, but the potted critiques are accurate, fair, and courteous. Marshall himself opts for the traditional evangelical "concursive action of the Spirit" theory, though he rejects as inadequate and misleading analogies drawn between the Bible and Jesus, both in some sense "Word of God," both in some sense simultaneously divine and human. Probably the weakest part of the chapter is the brief foray into epistemology at the end, a foray that reappears at several points in the book. Marshall could benefit by reading recent contributions by J. A. Passmore and George I. Mavrodes.[30]

Content and Critique of Chapter 3

The third and longest chapter answers the question, "What are the results of inspiration?" Here Marshall is his most innovative. He begins by quoting the definitions of *infallibility* and *inerrancy* in "The Chicago Statement on Biblical Inerrancy." Building on his foray into epistemology, he observes that acceptance of the Bible as the inspired word of God is a matter of faith and concludes therefore that "the claim that what the Bible says is true cannot be anything else than a statement of faith, which may or may not be ultimately justified" (p. 51). This and several similar statements in the book are almost meaningless because faith is not discussed or defined, but they strike me as naive about the nature of theological method[31] in a context that cries out for some reflection on the relations among truth, historical method, and faith.

The burden of this chapter, however, lies elsewhere. Marshall sets up a model contrasting Christians who begin with the actual characteristics of the Bible and

---

[29]See especially the work by Grudem that covers roughly the same territory but far more comprehensively (cf. n. 20, *supra*).

[30]J. A. Passmore, "The Objectivity of History," in *Philosophical Analysis and History*, ed. W. H. Dray (New York: Harper, 1966), 75–94; G. I. Mavrodes, *Belief in God: A Study in the Epistemology of Religion* (New York: Random House, 1970). The problem is related also to questions of theory formation and justification (see n. 18, *supra*).

[31]See nn. 18, 29.

who therefore conclude that inerrancy is an indefensible position, with those who hold to inerrancy and/or infallibility based largely on the proposition that it is God who cannot lie who stands behind this book. This classification is parallel to the inductivist/deductivist classification advanced by Beegle and others and already discussed in this article. Unfortunately Marshall, like Abraham, does not interact with the literature on this problem and therefore to some extent erects a straw man. Marshall at this point attempts to sidestep the problem by focusing on the question of what God actually wished to do by his concursive inspiration of Scripture. "The purpose of God in the composition of the Scriptures was to guide people to salvation and the associated way of life. . . . We may therefore suggest that 'infallible' means that the Bible is entirely trustworthy for the purposes for which God inspired it" (p. 53). Marshall argues that this analysis has the effect of shifting the focus away from the truth of the Bible to its adequacy for what God intends it to do. This step "opens up the possibility of a fresh approach to the Bible which may prove to be illuminating" (p. 53).

Pressing on with this fresh approach, Marshall points out that the true/false disjunction is applicable only to "propositions which convey factual information" (p. 56). A command such as "Take away the stone" (John 11:39) is neither true nor false. The proposition that Jesus said it may be labeled true or false, but the imperative itself is not amenable to this classification. The same is true of fictional narratives like parables, of much of the advice from Job's friends (cf. Job 42:7), and of much more. If all we mean by saying "Leviticus 11 is true" is that it is a true record of what God said to the Israelites, the statement is "somewhat banal" (p. 58) because the commands in that chapter are no longer directly relevant to us as Christians.

Even of statements that may legitimately be labeled true or false we must recognize, Marshall argues, how many are completely untestable, and therefore we must concede that the true/false category is sometimes unhelpful. Moreover, even the Chicago Statement is forced to point out that the proposition "Scripture is inerrant" must not be taken "in the sense of being absolutely precise by modern standards, but in the sense of making good its claims and achieving that measure of focused truth at which its authors aimed." Marshall concludes:

> Here it is admitted that certain phenomena, which might well be regarded as errors and contradictions, must not be counted as such. The reason for making this concession is that no amount of exegetical ingenuity can avoid recognizing the presence of such phenomena in the Bible. The significant point is that, once this has been admitted, then it has been implicitly agreed

that the definition of the kind of truth to be found in the Bible is dependent upon biblical interpretation of the difficult passages and cannot be drawn simply from statements in the Bible about its own nature. (p. 61)

So Marshall turns to an examination of some of these difficult biblical phenomena. The least that can be said for this approach is that it is methodologically superior to that of Abraham: at least we come down to hard cases. First Marshall introduces examples of "historical approximation" and other imprecision—condensation, reporting of general content and not actual words, and the like. He then turns to the manifest presence of interpretation of historical events in the biblical texts. For example, King Omri in 1 Kings 16 is dismissed as an evil man, without drawing attention to facts known by us from nonbiblical sources—Omri's great power, administrative genius, and international reputation. In these kinds of situations, Marshall suggests, such severe restraints are to be placed on the term *inerrancy* that its usefulness must be called into question. He then turns to a third kind of phenomenon, exemplified by Luke's ordering of Theudas and Judas (Acts 5:36–37) compared with that in Josephus. Marshall rejects as implausible suggestions that Josephus was the one who got it wrong or that the two authors were referring to different rebels. This is an instance, he charges, where regrettably the strict inerrantist retreats into his invulnerable position by holding to historical implausibilities. His problem, Marshall suggests, is that he has not permitted his doctrine of Scripture to be adequately informed by the phenomena of Scripture. If we adopt this more responsible course, then "our understanding of the truth of the Bible must allow" for "a genuine historical mistake . . . and other mistakes" (pp. 64–65). We must permit the phenomena of Scripture to determine our doctrine of Scripture. This should not alarm us unduly, Marshall suggests, for there are far more uncertainties about the Bible that are generated by textual variants, difficulties in interpretation, and problems of discerning appropriate application. Marshall asks: "[If] God's purposes did not include the provision of a guaranteed text, a guaranteed interpretation and a guaranteed application for today, what right have we to assume that he gave an original text that was guaranteed to be utterly precise?" (p. 69). And, finally, Marshall points out that the domino theory—if inerrancy falls, orthodoxy falls—is not a logically rigorous position. In any case, inerrancy is scarcely a guarantor of orthodoxy since many cultists are inerrantists. The upshot of the chapter is that Marshall thinks the term *inerrancy* should be abandoned because it "needs so much qualification, even by its defenders, that it is in danger of dying the death of a thousand qualifications. The term 'infallible' in the sense of 'entirely trustworthy' is undoubtedly preferable" (p. 72).

The issues are important enough to the readers of this journal that a measured response, however preliminary, may not be entirely out of place. First, although it is important to ask what God wished to accomplish by his concursive inspiration of the Scriptures, it does not follow that Marshall's formulation of that purpose ("to guide people to salvation and the associated way of life") justifies his shift in focus from the truth of the Bible to its adequacy for what God intends to do. One might equally argue that the purpose of Christ's coming was "to guide people to salvation and the associated way of life," but that does not render irrelevant questions about Christ's truthfulness nor sanction a corresponding shift in focus from the nature of Christ's truthfulness to the adequacy of his performance. The inherent instability of this position is perhaps underscored when we remember that Abraham argues that if the concursive theory is correct, it is hard to see how inerrancy does not follow—which is why Abraham rejects the concursive theory. Marshall accepts the validity of the concursive theory but seeks to sidestep the implications by shifting the focus from the truthfulness of the resulting text to the purpose of the resulting text. But one cannot legitimately duck a question in one category by introducing a question in another category. Moreover, it is not altogether clear that Marshall's formulation of the purpose of Scripture is fair to the issue at hand. One might have suggested with equal propriety that the purpose of Scripture as God inspired it is to bring glory to himself, or that its purpose is to explain truthfully God's plan of redemption to a fallen race in order to bring many sons to glory. Of these two suggested formulations of Scripture's purpose, the latter reintroduces the question of truth. All three of these formulations—Marshall's suggestion and my two—are biblically and theologically defensible and mutually complementary. It follows therefore that Marshall's formulation not only jumps categories in order to sidestep the truth question but does so by a questionable reductionism even of the purpose of Scripture.

Second, Marshall is certainly right to insist that the true/false disjunction is applicable only to statements of fact, but that rather misses the point. Very few one-word summaries of a Christian doctrine turn on a merely lexical unpacking of the term (e.g., doctrine of the church, doctrine of last things, doctrine of reconciliation, even doctrine of God). If therefore Marshall wants to dismiss the term *inerrancy* as inappropriate to the phenomena, he must analyze the term as a theological construct—the "doctrine of inerrancy," if you will—as handled by its best exponents (for no position is ever legitimately overthrown by exposing the weaknesses of its sloppiest defenders). Consider, then, the generally rigorous essay by Paul Feinberg on "The Meaning of Inerrancy" (to which, regrettably,

Marshall does not refer),[32] which offers the following as a proposed theological summary: "Inerrancy means that, when all facts are known, the Scriptures in their original autographs and properly interpreted will be shown to be wholly true in everything that they affirm, whether that has to do with doctrine or morality or with social, physical, or life sciences." Now I am aware of what phrases like "when all facts are known" and "in their original autographs" conjure up for some people, but such matters have been treated with some rigor not only by Feinberg but by many others. Carl Henry's *magnum opus*, for instance, receives no consideration at all in any of these three books.[33] But my main point here is that Marshall has failed to wrestle with inerrancy as a theological construct.

Third, even if inerrancy is restricted to its lexical meaning rather than allowed to stand for a theological construct and therefore is applicable only to statements, it is remarkable that it is a historical statement, a statement of fact (i.e., re Theudas and Judas) that Marshall advances as an instance where the Bible is not telling the truth. This kind of problem passage, however, cannot legitimately be lumped together with questions of precision or selective reporting. The latter is a necessary corollary of human finitude. Questions of precision are largely definitional and contextually delimited in some way. For instance, if I say I live about 15 miles from work, I speak the truth. If I say 16 miles, I also speak the truth, for the odometer testifies to 15.6, which is closer to 16 than 15. If I say 15.6, I am still speaking truth—even though if measured with an accurate laser in straight-line distance, 15.6 would be much too high—for in this case the context of conversation intimates driving or biking or train distance ("distance from work"), not straight-line distance. I would, however, be saying something untrue if I said I lived 15.02 miles from work, for this suggests a precision to the second decimal place when precision of that order would come out closer to 15.65. Thus the contextual parameters delimit the degree of precision expected. The book of 1 Kings does not pretend to give a pagan assessment of Omri: it openly assesses him on the basis of his idolatry and of his contribution to the seduction of Israel. Thus it would not be possible to begin to construct a comprehensive, modern biography of Omri from the slant offered by 1 Kings, but it is hard to see how truth has been compromised. A person or text may speak truly without speaking exhaustively, the more so when there are contextual clues as to the focus and perspective being adopted. (Fifty billion years into eternity, if I may speak of eternity in the categories of time, the assessment of Omri provided by 1 Kings will seem much more relevant than the assessment provided by his pagan neighbors anyway.) Similar judgments could

---

[32]See n. 18.

[33]C. F. H. Henry, *God, Revelation and Authority*, 6 vols. (Waco, TX: Word, 1976–1983).

be made about the range of reportage in the Gospels. But the Theudas/Judas listing belongs to quite a separate camp. Here there is no question of mere precision, but of truth versus error. The same confusion of category recurs throughout Marshall's book (e.g., p. 122).

Fourth, if at this point we are reminded that Luke's chief point is not to sort out which rebel came first but to draw attention to the transience of their rebellion, we are nevertheless still moving in a framework of the truth/error or true/false disjunction, not in the framework of mere precision. And matters that fall into the true/false classification were precisely the ones that were meant to be safeguarded by those who used the word *infallibility* thirty or forty years ago. But theological pressure from the left (I mean no insult or hurt) gradually restricted the word *infallible* to "matters of faith and practice" or to "what God intended to achieve," conceived in exclusively salvific categories. This development is one of the factors that has prompted some evangelical scholars to prefer the term *inerrancy*. They hope thereby to regain what has been lost by the shunt associated with *infallibility*. What is remarkable is that Marshall dislikes the word *inerrancy* and treats it as a purely lexical construct, while adhering to the term *infallibility* and treating it as a theological construct of recent vintage. If both terms are treated on a lexical basis alone, he would have equal problems with both (e.g., can a command be judged infallible any more easily than inerrant?), but if both terms are treated as theological constructs, it would quickly be discovered that the best theological construction on inerrancy is virtually indistinguishable from the best theological older construction on infallibility. It would then be obvious that those who champion the term *inerrancy* are not the theological innovators but merely the lexical innovators. And even this is to concede too much, for one can find countless examples of theologians insisting the Scriptures are without error—theologians going back all the way to the Fathers. Thus even the lexical "innovation," if it can be called that at all, is in the shift from *infallible* to *inerrant* as the focus of debate within evangelical circles now that the former term has become a little more slippery than it once was. This point is extraordinarily important for, as we have seen, there has arisen a revisionist historiography that tries to prove that the "inerrancy" view is historically innovative and therefore of dubious theological pedigree. So far as I am able to judge, the facts are quite otherwise.[34]

Fifth, for two reasons I am mildly surprised that Marshall makes so much of the Theudas/Judas passage. The first is that his judgments on possible solutions are offered without defense. "It could be argued," he writes, "that Josephus got his dates wrong (the view taken by the Jerusalem Bible). This, however, is very

---

[34]See n. 15.

unlikely" (p. 63). Why is it so unlikely? Marshall has done more than most schol-ars to show how reliable Luke is where he can be tested, and all agree that Josephus sometimes gets his facts wrong. And this is only one of two or three possible solu-tions. These reflections do not constitute a blind appeal to the merely possible in order to preserve an ill-founded doctrine. Rather, it is a responsible weigh-ing of probabilities that includes not only the data in this particular instance but the massive evidence that supports the (older) "infallibility" construct—i.e., the "inerrancy" construct. Part of the problem, again, is a failure to come to grips with the way any theological or scientific theory is formed. Second, I am surprised that for such an important step in his argument Marshall did not try to find a clear-cut, unambiguous example of what he calls "historical mistakes." Is this the worst that the classic doctrine of Scripture has to fear?

Sixth, although it is true that textual variants, difficulties in interpretation, and problems of discerning appropriate application all engender uncertainties of various kinds, Marshall's conclusion ("what right have we to assume that [God] gave an original text that was utterly precise?") can scarcely be said to follow, for: (1) The words "utterly precise" are probably a slip, for Marshall himself points out that inerrantists do not insist on utter precision. (2) But it is a slip of some significance, for it is again appealing to the "precision" category to allow through a historical error—i.e., something contrary to fact. If Marshall for "utterly precise" were to substitute the words "without historical error," he might perceive that his rhetorical question is a *non sequitur*. (3) But more important, the Scriptures nowhere encourage us to think there will not be textual variants, or that its ma-terial will be unambiguously clear, or that no problems of application will ever arise. But the Scriptures do encourage its readers to hold that all it says is reliable and true, along the lines of the theological construct I have sketched in.

There is far more biblical evidence for the classic view than is marshaled in this book. One of the interesting kinds of evidence not touched by Marshall is the range of historical tidbits from the Old Testament picked up by New Testament writers in order to make a point—e.g., Jacob gave a field to Joseph (John 4:5), Elijah was sent to the widow of Zarephath (Luke 4:25–26), Rahab received spies and sent them out another way (James 2:25), the Queen of the South came to hear Solomon (Matt. 12:42)—to mention only four of scores of examples. Never is there the faintest suggestion that previous Scripture gets its historically insignifi-cant details wrong. Much more evidence of many kinds could be adduced. And when it is amassed and contemplated, there is very good reason for thinking that historical difficulties (and of course there are some very tough ones) should not be treated exactly like textual variants. God has not declared himself on textual variants, but he has declared himself on the truthfulness of his Word.

Seventh, it is true that to interpret the proposition "Leviticus 11 is true" to mean no more than that Leviticus 11 is a true record of what God said to the Israelites at the time is not very satisfying. But even so, it may be of more importance than Marshall suggests. If someone denies that Leviticus 11 is true in that sense, it may be because he believes God cannot communicate propositionally, or because he so reconstructs the history of Israel that he does not believe the law was largely given before the advent of all the early prophets, or for several other reasons. Whatever the cause, the effect is to say something rather substantial about the veracity of Scripture, about God, and/or about Scripture's broad presentation of Israel's history. The order of major revelatory appointments in the Old Testament is not immaterial to the Bible as a whole, or even to the gospel itself (as Paul makes clear in Galatians 3).

Eighth, Marshall jumps categories yet again when he asks the question, "True for whom?" (p. 57). In Leviticus and Deuteronomy we find legislation distinguishing between clean and unclean foods, legislation that was binding on the Israelites of the time. But the New Testament seems to overthrow these laws (Mark 7:19; Acts 10:45). Thus the laws are not "true" for us as Christians today—i.e., they are not valid for us. This is the sort of argument that James D. G. Dunn makes much of in his recent pair of articles in the *Churchman*.[35] Interestingly, this criticism of his opponent's viewpoint is internally inconsistent with Marshall's earlier insistence that "truth" is inapplicable to imperatives. This new criticism is achieved by applying "true" to imperatives after all, but by taking it to mean "valid" or "currently legally binding" and then asking, "For whom?" I know no evangelical scholar who thinks every piece of legislation or every imperative is binding on all men everywhere in every age. And the thoughtful inerrantist has long since wrestled with problems of development and organic growth in redemptive history, struggling to understand the unity of the Bible in a broad framework that allows for prophecy and fulfillment, types, abrogation, and/or supersession of certain statutes and covenants in the light of fresh revelation, and much more. This is not to say there is widespread agreement on all these difficult matters, but it is to say that conservative scholars have thought about these matters a great deal, and it does them an injustice to raise a rather elementary legal change and introduce it as if it were a major obstacle to their view of Scripture. The fact of the matter is that the problem raised is irrelevant to the inerrantist's view of Scripture, and therefore to raise it in this context betrays either a substantial ignorance of historical theology

---

[35]J. D. G. Dunn, "The Authority of Scripture According to Scripture," *Chm* 96 (1982): 104–22, 201–25.

or a considerable failure to understand what the traditional doctrine of Scripture means. Moreover, if it were taken as a serious objection against inerrancy it could equally be posed as a serious objection against the (modern) form of infallibility that Marshall defends: We might ask, not "True for whom?" but "Infallible revelation of God's purposes for whom?"—and use the same example.

Ninth, Marshall is entirely right to point out that there is no logically cogent demonstration that the domino theory inevitably triumphs. Indeed there are some interesting counter-examples. Nevertheless, one might have expected an evenhanded treatment of these matters. We would then be reminded how often individuals and even denominations make shipwreck of their faith once the traditional view of Scripture is lost—if not in the first generation, then often in the second—even if this is not the inevitable result. This alone of course would not be an adequate reason for holding to the high view of Scripture that I am advancing: it is worth holding only if it is true. Similarly, although inerrancy does not guarantee orthodoxy, neither does, say, a high christology: One might be heterodox in other areas, or doctrinally orthodox but utterly callous and loveless. But that is scarcely an argument against orthodox christology or against orthodox views of Scripture.

What Marshall rightly says in this chapter, however—and it is important for his more conservative brothers to hear it—is that in practice his position is much closer to that of the inerrantist than it is to any other. This is a debate among brothers, among friends, among Christians, among those whose positions are close. I think Marshall's position is wrong, and I would go further and say that despite the immense good his books and learning have been to the church, I fear that on this issue he may do some damage. But we had better learn from one another, sharpening and correcting our own understanding of the Word of God, maintaining cool hands and warm hearts and avoiding hot heads and cold hearts.

Content and Critique of Chapter 4
The fourth chapter seeks to answer the question, "How are we to study the Bible?" Marshall begins by drawing sketches of the most antithetical positions: the mindless anti-intellectualism of one extreme and the ruthless antisupernaturalism of the other. He then turns to the interpretation of 1 Corinthians 16:22 as a test case and thoughtfully reasons his way through the problems. On the one hand, critical work is necessary even to produce translations, lexica, and dictionaries; on the other, the critical theories of Bousset about the genesis of "Lord" as applied to Jesus reflect poor historiography and unself-critical enslavement to reductionistic presuppositions.

Marshall proceeds to set up three models of biblical interpretation. The first he labels the "dogmatic approach." He criticizes it for thinking itself above historical, source-critical, and other questions, and rightly shows that such a position is in fact impossible: Every interpretation involves some "critical" judgments. The second approach is the "historical-critical method," which he identifies with the radical philosophical materialism and frankly atheistic historiographical presuppositions of Ernst Troeltsch, and which he therefore rejects, primarily because of its working presuppositions. But although this method "has failed to give a satisfying explanation of the Bible" (p. 85) —at which point I asked myself, "Satisfying to whom?" and wondered if satisfaction is a more important criterion than truth, and decided I was being too critical of what is doubtless a charitable scholarly euphemism—Marshall rightly points out that one "must not condemn all its works out of hand, since undoubtedly much valuable work has been done by proponents of it, and we would be the poorer without what has been done" (p. 85). True enough, and perhaps Marshall felt the need to say something like this because the chapter was "written with those readers especially in mind who are suspicious of biblical study because of the dangers which they see in it" (p. 93). I would have thought, however, that evenhandedness would have pointed out that although the church would have been poorer without much of this study, it would also have been considerably richer without much of it.

The third model, the *via media* Marshall himself prefers, is the "grammatico-historical method," an expression that is simply meant "to indicate that biblical study involves both linguistic and historical study" (p. 36). Using these three models Marshall returns to 1 Corinthians 16:22 and suggests how each approach might tackle the text.

The last four pages of the chapter then seek to relate these questions (to do with how the Bible is to be studied) with the concerns of the previous chapter. To focus his remarks Marshall points out that John refers to passages from Isaiah 6 and 53 as both being spoken by Isaiah (John 12:38–41), even though most scholars contend our "Isaiah" is a composite. One group will say that if John says Isaiah said it, that settles it. A second group will argue that John believed Isaiah wrote it but was wrong. A third will support the view that John was writing *ad hominem* and not intending to make a statement about the authorship of Isaiah one way or the other. Marshall argues that "if the weight of the evidence favors multiple authorship" (p. 90) then we are confined to one of the last two options. His next remarks are crucial:

The point is that it is dangerous to adopt a view of the Bible which rules out the findings of honest, unbiased study. To tread the path between the Scylla of suspending judgment on critical issues and the Charybdis of qualifying one's doctrine of the entire trustworthiness of Scripture is not easy. There is no simple formula which will enable us to solve all our difficulties. Faith is never free from risk or from the duties of self-examination and self-correction. If, however, we are prepared to take this attitude, then we may with good conscience defend ourselves against the objection that methods of biblical criticism which I have discussed are cunningly contrived to avoid any possibility of our doctrine of Scripture being disrupted by contradictory or erroneous teaching. . . . Nothing I have discovered in close study of the New Testament over a quarter of a century has caused me to have any serious doubts about its entire trustworthiness for the purposes for which God has given it; I cannot claim that I have studied the Old Testament so closely. (p. 91)

Several observations may extend the discussion a little further. First, Marshall's three models of approaches to biblical interpretation are painfully simplistic. Worse, they (doubtless unwittingly) manipulate the incautious reader into thinking there are dodos and twits on the right, apostates and rebels on the left, and reasonable people who agree with Marshall in the middle. I have no quarrel with Marshall's approach to 1 Corinthians 16:22, but surely there are many scholars who associate themselves with the historical-critical method while distancing themselves from Troeltsch's skepticism, and others who would align themselves with the grammatico-historical method while achieving conclusions considerably more radical, or more conservative, than Marshall's. The spectrum of approaches to biblical interpretation cannot be labeled so neatly.

Second, "the findings of honest, unbiased study" is a pleasant-sounding phrase that masks the astonishing faddishness of a substantial amount of biblical study. To take one example, most European university experts on John, writing before Strauss's *Das Leben Jesu*, ascribed to the Fourth Gospel a greater degree of historical reliability than they accorded the Synoptics, largely on the grounds that (1) John reports no exorcisms and (2) his reported miracles are called "signs" and frequently point toward discourses (which were judged less offensive to the post-Enlightenment mind than were miracles). After Strauss the tide turned and John was given lower marks for historical reliability, largely on the grounds that his christology was the highest and therefore the latest and least reliable. Several more shifts in the interpretation of the Gospel of John have of course taken place since then. At which point, then, may we profitably speak of "the findings of honest, unbiased study" in this regard?

But lest I be misunderstood, I insist that I am not trying to depreciate scholarly study or force it to bend the knee to undefended dogmatic considerations. I am arguing that scholarly results (conceived as those that are well justified and enduring) and the current consensus of scholars are not necessarily the same thing. Scientists remind us how difficult it is for them to develop, justify, and sustain a theory, even though they often have the great advantage of working in an experimental field that enables them to test their conclusions in ways unavailable to biblical scholars. Worse, biblical scholars (as Northrop Frye keeps pointing out) frequently resort to methods and judgments that are ruled inadmissible even in other literary fields. The entire area of biblical studies is ripe for some far-reaching methodological analysis. Marshall does not discuss the nature of the argumentation that leads many scholars to adopt, say, a theory of multiple authorship of Isaiah. Of course in a book of this nature he could scarcely be expected to do so. But that means his appeal is to little more than current majority scholarly opinion, which would, in its "findings of honest, unbiased study," equally reject even Marshall's brand of bibliography, not to mention matters even more central to Christian life and thought. We obviously need a more profound analysis than we are here offered.

Third, although Marshall's approach may preserve him from the criticism that conservatives use the tools of biblical criticism in a cunningly contrived way to avoid any possibility of disrupting their doctrine of Scripture, I am not sure he has considered the cost. Could it be that he has elevated literary tools that are not as objective as they are purported to be above the Scriptures, which on so many grounds rightly lay claim to a far greater authority? Might we not with equal propriety argue that many scholars abuse the critical and literary tools at their disposal by using them in a cunningly contrived way to make it impossible for them to come to the conclusion that the Scriptures are indeed by the concursive action of the Spirit nothing less than the words of God? In short, perhaps conservatives have been on the defensive for too long.

Fourth, I wonder how Marshall would handle a really different case of ascription, like that in Matthew 22:41–46 par. Here it is impossible to argue that the ascription of Psalm 110 to David is purely *ad hominem*, since the cogency of Jesus' argument depends on the correctness of that ascription. One wonders if this may have some bearing on how we judge other such remarks of Jesus as reported by the Evangelists.

And fifth, if Marshall has discovered nothing to have caused him serious doubts about the New Testament's "entire trustworthiness for the purposes for which God has given it," probably most New Testament scholars could say the same thing, if they interpreted "for the purposes for which God has given it" in an appropriate fashion. The formula does not seem very discriminating. In any case, testimonies of this sort are useful encouragements to those who know and trust the speaker but are of strictly limited usefulness when placed in the context of broader debate. I could testify equally, though obviously from the vantage point of fewer years of experience and less skill than Marshall can command, that I have not found anything contrary to the doctrine of infallibility (classically conceived). Such testimony is scarcely determinative, for other scholars have reached quite different conclusions. And that raises some formidable questions in epistemology not broached by this book. But what scholar is likely to testify that he has found examples of texts that run absolutely counter to his conclusions?

Content and Critique of Chapter 5

In his fifth chapter Marshall asks, "How are we to interpret the Bible?" The title does not very clearly distinguish the contents of this chapter from those of the last, but Marshall's aim here is to consider issues of exposition and application rather than exegesis proper. He offers a potted history of medieval interpretation and praises the Reformers for their return to the principle "that the exposition of the Bible must be based on its exegesis" (p. 97).

Most of the principles Marshall enunciates or hints at are in themselves elementary and not particularly contentious. We must be aware of phenomenological language, learn to identify commandments we must obey by observing their links with central biblical themes, and so forth. One or two of Marshall's examples, however, are problematic. For instance, he points out that Christians do not normally follow the Old Testament food laws, regarding them as something belonging to a past time (p. 100), and on this basis he wonders if it might be reasonable to jettison belief in the existence of demons:

> The New Testament certainly teaches that the demons may be conquered by the power of God, so that we do not need fear them, but the reality of demons is not denied. Is belief in the existence of demons and the like part of the package which we accept when we become Christian believers? Some Christians would want to insist that belief in Jesus Christ as the Son of God does not necessarily involve belief in demons as well. (p. 101)

Does not this line of reasoning confuse inner-canonical development with the bias against the supernatural prevalent in the West? Believers would not be free from the Old Testament's food laws if they did not hold that the coming and teaching of Jesus Messiah fulfilled certain Old Testament patterns and introduced a later and fuller revelation of God's will, introducing a new covenant that in measure supersedes the old. What new revelation frees us from holding to the reality of demons?

Of course one might argue that language about demons is merely phenomenological and should therefore not be taken as any more normative or ontologically descriptive than something like "the sun rises." But in that case it is not parallel to the question of foods prohibited under the Mosaic code, for no one argues that those prohibitions were mere instances of phenomenological language. Marshall for his part argues that some of the debates about the relevance of any particular command can be resolved by determining how central and persistent a theme is in biblical thought. For this reason he defends the truth and centrality to Christian thought of the notion of sacrifice and death as the foundation of forgiveness— e.g., in a passage like Hebrews 9:22 ("without the shedding of blood there is no forgiveness"). But interestingly enough he never applies this criterion to demons and devils. He would have found a great deal of material to contend with: Genesis 3, Job, parts of Daniel, crucial passages such as Matthew 12:28, much in Jesus' ministry, many texts in Paul, and more. But instead he makes appeal to the modern mind: "The important thing is that in the modern world many thinkers have expressed their belief in the existence of an evil power or influence in the universe which is greater than the individual evil wills of mankind: call it 'demonic' if you will" (p. 109). Marshall insists he is not denying "the *possibility* of such powers affecting individuals in the way described in the Gospels" (p. 110; italics mine), but this does not seem very reassuring. The rather personal demons of the Bible have become impersonal powers or influences, and statements of fact have become mere possibilities. In any case the Gospels do not present all illness and madness as the work of demons any more than they present it all as the immediate result of specific sin. But they do present some such cases as the direct result of one or the other of these two potential causes. I know many African believers, lay people and scholars alike, who would take Marshall's conclusions to be an index of unwitting but hopeless enslavement to Western culture, skepticism, and the inroads of philosophical materialism. My own limited experience in the area is too grim and unpleasant for me to want to write about it. But however such private judgments are assessed, the identification of demons with modern speculation about the structures of evil or macro-evil or cosmic evil is exegetically tenuous at best.[36]

The most disappointing part of this chapter is Marshall's reflection on his own procedure, which he identifies with "seeking a canon within the canon" (p. 110):

> For in practice all of us do work with a canon within the canon, drawing our main teaching from some books and passages and ignoring others. . . . It must, however, not be misused. It is one thing to use the principle to disqualify certain parts of the Bible as Scripture and effectively to reject them as Scripture; that way is not open to us. It is another thing to use the principle to identify the central message of the Bible and to assess the place of the various areas of the Bible in relation to it. (p. 111)

But the "canon within the canon" rubric has normally been used to refer to those procedures that so elevate and interpret certain parts of the Bible that other parts of the Bible lose all their authority—i.e., they effectively become non-canonical. Marshall reminds us of Luther's views on James, but when Luther labeled James "a right strawy epistle," he was still uncertain about the canonical status of James. But the expression is not usefully applied to those who lay more stress on some parts of the Bible than others as they attempt to synthesize their theology, for as long as they stand under the authority of the entire canon, there remains the possibility of self-correction, of correction by remonstration, or of debate based on an appeal to a common canon. If, however, one defends the retreat to "a canon within the canon" in the ordinary sense of that expression, it is possible to make the Bible say almost anything one wants. And in that sense, not only do the omitted bits lose their canonical status, but also the Bible as a whole can no longer meaningfully be thought of as a canon. The operative canon or rule or measure is the individual interpreter.

Marshall sees this danger, of course, and warns against it in the passage just cited. But because he extends the "canon within the canon" terminology to cover the procedures of those who are synthesizing their theology while unhesitatingly standing under the authority of the canon, he confuses quite different principles. What exactly does he mean by saying that we may identify the central message of the Bible and "assess the place of the various areas of the Bible in relation to it"? Does he mean that we may learn how to fit all the parts into the whole and make

---

[36]Cf. especially P. T. O'Brien, "Principalities and Powers," in *Biblical Interpretation and the Church: Text and Context*, ed. D. A. Carson (Exeter: Paternoster, forthcoming).

intelligent choices about which themes are more central—a procedure that still bows to the authority of the entire canon? Or does he mean that once we have identified the central themes, other parts may be written off without loss as errant or irrelevant to the modern setting—a procedure that is methodologically quite different from the other and in fact removes the locus of authority from Scripture as canon and transfers it to our more subjective choices about what is central in the Bible?

Marshall's discussion seems at this point to extend not only to the niceties of historical detail but to questions about the limits of Scripture's authority. This becomes explicit in the last chapter, where, after a helpful review of his arguments up to that point, he asks one last question: "What are we to do with the Bible?"—a way of introducing his "examination of the theme of 'authority'" (p. 118).

Marshall begins by helpfully distinguishing between authority based on force and authority based on truth, classifying the Bible in the latter category. But the Bible's authority is a derived authority; God alone has supreme authority. The Bible's authority is limited, Marshall suggests, by two factors: (1) the range of its topics: it is authoritative in matters of Christian faith and practice, not on medieval European history or polymer chemistry; and (2) its truthfulness: "Its authority depends not only on the truth of its statements (where they can be tested) but also on the authority of its writers as men inspired by God" (p. 120). The first is in one sense clearly right: the Bible cannot conceivably be regarded as an authoritative text on polymer chemistry or quantum mechanics. But the wording is slippery: I would prefer to say that the Bible is authoritative in every area with which it deals—whether Christian gospel or history or anything else. This way of putting things still needs qualification, for by "an authoritative text on quantum mechanics" we normally mean a work on quantum mechanics that is not only true but reasonably comprehensive, whereas an affirmation that the Bible is authoritative on all with which it deals says only that the Bible always speaks truth, not that it is broadly comprehensive on all it touches. For instance, the Bible deals with Pilate, and what it says about him (I would argue) is true, but the Bible does not give us a comprehensive treatment of Pilate. In that sense the Bible is not "an authoritative text" on Pilate.

We are thus driven to Marshall's second factor: the Bible's truthfulness. Here he returns to his earlier suggestion that the Bible may include historical mistakes. Since authority depends on truth, it follows that the Bible is not authoritative where it errs on such details. Marshall rhetorically asks, "May it not be the case that we are in danger of ascribing supreme authority to all that the Bible says instead of recognizing that it contains a mixture of material in different grades of authority?" (p. 122). His answer is "that we cannot suspend our mental and moral faculties" (p. 122). I agree with this bold statement, but wonder if Marshall really means not that we cannot suspend our mental and moral faculties but that we cannot submit our mental and moral faculties to the Bible's truth claims. If so, the reason is presumably because he finds insuperable difficulties. In that case, however, the debate must return to the broader questions of evidence and argumentation with which this book does not deal. But as matters stand, despite Marshall's laudable attempts to insist that the Bible is true and authoritative on the subject of Christian faith and practice, it is not entirely clear how he would respond to someone who holds that his or her "mental and moral faculties" require abandoning as nonessential or peripheral some element of Christian faith and practice that Marshall himself would defend. Despite a certain plausibility in Marshall's argument, one comes away with the uneasy suspicion that the ultimate measure of Christian truth and life is not what God chooses to reveal, but what man chooses to accept as true. That is not what Marshall is trying to say, of course, but I do not yet see how he can avoid this conclusion.

Marshall is always worth reading, and his tone is irenic throughout. There is very little trace of condescension toward those who are more conservative in their assessments than he—a common fault in this species of literature. But this is not Marshall's best work. I came away from his book with increased confidence that the traditional doctrine of Scripture espoused by evangelicals has very strong credentials indeed—and I doubt if that was what Marshall intended to achieve.

7

Three More Books on the Bible:
A Critical Review

John Webster, *Holy Scripture: A Dogmatic Sketch*. Cambridge: Cambridge University Press, 2003. 144 pp.

Peter Enns, *Inspiration and Incarnation: Evangelicals and the Problem of the Old Testament*. Grand Rapids: Baker, 2005. 179 pp.

N. T. Wright, *The Last Word: Beyond the Bible Wars to a New Understanding of the Authority of Scripture*. San Francisco: HarperSanFrancisco, 2005. 160 pp.

The last few years have witnessed the publication of several books on the Bible, most of which are in some measure innovative. In addition to the three I shall review in this essay, one cannot overlook Peter Jensen's *The Revelation of God*,[1] which makes the gospel central to his development of the theme of revelation; Timothy Ward's *Word and Supplement: Speech Acts, Biblical Texts, and the Sufficiency of Scripture*,[2] which relies rather heavily—a bit too heavily, in my view—on speech-act theory to address the accumulating problems that have arisen in recent decades over the notion of the sufficiency of Scripture; and Kevin Vanhoozer's *The Drama of Doctrine: A Canonical-Linguistic Approach to Christian Theology*,[3]

Reprint of D. A. Carson, "Three More Books on the Bible: A Critical Review," *TJ* 27 (2006): 1–62. The "more" in the title refers to an essay I wrote with a similar title more than twenty years ago, viz., "Three Books on the Bible: A Critical Review," *JETS* 26 (1983): 337–67. Peter Enns is now a senior fellow of biblical studies with the BioLogos Foundation.
[1]Downers Grove, IL: InterVarsity, 2002.
[2]Oxford: Oxford University Press, 2002.
[3]Louisville: Westminster John Knox, 2005.

which in some ways is as much a book about how to read the Bible—though, remarkably, without any need for a Scripture index—as it is a book about an innovative way to form a systematic theology. Reflecting on these three, which I am not going to discuss, makes me wonder if I should have doubled the length of this essay and titled it "Six More Books on the Bible"—but then I'd have to ask myself why I did not include several other recent contributions.[4] So I have restricted myself to the following three, all of which are interesting, helpful, and problematic—all three in very different ways. In other words, there may be some gain within the compass of one essay in reflecting on three such different books, for the stance each adopts and the innovations each introduces shed light on the other two.

John Webster, *Holy Scripture: A Dogmatic Sketch*

Content

Webster's book, *Holy Scripture: A Dogmatic Sketch*,[5] is the most intellectually demanding of the three. Professor of systematic theology at the University of Aberdeen and the editor of the *International Journal of Systematic Theology*, Webster first presented the four chapters of this book as the *Scottish Journal of Theology* lectures in 2001. The first of the four chapters is the most innovative.

"'Holy Scripture,'" Webster writes, "is a shorthand term for the nature and function of the biblical writings in a set of communicative acts which stretch from God's merciful self-manifestation to the obedient hearing of the community of faith" (p. 5). The definition is important to Webster, not least because it focuses on God himself. Even while his definition speaks of "texts in relation to revelation and reception" (p. 6), the most important thing is that "both the texts and the processes surrounding their reception are subservient to the self-presentation of the triune God, of which the text is a servant and by which readers are accosted, as by a word of supreme dignity, legitimacy and effectiveness" (p. 6). Otherwise put: "Holy Scripture is dogmatically explicated in terms of its role in God's self-communication, that is, the acts of Father, Son and Spirit which establish and

---

[4]To mention only a few: R. C. Sproul, *Scripture Alone: The Evangelical Doctrine* (Phillipsburg, NJ: P&R, 2005); Mark D. Thompson, *A Sure Ground on Which to Stand: The Relation of Authority and Interpretive Method in Luther's Approach to Scripture* (Carlisle: Paternoster, 2004); I. Howard Marshall, *Beyond the Bible: Moving from Scripture to Theology* (Grand Rapids: Baker, 2004); David S. Katz, *God's Last Words: Reading the English Bible from the Reformation to Fundamentalism* (New Haven, CT: Yale University Press, 2004); Robert M. Fowler, Edith Blumhofer, and Fernando F. Segovia, eds., *New Paradigms for Bible Study: The Bible in the Third Millennium* (London: T&T Clark, 2004); David Daniell, *The Bible in English: Its History and Influence* (New Haven, CT: Yale University Press, 2003); Scott McKendrick and Orlaith O'Sullivan, eds., *The Bible as Book: The Transmission of the Greek Text* (London: The British Academy, 2003). Many more could be adduced, not to mention a far greater number of essays.
[5]Cambridge: Cambridge University Press, 2003.

maintain that saving fellowship with humankind in which God makes himself known to us and by us" (p. 8).

Webster's first task in unpacking this definition is "to offer an overall sketch of the doctrine of Holy Scripture by examining three primary concepts: revelation, sanctification and inspiration" (p. 9).

REVELATION

Webster asserts that for a long time the doctrine of revelation has been pummeled and distorted by attempts to formulate it in relation to "dominant modern intellectual and spiritual conventions" (p. 11) and not in relation to the self-disclosing Trinity. Scholars have discussed "revelation" as a feature of a merely "theistic" metaphysical outlook, with scarcely any material reference to such aspects of Christian thought as christology, pneumatology, soteriology, "and—embracing them all—the doctrine of the Trinity" (p. 12). Ironically, while the doctrine of revelation was thus being eviscerated, more and more demands were placed on it, "to a point where they became insupportable" (p. 12). "Perhaps the most significant symptom of this is the way in which Christian theological talk of revelation migrates to the beginning of the dogmatic corpus, and has to take on the job of furnishing the epistemological warrants for Christian claims"(p. 12). "What we do *not* need is a still "more effective defence of the viability of Christian talk about revelation before the tribunal of impartial reason" (p. 13). Rather, we must

call into question the idea that the doctrine of revelation is a tract of Christian teaching with quasi-independent status; this will in turn offer the possibility of an orderly exposition of revelation as a corollary of more primary Christian affirmations about the nature, purposes and saving presence of the triune God. (p. 13)

So Webster provides us with his definition: *"Revelation is the self-presentation of the triune God, the free work of sovereign mercy in which God wills, establishes and perfects saving fellowship with himself in which humankind comes to know, love and fear him above all things"* (p. 13; italics his). Thus the *content* of revelation is "God's own proper reality" (p. 14); the agent is God himself; and it follows that revelation "is identical with God's triune being in its active self-presence" (p. 14)—which is precisely why "revelation is *mystery*, a making known of 'the mystery of God's will' (Eph. 1.9)" (p. 15). "That is to say, revelation is the manifest presence of God which can only be had on its own terms, and which cannot be converted into something plain and available for classification. Revelation is God's *presence*; but it is *God's* presence" (p. 15). Its purpose is *saving fellowship*, and thus its end "is not simply divine self-display, but the overcoming of human opposition, alienation and pride, and their replacement by knowledge, love and fear of God. In short: revelation is reconciliation" (pp. 15–16). Webster quotes Barth: "Reconciliation is not a truth which revelation makes known to us; reconciliation is the truth of God Himself who grants Himself freely to us in His revelation" (p. 16).[6] In other words, "revelation is itself the establishment of fellowship" (p. 16). For "knowledge of God in his revelation is no mere cognitive affair: it is to know *God* and therefore to love and fear the God who appoints us to fellowship with himself, and not merely to entertain God as a mental object, however exalted" (p. 16).

It follows that "the proper doctrinal location for talk of revelation is the Christian doctrine of the Trinity, and, in particular, the outgoing, communicative mercy of the triune God in the economy of salvation" (pp. 16–17). In sum: "'Revelation' denotes the communicative, fellowship-establishing trajectory of the acts of God in the election, creation, providential ordering, reconciliation, judgement and glorification of God's creatures" (p. 17).

SANCTIFICATION

Webster understands that the application of this term to the doctrine of revelation is nonstandard, but he argues that much can be said for it. Sanctification he understands to be "the act of God the Holy Spirit in hallowing creaturely processes, employing them in the service of the taking form of revelation within the history of the creation" (pp. 17–18). What Webster is attempting to address is a perennial and deepening problem in "modern intellectual culture" (p. 18), viz., "how we are to conceive the relation between the biblical texts as so-called 'natural' or 'historical' entities and theological claims about the self-manifesting activity of God" (p. 18). The more that "modern Western divinity" has stressed the "natural" and the "historical," the less space remains for a justifiable revelatory function "within the communicative divine economy" (pp. 18–19). Otherwise put, this is the challenge of "the dualistic framework of modern historical naturalism as applied to the study of the biblical texts" (p. 20), dominant from the time of Spinoza. It is no solution to follow those theologians who

> leapt to the defence of Scripture by espousing a strident supernaturalism, defending the relation of the Bible to divine revelation by almost entirely removing it from the sphere of historical contingency, through the elaboration of an increasingly formalized and doctrinally isolated theory of inspiration. Rather than deploying theological resources to demonstrate how

[6]Karl Barth, "Revelation," in his *God in Action* (Edinburgh: T&T Clark, 1936), 17.

creaturely entities may be the servants of the divine self-presence, they sought to dissolve the problem by as good as eliminating one of its terms: the creatureliness of the text. (p. 20)

This is the problem that Webster seeks to address by his use of the term *sanctification*. The biblical texts, he asserts, are "creaturely realities" that have been "set apart by the triune God to serve his self-presence" (p. 21). Alternative expressions often deployed to describe the nature of Scripture (Webster discusses five of them) are less satisfactory. As developed in Protestant scholasticism, accommodation depends on too neat a distinction between the mode and the content of revelation. The analogy with the hypostatic union Webster finds deficient, because the Word made flesh and the scriptural word "are in no way equivalent realities" (p. 23):

> The application of an analogy from the hypostatic union can scarcely avoid divinising the Bible by claiming some sort of ontological identity between the biblical texts and the self-communication of God. Over against this, it has to be asserted that no divine nature or properties are to be predicated of Scripture; its substance is that of a creaturely reality (even if it is a creaturely reality annexed to the self-presentation of God); and its relation to God is instrumental. In the case of the Bible, there can be no question of "a union of divine and human factors," but only of "the mystery of the human words *as* God's Word."[7]

Less dangerous is the concept of prophetic and apostolic testimony, much loved by Barth. Yet this, too, requires careful handling, "because the notion of Scripture as human testimony to God's revealing activity can suggest a somewhat accidental relation between the text and revelation" (p. 24). The fourth concept, "means of grace," is not necessarily faulty, but much depends on the way "means" is understood: *any* theology of mediation (not only textual, but also sacramental, ministerial, or symbolic) is in at least some danger of eclipsing "the self-mediation of God in Christ and Spirit" (p. 25). A happier expression thinks of the "servant-form" of Scripture—an expression much loved by Berkouwer, but advanced by Herman Bavinck—which thinks of God's active presence as Word in terms of "treasure in earthen vessels" (2 Cor. 4:7 kjv).

But Webster prefers to speak of the biblical text as "sanctified." As with human beings, so with texts: sanctification does not diminish creatureliness. "A sanctified

---

[7]Page 23, citing G. C. Berkouwer, *Holy Scripture* (Grand Rapids: Eerdmans, 1975), 203.

text is creaturely, not divine" (p. 28). Because the text is creaturely, all the tools of its creatureliness are legitimate: grammar, source criticism, redaction criticism, and so forth. Yet creatureliness is not to be confused with naturalness. The text is sanctified, set apart by the triune God for his revelatory purposes. Initially, this might sound as if Webster sees a *chronological* development: the text first comes into being as the product of creaturely activity, and then God opts to set the text apart, to sanctify it. In reality, however, Webster avoids the trap:

> Sanctification is not to be restricted to the text as finished product; it may legitimately be extended to the larger field of agents and actions of which the text is part. The Spirit's relation to the text broadens out into the Spirit's activity in the life of the people of God which forms the environment within which the text takes shape and serves the divine self-presence. Sanctification can thus properly be extended to the processes of the production of the text—not simply authorship . . . but also the complex histories of pre-literary and literary tradition, redaction and compilation. It will, likewise, be extended to the post-history of the text, most particularly to canonisation (understood as the church's Spirit-produced acknowledgement of the testimony of Scripture) and interpretation (understood as Spirit-illumined repentant and faithful attention to the presence of God). (pp. 29–30)

INSPIRATION

Webster urges that there are three requirements if talk of inspiration is to be profitable. *First*, it "needs to be strictly subordinate to and dependent upon the broader concept of revelation" (p. 31); it must not become the hinge on which all else turns, for "inspiration is not foundational but derivative, a corollary of the self-presence of God which takes form through the providential ordering and sanctification of creaturely auxiliaries" (p. 32). Webster wants to avoid grounding Christian certainty on some notion or other of inspiration. Instead, he says, he wants to follow Calvin, who asserts that "since certainty of faith should be sought from none but God only, we conclude that true faith is founded only on the Scriptures which proceeded from him, since therein he has been pleased to teach not partially, but fully, whatever he would have us know, and knew to be useful" (p. 32).[8] *Second*, the notion of inspiration must avoid both objectifying (i.e., the inspired *product* must not take precedence over the "revelatory, sanctifying and inspiring activities of the divine agent" [p. 33]) and spiritualizing of the divine activity (so that the center of gravity is pulled away from the text toward

---

[8]Webster is citing *Articles Agreed Upon by the Faculty of Sacred Theology of Paris, with the Antidote*, in *Tracts and Treatises*, vol. 1 (Edinburgh: Oliver and Boyd, 1958), 106.

the persons associated with the text). And *third*, the notion of inspiration must be expounded "in clear connection to the end or purpose of Holy Scripture, which is service to God's self-manifestation" (p. 35).

This brings Webster to his "conceptual paraphrase" (p. 36) of 2 Peter 1:21. I mention only one of his four points: "the Spirit generates language" (p. 37). This, and not dictation, is what is properly meant by "verbal inspiration." "What is inspired is not simply the *matter* (*res*) of Scripture but its verbal *form* (*forma*)" (p. 38). Webster writes:

> Inspiration is the specific textual application of the broader notion of sanctification as the hallowing of creaturely realities to serve revelation's taking form. Where sanctification indicates the dogmatic ontology of the text as the servant of the divine self-communicative presence, inspiration indicates the specific work of the Spirit of Christ with respect to the text. (pp. 30–31)

I cannot devote equivalent space to the detailed description of the remaining three chapters of Webster's book, but I may attempt very brief summaries.

In his second chapter, "Scripture, Church and Canon," Webster provides what is in fact an elegant defense of the classic Protestant view of the processes of canon-ization during the patristic period (though he doesn't call it that). He begins with a "dogmatic sketch" (p. 42) of the relations between Scripture and the church, describing the latter (i) as a "hearing church": "the definitive act of the church is faithful hearing of the gospel of salvation announced by the risen Christ in the Spirit's power through the service of Holy Scripture" (p. 44); (ii) as a "spiritually visible" church (p. 42):

> The church's visibility, of which Holy Scripture is part, is spiritual visibility. ... Positively, this means that the church has true form and visibility in so far as it receives the grace of God through the life-giving presence of Word and Spirit. Its visibility is therefore spiritual visibility; (pp. 47–48)

(iii) as an apostolic church: "The church's history, of which Holy Scripture is part, is apostolic history" (p. 50). By the latter, Webster means more than the affirmation that the gospel came to us through the first witnesses, the apostles, who therefore have a certain status—for this converts apostolicity "into a given form of social order" (p. 51). It is better to think of apostolicity as "a matter of *being accosted* by a mandate from outside. It is a Christological-pneumatological concept, and only by derivation is it ecclesiological. Apostolicity is the church's standing beneath the imperious directive: 'Go'" (p. 51).

With these matters understood, Webster insists that "the church is not competent to confer authority on Holy Scripture, any more than it is competent to be a speaking church before it is a hearing church, or competent to give itself the mandate to be apostolic" (p. 53). Of course, the authority of Scripture cannot be "abstracted from the life and acts of the church as the place where the saving presence of God is encountered" (p. 55).

> To sum up: the authority of Scripture is the authority of the church's Lord and his gospel, and so cannot be made an immanent feature of ecclesial existence. Scripture's authority *within* the church is a function of Scripture's authority *over* the church. The church's acknowledgement of Scripture's authority is not an act of self-government, but an exposure to judgement, to a source not simply of authorisation but also and supremely of interrogation. (pp. 56–57)

So it is not surprising that Webster, while acknowledging the element of human decision in the process of canonization, follows Calvin approvingly: Scripture does not take its approbation from the church; rather, "this act of confession, the church's judgement with respect to the canon, is an act of submission before it is an act of authority" (p. 63). By it, "the church affirms that all truthful speech in the church can proceed only from the prior apostolic testimony" (p. 64).

Webster's third chapter, "Reading in the Economy of Grace," is a penetrating and sometimes moving contrast of two theologies of reading, or, more precisely, two anthropologies of reading. On the one side stands Schopenhauer, who embodies attitudes to reading that dominate today's culture; on the other side stand Calvin and Bonhoeffer, with quite different approaches to reading Scripture. Schopenhauer contrasts reading with "thinking for yourself": too much reading may so swamp the mind that the mind's originality is squashed. The *summum bonum*, then, remains the human mind, the mind's autonomy, its originality. By contrast, Calvin and Bonhoeffer insist that thought must be subordinate to the Word. For the Christian, reading Scripture "thus involves mortification of the free-range intellect which believes itself to be at liberty to devote itself to all manner of sources of fascination" (p. 90). Or again:

> For Calvin, the counter to the vanity, instability and sheer artfulness of the impious self is "another and better help," namely "the light of his Word" by which God becomes "known unto salvation." God counters pride by self-

revelation through Scripture. Scripture is on Calvin's account "a special gift, where God, to instruct the church, not merely uses mute teachers but also opens his most hallowed lips. Not only does he teach the elect to look upon a God, but also shows himself as the God upon whom they are to look." . . . This does *not* entail wholesale abandonment of any appropriation of the tools of historical inquiry, but raises a question about their usefulness by asking whether they can foster *childlike* reading of the text. (p. 77)[9]

Webster's final chapter, "Scripture, Theology and the Theological School," takes its departure from interaction with Ursinus (who drafted the Heidelberg Catechism). In prestigious theological schools today, universal reason reigns, and divides (not to say fragments) the subject matter into the well-known fourfold division: biblical, historical, systematic, and practical theology. By contrast, Ursinus saw catechism and systematic theology as helping tools to enable the Christian more productively to read the Scriptures and thereby encounter God. In other words, the reading of Scripture is not the starting point for the creation of a reason-generated theological superstructure, but the end point, the *telos* of all the disciplines—the fruitful encounter with God in the Scriptures. Webster calls for major revision of the theological curriculum. "Christian theology is properly an undertaking of the speaking and hearing church of Jesus Christ" (p. 123), and therefore can claim only marginal connection with the atmosphere in the university. If that means theology is squeezed to the periphery of university life, so be it: "In contexts committed to the sufficiency of natural reason (or at least to the unavailability of anything other than natural reason), theology will have something of the scandalous about it" (p. 134). Webster wants the curriculum overhauled to reflect these sorts of concerns. Indeed, Calvin's understanding of the role of theology becomes, for Webster, the high point of wisdom in this arena.

Critique

This book is one of the freshest things I have read on Scripture in some time. It must be evaluated, of course, on its own terms: it is a "dogmatic *sketch*," and so makes no pretensions of being comprehensive; it is a "*dogmatic* sketch," and therefore makes limited appeal to historical development, exegesis of Scripture itself, contemporary communication theory, and the like. But as a dogmatic sketch, even where it is articulating positions that are in fact traditional, Webster's freshness of thought and probing intelligence make the book a delight to read. Better yet: Webster writes as a churchman who thinks and serves by self-consciously put-

---

[9]The references in Calvin are to *Institutes* 1.6.1.

ting himself *under* the authority of the Word. On many fronts, the work is quietly edifying, which of course will damn it in some academic circles.

Nevertheless, some questions must be raised, and these are of various kinds. In some instances I am not quite sure what Webster means: I am simply inquiring. In other cases, I suspect the balance of things is not quite right—but I acknowledge that the disagreement may sometimes spring from Webster's brevity. In still others, I am not sure Webster is right, which is of course a polite way of saying that I am pretty sure he is wrong, and I hope that by this sort of interaction we may sharpen each other's thinking.

(1) It should be obvious that the terminology Webster uses in this dogmatic sketch of the doctrine of Holy Scripture is not the terminology found in Holy Scripture to describe itself. This is not necessarily a disastrous weakness, of course; indeed, it is commonplace in dogmatics. For instance, the καταλάσσω word-group in Paul, as is well known, invariably depicts human beings being reconciled to God, never God being reconciled to human beings, even though, conceptually speaking, there is space for the latter idea in the field of dogmatics, not least because that idea is found in Scripture, even though it is never connected with this word-group. Again, only rarely in the field of systematic theology does *sanctification* mean what it means in the New Testament—though what is meant by the use of the term in systematics is common enough in the pages of the Greek Testament, but without using the term. The domain of dogmatic discussion is often quite different from the domain of exegetical discussion. This is a well-known phenomenon, of course, but it raises a deeper question: At what point do terms found in the Scriptures but which are deployed within the field of systematic theology in ways quite different from that found in the Scriptures generate unfortunate confusion, finally producing a dogmatic structure that is more than a little problematic? Several of the points raised below reflect this problem.

(2) The definition of Scripture that Webster provides, for all its strengths, is simultaneously too large and too restrictive. He writes (as we have seen), "'Holy Scripture' is a shorthand term for the nature and function of the biblical writings in a set of communicative acts which stretch from God's merciful self-manifestation to the obedient hearing of the community of faith" (p. 5). The strength of the definition is in the resolve to connect Scripture to God himself; the notion of "Scripture" is incoherent if it is abstracted from God, who reveals himself by this means. But what is gained by saying that Holy Scripture is a shorthand "for the nature *and function* of the biblical text"? It is entirely proper to discuss the function of Scripture, of course; is it wise to make the function of Scripture part of the definition of what Scripture *is* as opposed to what it *does*? The next phrase is ambiguous: "in a

set of communicative acts which stretch from God's merciful self-manifestation to the obedient hearing of the community of faith." Does this mean: (i) Scripture is the God-given means for linking the communicative acts of God to their reception by obedience in the community of faith? Or: (ii) as a category, "Holy Scripture" *includes* the entire sweep of movement from the communicative acts of God all the way to their reception by obedience in the community of faith? Judging by what he goes on to say, Webster has the latter in view—but both readings are problematic. If the former, then Scripture itself is not revelation, but constitutes part of the link from revelation to reception of revelation; if the latter, then what "Holy Scripture" includes is much *more* than what is meant by ἡ γραφή: it goes way beyond the *writing* to include the entire communicative act, from its giving to its reception. Not for a moment should we deny the importance of the *entire* sweep when it comes to discussion of the ways in which God graciously presences himself with his image-bearers, but that is not the same thing as saying that the word *Scripture* is *itself* the appropriate term to refer to this entire sweep. Such usage is too all-embracing; worse, the effect, ironically, is to reduce what *Scripture itself is*, what the written thing is. For whatever the written thing is, it remains that, *even if people ignore it, even if people turn blind eyes to it and fail to see it for what it is, and receive none of God's self-presencing by this means.* By opening the aperture to include the sweep of God's self-disclosure, Webster fails to acknowledge, as we shall see, what Scripture says about itself.

The same problem can be seen in Webster's treatment of revelation. Recall his definition: *"Revelation is the self-presentation of the triune God, the free work of sovereign mercy in which God wills, establishes and perfects saving fellowship with himself in which humankind comes to know, love and fear him above all things"* (p. 13; italics his). Thus the *content* of revelation is "God's own proper reality" (p. 14); the agent is God himself; and it follows that revelation "is identical with God's triune being in its active self-presence" (p. 14). He stipulates further:

> Revelation is purposive. Its end is not simply divine self-display, but the overcoming of human opposition, alienation and pride, and their replacement by knowledge, love and fear of God. In short: revelation is reconciliation. "This is what revelation means," writes Barth, "this is its content and dynamic: Reconciliation has been made and accomplished. Reconciliation is not a truth which revelation makes known to us; reconciliation is the truth of God Himself who grants Himself freely to us in His revelation."[10]

As the gracious presence of God, revelation is itself the establishment of

---

[10]Webster is citing Barth, "Revelation," 17.

fellowship. . . . God is present as saviour, and so communicatively present. (pp. 15–16)

Once again, however, there is a hasty leap from the assertion that revelation is purposive (which of us would disagree?), and that its "end" is reconciliation, to the assertion that "revelation *is* reconciliation." We must applaud Webster's insistence that revelation not be cut off from God and from the larger sweep of God's purposes. Nevertheless, by *identifying* revelation with its purposes so closely, Webster is more Barthian than biblical: the Bible, as we shall see, is quite prepared to talk about the reality of God's revelation *even where no reconciliation takes place, even when God's revelation is spurned.* It is true to say that the conceptual range of revelation *includes* the personal, the reconciling, the communication of God himself; it is entirely reductionistic to say that all those ingredients must be present in *every* display of revelation. This analysis seems to have no purpose other than to deny that Scripture *is* revelation even when people do not receive it.

(3) Another way of getting at the same problem is by observing that Webster has an understanding of revelation and of Holy Scripture in his mind that he carefully and thoughtfully works out, but without testing it against the sheer phenomena of the documents that make up Scripture. At one level, this is related to what I said at the beginning of this critique: systematicians often use categories that are somewhat removed from the categories of the Scriptures themselves. But if the synthetic categories are too far removed from what the Bible says—in this instance, what the biblical documents say about themselves—then sooner or later a question mark is raised over the validity of the synthesis.

To begin with what initially appears a small thing: Webster can comfortably speak of God's Word, but never of God's words. Yet the biblical writers can oscillate between the two without a trace of embarrassment (e.g., Ex. 4:12; Num. 22:38; Deut. 18:18–20; Jer. 14:14; 23:16–40; 29:31–32; Ezek. 2:7; 13:1–19; passim). Sometimes the biblical writers refer to the words of YHWH that he spoke through his prophet (e.g., 1 Kings 16:34; 2 Kings 9:36; 24:2; 2 Chron. 29:25; Ezra 9:10–11; Neh. 9:30; Jer. 37:2; Zech. 7:7, 12; passim). Sometimes God's words are said to be written (e.g., Ex. 24:4; 34:27; Josh. 24:26). Even when God is not cast as immediately being the speaker (as in a "Thus says the Lord" utterance), later writers can say, "The Scripture had to be fulfilled which the Holy Spirit spoke long ago through the mouth of David" (Acts 1:16; see the diverse formulae in Hebrews, for instance) or the like.[11] Scripture itself can be personified (e.g., Scrip-

---

[11] Although he attempts no sophisticated theological integration—after all, that was not his assignment—in his essay, Wayne Grudem's survey of the ways in which Scripture refers to itself ("Scriptures' Self-Attestation and the Problem of

ture foresees, Gal. 3:8), because it is a colorful way of saying that God foresees, as reported in Scripture.

This neglect of what Scripture says gets worse. As we have seen, Webster denies any appropriate analogical connection between the Word made flesh and the inscripturated word. He writes:

> But the Word made flesh and the scriptural word are in no way equivalent realities. Moreover, the application of an analogy from the hypostatic union can scarcely avoid divinising the Bible by claiming some sort of ontological identity between the biblical texts and the self-communication of God. Over against this, it has to be asserted that no divine nature or properties are to be predicated of Scripture; its substance is that of a creaturely reality (even if it is a creaturely reality annexed to the self-presentation of God) and its relation to God is instrumental. In the case of the Bible, there can be no question of "a union of divine and human factors," but only of "the mystery of the human words as God's Word." (p. 23)[12]

Here several things must be said. (i) Of course it is true that the Word made flesh and the scriptural word are not "equivalent realities." No one says they are. The question, rather, is whether an appropriate *analogy* may be drawn between them. (ii) There is at least some biblical hint that an analogy might be appropriate, viz., the frequency with which "word" and "words" refer to Scripture, on the one hand, and the fact that "Word" can be applied to Christ, on the other—applied both directly (John 1:1, 14; Rev. 19:13) and by implication (Heb. 1:1–4). (iii) In passing, observe once again the unfortunate and unnecessary distinction—the biblically unsanctioned distinction—between "human words" and "God's Word." (iv) I am not sure what Webster means when he speaks of the danger of "divinising the Bible." Perhaps he is thinking of well-meaning but not very well-informed believers who understand correctly that, however mediated, this book has been given by God, but who understand so little of the humanness of the Bible that they have no categories for the idiolects of the individual corpora, the complex array of literary genres and their diverse rhetorical appeals, and so forth. But this is not so much the "divinising" of the Bible as the dehumanizing of the Bible. As far as I can see, the greatest contemporary danger of divinizing the Bible does *not* lie with the fundamentalists who, however conservative their views, invariably understand that the Bible *is talking about something outside itself*, about God, Christ, people, the

---

Formulating a Doctrine of Scripture," in *Scripture and Truth*, ed. D. A. Carson and John D. Woodbridge [Grand Rapids: Zondervan, 1983], 19–59, 359–68) should be required reading for those, like Webster, who do make the attempt.
[12] The words quoted by Webster are from Berkouwer, *Holy Scripture*, 203.

world, atonement, the gospel, and that it is this God of the gospel who saves us, not the Bible itself. In other words, they understand that the Bible is a graciously provided means to refer to extrabiblical reality, to God himself. In that sense, they do not so "divinise the Bible" that they are tempted to worship it. No, the greatest danger of bibliolatry today lies with some in the Yale school who are loath to say clearly that the Bible actually does refer to extrabiblical realities, or, if they concede it does, they give the impression that we cannot know them. They speak of the importance of reading the Bible, memorizing the Bible, firing our imaginations by much meditation on the Bible, but can scarcely bring themselves to say that what saves us is something extrabiblical: the gospel of God, which has both historical and super-historical content, both natural and supernatural content. Clearly, Webster is not addressing that problem, at least not here. So is the warning against "divinising the Bible" merely a rhetorical condemnation of those who buy into what is in fact the more traditional view of what Scripture actually is throughout the centuries of the church?[13] (v) Above all, is it justified to assert that "no divine nature or properties are to be predicated of Scripture"? Here again, Webster has not listened carefully enough to what Scripture says of God's word or of God's words. *Like God himself,* God's words and God's word (the biblical writers can use both the singular and the plural) are frequently asserted to be faithful, true (Ps. 119:160), righteous (Prov. 8:8), pure or flawless (Ps. 12:6; 18:30). Small wonder that the appropriate response to God's word is humility, contrition, trembling (Isa. 66:2)—exactly the appropriate response to God himself.

(4) The use of "sanctification" to try to describe the way in which God uses Scripture and manifests himself in Scripture, even while the Scriptures are the product of human, historical contingencies, certainly opens up some windows, and is worth pondering. The biblical texts, Webster writes, are "creaturely realities" that have been "set apart by the triune God to serve his self-presence" (p. 21). Yet the category of "sanctification," applied to Scripture, has at least as many problems connected with it as the terms Webster wants to displace.

(a) Webster's definition of sanctification could easily be contested: sanctification is "the act of God the Holy Spirit in hallowing creaturely processes, employing them in the service of the taking form of revelation within the history of the creation" (pp. 17–18). Remembering that in the original, "sanctification" and "hallowing" share the same lemma, the definition breaks one of the cardinal rules of all definitions: one cannot use the same or a cognate word to define what is being defined. But the problem with the definition runs deeper. Sanctification

---

[13]For an excellent survey of the primary sources on this subject, see John D. Woodbridge, *Biblical Authority: A Critique of the Rogers/McKim Proposal* (Grand Rapids: Zondervan, 1982).

is "the act of God the Holy Spirit in hallowing *creaturely processes*": when the shovel that removes the ash from the altar before the tabernacle is "sanctified" or "hallowed," is it a process? Or is the word "process" used to call to mind the dominant use in Reformed dogmatics, to refer to ongoing patterns of *growth* or *improvement* in the people of God? Even here, however, one needs to be very careful, since exegesis has often shown that the "sanctification" vocabulary in Paul can refer, not to process, but to something positional, instantaneous—which is why many have dubbed such passages "positional sanctification" or "definitional sanctification." Indeed, some argue that most "sanctification" passages in the New Testament rightly belong in that camp,[14] while biblical texts that speak of the Christian's growing conformity to Christ (e.g., Philippians 3) do not use the term "sanctification." In other words, we often find sanctification without "sanctification," i.e., we find the theme of sanctification (in the dogmatic sense) without the word being present. Even if we manage to negotiate around such details in Webster's definition, what is meant by saying that God the Holy Spirit employs the said creaturely processes "in the service of the taking form of revelation within the history of the creation"? I suppose that in some very broad sense this could be said of the Spirit's "employment" of the shovel that takes out the ash, and of the Christian who is set aside to do God's will: both are used of the "taking form of revelation within the history of the creation." Yet the extension of such usage to Scripture is not obvious. At least in the case of the analogy between Scripture and the hypostatic union, there is, as we have seen, some Scripture-given common terminology. What precisely is the warrant for this extension of sanctification to Scripture? Merely the fact that it too belongs to "creaturely processes"? But so also does the thermonuclear burning of the sun and the stars, the writing of a pornographic book, a sunset, and the rape of Nanking.

(b) More precisely, the application of "sanctification" to cover the God-sanction of Scripture is extraordinarily ambiguous. One could take it positively and appreciatively, and find little fault with it; but one could use the term so loosely that almost anything could slip under it. The shovel that is "sanctified" and thus set apart for God's use is in itself amoral; the believers who are "sanctified" and thus set apart for God's use are not only moral beings, but still flawed, frequently rebellious, frankly guilty. So what kind of "thing" is Scripture, which is also said to be "sanctified" and thus set apart for God's use?

(c) Despite the powerful and sometimes moving passages Webster has written to foster childlike reading of the text and wholehearted submission to Scripture,

---

[14]See especially David Peterson, *Possessed by God: A New Testament Theology of Sanctification and Holiness*, NSBT 4 (Leicester: Inter-Varsity, 1995).

passages by which we are challenged and for which we are grateful, the "sanctifica-tion" category does not lead him to address the hard questions. In fact, he rather ruthlessly avoids them. On the one hand, because the Scriptures are "creaturely realities," the full panoply of human literary and historical criticism is appropriate, he says: source criticism, redaction criticism, and so forth; yet on the other, the Bible is so "sanctified" by God that we are to submit before it, not stand in judg-ment over it, for it is nothing less than the self-disclosing self-presencing of God. But suppose the historical criticism leads many to the conclusion that what is actu-ally said in the Bible is not true? For instance, many "minimalists," and even some mainstream Old Testament critics, do not think a person by the name of Abraham really existed, and do not think that the giving of the law, depicted in Moses, has any reality in history. It is a late creation, about the sixth century BC (or, in the case of the minimalists, datable to the Persian period). But Paul's argument for the way promise and law fit together turns absolutely on their relative historical sequenc-ing (Galatians 3); the argument for the supremacy of the Melchizedekian priest-hood depends on Psalm 110 being written *after* the giving of the law-covenant that prescribes the Levitical priesthood (Hebrews 7). Elsewhere, the argument for the obsolescence, in principle, of the Mosaic covenant, once the new covenant has been announced, depends on which came first (Hebrews 8); the argument for the identity and stature of the one David refers to as "my Lord" depends on the truthfulness of the superscription of Psalm 110; and on and on. Does the "sanctification" of the biblical texts mean that they are telling the truth? If so, does that not impose at least some sort of curb on ostensibly "historical" reconstruc-tions? Alternatively, if we are to submit to these texts even where they are not telling the truth about such fundamental matters, are we being encouraged to bow to what is untrue, simply because the text is in some sense "sanctified"? This is not to deny the historical, literary, and idiolectical particularities of the biblical texts. Any robust doctrine of Scripture must account for these realities. But how would Webster address them? Quite frankly, he does not say, and his exposition of "sanctification" of Scripture gives no clue of the direction in which he would go. And that is the problem. These sorts of issues cannot be ducked. Moreover, they become even more acute when we recall that Webster applies the "sanctification" label to the entire process of the development of the text, not to mention also its reception among readers, for many historical and literary critics create processes of ostensible development that portray the components of texts to be saying the diametric opposite of what the final text says. What does the "sanctification" of these "processes" of text-development mean? Does it mean the same thing as the "sanctification" of the final product?

(5) Related to these problems are some of the antitheses that Webster creates. Here are a batch of them:

> In an objectified account of revelation [which Webster rejects], the inspired *product* is given priority over the revelatory, sanctifying and inspiring activities of the divine agent. But properly understood, inspiration does not mean that the truth of the gospel which Scripture sets before us becomes something to hand, constantly available independent of the Word and work of God, an entity which *embodies* rather than *serves* the presence of God. Inspiration does not spell the end of the mystery of God; it is simply that act of the Spirit through which this set of texts proceeds from God to attest his ineffable presence. Inspiration is a mode of the Spirit's freedom, not its inhibition by the letter. (p. 33)

Observe: (i) Webster sets the *product* over against the *activities of the divine agent*. Why the antithesis? Why not rather say that *because* of the activities of the divine agent, the product is what it is? (ii) This is all the more pertinent when θεόπνευστος, the Greek word closest to what we mean by "inspired," is explicitly tied by the Pastoral Epistles to the *text* of Scripture, to the γραφή, not to the process (2 Tim. 3:16)—a point exquisitely demonstrated by Warfield a century ago.[15] (iii) Webster characterizes any inspired *product* as having a certain "independent" status, of being "constantly available independent of the Word and work of God." But would it not be closer to what Scripture says of itself to say that Scripture must never be seen as anything other than the Word and work of God? How does an inspired product diminish such a view—unless, of course, one has rejected the way in which θεόπνευστος explicitly refers to γραφή, in favor of some other dogmatic structure? (iv) Similarly, Webster says that having an inspired *product* makes it "an entity which *embodies* rather than *serves* the presence of God." The antithesis is misleading, for it would be closer to the evidence to say that precisely because this inspired product *embodies* the presence of God, it also *serves* the presence of God. (v) Webster implies that the view he wishes to confute "spell[s] the end of the mystery of God." But why? There is plenty of mystery in how these biblical texts came into being, plenty of mystery remains in how the Spirit of God uses them to bring conviction of sin and to awaken faith, plenty of mystery in how God presences himself through them, plenty of mystery in what the Scriptures themselves tell us remains unknown (e.g., Deut. 29:29; Rom. 11:33–36).[16] Just

---

[15]B. B. Warfield, *The Inspiration and Authority of the Bible* (Philadelphia: Presbyterian and Reformed, 1948), 245–96.

[16]Incidentally, I cannot forbear to mention that Webster's prooftext for the "mystery" of God's revelation, viz., Eph. 1:9 (15), clearly misunderstands what μυστήριον means in the Pauline corpus. I am certainly not denying that there are

because God is so great and so hidden, that there are lots of things we do not know of him and therefore cannot say of him, does not mean that there are no true things that we can say of him—the more so if God himself insists he is the One who has disclosed them. And finally, (vi) Webster's final sentence, another antithesis, is baffling: "Inspiration is a mode of the Spirit's freedom, not its inhibition by the letter." Is not the Spirit free to say things in words, as the Scriptures themselves attest? In the light of what Webster himself later says about "verbal inspiration," why is an inspired *product* a sad instance of "inhibition by the letter"?

(6) One sometimes wonders who Webster's theological sparring partners are. At the risk of speculation, I suggest they fall into two groups. On the one hand are pure rationalists, philosophical materialists, scholars who are trying to maintain an "objectivity" over against Scripture and who really have no place for God himself. Webster sometimes names them, and in any case handles them fairly and well. For convenience, we'll place them on Webster's left. On the other hand are those who seem to be on Webster's right. It is hard to know exactly who they are, because Webster never names them or interacts with them. Who are they? Maybe he thinks they are evangelicals, or conservative evangelicals, or some conservative evangelicals, but the positions Webster deplores do not fit them very well. He worries about those who abstract Scripture from God and from the gospel: well and good, and Peter Jensen shares his concern.[17] He warns against the "strident supernaturalism" of those who leap to the Bible's defense by "almost removing it from the sphere of historical contingency" (p. 20), but few have thought more deeply about such matters, and avoided the dualism Webster deplores, than Warfield (even if Warfield's dogmatic conclusions about Scripture are different from Webster's). He wants to anchor the Scriptures in the self-disclosure of God, and he is right to do so—but of course, in his own way, that is exactly what John Wenham was trying to do.[18] He is highly suspicious of the category of accommodation, which he blames on the Protestant scholastics (p. 32): indeed, he has only negative things to say about "Reformed scholastics." Interestingly enough, however, he has only positive things to say about Calvin (who is quoted more than anyone else in the book), even though there is a rising chorus of scholars who have argued that the ostensible distance between Calvin and the Reformed scholastics is not nearly as great as many like to think it is (Webster refers to none of that literature),[19] and even though Calvin's own treatment of accommoda-

---

massive emphases on the ineffability of God in Scripture, but only that this word, and this text, supports them.
[17] *The Revelation of God.*
[18] *Christ and the Bible,* 3d ed. (Grand Rapids: Baker, 1994).
[19] The most important contribution, not only because of its comprehensiveness but also because of its subtlety, is doubtless that of Richard A. Muller, *Post-Reformation Reformed Orthodoxy: The Rise and Development of Reformed Orthodoxy,*

tion is rich, nuanced, and not mentioned by Webster. He wants to see systematic theology as the handmaid of Scripture, that which helps us read Scripture better, the ultimate goal being encounter with God in the Scriptures, not the production of systematic theology—a point repeatedly made over the years by J. I. Packer. But because Webster does not mention any of these contemporary scholars by name, or refer even once to their writings, it is not entirely clear whom he has in mind when he levels his guns toward the right. But sometimes, I fear, he is shooting at a caricature.

(7) Would it be churlish of me to wonder why a scholar as helpfully committed to reforming theological education as he is, distancing it from the prevailing mindset of university faculties, isn't teaching at a church-based theological college instead of in a university department?

In short: this is a thought-provoking book by a mature theologian with a coherent thesis to defend. It cannot be skimmed; it must be read slowly and pondered, and there is much to gain from it. Yet its distance from what the texts of Scripture actually say contributes to its serious flaws.

Peter Enns, *Inspiration and Incarnation: Evangelicals and the Problem of the Old Testament*

Content
The subtitle of the book by Enns, *Inspiration and Incarnation: Evangelicals and the Problem of the Old Testament*,[20] shows it to have a very different purpose from that of Webster's volume. Enns, associate professor of Old Testament at Westminster Theological Seminary, is not trying to make a positive statement about the nature of Scripture, except incidentally; rather, he is trying to refute what he judges to be the failure of evangelicals to face up to real problems in the nature of the Bible that they tend to skirt. These he breaks down into three large categories. After an opening chapter, he devotes a long chapter to each of these problem areas, and then concludes with a final chapter that draws his discussion to a close and points the way forward. Each chapter except the last ends with a list of "Further Readings." The book provides an excellent glossary, making it accessible to almost any competent reader.

In his opening chapter, "Getting Our Bearings" (pp. 13–22), Enns tells us that his purpose "is to bring an evangelical doctrine of Scripture into conversation with the implications generated by some important themes in modern biblical

---

ca. 1520 to ca. 1725: vol. 1, *Prolegomena to Theology*; vol. 2, *Holy Scripture: The Cognitive Foundation of Theology*; vol. 3, *The Divine Essence and Attributes*; vol. 4, *The Triunity of God* (Grand Rapids: Baker, 2003).
[20]Grand Rapids: Baker, 2005.

scholarship—particularly Old Testament scholarship—over the past 150 years"
(p. 13). He is not suggesting that such a conversation has not taken place: it has,
he admits, but "what is needed is not simply for evangelicals to work *in* these areas,
but to engage the *doctrinal implications* that work in these areas raises" (p. 13). His
primary envisaged readers are the "fair number of Christians who conclude that
the contemporary state of biblical scholarship makes an evangelical faith unviable"
(p. 13). Enns writes that evangelicals must maintain their conviction "that the
Bible is ultimately from God and that it is God's gift to the church" (p. 14), but
how "these fundamental instincts" are fleshed out is another matter. The kind of
adjustment Enns thinks is necessary is akin to the kind of reinterpretation of the
Bible that took place in the wake of Copernicus. In other words, "Reassessment
of doctrine on the basis of external evidence . . . is nothing new" (p. 14). Enns
is not proposing to solve "Bible difficulties" (his expression, p. 14). Rather, by
focusing on "three problems raised by the modern study of the Old Testament,"
he hopes to suggest

> ways in which our conversation can be shifted somewhat, so that what are
> often *perceived* as problems with the Old Testament are put into a different
> perspective. To put it another way, my aim is to allow the collective evidence
> to affect not just how we understand a biblical passage or story here and
> there within the parameters of earlier doctrinal formulations. Rather, I want
> to move beyond that by allowing the evidence to affect how we think about
> what Scripture as a whole *is*. (p. 15)

The three issues Enns proposes to take up in the following three chapters are,
respectively, the Old Testament's relation to other literature of the ancient world
(i.e., the issue of the Bible's uniqueness); the theological diversity of the Old Testament (the issue of the Bible's integrity); and the way in which the New Testament
authors handle the Old Testament (the issue of the Bible's interpretation).

Before embarking on this exercise, Enns devotes a few pages to suggesting that
the "incarnational analogy" is a good way to address the problem (pp. 17–21).
Just as the ancient church had to come to grips with the heresy of docetism, so
we must come to terms with "scriptural docetism" (p. 18): we must come to grips
with "the human marks of the Bible" which are "*everywhere, thoroughly integrated
into the nature of Scripture itself*" (p. 18, emphasis his). Thus the Bible is written
in human languages, not some heavenly dialect. The Old Testament is a world
of temples, priests, sacrifices, and both Israel and the surrounding nations "had
prophets that mediated the divine will to them" (p. 19). Both Israel and the sur-

rounding nations were ruled by kings, and "Israel's legal system has some striking similarities with those of surrounding nations" (p. 20).

In short, if we take Jesus' humanness seriously, we ought to take the Bible's "situatedness" equally seriously. To put the matter in two statements that Enns italicizes:

> *That the Bible, at every turn, shows how "connected" it is to its own world is a necessary consequence of God incarnating himself. . . . It is essential to the very nature of revelation that the Bible is not unique to its environment. The human dimension of Scripture is essential to its being Scripture.* (p. 20)

In the second chapter (pp. 23–70)—the first of the three lengthy, substantive chapters—Enns begins by surveying the contents of ten ANE (=Ancient Near Eastern) texts. Any graduate from a decent seminary will have been exposed to the first batch of these, and probably read them in English translation.[21] The Akkadian texts introduced us to *Enuma Elish*, the so-called "Babylonian Genesis," with distinct parallels to the Genesis account of creation; and to *Atrahasis* and *Gilgamesh*, not to mention the still older Sumerian version. These two documents give us parallels to the flood accounts. Enns points out that the parallels are not the sort that demonstrate direct borrowing, but are adequate to demonstrate a connection of some kind, perhaps through some even older precursor. The *Nuzi* tablets (for which there is no standard English translation) preserve various legal, administrative, and economic texts that show remarkable parallels to the patriarchal period reported in the Bible. But if these depictions of life in ancient Mesopotamia are so close to the cultural practices of the Bible, "the reasonable question is raised of how *different* the Bible really is. If the Bible reflects these ancient customs and practices, in what sense can we speak of it as revelation?" (p. 31). Similarly, the *Code of Hammurabi* provides parallels to the Mosaic legislation; Hittite suzerainty treaties provide parallels to Deuteronomy. (Enns is careful to admit that some scholars do not think that the Decalogue and Deuteronomy directly reflect the structure of Hittite suzerainty treaties, though most accept some sort of connection.) The recently discovered Tel Dan inscription speaks of the house of David, and the consensus is that the Davidic dynasty is in view. The Siloam tunnel inscription is linked to the time of Hezekiah; the *Mesha* inscription to the time of Omri; and the book of Proverbs certainly reflects influence of Egyptian wisdom literature, in particular the *Instruction of Amenemope*.

---

[21] I first read them when I was a beginning seminary student in the 1960s, devouring them in an early edition of what we all called "Pritchard": James B. Pritchard, ed., *The Ancient Near East: An Anthology of Texts and Pictures* (Princeton: Princeton University Press, 1958).

So what is the problem? Enns specifies it with three questions:

1. Does the Bible, particularly Genesis, report historical fact, or is it just a bunch of stories culled from other ancient literature?
2. What does it mean for other cultures to have an influence on the Bible that we believe is revealed by God? Can we say that the Bible is unique or special? If the Bible is such a "culturally conditioned" product, what possible relevance can it have for us today?
3. Does this mean that the history of the church, which carried on for many centuries before this evidence came to light, was wrong in how it thought about its Bible? (pp. 38–39)

Enns develops his argument by placing the ten sources to which he has already referred into three groups, which, he says, reflect these three problems. First, *Enuma Elish, Atrahasis,* and *Gilgamesh,* all dealing with creation and the flood, raise the question, "Is Genesis myth or history?" (p. 39). After all, "how can we say logically that the biblical stories are true and the Akkadian stories are false when they both look so very much alike?" (p. 40). Enns argues that the way forward is to refuse to think of "myth" as a "made-up" story, but to define myth in "more generous" terms: myth is *"an ancient, premodern, prescientific way of addressing questions of ultimate origins and meaning in the form of stories: Who are we? Where do we come from?"* (p. 40; the italics are his). After all, the "scientific world in which we live and that we take so much for granted was inconceivable to the ancient Mesopotamians" (p. 40). But if the ANE stories are "myth," and the biblical parallels are similar, "does this indicate that myth is the proper category for understanding Genesis? Before the discovery of the Akkadian stories, one could quite safely steer clear of such a question, but that is no longer the case."

Second, Enns groups together the *Nuzi* documents, the *Code of Hammurabi,* the Hittite suzerainty treaties, and *Instruction of Amenemope*—all reflecting customs, laws, and proverbs. On any dating, the *Code of Hammurabi* predates Moses by several hundred years. Granted the parallels with the Bible, don't these facts make the Bible look a good deal less than unique? "In other words, the Bible seems to be relativized" (p. 43).

Third, Enns groups together the Tel Dan inscription, the Siloam tunnel inscription, and the *Mesha* inscription, all dealing with Israel and her kings. In some ways, these support the historicity of the monarchs. The first two inscriptions attest the reigns of David and Hezekiah respectively. But the *Mesha* inscription introduces a new problem. It is an account of King Mesha of Moab, and transparently it is a seriously biased, self-serving account. The conflict with King Omri of Israel is introduced, but in the *Mesha* inscription, Moab got out of that one because their god Chemosh came to the rescue. "In other words, the Mesha Inscription raises the following problem: do biblical authors have an ax to grind as well?" (p. 45).

In the past, Enns avers, as these documents became available, the sure ground of Scripture was eroded by liberals who argued that these historical contexts unavoidably relativize the Bible, which can no longer be taken as the unique Word of God. But evangelicals, implicitly assuming that "the Bible, being the Word of God, ought to be historically accurate in all its details (since God would not lie or make errors) and unique in its own setting (since God's word is revealed, which implies a specific type of uniqueness)" (p. 47), opted for selective engagement, and embraced evidence that seems to support the biblical text, while retreating from or criticizing "evidence that seems to undercut these assumptions" (p. 47). Worse, "the *doctrinal implications of the Bible being so much a part of its ancient contexts* are still not being addressed as much as they should" (p. 47).

So what is the way ahead? Before proceeding, Enns articulates two assumptions: (a) he rejects the notion "that a modern doctrine of Scripture can be articulated in blissful isolation from the evidence we have" (p. 48); and (b) all articulations of the nature of Scripture, including his own, are corrigible. He then circles around his three problem questions again, this time with his own proposals for the way ahead.

First, "Is Genesis myth or history?" (pp. 49–56). Enns rejects the disjunction, "myth" or "history." Israelite culture is a relative latecomer on the ANE scene, so it seems unlikely that late Israelite texts preserve the earliest form of these accounts in Israel's much later texts. So when "God adopted Abraham as the forefather of a new people . . . he also adopted the mythic categories within which Abraham— and everyone else—thought" (p. 53). Of course, he did not leave these myths unchanged: "God *transformed* the ancient myths so that Israel's story would come to focus on its God, the real one" (p. 54). Still, Enns preserves a schematized drawing of this ostensible ANE universe, taken over from Alan P. Dickin, complete with the foundations of the earth, the pillars of the earth, the location of Sheol, the distinction between the upper waters and the lower waters, the actual floodgates of heaven, the roof of the sky, and the throne of God. It is almost inconceivable to think that God would have given his revelation to people of the time in the terms and categories that make sense to twenty-first-century Westerners. Rather: "This is what it means for God to speak to a certain time and place—he enters *their* world. He speaks and acts in ways that make sense to *them*. This is surely what it means for God to reveal himself to people—he accommodates, condescends, meets them where they are" (p. 56).

Second, "Is revelation unique?" (pp. 56–59). With respect to the second group of texts, Enns argues that ancient Israelite laws and proverbs, Israel's customs and ethical standards, "are not absolutely unique to Israel" (p. 56). In short, it is not the *content* of Israel's laws and customs that is unique, but something else, exemplified, for instance, in the introduction to the Decalogue (Exodus 20): the "motivation and the historical conditions of Israel's law code are very different from its neighbors [*sic*]" (p. 58).

Third, "Is good historiography objective or biased?" (pp. 59–66). Historiography, after all, is not a mere statement of facts, "but the *shaping* of these facts for a particular *purpose*. To put it another way, historiography is an attempt to relay to someone the *significance* of history" (p. 60). Moreover, there is plenty of evidence that this takes place in Scripture: one need only compare 1–2 Chronicles with Samuel–Kings to see that there is a somewhat different agenda, an independent point of view, even though roughly the same material is being covered. One could say much the same with respect to the Gospels.

> Of course, the Bible is different. It is God's word. But what is true of all historiography is also true of biblical historiography—it is not objective. In fact—and this is getting more to the heart of the matter—in the strict sense of the word, there really is no such thing as objective historiography. . . . What makes biblical historiography the word of God is not that it is somehow immune from such things. It is God's word because it is—this is how God did it. To be able to *confess* that the Bible is God's word is the gift of faith. To *understand* this confession is an ongoing process of greater clarification and insight, a process that will not end. (p. 66)

In the second substantive chapter, the third chapter of the book (pp. 71–112), Enns treats the theological diversity within the Old Testament. He begins by summarizing three quite distinct approaches to reading the Scriptures. Jewish interpreters delight in the diversity, tensions, and ambiguities, which spur Jewish scholars on to more profound reflection. The effort is not so much to resolve tensions as to enter the conversation. By contrast, both liberal-critical scholars and evangelical scholars adopt quite a different assumption: "God's word and diversity at the level of factual content and theological message are incompatible" (p. 73). The liberal-critical scholars make the assumption and conclude that this is not God's word in any meaningful way; the evangelical scholars, with the same assumption, feel awkward in the face of the diversity and expend their energies explaining it away. Enns's purpose in this chapter is "to outline some examples of diversity in the Old Testament in order to demonstrate that diversity is inherent to the Old Testament text and not imposed onto the Bible from outside attacks on its unity.... It is an important part of Scripture's own dynamic" (p. 73).

I do not have space here to summarize all of the evidence that Enns adduces, but I will try to convey something of its sweep. He begins with the Wisdom Literature, in particular Proverbs, Ecclesiastes, and Job (pp. 74–82). Proverbs can tell us not to answer a fool according to his folly, and to answer a fool according to his folly (Prov. 26:4–5); it can treat wealth as a blessing that secures them while the poor are left unprotected (Prov. 10:15), but it can treat wealth as something unstable and thus a false security (18:11; cf. 11:28), while yet again treating wealth as a more or less neutral thing whose benefits depend on the quality of the person who possesses it (10:16).

> The point to be stressed here is that *all* of these proverbs are wise. *All* are correct. The question is not *whether* they are correct, but *when*. It is, therefore, wrong to think of "the teaching of Proverbs on wealth" with the expectation that all its statements about wealth "say the same thing" or are compatible on the level of isolated concepts. The wisdom derived from Proverbs on the question of wealth differs depending on what proverb you read. To isolate any one proverb and claim universal validity is in fact a fundamental misreading of the trajectory of the book. (p. 76)

Ecclesiastes goes further, and displays two kinds of diversity: (a) diversity within the book itself, as Qoheleth adopts different stances amid the contradictions of life to try to make sense of existence; and (b) diversity between what this book says and what mainstream Old Testament theology says—including the insistence that with much wisdom comes much sorrow (1:18), which is scarcely what Proverbs says (cf. Prov. 4:7), or its approach to the afterlife (Eccles. 2:18–21). As for Job, while much of the Old Testament "presents the notion that deeds have consequences" (p. 80; cf. Deut. 5:32–33; Prov. 3:1–2), this is the stance of the three miserable comforters (Eliphaz, Job 5:17–18; Bildad, 8:20–22; Zophar, 11:13–15—all of whom are condemned) and even of Elihu (36:5–7). For Job is in the position of a man who is suffering even though he does not deserve it.

Enns turns next to diversity in Chronicles (pp. 82–85). He places Samuel and Kings within the sweep of the Deuteronomistic History, affirming that the purpose of these books, at least in part, is to explain the exile to an exilic audi-

ence: Why did we get into this mess? By contrast, the purpose of Chronicles is
to address those who have returned to the land. "The burning question was not,
'What did we do to get us kicked out of the land?' but, 'Now that we are back,
what do we do?'; or, perhaps a better way of putting it, 'Who are we? Are we still
God's people? How can we be sure he'll have us back?'" (p. 84). In consequence,
the books of Chronicles greatly diminish the sins of David, emphasize the unity
of God's people, strongly emphasize the temple and Solomon's role, and articulate
a theology of "immediate retribution" (p. 84). "The basic point . . . is that there is
considerable theological diversity between the two accounts of Israel's history"
(p. 85).

As for diversity in law (pp. 85–97), Enns notes the differences between the two
reports of the Decalogue (Ex. 20:2–17 and Deut. 5:6–21) and infers, "God seems
to be perfectly willing to allow his law to be adjusted over time" (p. 87). Moreover, the Decalogue insists that God is a jealous God who punishes the children
for the sins of the fathers to the third and fourth generation (Ex. 20:5–6; Deut.
5:9–10), while Ezekiel 18 seems to restrict the punishment to the individual: "the
soul who sins is the one who will die" (18:4; see esp. vv. 19–20). Enns goes on to
detail differences he finds in laws regarding slaves, the Passover, and the contrast
between the central importance of sacrifices in the Pentateuch and the casual
relegation of sacrifice to at best secondary importance in some of the prophets
(Hos. 6:6 ["For I desire mercy, not sacrifice, and acknowledgment of God rather
than burnt offerings"]; Amos 5:21–27; Mic. 6:6–8; Isa. 1:11–14; Jer. 7:21–23).
Of course, Enns is careful to recognize these assorted texts were never meant
to be taken in isolation: "They were speaking to the mere institutionalizing of
sacrifice, that is, sacrifice without heartfelt obedience in the remainder of one's
life" (p. 94). But Enns insists his point stands firm anyway: "What is important
for us to note, however, is that within the Old Testament itself there is a dynamic
quality. Even something so fundamental to Israel's religious system as sacrifice is
open to critical reflection" (p. 94).

This is exactly the same sort of flexibility Enns finds in Paul, when on the one
hand the apostle insists that "circumcision is no longer binding for Gentiles to
enter God's family" (p. 95; see Acts 15:1–35; Enns could have added Gal. 2:1–4),
but on the other hand happily circumcises Timothy (Acts 16:1–3). "Paul does
what he does because the *situation* calls for it" (p. 95). Or again, the Old Testament's stance toward Gentiles is highly diverse. For instance, on the one hand we
are told that no Ammonite or Moabite may enter the Lord's assembly, down to the
tenth generation (Deut. 23:3); on the other hand, Ruth is a Moabitess whose first
husband, Mahlon, is an Israelite from the tribe of Judah, and whose next husband,

Boaz, joins with her to form the line that sires David and thus begins the David dynasty—all within four generations.

Even what the Old Testament says about God is diverse (pp. 97–107). On the one hand, there are passages that stress God's superiority over other gods (e.g., Pss. 86:8; 95:3; 135:5; 136:2). The Israelites are told to serve the Lord *alone* (e.g., Josh. 24:2, 14–15). When the Decalogue is disclosed (Ex. 20), God does not reveal himself as the only God, but as the God who brought the Israelites out of the land of slavery (Ex. 20:2). But on the other hand, there are "high points" of insistent monotheism in which the gods of the surrounding nations are dismissed as nothings (e.g., Isa. 44:6–20; 1 Kings 18:16–46). Moreover, though the Bible can say some powerful things about God being the Creator of everything, who thus stands sovereignly over the whole, it often depicts God as someone *within* the story. God "changes his mind" (p. 103)—not only in the context of massive movements (e.g., Gen. 6:5–8), but also in consequence of Moses interceding with him (Ex. 32–34). Enns insists he is not entering the "openness of God" debate; rather, he writes,

> I feel bound to talk about God *in the way(s) the Bible does*, even if I am not comfortable with it. . . . God reveals himself *throughout* the Old Testament. There is no part that gets it "more right" than others. Rather, they get at different sides of God. Or, to use the well-worn analogy, the different descriptions of God in the Old Testament are like the different colors and textures that *together* combine to make a portrait. In keeping with the incarnational analogy, we can appreciate that the *entire* Bible, through and through, has that human dimension. So, for the Old Testament to speak of God as changing his mind means that this is *his* choice for how *he* wants us to know him. (p. 106)

Enns ends the chapter by asking what such diversity tells us about Scripture. He must again be quoted at length:

> It seems to me that there is a significant strand of contemporary Christian thinking on the Old Testament that feels that these sorts of things just shouldn't happen. And, if they do, they just *appear* to be a problem. You just need to read a bit more closely or do a little more research, and if you're patient enough, you'll get the right answer eventually. For others, however (including myself), such an approach comes close to intellectual dishonesty. To accept the diversity of the Old Testament is not to "cave in to liberalism," nor is it to seek after novelty. It is rather, to read the Old

Testament quite honestly and seriously. And if diversity is such a prevalent phenomenon in the Old Testament, it would seem to be important to do more than simply take note of diversity and file it away for future reference. We must ask why God would do it *this* way. Why does God's word look the way it does? (p. 107)

What this diversity shows is that "there is no superficial unity" to the Bible (p. 108). The unity that exists is "not a superficial unity based on the surface content of the words of passages taken in isolation" (p. 110). It is something more subtle and simultaneously deeper:

> It is a unity that should ultimately be sought in Christ himself, the living word. . . . It is . . . a broad and foundational theological commitment based on the analogy between Christ and Scripture. . . . Christ is supreme, and it is in him, the embodied word, that the written word ultimately finds its unity. Christ is the final destiny of Israel's story, and it is to him that the Bible as a whole bears witness. (p. 110)

That brings us to Enns's final substantive chapter, his fourth chapter (pp. 113–65). Here Enns surveys the way the Old Testament is interpreted by and in the New. Beginning with the requisite example of a preacher who abuses an Old Testament text—the choice is Genesis 31:22, "On the third day Laban was told that Jacob had fled," with the preacher explaining that Jesus rose on the "third day" and "fled" from the grave—Enns wants, rather, to affirm the basic instinct to respect the author's intention. Nevertheless, he asserts, the New Testament appeals to the Old Testament, or makes use of it, in ways that are so strange that they make us uncomfortable. Enns rejects solutions (a) that try to show the New Testament authors really do respect the Old Testament context; (b) that concede the New Testament author is not using the Old Testament text "in a manner in which it was intended," but which then argues the New Testament author is not really interpreting the Old Testament text but merely *applying* it (p. 115); (c) that concede the Old Testament text is being stretched way beyond its context, but which then simply appeals to apostolic authority to cover the breach. Enns is happy to summarize his alternative:

1. The New Testament authors were not engaging the Old Testament in an effort to remain consistent with the original context and intention of the Old Testament author.
2. They were indeed commenting on what the text *meant*.

3. The hermeneutical attitude they embodied should be embraced and followed by the church today.

To put it succinctly, the New Testament authors were explaining what the Old Testament means *in light of Christ's coming*. (pp. 115–16)

And if we are to begin to understand apostolic hermeneutics, Enns says, the first thing to be done is to try to understand, "*as best we can, the interpretive world in which the New Testament was written*" (p. 116; italics his).

So that is what he turns to (pp. 116–32). He begins with inner-biblical interpretation—not simply the rewriting implicit in the work of the Chronicler, but how Daniel interprets Jeremiah's prophecy of the seventy years (Jer. 25:11; 29:10; Dan. 9:1–2, 21–24): because Gabriel provides him with "insight and understanding," Daniel is able to interpret the seventy years as "seventy sevens" of years. "It is by heavenly illumination that Daniel comes to understand the fuller, deeper measure of Jeremiah's prophecy" (p. 118). This, Enns says, is akin to the way the resurrected Christ had to "open the minds" of his disciples to enable them to "understand" the Scriptures written about him in the Law of Moses, the Prophets, and the Psalms (Luke 24:44–48).

With this sort of "interpretation" in mind, Enns scans some of the literature of Second Temple Judaism. The Wisdom of Solomon not only retells some aspects or other of biblical stories, but adds interpretive traditions that had become commonplace in the understanding of those stories. Enns finds similar phenomena in the *Book of Biblical Antiquities*, certain rabbinic texts, Jubilees, some of Philo's writings, and the Targum of Pseudo-Jonathan. The much-quoted *pesher* on Habakkuk 1:5, 1QpHab, puts in an appearance so that a comparison can be drawn between the form of this *pesher* and the form of reference to Scripture in Luke 24. The point Enns is attempting to establish from all this is that the New Testament writers adopted similar interpretive *methods* and interpretive *traditions* as these writers (p. 128).

To clarify and justify this conclusion, Enns devotes the next section to New Testament interpretive methods (pp. 132–42) and the subsequent section to New Testament interpretive traditions (pp. 142–51). As for methods: Enns briefly analyzes a number of texts to demonstrate his point, including the use of Hosea 11:1 in Matthew 2:15, of Isaiah 49:8 in 2 Corinthians 6:2, of the use of Abraham's "seed" in Galatians 3:16, 29, of Isaiah 59:20 in Romans 11:26–27, and of Psalm 95:9–10 in Hebrews 3:7–11. I will pick up on one or two or these below; for now it is enough to note that in each case Enns thinks that the New Testament writer, adopting Jewish hermeneutical methods, felt free to add words or change the referent or the like, in order to establish his point, even if that point was sub-stantively different from the Old Testament text itself. As for the willingness of New Testament writers to adopt the interpretive *traditions* of Second Temple Judaism, Enns adduces the mention of Jannes and Jambres in 2 Timothy 3:8; the mention of Noah as "a preacher of righteousness" in 2 Peter 2:5; the dispute over Moses' body picked up in Jude 9; the allusion to *1 Enoch* in Jude 14–15 (though Enns thinks of it as a citation); the reference to Moses' Egyptian education (Acts 7:21–22); the triple New Testament reference to the fact that the law was put into effect through angels (Acts 7:52–53; Gal. 3:19; Heb. 2:2–3); and the rather strange mention of what Enns calls "Paul's movable well" (1 Cor. 10:4). In each instance there are analogous passages in the literature of Second Temple Judaism, and on the face of it the New Testament writers seem to be picking up on these traditions without any discomfort, even though they are not clearly found, or not found at all, within the canonical Old Testament text.

So what makes apostolic hermeneutics unique? Neither the methods nor the traditions adopted by the New Testament writers qualify as unique, Enns avers. The difference is this: the New Testament writers came to believe that Jesus is Lord; they knew that the historical death and resurrection of the Son of God had taken place, "and on the basis of that fact reread their Scripture in a fresh way" (p. 152). By our standards, the result is eisegesis; by their own, their reading of the Old Testament is "*christotelic*" (p. 153)—i.e., "To read the Old Testament 'christotelically' is to read it *already knowing* that Christ is somehow the *end* to which the Old Testament story is heading" (p. 154). And we must read the Old Testament the same way (pp. 156–60).

In his final brief chapter (pp. 167–73), Enns summarizes his argument and encourages his readers in humility, love, and patience. And he returns to his "incar-national paradigm":

> To work within an incarnational paradigm means that our expectations of the Bible must be in conversation with the data, otherwise we run the very real risk of trying to understand the Bible in fundamental isolation from the cultures in which it was written—which is to say, we would be working with a very nonincarnate understanding of Scripture. Whatever words Christians employ to speak of the Bible (inerrant, infallible, authoritative, revelational, inspired), either today or in the past, must be seen as attempts to describe what can never be fully understood. (p. 168)

Critique

In some ways, this is the most traditional of the three volumes reviewed in this article. Appearances to the contrary, it advances no new theory or grand hypothesis. At least one of its aims is to enlighten the less informed constituents of evangelicalism, and Enns tackles this assignment with verve. As a result, the book is easy to read and assimilate. And of course, it must be evaluated against the standard of its own objectives.

(1) That introduces the first problem: Who are the intended readers? The answer to that question, in the case of this book, must be an integral part of the evaluation. Enns himself, it must be recalled, states that his envisaged readers are the "fair number of Christians who conclude that the contemporary state of biblical scholarship makes an evangelical faith unviable" (p. 13). In other words, granted the historical/literary/archaeological difficulties cast up by "biblical scholarship," how can "evangelical faith"—presumably what evangelical faith says about the Bible—be viable? Taking this at face value, the difficulties should be the "given" in the minds of the envisaged readers, and the book would then either challenge some of those "difficulties" in order to maintain evangelicalism's stance on the Bible, or it would accommodate the difficulties and provide a more sophisticated understanding of "evangelical faith," or perhaps a revision of it. Yet in the three substantive chapters, most of the space is devoted instead to convincing the reader that the difficulties Enns isolates are real and must be taken more seriously by evangelicals than is usually the case. In other words, despite his initial claim that he is writing the book to comfort the disturbed, as it were, the actual performance aims to disturb the comfortable. This makes the book rather difficult to evaluate. Moreover, Enns's ambitions are vaulting: the evidence cast up by biblical scholarship, we are told, is of the sort that requires that an "adjustment" be made in how we think of Scripture, akin to the reinterpretation generated by the Copernican revolution (p. 13). Wow. So are we explaining how evangelical faith accommodates biblical scholarship, or are we asserting that a Copernican revolution must take place within evangelical faith so as to accommodate biblical scholarship?

Either way, a fair evaluation must probe the status of the problems that Enns adduces, the nature of the solution he advances, and the pastoral wisdom and effectiveness of the presentation.

(2) The controlling analogy that Enns advances is the incarnation: the title of the book is not accidental. In choosing the incarnation as the fundamental way to think about the nature of Scripture, Enns is adopting a path diametrically opposite to what Webster judges to be appropriate. We have already seen that there is

at least a superficial parallel to be drawn between, on the one hand, confessing Jesus to be God and a human being, and, on the other, confessing that Scripture is both God's word and human word—not least when the Scriptures themselves can speak of Jesus as the Word made flesh. Enns, of course, is not the first to draw attention to the parallels between Christ and Scripture. Yet this is the place where Enns's discussion becomes disturbingly inadequate, not to say seriously slanted. Three things stand out.

First, Enns offers no discussion whatsoever of what the doctrine of the incarnation actually looks like. If the incarnation is to become the controlling model for our understanding of the nature of Scripture, then are we not owed some exposition, however brief, of what "incarnation" means to Enns? The word is thrown around in contemporary discussion with an enormous array of meanings; it is entirely unclear what Enns means. But let us suppose, for charity's sake, that he stands roughly in line with Nicea and Chalcedon.

That brings up the *second* problem. The *only* thing that Enns draws from the doctrine of the incarnation is that Jesus is *truly* a human being; he does not merely *appear* to be a human being. In other words, for Enns an adequate affirmation of the incarnation entails the abolition of docetism, and the parallel with Scripture entails the abolition of a kind of scriptural docetism, in which Scripture only *appears* to be human, but is not *truly* human. So far so good. But the doctrine of the incarnation was used to fight off multiple errors, not just docetism. For instance, it equally fights off Arianism, in which Jesus is not *truly* God, but at most is an inferior god, or perhaps merely godlike. If incarnation is to serve as the controlling model for how Scripture is to be understood, why does not Enns use it to refute the voices that confess the Bible to be *only* a human document, or a collection of human documents? In what sense is the Bible *God's* word, or, as we have noted in biblical usage, a collection of *God's words*? And how do the human and the divine dimensions of Scripture cohere? Is there some point where we appeal to mystery, as we appeal to mystery when we are talking about the divine nature and the human nature cohering in the one person, Jesus the Messiah? Without ever discussing the nature of the incarnation, Enns is using the incarnation as a positive "buzz" word to fight off his opponents to the right, but he never develops the doctrine, or the argument, to warn against dangers at least as great on the left (if we may resort to that old left/right spectrum). Nor is it merely a question of balance that could be remedied by another book treating the other side. The doctrine of the incarnation is powerful and central to Christian confessionalism not only because it counters "left" and "right" alike, but because it carefully formulates what it *means* to confess Jesus as the God/man. If the incarnation were deployed *only* to fight off docetism, pretty soon we would have a thoroughly human Jesus, but nothing more; if it were deployed *only* to fight off Arianism, pretty soon we would have a thoroughly divine Jesus, but nothing more. The doctrine of the incarnation tries, with appropriate caution, hesitation, and adoration, to get it right. But the only way it functions in Enns's analogical argument is to confirm that docetism is bad, and therefore a failure to confess the truly human nature of Scripture is bad. Enns adduces all the evidence he can for the Bible's humanness, and reflects on it at length; he does not attempt to adduce all the evidence he can for the Bible's rootedness in God himself, and reflect at length on that—not even the very sketchy bits of evidence I mentioned in discussing Webster's book. It is not just that the view of Scripture that Enns paints is lopsided, but that the *heart* of the issue is sidestepped, i.e., how it must all cohere. Think "incarnation" in any historic, confessional sense of "incarnation," and you are never far away from mystery (in the modern sense of that word); apply it as Enns has done to the nature of Scripture, and there is very little that is mysterious at all. Apply it to Jesus, and you think "God/man"; apply it to the Bible in the way that Enns does and you think "not docetic; thoroughly human." True, Enns repeatedly concedes that the Bible is God's word, but because he does not tie that confession to incarnation, or warn against a kind of scriptural Arianism, or probe the difficulties inherent in Scripture's dual nature, the result is remarkably distorted.

Third, whenever one makes an entire argument turn on analogy, it is imperative to explain in what ways the two poles of the analogy are alike and unlike. In christology, for instance, we speak of two natures and one person; we cannot deploy exactly that terminology in talking about the Bible. When we speak of Jesus as truly human, as truly a man, we carefully insist that he is a *perfect* man, i.e., a man without sin, and that there is nothing intrinsic to humanness that requires that humans be sinners. In that sense, Jesus is thoroughly like us, human; he is also thoroughly unlike all of us, since he alone is sinlessly perfect. If the incarnation is to be our model for how we think of Scripture, or even of Scripture's humanness, how do such elementary distinctions as these play out? What might it mean to say that Scripture is composed of thoroughly human, but perfect, documents? Or does the analogy break down? If so, why and where? None of this is discussed. "Incarnation" is merely a rhetorically positive word to approve Enns's argument; it is not a word with real substance that can clarify or illuminate the nature of Scripture by really careful analogical argumentation. Thus, when Enns writes (his italics), *"It is essential to the very nature of revelation that the Bible is not unique to its environment. The human dimension of Scripture is essential to its being Scripture"* (p. 20), the statement is formally true and hopelessly muddled. Using the incarnational analogy, the "human dimension" of the God/man not only places him in the human environment, but leaves him unique in that environment since only he is without sin. And even more strikingly, of course, what makes Jesus most strikingly unique to the human environment is that, without gainsaying his thorough, perfect, humanness for an instant, he is also God, and thus the perfect revealer of God, such that what Jesus says and does, God says and does. But when Enns speaks of "the very nature of the revelation of the Bible" as "not unique in its environment," he looks *only* at its "human dimension" and integrates nothing of what else *must* be said if we are to understand what the Bible *is* in this "human environment." I hasten to add that I am as rigorously opposed to what he thinks of as a docetic understanding of Scripture as he. But I am no less suspicious of an Arian understanding of Scripture—or, if we may get away from the incarnational analogy, I am no less suspicious of assorted non-supernatural and domesticated understandings of the Bible, understandings of the Bible that are far removed from, say, that of the Lord Jesus. Methodologically, Enns gets himself into these problems because he has spelled out neither what he understands of the doctrine of the incarnation, nor how well analogical arguments work in this case, and what limitations might be applicable.

(3) The argument as to whether Genesis 1–11 is myth or history is freighted with generalizations and antitheses that leave the informed reader saying, "Yes, but . . ." Basing his argument on comparisons between the biblical accounts and other ANE accounts, Enns is surely right to ask hard questions, and he is commendably careful not to rush toward any theory of direct literary dependence. The same sorts of questions could be raised by asking what literary genre(s) these chapters belong to, for different literary genres have different ways of making their rhetorical effects, of talking about reality, and so forth. Enns is certainly right to insist that we should not expect Genesis to use the scientific terminology of twenty-first-century science—for why not seventeenth-century science, or twenty-third-century science (which option, of course, makes a small assumption!)? Nevertheless:

First, the "myth" category is not so much wrong as loaded. Enns's definition, we recall, is that myth is *"an ancient, premodern, prescientific way of addressing questions of ultimate origins and meaning in the form of stories: Who are we? Where do we come from?"* (p. 40; the italics are his). By itself, of course, this definition is fairly innocuous, for it does not even glance at the question of how we should relate this "ancient, premodern, prescientific" way of thinking about origins with reality. Yet the history of the use of "myth" in the study of the Bible—not only with respect to origins, but also with respect to who Jesus is: one cannot easily forget the influence of David Friedrich Strauss—warns us that unless one asks a lot of pressing questions, "myth" becomes the proverbial nose of the camel in the tent.[22] Are there not some slightly better ways of proceeding than a choice between "twenty-first century science" and "myth"?

Second, the choice between "history" and "myth" seems to control Enns's discussion for a while, and then he carefully debunks the choice (p. 49). The distinction

> seems to be a modern invention. It presupposes—without stating explic-
> itly—that what is historical, in a modern sense of the word, is more real, of
> more value, more like something God would do, than myth. So, the argu-
> ment goes, if Genesis is myth, then it is not "of God." Conversely, if Genesis
> is history, only then is it something worthy of the name "Bible." (p. 49)

The argument rushes on, and it takes a moment before you realize you've just been had. Doubtless it is true that the *modern* definition of "myth" and the *modern* definition of history is a *modern* invention: that is mere truism. But in that case, why apply the *modern* sense of "myth" to this ancient literature? The fact remains that the ancient writers could distinguish between, say, what they understood to be actually taking place in the domain of human existence and a fable: observe how Judges 9 stands out from the surrounding chapters. The ancient literary categories do not overlap exactly with ours, of course, and that is why we must always take care when we talk about biblical genres (lament, poetry, oracle, letter, apocalyptic, and so forth). It is also why sometimes our label must be carefully distinguished from the use of the formally identical label in the text (e.g., the word παραβολή covers a far wider array of forms than what we mean by "parable" today, which is almost entirely restricted to narrative parables; what Paul means by "allegory" is not exactly what we usually mean by "allegory"—indeed, it is not even quite what Paul's contemporary Philo meant by "allegory," since the word then covered a broader semantic swath than we sometimes think). So whatever we decide is the most helpful and insightful genre-label for the opening chapters of the Bible, a fair bit of sophistication is needed. And isn't it proper to ask (however difficult it may be to answer) what the ancients themselves thought was the connection between, on the one hand, their accounts of creation and the flood, and what actually happened? Isn't that a question we must ask of *Enuma Elish* every bit as much as we ask it of Genesis? And if they *did* think that their accounts really did

---

[22]Cf. the wise words of Tremper Longman III, *How to Read Genesis* (Downers Grove, IL: InterVarsity, 2005), 61, who prefers something generic such as "theological history," and says, regarding other proposed genre labels such as "novella, legend, fable, etiology, and myth": "Such terms are clearly prejudicial to the historical intentionality of the book."

describe things, more or less, as they occurred, what, precisely, are we to infer? If they did *not* think of their accounts as describing, more or less, what occurred, what *did* they think? Or do we know too little to say? I can imagine half a dozen ways of proceeding from here, some of which would be seen as widely acceptable to traditional understandings of the nature of Scripture, and some of which would not be. What I cannot imagine is a responsible handling of the nexus of Scripture, myth, and history, *without* addressing some of these questions.

Third, while Enns rightly asserts that there is no convincing evidence of direct borrowing between Genesis and the relevant ANE accounts of creation and flood, he does little to point out the differences. That the categories of thought are remarkably similar is obvious, and should cause no surprise among those who fully recognize how much the biblical revelation is grounded in history (more on that below); yet competent scholars have laid out the differences between Genesis and the other ANE accounts with penetrating attention both to detail and the big picture, and Enns does not interact with that literature.[23] Had he done so, perhaps his argument would have been a tad less tendentious.

Fourth, the much published line-drawing of Dickin, complete with foundations of the earth, pillars of the earth, sheol, lower and higher waters, and all the rest (p. 54), raises interesting questions about how the Old Testament writers themselves understood these expressions. Did they think of literal pillars, as the drawing suggests? Perhaps so—but I wonder, and I have my doubts. Does the reference to "the circle of the earth" in Isaiah 40:22 mean that the writer thought of the world as a sphere? Or that at the very least he was aware of the curvature of the world? And in that case doesn't Dickin's rather flat surface beg a few questions? Or if the Isaiah reference should be understood in some sort of poetic/ metaphorical sense, may "pillars of the earth" be understood similarly? When I was a boy of about nine or ten, my father called me over to listen to him reading an editorial or a letter to the editor (I cannot remember which) in *The Montreal Star*, one of the leading papers in eastern Canada at the time. The writer was inveighing against all those stupid Christians who believe the Bible is the word of God, when it speaks so ignorantly of the sun "rising" in the east: any schoolboy knows that the sun does not rise, but that the earth rotates on its axis. My father asked me what I thought of the argument. I looked at him rather nonplused. He grinned, and calmly turned to the front page of the paper, and drew my attention to the line, "Sunrise: 6:36 am."

---

[23]One thinks, for instance, of the important book by David Tsumura, *Creation and Destruction: A Reappraisal of the Chaoskampf Theory in the Old Testament* (Winona Lake, IN: Eisenbrauns, 2005). If this edition of the book appeared too late for inclusion in Enns's volume, the earlier edition, under the title *Genesis 1 and 2: A Linguistic Evaluation*, made the same points in 1989, with somewhat less detail.

Fifth, all this reflection is decidedly lacking in pastoral sensitivity. I do not mean to ask Enns to write an entirely different book. But when I compare this book with the one by Tremper Longman, to which I have already referred (viz., *How to Read Genesis*), I know which one I would be happy to put into the hands of students. Longman covers much of the same turf, but his judgments are subtler, there is no hint of the "angry young man" syndrome, he maintains a serene evaluative stance that does not project itself into the position of correcting everybody, and he happily lays out the kinds of themes that the Genesis text is certainly establishing. On the latter point, he reminds me of the book by Francis Schaeffer, *Genesis in Space and Time*, now more than three decades old.[24] Schaeffer raises some of the questions that are extremely difficult to resolve to everyone's satisfaction, and then asks the disarming question, in effect, "What is the least that Genesis 1–11 must be saying if we are to maintain that the Bible is true and hangs together?" Longman does not ask exactly the same question, but he happily reflects on the "theological teaching" of the book of Genesis.[25] Or again, the volume by Henri Blocher tackles many of the questions raised by Enns, but he integrates his discussion into a much more integrated framework that includes exegesis, science, ANE literature, historical and systematic theology, and more. Enns refers to neither work. Moreover, some of the best recent commentaries on Genesis, not least those written by evangelicals, display the same merits. This is not to say that every Christian reader will want to adopt all of the conclusions put forward by Blocher, or by Schaeffer and recent commentators, or, for that matter, by Enns. But with Blocher and Schaeffer, one does not feel "got at," and it is easy to admire both the largeness of their vision and their pastoral wisdom.

(4) Enns repeatedly asks his readers to reflect on the questions, If Genesis is so much like other ANE literature, how can we think that Genesis alone is revelation? More generally, if laws and "historical" records in the Bible are so much like parallel ANE sources, in what sense is the Bible unique? Or more pointedly yet, if the parallel "historical" sources are biased, shouldn't we admit that the biblical documents are no less biased? Isn't it best to admit that there is no such thing as objective historiography?

After a while, these questions begin to feel as if I am being squeezed into a Sophie's choice, into a "damned if you do and damned if you don't" pair of alternatives. If Bible readers think that what is found in the text of Scripture is rather different from what one finds in parallel ANE literature, obviously they are flirting with a docetic (mis)understanding of Scripture. Alternatively, if they find the text

---

[24]London: Hodder & Stoughton, 1972.
[25]E.g., *How to Read Genesis*, 27–34.

of Scripture is rather similar to what one finds in parallel ANE literature, obviously Scripture is as biased and as guilty of subjective historiography as are those sources, threatening the very foundations of what we mean by revelation.

But why? Most of us glory in the fact that God has disclosed himself to us in space-time history, in real words, to real people, in real languages. This is one crucial component of the doctrine of accommodation. Almost half a millennium ago, Calvin treated that subject with more imagination and flourish, more rigor and comprehension, than the occasional reference to accommodation in this book, which makes it all the more irritating to be told that evangelicals have not thought much about these matters. Moreover, the notion of "objective historiography," which Enns dismisses so confidently, deserves more thoughtful treatment. If by "objective historiography" Enns is holding out for an ideal in which historical events are portrayed in absolute comprehensiveness and perfect proportion, then it is a mere truism that there is no such thing as "objective historiography": the bar has been raised so high that objective historiography is open only to Omniscience. Moreover, since God himself cannot dump his omniscient knowledge into the minds of finite beings, even the most staggeringly immediate notion of revelation could not alleviate the problem: human knowledge will always be partial, even in eternity, since omniscience is not a communicable attribute of God. That is one of the reasons why the notion of accommodation must be thought through. The problem is that to ordinary readers whom Enns wants to help, the disavowal of objective historiography will sound, rather, like the disavowal of historiography that tells the truth, which is quite a different thing. King Mesha provides a rather self-serving report: good observation. But one of the remarkable things about biblical treatment of biblical "heroes" is that they are portrayed warts and all: think of David, Abraham, Moses, Peter, Barnabas, and so forth. Where are Mesha's warts? Of course the biblical records regarding King Omri do not tell *everything* that Omniscience knows about him: in that sense, the selection itself guarantees that the report is "biased." But does the report that is transparently and inevitably "biased" in this sense nevertheless tell the truth about him? Yes, the biblical report of the new Persian policy that permits the Jewish exiles to return home focuses almost all attention on the Jews themselves, without discussing how the policy affected a lot of other national/tribal groups: in that sense, it is "biased." But does it tell the truth about what is actually reported? And if we are going to maintain the incarnation as a useful analogy for our understanding of Scripture, doesn't the "humanness" of Scripture's approach to reportage have to be tied, somehow, to the evidence that these words are also God's words, duly accommodated?

(5) Enns is right, of course, to point out that Scripture includes diverse theological emphases. And he is right to point out that Scripture is being domesticated if this diversity is flattened, whether by reading Mark and John as if they boasted identical emphases, or by reading 1 and 2 Chronicles as if their theological emphases cannot be properly differentiated from those of Samuel and Kings. But Enns expends too little energy in showing how these diverse voices sing in the same choir and harmonize rather well.

I cannot take the space to deal with every instance Enns adduces, but a few examples will demonstrate that the diversity is not quite as problematic as he wants us to think. Consider the two Proverbs, 26:4 and 26:5:

> Do not answer a fool according to his folly,
>> or you will be like him yourself.
>
> Answer a fool according to his folly,
>> or he will be wise in his own eyes.

The fact that these two lie side by side is strong evidence that the compiler did not think they are mutually irreconcilable. Indeed, the second part of each proverb hints at the different situations when one or the other might be most appropriate. I have often appealed to this pair of verses to demonstrate the way proverbs work: they are not universal case law. The formal divergence in this instance powerfully embraces more comprehensive reflection than either proverb alone could have done. Yes, Proverbs includes divergent emphases on wealth. But far from being irreconcilable, these diverging emphases—wealth as an evil, wealth as a blessing; poverty as an evil, poverty as a blessing—are utterly realistic, and together paint a more comprehensive picture than one emphasis alone could have done. Why should anyone find these divergent emphases in any sense problematic?[26] True, at a superficial level, passages such as Hosea 6:6; Amos 5:21–27; Micah 6:6–8 and others might be taken to be in conflict with the insistence of the Mosaic code that the prescribed sacrifices be offered. But apart from the fact that, as a literary form, Hebrew prophets regularly use a "not this . . . but that" form to articulate strong preference or ultimate preference, these verses are also part of the fabric of Old Testament theology that slightly relativizes the Sinai law, thereby preparing the way for that to which, canonically speaking, the law was pointing (as Hebrews 10, and many other passages, insist: more on this below). As for diverse emphases in

---

[26]Indeed, one of the strengths of the book by Craig L. Blomberg (*Neither Poverty Nor Riches: A Biblical Theology of Possessions*, NSBT 7 [Downers Grove, IL: InterVarsity, 1999]) on this subject is its wisdom in knitting the divergent biblical emphases together in faithful proportion and with prophetic application.

Ecclesiastes, Enns criticizes those who see "Qoheleth as a fool himself, someone whose lack of faith will not allow him to see past the end of his nose. The end of the book does not cancel out the words of Qoheleth" (p. 79). But as one reviewer comments in this regard, "No, they don't cancel them out, but they situate them, especially when it is realized that Qoheleth is speaking from an 'under the sun' perspective and that the second wise man who is quoting him to his son (12:8–14) is trying to lift his son to an above the sun perspective."[27]

It is easy to adduce other examples of formal divergence where the disparate emphases must be given full voice, but where the unity is not only fairly transparent, but also more powerful precisely because it is layered and complex. For instance, Deuteronomy 6 commands the Israelites to take their oaths in YHWH's name; the Sermon on the Mount reports Jesus saying that his followers are not to swear at all, but simply let their "Yes" be yes and their "No" no (Matt. 5:33–37; cf. 23:16–22). But is this so very problematic? One swears by what one values most highly. When ancient Israel was constantly tempted by polytheism, taking solemn oaths in the name of their covenant Lord, YHWH, was one small sign of continuing faithfulness. But where swearing by something sacred could be construed as more or less binding depending on antecedent decisions about just how sacred the thing was, then swearing by something sacred became a complex justification for evasive lying: hence Matthew 5 and 23. Paul joins with others in refusing to allow Titus to be circumcised (Gal. 2:1–3), yet circumcises Timothy (Acts 16:1–3). This polarity owes nothing to the fact that the latter incident is written up by Luke and not Paul. Rather, if anyone is suggesting that Gentiles *must* be circumcised if they are to accept the Jewish Messiah and belong to the messianic community, Paul will vehemently refuse, for such a stance jeopardizes the exclusive sufficiency of Jesus Christ. By contrast, where no one is making that assertion, and being circumcised removes barriers and opens the door to synagogues for the sake of evangelism, Paul is eager to comply—and this is entirely in line with Paul's own flexibility when evangelism is at stake (1 Cor. 9:19–23). Enns himself points out that the contrast between Deuteronomy 23:3, where Moabites are prohibited from entering the assembly of the Lord all the way down to the tenth generation, and the book of Ruth, which tells of a Moabitess only four generations removed from King David himself, is in fact of a piece with other Old Testament polarities. In the book of Jonah, God promises the destruction of the Ninevites, yet forgives them when they repent. The Assyrians and the Egyptians are under God's curse, yet the prophet anticipates the time when they will be part of the eschatological people of God (Isa. 19:23–25). Note well that these

---

[27]Tremper Longman III, review of Enns in *Modern Reformation* 14, no. 6 (November–December 2005): 34.

polarities do not require different authors writing at different times: they can be tied up in one book (e.g., Jonah). Yes, Exodus 32–34 depicts God "changing his mind" in response to the prayer of Moses,[28] but Pierre Berthoud, in a paper not yet published, traces out what he calls the "extreme tension" *within* these chapters in the depiction of God himself: for instance, he is not only the God who responds to Moses' prayer, but also the God who insists that his mercy and compassion are his to dispense (33:19).[29] Why, then, should these polarities be viewed as "problems" at all? Why not simply rejoice in the just severity and joyous mercy of God? The disparate emphases regarding the nature of God leave us with a God who is utterly sovereign and transcendent (i.e., "above" space and time), yet who interacts with us as persons in "our" space and time.

Sometimes I think Enns sees this clearly, for several times he wisely avoids the obvious traps characterized by reductionism (e.g., he disavows the theology of the "openness of God" movement). He thus aligns with many generations of commentators and theologians who have wrestled with these things before him. And then suddenly he insists that we must not say that these polarities merely *appear* to be a problem: what people fail to see is that these divergences tell us something about Scripture that everyone seems to be missing (e.g., pp. 107–11). But what? Of course, there have always been Christian preachers and teachers who have veered toward reductionism, and they need to be challenged—but by the same token there have always been preachers and teachers who, precisely because they listen well to Scripture, reflect Scripture's richness and diversity, within a holistic faithfulness, remarkably well. Will Enns join them and speak of the unity of the Bible? Well, yes and no: he asserts that we can speak of "a unity to the Bible . . . but it is not a superficial unity based on the surface content of the words of passages taken in isolation" (p. 110). Well and good: so far, I do not know any serious Christian thinker who would disagree. But then this:

> The unity of the Bible is more subtle but at the same time deeper. It is a unity that should ultimately be sought in Christ himself, the living word. This itself is not a superficial unity, as if we can "find Jesus" in every passage of the Old Testament (a point we will address from a different angle in the next chapter). It is, rather, a broad and foundational commitment based on the analogy between Christ and Scripture. (p. 110)

---

[28]Though many have pointed out that "change one's mind" is not the most obvious rendering of the Hebrew.
[29]See also Michael Widmer, *Moses, God and the Dynamics of Intercessory Prayer* (Tübingen: Mohr Siebeck, 2004).

Yet this is just one more reductionism, gently masked by sloganeering. What Christian wants to deny that in some sense the Bible finds its unity in Christ? Indeed, in recent decades quite a number of Christian thinkers have traced out inner-canonical themes to show how the Bible hangs together and comes to a genuine focus in him. And some of the polarities Enns adduces find some sort of further resolution in Jesus: e.g., texts that relativize the place of the sacrificial system, while people are still under the law-covenant that demands that certain sacrifices be offered. But appeal to Christ does not explain how the divergent emphases on wealth in the Wisdom Literature belong together. There is a deep unity to the Old Testament picture of God, which is then deepened further in the depictions of Christ—or, better, further exemplified in him—but Christ does not somehow resolve the polarities of transcendence/sovereignty on the one hand, and personal interaction with finite creatures on the other. And what Enns means by the last sentence of the block quote—the unity he stipulates is "a broad and foundational theological commitment based on the analogy between Christ and Scripture"—I have no idea. I'm not even sure what Enns means when he says that this unity is a commitment, "a broad and foundational theological commitment," let alone that this commitment is "based on the analogy between Christ and Scripture." With the best will in the world, I cannot see how this is anything more than an attempt to keep alive the title of his book. It does not unpack how Christ unifies the assorted polarities and divergences that Enns has set out.

(6) The extended chapter on the use of the Old Testament in the New addresses one of the areas of biblical hermeneutics that has occupied my attention for several decades, so the temptation to write an entire book by way of interaction is pathetically strong. So I shall strive the more valiantly for brevity.

First, the thrust of the approach Enns adopts is that the hermeneutics deployed by the New Testament writers is indifferentiable from the hermeneutics of other first-century Jewish writers. However alien such interpretive principles may be to those of us weaned on grammatical-historical exegesis, those are the realities, and we need to come to terms with them. With much of this I am in happy concurrence. Indeed, this argument has been made by many people in recent decades, not a few of them evangelicals.[30] Enns's treatment is a popularizing of much of that work: e.g., he does not set out for us the *middoth* (more or less "rules of interpretation," usually numbering between seven and thirteen, depending on the ancient Jewish authority) and demonstrate the extent to which they are duplicated in the New Testament.

---

[30]E.g., one thinks of the many publications of E. Earle Ellis.

Yet the more one insists on the commonality of Jewish and Christian hermeneutics in the first century, the more urgently one faces two crucial needs. (i) One
should try to identify *differences* as well as similarities in their respective hermeneutical approaches. For instance, many have pointed out ways in which New
Testament *pesher* interpretation is rather *unlike pesher* found in 1QpHab.[31] But
we'll let that pass. (ii) It becomes important to raise a question of warrant. If Paul's
way of reading the Hebrew Bible, the Old Testament, is methodologically indifferentiable from the way of reading deployed by his unconverted Jewish colleagues,
how are they managing to come to such different conclusions while reading the
same texts? We'll see in a moment that it is inadequate simply to say, "Well, Paul
now believes Jesus has risen from the grave, and is the long-promised Messiah."
That is true, but, as we shall see, not sufficient to address the question. To put it differently, how does Paul think his own reading of the Old Testament has changed
from three months before his Damascus Road experience to three months after?
Is there *any* change in his hermeneutics? Or is it only that his *answers* are now different, so that he manipulates the hermeneutical axioms in rather creative ways?
What hermeneutical change in his thinking *warrants* the christological readings
of the Old Testament he adopts?

That is an important question. It is possible to identify several *hermeneutical*
differences. I can take the space to mention only one, and it needs much more
development than I will give it here. First-century Palestinian Jews who were asked
the question, "How does a person please God?" were likely to answer, "By obeying
the law." This answer they could apply not only to figures such as Hezekiah and
David and Moses, all of whom are found *this* side of Sinai, but even to figures such
as Abraham and Enoch, who are found on the *other* side of Sinai. After all, Genesis
tells us that Abraham kept all God's statutes, and we know what they must have
been; Enoch walked with God, and we know full well what is required for that to
take place. One must infer that they received private revelations of the law. What
this does, hermeneutically speaking, is elevate the law to the level of hermeneutical hegemony: it is the grid that controls how you read the Old Testament. It is,
in substantial measure, an ahistorical reading. But when Paul as a Christian and
an apostle reads the same texts, he insists on preserving the significance of the
historical sequence. Thus in Galatians 3, Abraham was justified by faith *before* the
giving of the law, and the promise to him and to his seed similarly came *before* the
giving of the law. That means that the law given by Moses has been relativized;
one must now think afresh exactly why it was given, "added" to the promise. Again,

---

[31]E.g., see the discussion in Timothy H. Lim, *Pesharim*, Companion to the Qumran Scrolls 3 (London: Sheffield
Academic Press, 2002).

in Romans 4 Paul analyzes the relation between faith and circumcision *on the basis of which came first*: it is the historical sequence that is determinative for his argument. Nor is this approach exclusively Pauline. In Hebrews, for instance, the validity of *Auctor's* argument in chapter 7 turns on historical sequence. If Psalm 110, written *after* the establishment of the Levitical priesthood at Sinai, promises a priesthood that is tied *not* to the tribe of Levi but to the tribe of Judah, and is thus bringing together royal and priestly prerogatives in one person, then the Levitical priesthood has been declared obsolete in principle. Moreover, if this new king-priest is modeled on ancient Melchizedek, himself a priest-king, there is also an anticipation of this arrangement as far back as Genesis 14. In other words, where one pays attention to links that depend on historical sequencing, one has laid the groundwork for careful typology. The argument in Hebrews 3:7–4:13 similarly depends on reading the Old Testament texts in their historical sequence: the fact that Psalm 95, written *after* the people have entered the Promised Land, is still calling the covenant people to enter into God's rest, demonstrates that entry into the land was not *itself* a final delivery of the promise to give them rest. Moreover, the reference to "God's rest" triggers reflection on how God rested as far back as Genesis 1–2—and thus another typological line is set up, filled in with a variety of pieces along the *historical* trajectory.

Ultimately, this insistence on reading the Old Testament historically can be traced back to Jesus himself. But the only point I am making here is that this is one of the *hermeneutical* differences between the apostolic interpreters of Scripture and their unconverted Jewish counterparts. But none of this is unpacked by Enns, even though such considerations must play a considerable role in any evaluation of how the New Testament writers are reading Scripture.

Second, as a result of these points being ignored, in quite a number of Enns's discussions I wish the presentation went in slightly different directions. I will not here treat the use of Hosea 11:1 in Matthew 2, as I have discussed that quotation at rather too much length in my commentary on Matthew in the EBC series. But consider how Psalm 95:7–11 is used in Hebrews 3 and 4. Enns makes much of the shift in the position of διό: he thinks that this means that, whereas in Psalm 95 God is angry with his people *for* the forty years of the wilderness wanderings, in Hebrews 3–4 God's anger comes *only at the end of the forty years* of wilderness wandering (pp. 140–42). But this is seriously overstated. Even in the account in Hebrews, it is clear that during the forty years the people are hardening their hearts, rebelling, and testing the Lord and trying him. That is why (διό) God was angry with that generation—i.e., because of this rebellious behavior *during* the forty years. The assumption, surely, is that God's response has been wrath as long as there has been rebellion. The text does not say that God was *not* wrathful during the forty years, but suddenly became wrathful at the end of forty years: the latter way of taking the text demands an antithesis that is simply not there. Instead, what one finds is a small difference in emphasis. One can even venture a guess as to why this small difference in emphasis has taken place: in Hebrews, *Auctor* wants to show his readers how God's wrath finally issued in his refusal to let his covenant people enter the Promised Land. The readers are thereby warned that they, too, might not enter into the ultimate rest, if, like the generation of the exodus, they begin well, but do not persevere to the end. Of course, that lesson was already there in the words of Psalm 95; all that *Auctor* has done is strengthen that point. And meanwhile, what Enns has overlooked in *Auctor*'s brilliant exposition of Psalm 95 is (as we have seen) the way he situates the psalm within the trajectories of redemptive history to show that even the Old Testament writers did not think that entrance into Canaan constituted the ultimate rest. Collectively they generated a typological trajectory that *necessarily* outstrips the rest of Canaan.

It would be tedious to go through all of Enns's examples, but I cannot forbear to mention that readers would do well to compare Enns's treatment of "Paul's movable well" with that of, say, Thiselton.[32]

(7) Enns draws attention to Luke 24:45: the resurrected Jesus "opened the minds" of the two Emmaus Road disciples "so they could understand the Scriptures." Enns takes this to be the kind of claimed revelation the Teacher of Righteousness enjoyed at Qumran, reorienting the reader to a new understanding of Scripture along lines that are not transparently there on the surface of the Old Testament text. But the context shows another dimension to this exchange between Jesus and the two Emmaus believers that must not be overlooked: toward the beginning of the conversation, Jesus tells them, "'How foolish you are, and how slow of heart to believe all that the prophets have spoken! Did not the Christ have to suffer these things and then enter his glory?' And beginning with Moses and all the Prophets, he explained to them what was said in all the Scriptures concerning himself" (24:25–26). Toward the end, Jesus adds, "Everything must be fulfilled that is written about me in the Law of Moses, the Prophets and the Psalms" (24:44).

This is quite striking. On the one hand, even the apostles and other disciples did not understand, before the cross and resurrection, that the Messiah would be crucified and would rise the third day, even though Jesus had told them. They simply did not have the categories to absorb such information. Transparently, when they had become convinced of his resurrection, they had to undergo a transforma-

[32]Anthony C. Thiselton, *The First Epistle to the Corinthians*, NIGTC (Grand Rapids: Eerdmans, 2000), 737–40.

tion of their understanding of the Scriptures. In other words, in the psychological development of their understanding, the resurrection of Christ comes before their Christianized understanding of the Old Testament text. That is the point Enns is making. But on the other hand, *even before his resurrection,* Jesus himself holds his followers responsible for understanding the Old Testament text in a Christianized way, and labels them foolish when they fail in this regard. He himself, and all the major New Testament writers, speak of the events of his life as *fulfilling* what the Old Testament says, not as adding brand new meaning to what the Old Testament says. (This, as we shall see, is one of the dominating themes in Wright's book.) Enns never explores what this side of things might mean.

Sometimes the two points come together in dramatic ways. For instance, in Romans 16:25–27, Paul's gospel is in line with "the revelation of the mystery hidden for long ages past"; but it is also "now revealed and made known *through the prophetic writings.*" On the one hand, the gospel has been long hidden; but when it is revealed and made known, this revelation takes place *through the prophetic writings.* Quite a number of the "mystery" passages of the New Testament turn on unpacking some things that are *genuinely there in the biblical texts,* but which have been "hidden" in the past until the great revelatory event of Jesus Messiah has taken place. Because they truly are there in the text, readers can be berated for not having seen them—i.e., the assumption is that if it were not for their moral turpitude and their ignorance of God, they would have seen how the texts are put together, would have grasped more clearly what this God is truly like, and would have understood their Bibles properly. That is also why the New Testament writers do not restrict their apologetic to the stance, "If only you will believe that Jesus is the Messiah and that he rose from the dead, then you will be transformed and come to read the Bible the way we do." Rather, they urge upon their Jewish counterparts the *right* way to read the Bible. Their apologetic often consists of showing *from the Scriptures* that Jesus Messiah *had* to die and rise again. Their hermeneutic in such exposition, though it overlaps with that of the Jews, is distinguishable from it, and at certain points is much more in line with the actual shape of Scripture: it rests on the unpacking of the Bible's storyline.[33]

(8) The failure to get this tension right—by "right," I mean in line with what Scripture actually says of itself—is what makes Enns sound disturbingly like my *Doktorvater* on one point. Barnabas Lindars's first book was *New Testament Apologetic.*[34] The thesis was very simple, the writing elegant: the New Testament

---

[33]I have dealt with this in some detail in "Mystery and Fulfillment: Toward a More Comprehensive Paradigm of Paul's Understanding of the Old and the New," in *Justification and Variegated Nomism,* vol. 2, *The Paradoxes of Paul,* ed. D. A. Carson, Peter T. O'Brien, and Mark A. Seifrid, WUNT 181 (Tübingen: Mohr Siebeck, 2004), 393–436.

[34]*New Testament Apologetic: The Doctrinal Significance of the Old Testament Quotations* (London: SCM, 1961).

writers came to believe that Jesus was the Messiah, and that he had been crucified and raised from the dead. They then ransacked their Bible, what we call the Old Testament, to find prooftexts to justify their new-found theology, and ended up yanking things out of context, distorting the original context, and so forth. Enns is more respectful, but it is difficult to see how his position differs substantively from that of Lindars, except that he wants to validate these various approaches to the Old Testament partly on the ground that the hermeneutics involved were already in use (we might call this the "Hey, everybody's doing it" defense), and partly on the ground that he himself accepts, as a "gift of faith," that Jesus really is the Messiah. This really will not do. The New Testament writers, for all that they understand that acceptance of who Jesus is comes as a gift of the Spirit (1 Cor. 2:14), never stint at giving *reasons* for the hope that lies within them, *including reasons for reading the Bible as they do.* The "fulfillment" terminology they deploy is too rich and varied to allow us to imagine that they are merely reading in what is in fact not there. They would be the first to admit that *in their own psychological history* the recognition of Jesus came before their understanding of the Old Testament; but they would see this as evidence of moral blindness. As a result, they would be the first to insist, with their transformed hermeneutic (not least the reading of the sacred texts in salvation-historical sequence), that *the Scriptures themselves can be shown to anticipate a suffering Servant-King, a Priest-King, a new High Priest,* and so forth. In other words, Enns develops the first point but disavows the second. The result is that he fails to see how Christian belief is *genuinely* warranted by Scripture. No amount of appeal to the analogy of the incarnation will make up the loss.

N. T. Wright, *The Last Word: Beyond the Bible Wars to a New Understanding of the Authority of Scripture*

Content

Tom Wright, one of the most influential and prolific New Testament scholars of our day, is currently Bishop of Durham. In comparison with some of his own weighty tomes, his little book on Scripture is slight. On the other hand, it is easily the best written of the three books under review here: Wright finds it difficult to draft a boring sentence. In some ways it is a simple book, pitched at the common reader; it does not require detailed technical interaction. Yet because it develops an independent proposal regarding how we are to think about Scripture, it demands evaluation that is prepared to think "outside the box." I should say right away that the American title is different from the British original, so we had better get that squared away: the original is *Scripture and the Authority of God*, which admirably

summarizes the book;[35] the American title, I'm afraid, has opted for a full dose of
pompous nonsense, attributable, I hope, to the publisher: *The Last Word: Beyond
the Bible Wars to a New Understanding of the Authority of Scripture.*[36] The pagination
of the two is different; references below are to the British edition.

Title aside, the book is made up of ten short chapters and a concluding appendix (briefly mentioned below). As for the other end of this volume—well, anyone
who opens his preface with the sentence, "Writing a book about the Bible is like
building a sandcastle in front of the Matterhorn" (p. xiii) has my interest already.
The first chapter (pp. 1–3) gives a potted survey of the role of Scripture within
the church from the first century until the present. This is cast as a sermonette to
encourage us to keep reading.

In chapter 2, Wright sets the stage for his discussion by talking about "Scripture
within Contemporary Culture" along five axes. The first is Scripture's relation
to culture. The interplay between modernity and postmodernity has "created a
mood of uncertainty within Western society at least" (p. 4). Modernity challenged "the overarching story of the church" (p. 4); postmodernity deconstructs
it. Truth is often now reduced to power claims or the perspective of a particular community, with no obvious connection to "what happened," to "reality." In
all this, personal identity has become squishy and uncertain. The second axis is
Scripture's relation to politics: "The map of what we might call political morality has shrunk" (p. 7): this Wright attributes to the Enlightenment. The third
surveys the relation between Scripture and philosophy: the substantial removal
of God from the arena of philosophical discussion was supposed to eliminate the
internecine wars generated by religious conflict, but in fact gave us Hitler and
Stalin. Scarcely less sad, as Scripture has interacted with theology, theology has
become disconnected from Scripture. Even the books that talk about Scripture
devote very little space to wrestling with what Scripture actually says: here Wright
mentions Webster's *Holy Scripture*, reviewed above, and the "radical orthodoxy"
movement, which says a great deal about tradition but rather little about the Bible.
And in the domain of ethics, the dominant categories of discussion bounce topics
like homosexuality and gender ethics around culture, politics, philosophy, and
theology with all too little wrestling with the text of Scripture. Prooftexting is not
the way ahead. What we must face, Wright says, are three questions, which the
rest of his book addresses:

1. In what sense is the Bible authoritative in the first place?

---

[35]London: SPCK, 2005.
[36]San Francisco: HarperSanFrancisco, 2005 (the paperback appeared in 2006).

2. How can the Bible be appropriately understood and interpreted?

3. How can its authority, assuming such appropriate interpretation, be brought to bear on the church itself, let alone on the world? (p. 13)

The rest of the chapter basically argues that the present debate cannot be cast in the categories of earlier centuries, and that much of it is shallow. The problems of shallowness, Wright says,

> occur when people push the Bible to one side because it appears to be telling them something they do not wish to hear. This happens secretly in the case of the so-called "conservative," who may well choose to ignore the ecclesial, ecumenical, sacramental and ecological dimensions of Paul's soteriology, in order to highlight and privilege a doctrine of justification or "personal salvation" which owes its real shape to a blend of Reformation, enlightenment, romantic and existentialist influences. It may well happen in a bold, in-your-face manner in the case of the so-called "radical," who will often take pleasure in saying things like, "Paul says this, and we now know he's wrong," playing to a gallery stacked with iconoclasts. All this has to be named, shamed and got rid of if we are to seek and find fresh wisdom. (p. 15)

Nevertheless, Wright concedes that some "thorough, indeed magisterial" (p. 15) work has been done, and that is why he provides the appendix, "Recent Resources on Scripture," as he will not be interacting with such materials in this short book.[37]

The third chapter sets out one major plank in Wright's argument: "'Authority of Scripture' as Part of a Larger Whole" (pp. 17–25). "We now arrive at the central claim of this book: that the phrase 'authority of scripture' can only make Christian sense if it is a shorthand for 'the authority of the triune God, exercised somehow *through* scripture'" (p. 17). But since whatever else the Bible is, it is a massive story, this raises the question of what it means to speak of the authority of a story, or of how God's authority is exercised *through* this story. We should be nervous of preachers like Martin Luther and Charles Spurgeon who kept quoting the Bible as a protest against other positions: people appeal to "the authority of the Bible" when they want to stop other people from acting in some way of which they disapprove. Of course, Wright says, "there is a positive use [of the phrase

---

[37] The appendix is pitched at an entirely different level than the book itself: one would need to be a serious student, and sometimes a rather advanced student, to understand some of the books Wright lists. The selection is seriously slanted on some of the subjects covered, but doubtless that is a picky criticism.

'the authority of Scripture'] as well, exemplified in the teaching and preaching of scripture" (p. 20), but he judges it important to reiterate the warning. As for *God's* authority, it is best thought of in the context of God's kingdom—and that draws us toward the running tension between God's constant sovereign rule over everything, and the way his sovereignty breaks into this world of corruption and decay: Yahweh will be king over all the world (Zech. 14:9). As God's authority is worked out in this advancing kingdom, the right question to ask is this: "What *role* does scripture play *within* God's accomplishment of this goal?" (p. 22).

> "The authority of scripture" is thus a sub-branch of several other theological topics: the mission of the church, the work of the Spirit, the ultimate future hope and the way it is anticipated in the present, and of course the nature of the church. Failure to pay attention to all of these in discussing how scripture functions is part of the problem, as we can see when people, hearing the word "scripture," instantly think of a rule-book—and then, according to taste, either assume that all the rules are to be followed without question or assume that they can all now be broken. (p. 22)

All of this means that Scripture transcends revelation, in the sense of conveying information; it is more than a devotional manual, not least when the Bible is used for personal guidance. What we *should* remember is that the role of the Bible within the Christian church indicates three things of central importance; first, God is a speaking God; second, the Bible is "central to early Christian instruction so that we can be transformed by the renewal of our minds" (p. 25); and third, it reminds us that "the God we worship is the God of world-conquering power, seen in action in the resurrection of Jesus" (p. 25).

The fourth chapter invites us to look at "Scripture Within the Kingdom-People, BC" (pp. 26–30). Here Wright makes three points. First, in the Old Testament, the purpose of God's kingdom is to rescue his people and to complete creation, and the Scriptures, Israel's sacred writings, even allowing for all their diversity of literary genres, "were the place where, and the means by which, Israel discovered again and again who the true God was, and how his kingdom-purposes were being taken forward" (p. 27). Second, basing himself on Psalm 33:6; Jeremiah 23:29; Isaiah 40:8; 55:10–11; and Deuteronomy 30:14, Wright likens "the word of the Lord" to "an enormous reservoir, full of creative divine wisdom and power, into which the prophets and other writers tap by God's call and grace, so that the word may flow through them to do God's work of flooding or irrigating his people" (p. 28). And third, this Scripture "was never simply about the imparting of information, reminding people of previous religious experience" (p. 29), but actually constituted Israel as the Scripture-hearing people. Moreover, within Second Temple Judaism, these Scriptures "formed the controlling *story* in which Israel struggled to find its identity and destiny as the covenant people," and "formed the call to a present *obedience* . . . through which Israel could respond appropriately to God's call" (p. 30).

As for the relationship between Scripture and Jesus (chap. 5, pp. 31–34), two things must be said. First, Jesus understands that the (Old Testament) Scriptures point to him; he accomplishes and fulfills "an entire world of hints and shadows now coming to plain statement and full light" (p. 32)—which is the way Wright understands Matthew 5:17–18.[38] Second, Jesus insists on Scripture's authority. But even this authority must be understood within the storyline in which Jesus fulfills Scripture, for otherwise it would not make sense to find Jesus declaring foods to be clean, formally modifying the law on oaths, and so forth.

The sixth chapter is devoted to "'Word of God' and Scripture in the Apostolic Church" (pp. 35–44). The earliest apostolic preaching did not announce a brand-new religion, but told "the story of Jesus *understood as* the fulfillment of the OT covenant narrative" (p. 35). This preached "word" was the gospel itself, and it not only conveyed information—Jesus' story as the fulfillment of the old covenant narrative—but was itself charged with power to transform lives (e.g., Rom. 1:16).

> Here we have the roots of a fully Christian theology of scriptural author-
> ity: planted firmly in the soil of the missionary community, confronting
> the powers of the world with the news of the kingdom of God, refreshed
> and invigorated by the Spirit, growing particularly through the preaching
> and teaching of the apostles, and bearing fruit in the transformation of
> human lives as the start of God's project to put the whole cosmos to rights.
> (p. 37)

In that way, the writers of the New Testament intended to "energize, shape, and direct the church," and thus their writings "were intended to be vehicles of the Spirit's authority" (p. 37), and that is in fact how they were viewed. The modern penchant for detecting mutually contradictory communities behind the various New Testament corpora is indefensible; in fact, the early Christians worked out a remarkably "multi-layered reading of the OT: not arbitrarily, but reflecting their

---

[38]This chapter is, of course, in some ways the briefest possible digest of Wright's *Jesus and the Victory of God* (Minneapolis: Fortress, 1996).

understanding of the church as God's new covenant people and their place in the ongoing story" (p. 39).[39] These documents work out thoughtful continuity and discontinuity with the Old Testament Scriptures, and stand as well "in dialogical relation with all human culture" (p. 43). Some things in the culture were approved, but often Christians found themselves in sharp opposition to the prevailing evils of the day, and pronounced against them by calling believers to "a costly and contested redemption" (p. 44). In short, the New Testament writings "guided the early Church in discerning the relationship between cultural context and the path of new, renewed humanity" (p. 44). But Wright again insists:

> Yet this has nothing to do with the declaration of an arbitrary or "controlling" ethic, a standard imposed from without by constricting or bullying authority in the early church. It has everything to do with understanding human renewal as the beginning, the pointer towards, and even the means of, God's eventual eradication of evil from the world and the bringing to birth of the new creation itself. . . . We can summarize it like this: the New Testament understands itself as the new covenant charter, the book that forms the basis for the new telling of the story through which Christians are formed, reformed and transformed so as to be God's people for God's world. That is the challenge the early Christians bequeath to us as we reconsider what "the authority of scripture" might mean in practice today. (p. 44)

In chapter 7, Wright surveys "Scripture from the Second to the Seventeenth Century" (pp. 45–60). In the patristic period, he covers early challenges (Marcion, the Gnostics, and so forth), and the response of the church by appealing to early tradition and "good exegesis" (p. 45). For Wright, the most important thing is that the scriptural narrative ("creation spoiled and restored, covenant broken and renewed," p. 46) was reaffirmed over against approaches that were non-Jewish, atemporal ("de-storied"), and anti-creation. Sadly, however, this emphasis was gradually lost as Scripture became mere "court of appeal" or the focus of *lectio divina*. In time, the drift toward allegorical exegesis, which testifies to the willingness of Christians to stick with Scripture even when they themselves were finding it problematic, brought more problems. The oft-discussed "four senses" of the medieval church became "a way of trying to get at the rich contours of Scripture without grasping the early Christians' own theological method" (p. 51). "As even apologists for the medieval period will admit, once allegory had taken over almost

---

[39]Here and elsewhere, I have sometimes drawn on the exact words Wright uses in one of his lengthy subtitles, where he has in fact preserved capital letters. I have taken the liberty of removing the caps for the sake of the flow of my summary.

anything could be 'proved' from scripture, resulting in fantastic and highly speculative theories" (p. 52). Wright asserts that the popularity of the "four senses" went hand in hand with the development of "tradition" as a parallel authority to Scripture. That brings us to the Reformation. The Reformers' *sola scriptura* slogan "was part of its protest against perceived medieval corruptions" (p. 53).

> The Reformers thus set scripture over against the traditions of the church; the recovery of the literal sense over against the lush growth of the three other senses; and the right of ordinary Christians to read scripture for themselves over against the protection of the sacred text by the Latin-reading elite. They did so in order to insist that the church had got off the right track and that the living God was using scripture itself to get it back on the right one. (p. 54)

Of course, "literal sense" in this context means the first of the four medieval senses, not exactly what we mean by "literal" today. But where the Reformers fell short, Wright insists, is in their failure to deal adequately with "the great *narrative* of God, Israel, Jesus and the world, coming forwards into our own day and looking ahead to the eventual renewal of all things" (p. 56). Their readings of the Gospels, for instance, "show little awareness of them as anything other than repositories of dominical teaching, concluding with the saving events of Good Friday and Easter but without integrating those events into the kingdom-proclamation that preceded them" (p. 57).

As for the English Reformation, Wright is eager to point out that Hooker's insistence on "reason" must not be seen in the light of later Enlightenment debates. "Reason" was not a way of undervaluing Scripture, but a way of thinking in the light of Scripture "and in harmony with the natural law which stemmed from the creator God in the first place" (p. 59). "The thought of 'reason' as an entirely separate source of information, which could then be *played off against* scripture and/or tradition, flies in the face of [Hooker's] whole way of thinking" (p. 60).

That brings us to "The Challenge of the Enlightenment," chapter 8 (pp. 61–77). Wright again paints with a broad brush. The Enlightenment was helpful to the church in that it insisted on *historical* readings of texts. Unfortunately, it soon offered its own rival eschatology, borne along by "rationalism," which understood "reason" as a faculty utterly independent of Scripture. God and religion became private matters; evil was primarily a matter of ignorance, to be met with education and good government policies. In the light of these developments, modern biblical scholarship made some advances, but generated "muddled debates" and precipitated "complex interplay with cultural movements" (p. 66). Wright dumps fundamentalism and liberalism into the same pot: both are the products, he avers, of Enlightenment thought that screen out huge swaths of what the Bible actually says. More recently, postmodernism's challenge to modernism is appropriate, a necessary corrective, yet it veers constantly toward "nihilistic deconstruction" (p. 71). One of the signs of postmodernism's impotence, Wright asserts, is this: "It can protest against empire, but cannot bring Scripture's power to bear against it" (p. 73).

In chapter 9, Wright offers us two lists of misreadings of Scripture (pp. 78–83). Misreadings of the "right" include dispensational understandings of the "rapture," the prosperity gospel, support for slavery, endemic racialism of much Western culture, undifferentiated readings of the Old and New Testaments, assorted "new Israel" ideas applied to various Enlightenment projects, support for the death penalty, and overlooking political meanings in the text. Misreadings on the "left" include claims to objectivity, claims that modern science has disproved the Bible, various caricatures of biblical teaching, the "cultural relativity" argument, discovery of "political" meanings to the exclusion of religious meanings, the claim that the New Testament writers did not think they were writing "Scripture," and more of the same. (Neither list is as full as Wright's lists.) "The polarization of debates, especially in North America, leaves us in urgent need of fresh, kingdom-oriented, historically rooted exegesis" (p. 81).

The last chapter tells us "How to Get Back on Track" (pp. 84–104). Wright offers a paragraph that tells where the rest of the chapter is going:

> We urgently need an *integrated* view of the dense and complex phrase "the authority of scripture." Such an integrated view needs to highlight the role of the Spirit as the powerful, transformative agent. It needs to keep as its central focus the goal of God's kingdom, inaugurated by Jesus on earth as in heaven and one day to be completed under that same rubric. It must envisage the church as characterized, at the very heart of its life, by prayerful listening to, strenuous wrestling with, humble obedience before, and powerful proclamation of scripture, particularly in the ministries of its authorized leaders. (p. 84)

Among the points that are then unpacked in the following pages are these: The authority of Scripture "is most truly put into operation as the church goes to work in the world on behalf of the gospel, the good news that in Jesus Christ the living God has defeated the powers of evil and begun the work of new creation" (p. 85).

The proper way to think of Scripture's relation to tradition is in terms of dialog with previous readings (p. 86). To appeal to "reason" "will mean giving up merely arbitrary or whimsical readings of texts, and paying attention to lexical, contextual, and historical considerations" (p. 88).

> "Reason" will mean giving attention to, and celebrating, the many massive discoveries in biology, archaeology, physics, astronomy, and so on, which shed great light on God's world and the human condition. This does not, of course, mean giving in to the pressure which comes from atheistic or rationalistic science. (p. 88)

A truly multilayered view of Scripture recognizes the "vital and theologically coherent differences between OT and NT" (p. 89)—and this means adopting Wright's five-act model.[40] When we read Genesis 1–2, we read it as "the first act of a play of which we are the fifth" (p. 91); Genesis 3–11 is the second act of the play of which we are the fifth; the entire history of Israel from Abraham to the Messiah is the third act; the story of Jesus is "the decisive and climactic fourth act" (p. 91) of this play of which we are the fifth. "To live in the fifth act is thus to presuppose all of the above, and to be conscious of living as the people through whom the narrative in question is now moving towards its final destination" (p. 91). And so our relation to the New Testament is not the same as our relation to the Old. We must also be committed to "a totally contextual reading of Scripture" (p. 93); "a liturgically grounded reading of Scripture" (p. 95); "a privately studied reading of Scripture" (p. 98); a reading of Scripture "refreshed by appropriate scholarship" (p. 98) and "taught by the church's accredited leaders" (p. 100).

> In other words, if we are to be true, at the deepest level, to what scriptural authority really means, we must understand it like this. God is at work, through Scripture (in other words, through the Spirit who is at work as people read, study, teach and preach scripture) to energize, enable and direct the outgoing mission of the church, genuinely anticipating thereby the time when all things will be made new in Christ. At the same time, God is at work by the same means to order the life of the church, and of individual Christians, to model and embody his project of new creation in their unity and holiness. (p. 101)

---

[40] This he develops at length in *The New Testament and the People of God* (London: SPCK, 1992), chap. 5.

Critique

Despite its brevity, this little book leaves us with plenty to appreciate. Not least is Wright's running concern to trace the authority of Scripture back to the authority of God himself. The long-standing habit of beginning works of systematic theology with bibliology instead of with theology proper may not set up Scripture as an independent authority (as Wright avers), since even in such treatments of bibliology theologians typically talk about how God himself has (or has not) given Scripture, inspired Scripture, and the like; but the habit nevertheless focuses on human epistemology—i.e., how we know God—before focusing on God himself, and that is a very post-Enlightenment thing to do. Equally praiseworthy is Wright's attempt to tie the notion of the authority of Scripture to the Bible's storyline, even if I'll pick away at parts of his proposal. In some ways, this is in line with the retrieval of biblical theology that has been going on for some time (though Wright does not cast his work in such categories). Again, Wright's underscoring of Jesus, in the New Testament's presentation of him, as the *fulfillment* of the Old Testament narrative about Israel, is essentially right. Moreover, in remarkably brief compass, Wright has both appreciated postmodernism and skewered it. This little book is worth reading for that section alone.

In his preface, Wright disarmingly warns his readers,

> The present book makes no pretence at completeness, in terms either of the topics covered or the debate with other writers that might be expected. It is more a tract for the times. I trust that those who have grumbled at the length of some of my other books will not now grumble at all the things I have left unsaid. (p. xiv)

Quite—with one exception: where Wright lays out what he thinks Scripture is saying in some area, and in effect claims that his summary is at the heart of things and is an accurate reflection of Scripture (however much it is a mere snapshot), we may legitimately raise questions if we judge that by omission of complementary themes the center has been lost or moved. Some of the following evaluative comments take that line.

(1) Wright's use of the conservative/liberal or fundamentalist/liberal polarity is a bit grating at times.[41] Everyone understands how such polarities work, of course: there are twits to my left, and twits to my right, and I am situated in the sensible middle. That is a standard ploy in all discussion, especially polemical

---

[41]As an aside: Wright often treats "fundamentalist" and "conservative" as synonyms, which works well in much British academic polemics, but is linguistically four decades out of date in America.

discussion, so I am not objecting to it. But since the way the polarity is deployed in this book sometimes distorts the subject of the book, i.e., the authority of Scripture, it must be probed a little. I give three examples.

First, recall how Wright condemns the "shallowness" of both the "conservative" and the "radical": the former

> may well choose to ignore the ecclesial, ecumenical, sacramental and ecological dimensions of Paul's soteriology, in order to highlight and privilege a doctrine of justification or "personal salvation" which owes its real shape to a blend of Reformation, enlightenment, romantic and existentialist influences;

but shallowness may well

> happen in a bold, in-your-face manner in the case of the so-called "radical," who will often take pleasure in saying things like, "Paul says this, and we now know he's wrong," playing to a gallery stacked with iconoclasts. All this has to be named, shamed and got rid of if we are to seek and find fresh wisdom. (p. 15)

But there is a *qualitative* difference between the two. The "radical" is *dismissing* what Paul says, i.e., he is denying its authority. The "conservative" may well misinterpret the text, but is, within his or her own lights, bowing to it. Wright may be convinced that there is little difference between the two, since both end up missing a substantial part of what the text says. By this, of course, he means something like "what the text says *as I interpret it*"—and I shall show in a moment that, according to *my* lights, Wright himself is missing and downplaying some major themes in the text. But that does not warrant an accusation that Wright is thereby self-consciously shunting aside the authority of Scripture, in the way that the "radical" is. Wright perpetually charges those who disagree with his *interpretations* with disowning Scripture's *authority*: this is a major category mistake, for it will apply to Wright as much as to anyone else. Even if he were to insist that the result is the same—viz., the disavowal of certain content that Wright himself finds in the Bible—the way of getting there is not the same, and the solution to the problem is not the same. The one disavowal stems from the fact that the "conservative" simply does not think those themes are there; the other disavowal stems from the fact that, whether the "radical" thinks they are there or not, he thinks they are ridiculous, or unimportant, or against his own atheism, or whatever, and thus not *authoritative* for him. Similarly, the solution to the conservative's shortcoming is cogent exegesis and biblical theology, because in principle he or she already submits to Scripture's authority. Of course, the conservative may or may not be convinced by the exegesis, on various grounds; but that is still a long leap away from the stance of the radical who must abandon his or her atheism or liberalism or whatever, even to be open to such correction from Scripture.

A *second* example cements the problem. The brief linking of Martin Luther and Charles Spurgeon as two men who illustrate how the appeal to "the authority of Scripture" can merely be the language of protest, sometimes resulting in the protestor starting a new denomination or movement (p. 20), is singularly inapt. Of course it's possible to claim Scripture's authority in order to enhance one's own, but I have not found that fault to be worse among those who protest current developments than among those who endorse them. Wright repeatedly emphasizes the special responsibility of those who are "authorized teachers" or "accredited teachers" of the church: I had not noticed him using that expression until he himself was elevated to the see of Durham. But I'll let that pass, and notice how often those who occupy the role of "authorized teacher" in his own denomination have been happy to disown the bodily resurrection of Jesus, deny the incarnation (except in the most metaphorical sense), to go no further, without any serious repercussions whatsoever, except for a little charming notoriety. Thank God for those, then, like Luther and Spurgeon, who, in the name of what Scripture says, were willing to sacrifice their reputations[42] to call people to the truth of the Bible *precisely because they submit to the authority of Scripture*. Shall we condemn Athanasius for standing alone? Shall we condemn Paul for confronting Peter? Once again, then, Wright is sometimes not really wrestling with the questions surrounding the authority of Scripture, but is scoring points on somewhat adjacent subjects related to his own theological agendas.

A *third* example:

> The protest of that kind of fundamentalism [i.e., the kind that jumps from "Christ" to the divinity of Jesus without stopping along the way to think through first-century understandings of "Messiah"] against the "liberalism" of so-called modernist biblical scholarship (which often held the form of religion but denied its power) is simply a battle between one kind of Enlightenment vision and another. (p. 68)

---

[42]Luther, of course, risked his life; in the middle of the "Downgrade" controversy, Spurgeon said he was willing to be eaten by dogs for the next fifty years, but he was sure that the later history would exonerate him—so certain was he that he was bowing to the truth of Scripture, and that the truth itself would prevail.

This is an adaptation of the argument of Hans Frei, discussed above in my discussion of Webster. I am far from convinced that this is quite fair, though it is a mere truism in many contemporary academic circles. There is something to it, of course, for the influence of the Enlightenment has (as we have seen) shaped the way several generations of systematicians advanced bibliology to the first place of consideration, displacing God himself. Yet the charge that fundamentalism is merely another form of modernism, and thus one with liberalism, is surely not quite fair. In the words of one of Wright's reviewers:

> Now I confess that it is one of history's high ironies that the vast majority of those in the 20th century who believed the words of the Apostles' Creed in the same way they were believed from the 2nd to the 19th century were also the kind of people who believed that Hal Lindsey knew what he was talking about. Okay, so God has a sense of humor. But I think it more accurate to describe all this as a rude and unlettered reaction to modernity than an expression of it.[43]

Clearly, one of the reasons *why* these "conservatives" or "fundamentalists" tried to withstand the unbelief of late modernism was precisely *because* they wanted to remain under the authority of Scripture, as they understood it.

(2) Here and there, Wright's argument is tendentious in other ways. Consider two examples. At times, Wright seems to confuse function and essence, i.e., he talks about the right outworking of the authority of Scripture as if it were the theology of the authority of Scripture. Recall his comments on the preached word in Acts, and on Romans 1:16:

> Here we have the roots of a fully Christian theology of scriptural authority: planted firmly in the soil of the missionary community, confronting the powers of the world with the news of the kingdom of God, refreshed and invigorated by the Spirit, growing particularly through the preaching and teaching of the apostles, and bearing fruit in the transformation of human lives as the start of God's project to put the whole cosmos to rights. (p. 37)

But these are *not* the "roots of a fully Christian theology of scriptural authority." Rather, they are the powerful outworking of that authority in the lives of the early Christians. This is a repeated confusion of category in Wright's book. The

---

[43]Douglas Wilson, on his "Blog and Mablog," posted January 14, 2006: http://dougwils.com/index.asp?Action=A nchor&CategoryID=1&Bl.

problem is crystallized by asking a few questions. Suppose missionaries lived and preached Scripture in some cultural setting or other where there was little or no "bearing fruit in the transformation of human lives as the start of God's project to put the whole cosmos to rights," where "confronting the powers of the world" resulted in martyrdom after martyrdom but no transformation. Would the authority of Scripture be in any way diminished simply because no one but the missionaries themselves were responding positively to it?

For a second example, recall Wright's description of the "word of the Lord" in the Old Testament as a "reservoir" into which the prophets and others can "tap"— basing himself on Psalm 33:6; Jeremiah 23:29; Isaiah 40:8; 55:10–11; and Deuteronomy 30:14 (p. 28). Well, at the risk of being picky, I confess I'm not sure the prophets can simply tap into this reservoir: they typically seem, rather, to have had to wait until God gave them something: note the repeated expression, "The word of the Lord came to the prophet So-and-So." More importantly, why not survey the large and diverse ways the Bible speaks of itself, that Jesus speaks of biblical texts, and so forth? I briefly mentioned some of the evidence when I noted how little attention to it Webster had paid. Wright's course is rather different: he pays a lot of attention to a handful of biblical expressions, and entirely ignores others, thus giving the impression that he has summarized biblical teaching on how the Bible or "the word of the Lord" or related expressions are to be viewed, when in reality the evidence is so selective that it is mildly distorting.

(3) One of Wright's great strengths, viz., the careful way he ties his thesis to the Bible's "story," opens the door to one of his great weaknesses. The Bible's "story" for him is central to his understanding of Scripture: whatever else the Bible is, it is story. Israel's "story" is "fulfilled" in "Jesus' story." Yet the exclusiveness of this category to explain how the Bible hangs together rings gentle warning bells. I am sure this is a better category than law (as in the theonomy movement). Yet others trace out the relationships among the covenants, worry away at promise and fulfillment, or use "salvation history" as the controlling vector. Of course, any one of these can "control" the others. But would it not be a richer analysis to show how these and other trajectories intertwine?

The extent to which "story" controls Wright's thought is clearly seen when he discusses Second Temple Judaism: the Scriptures, he said, "formed the controlling *story* in which Israel struggled to find its identity and destiny as the covenant people," and "formed the call to a present *obedience* . . . through which Israel could respond appropriately to God's call" (p. 30). Well, yes, I suppose one could say that. But equally, large swaths of Judaism devoted enormous energy to thinking through how *law* should be worked out in their day, generating new *halakah*.

Again, we are told that modernity challenged "the overarching story of the church" (p. 4). Why word it like this? Why not say that modernity challenged the truth claims of Scripture and sought to undermine its *authority*? For transparently, *one* of the things that goes into making a document *authoritative* is its reliability, its "truthfulness" in that sense, when it speaks on whatever topic is the focus of its attention. But Wright ignores that facet of authority, so as to focus on the inbreaking kingdom and the Bible's story. I'm far from saying that all of his emphases are mistaken; but they soon appear distorted and troubling because they are so narrow, so reductionistic.

Moreover, the actual story Wright finds in the Bible is again so narrowly construed as to miss or reduce matters of central importance. We have repeatedly seen how the "story" of God's advancing kingdom is cast in terms of rescuing human beings and completing creation, or perhaps in terms of defeating the powers of darkness. Not for a moment do I want to reduce or minimize those themes. Yet *from what* are human beings to be rescued? Their sin, yes; the powers of darkness; yes. But what is striking is the utter absence of any mention of the wrath of God. This is not a minor omission. Section after section *of the Bible's story* turns on the fact that God's image-bearers attract God's righteous wrath. The entire created order is under God's curse because of human sin. Sin is not first and foremost horizontal, social (though of course it is all of that): it is vertical, the defiance of almighty God. The sin that most consistently is said to bring down God's wrath on the heads of his people or on entire nations is idolatry— the de-godding of God. And it is the overcoming of this most fundamental sin that the cross and resurrection of Jesus achieve. The most urgent need of human beings is to be reconciled to God. That is not to deny that such reconciliation entails reconciliation with other human beings, and transformed living in God's fallen creation, in anticipation of the final transformation at the time of the consummation of all things. But to speak constantly of the advance of the kingdom without tying kingdom themes to the passion narrative, the way the canonical Gospels do, is a terrible reductionism.[44] To speak a couple of times of the cross in terms of the *Christus Victor* theme, as Wright does (though without using that expression), is unexceptional; to do so without burning with Paul's "I resolved to know nothing while I was with you except Jesus Christ and him crucified" (1 Cor. 2:2) and showing how this is tied in Paul's thought to the setting aside of God's wrath, and to the reconciliation of alienated rebels *to their Maker*, is irresponsible. I know that Tom Wright affirms substitutionary atonement: I have

---

[44]See, for instance, Peter G. Bolt, *The Cross From a Distance: Atonement in Mark's Gospel*, NSBT 18 (Downers Grove, IL: InterVarsity, 2004).

heard him defend it, for instance, from Romans 8:3–4. Yet the massive story of Israel is replete with sacrificial references—e.g., to Passover, to the slaughter of bull and goat on *yom kippurim*—which are then *explicitly* said to be fulfilled by Jesus in the New Testament. Yet not a word on this from Wright. While he berates Luther and the other Reformers for what they do not see, not to mention Spurgeon and assorted brands of "conservatives" and "fundamentalists," I confess I am more than a little worried by what Wright himself does not see—or, if he does see it, what he barely alludes to. We all have our blind spots, and most of the time I'm glad to be helped to see what Wright sees. But it is highly troubling that what Wright himself does not see lies at least as close to the heart of the gospel, in Paul's view, as what Wright does see. I would not want to take the step that Wright himself takes at this juncture, when he charges his opponents with stepping away from the authority of Scripture. All I would say is that we not only need to come under the authority of Scripture, and above all of the God whose authority establishes the authority of Scripture, but we must strive with all our might not to do so in such a selective way.

(4) Wright repeatedly warns us against a "rule-book" approach to the Bible. If all he means by this is that the Bible cannot be *reduced* to a "rule-book," that the "rules" of, say, the Sinai covenant must be read along the axis of the Bible's story to try to discern in what way they find their "fulfillment" in the next "act," then of course this is right. In itself, this is not an issue of scriptural authority; rather, it is a matter of interpretation by recognizing the different genres of Scripture and, above all, the story—the metanarrative—that holds it all together. Yet Wright seems to go farther than this. For instance, recall that he says that what he is proposing

> has nothing to do with the declaration of an arbitrary or "controlling" ethic, a standard imposed from without by constricting or bullying authority in the early church. It has everything to do with understanding human renewal as the beginning, the pointer towards, and even the means of, God's eventual eradication of evil from the world and the bringing to birth of the new creation itself. . . . We can summarize it like this: the New Testament understands itself as the new covenant charter, the book that forms the basis for the new telling of the story through which Christians are formed, reformed and transformed so as to be God's people for God's world. That is the challenge the early Christians bequeath to us as we reconsider what "the authority of scripture" might mean in practice today. (p. 44)

One gets the impression that this is largely right in what is being affirmed, but dangerously wrong in what is being denied by appeal to pejorative language (e.g., "bullying authority"). Precisely because of the way that the New Testament writers establish the links between the covenants along the axis of redemptive history, very strong "rules" (for want of a better word) are enforced. The man sleeping with his stepmother is to be excommunicated (1 Corinthians 5); those who are preaching "another Jesus" are to be turfed out of the Corinthian church before Paul gets there, or he will impose discipline himself (2 Corinthians 11–13). Passage after passage is replete with moral exhortation, commands, threat of sanctions, promise of strength to enable believers to live out the right conduct, and so forth. These are things that *Scripture* mandates, things that we cannot ignore without disowning the authority of Scripture. Perhaps Wright has a place for all of this, but if so, I wish he would make it clear. Perhaps his presentation is so antithetical—that is part of Wright's pedagogical style—that if he arrived in the same room as a few interlocutors who challenged him, he would work a little harder at the integration he nominally espouses. Perhaps it would help if he gave us a batch of ethical examples where the New Testament writers *do* speak. But his own role in *The Windsor Report*, which is a remarkably woolly piece on one of the most pressing and divisive issues of our day, is not reassuring. As they stand, the antitheses he generates in defense of his "story" sound perilously close to skirting such "rules" as *are* found in the New Testament texts. What does that do for becoming obedient to the Scriptures—a stance that Wright himself forcefully advocates?

(5) Finally, Wright's important insistence that the authority of Scripture is nothing other than the authority of God exercised *through* the Scripture, as important as that is (and of course many others have said the same thing), rapidly becomes skewed by Wright's next moves. Wright does not leap to a meditation on, say, Psalm 119, with all the things said there about God's word, God's statutes, God's words, etc.—a lot of them in remarkably atemporal categories. Instead, he stipulates that God's authority must be thought of in terms of his *kingdom*, whether the eternal sovereignty God always manifests, or kingdom understood as the inbreaking of his transforming power to rescue human beings and to bring the creation to its completion. The former notion of kingdom Wright does not take up in connection with Scripture; everything depends on the latter notion of kingdom. As a result, the authority of Scripture becomes one vehicle (perhaps the most important one) of the authority of God as he displays his transforming kingly rule in rescuing people and transforming the world. The result of this is that the authority of Scripture becomes, as we have seen, "a sub-branch of several other theological topics: the mission of the church, the work of the Spirit, the ultimate

future hope and the way it is anticipated in the present, and of course the nature of the church." In one sense, this is the same mistake that Webster makes: Webster, it will be recalled, attempts to tie "Scripture" to the entire communicative act, and loses clarity on what *Scripture itself* is. Wright doesn't do that, exactly; instead, he links the authority of Scripture to God's authority (a good move), reduces God's authority to his redemptive-kingdom display of authority (a bad move), associates the purpose of Scripture with this notion of kingdom (a reductionistic move)— and loses clarity as to what *Scripture itself* is, as to what *the authority of Scripture itself* is as God displays his authority *through Scripture itself*. We ask again, Does not Scripture's authority stand, even if the church is failing in its mission, and people do not believe this word?

> Failure to pay attention to all of these [themes] in discussing how scripture functions [note again: we have leapt from Scripture *is* to how it *functions*] is part of the problem, as we can see when people, hearing the word "scripture," instantly think of a rule-book—and then, according to taste, either assume that all the rules are to be followed without question or assume that they can all now be broken. (p. 22)

But the problem that Wright has himself introduced is so to tie God's authority to the inbreaking kingdom that the authority of Scripture becomes a "sub-branch" of such topics as mission, transformation, ultimate hope, and so forth. How does this follow? Where is the notion, expressed in both Testaments, that God's word is forever settled in heaven, that the grass withers and the flower fades, but the word of the Lord endures forever? Is *God's* authority diminished when mission is not accomplished? Is this not rather an instance of God's authority being undiminished, but liable to be manifest now in judgment? Why then should Scripture's authority be diminished, demoted to a "sub-branch" of mission? True, God's authority is *displayed* in his kingly advance to reconcile rebels to himself and bring in the new heaven and the new earth, but it is not to be *identified* with this king-dominion. God's authority is also displayed in the courts of heaven; it is displayed in his sweeping, universal sovereignty (which Wright, as I've said, does not develop in connection with Scripture). In both Testaments, the authority of Scripture is sometimes tied to God's reliability in both word and deed—and when in word, to God's reliability in speech, and thus to his truthfulness, whether he is believed or not. God's authority is chimerical and deceptive if he himself is not reliable: the point is developed at length by the prophets and by some of the psalmists. By the same token, insofar as God's authority is displayed in Scripture, the authority of Scripture is chimerical and deceptive if it is not reliable. It is certainly true that God's word is often described in performative categories, to use a term much loved by speech-act theorists: God's word *accomplishes* things, and these things are regularly bound up with God's redemptive purposes, and thus with the kingdom. But God's word is also often described in truth categories (which of course are also allowed by speech-act theorists), which inform, instruct, reform, teach, and so forth, and this word is true and reliable (as God himself is, for God discloses himself by this means) whether people accept it or not.

Sadly, this more comprehensive way of looking at things, clear from the very surface of Scripture, is lost when God's authority is tied exclusively to the notion of kingdom, understood to be advancing through the four acts of Scripture, and still advancing today in the fifth act. We have already seen how the actors in the fourth act, Jesus and the apostolic church, habitually speak of antecedent Scripture in more comprehensive terms than Wright deploys, including terms of truth, God speaking, the fact that Scripture cannot be broken, and the like—the kind of ways that Jesus himself spoke of Scripture.[45] Shouldn't those who live in the fifth act adopt the same stance toward Scripture as that held by Jesus himself, the star of the fourth act?

Wright's moves have made the authority of Scripture a "sub-branch" of mission and related themes. I'm afraid that this is of a piece with other moves he has made. At the risk of using theological labels as mere slogans, we might put it this way: as his understanding of justification, developed elsewhere, has in effect elevated ecclesiology over soteriology, so his linking of God's authority with the kingdom of rescue and transformation has in effect elevated ecclesiology over bibliology. It is better to recognize that God does not speak of his word and its authority as a sub-branch of mission or of anything else. Instead, he declares, "This is the one I esteem: he who is humble and contrite in spirit, and trembles at my word" (Isa. 66:2).

---

[45]The classic on this point remains John Wenham, *Christ and the Bible*, 3d ed. (Grand Rapids: Baker, 1994).

8

Review of Jeffrey L. Sheler, *Is the Bible True? How Modern Debates and Discoveries Affirm the Essence of the Scriptures*

Jeffery L. Sheler. *Is the Bible True? How Modern Debates and Discoveries Affirm the Essence of the Scriptures*. San Francisco: HarperSanFrancisco, 1999. 288 pp.

Rightly Dividing Biblical History: A Journalist Makes a Case for Scripture's Reliability

Jeffery Sheler's book is not interested in ascertaining whether Jesus is "the way, the truth, and the life." But Sheler does want to learn "whether he might have said he is." His book is about the history in the Bible, about the evidence and arguments used to verify that history, about what can be proved, and with what probability. Ultimately, though, it is this commitment to historical inquiry that gives *Is the Bible True?* a certain apologetic value.

Sheler, a religion writer at *U.S. News & World Report* for the last nine years and a correspondent for *Religion & Ethics News Weekly* on PBS, is not a biblical scholar, but he has read widely from most sides of any debate he treats. He brings to his task an admirable ability to write lucid prose without technical jargon. An ordained

Reprint of D. A. Carson, review of Jeffery L. Sheler, *Is the Bible True? How Modern Debates and Discoveries Affirm the Essence of the Scriptures*, Christianity Today 44, no. 6 (May 22, 2000): 87–88.

elder at National Presbyterian Church in Washington, D.C., Sheler remains true to his journalistic trade and presents his arguments as the dispassionate observer, the evenhanded evaluator.

The book is divided into six parts, beginning with a discussion of canon, as well as authorship and source theories. Sheler tends toward conservative conclusions without being dogmatic. For example, Moses himself is at the core of the Pentateuch, even if some later editors updated some strands of these books. The canonical Gospels are formally anonymous, but the early patristic evidence assigning the traditional authors to them cannot be ignored.

Regarding the disputed Pauline authorship of the Pastoral Epistles, he notes: "Modern scholarship remains divided over these questions. But barring firm proof to the contrary—proof that to date has not been shown to exist—it seems reasonable to take the letters at their word as having come from the hand, or at least the lips [under the assumption of an amanuensis], of Paul."

Sheler also attempts to sort out in what sense the Bible is "history," admittedly "theological history." He cuts a swath between fundamentalism and historical skepticism. Though he treats all sides fairly, Sheler concludes: "When biblical writings that are unambiguously historical in their intent are critically examined, they consistently show themselves to be remarkably dependable"—a conclusion with which an extraordinarily broad group of scholars can agree. Sheler then reviews biblical archaeology, including a brief history of the discipline and surveys of one or more sites connected with various periods (the patriarchs, the exodus, the conquest, the monarchy, the days of Jesus). He notes that at most of the sites, archaeological discoveries support the Bible's historical claims, such as the famous ninth-century BC Dan inscription that refers to the dynasty of David and distinguishes the kingdoms of Israel and Judah.

On the other hand, Sheler argues that the biblical account of the exodus may be a typological telescoping of many small exoduses, each archaeologically unrecoverable. (Alternatively, he concedes, there may be more to discover.)

Sheler also carefully records the scholarly debate surrounding the fall of Jericho and the conquest of Canaan, concluding: "Despite all the remaining uncertainties, however, most scholars would agree that there is a historical core behind the biblical stories of Israel's emergence in Canaan."

Sheler follows this with a discussion of the Dead Sea Scrolls, giving a sensible introduction and evaluation for people who know nothing about them.

The historical Jesus is the subject of part four. Once more Sheler provides a brief history of scholarly debate, from the so-called "old quest" (so ably criticized by Albert Schweitzer) to the "third quest," which pits the scholars of the (in)famous Jesus Seminar against their mainline and conservative counterparts. This third quest is in part a conflict over the correct "background" against which the New Testament documents are to be read. This survey is probably the best in the book. Sheler gives brief biographies of the Jesus Seminar's three leading lights (Robert Funk, Marcus Borg, and John Dominic Crossan), and two of their most influential opponents (John Meier and N. T. Wright). After laying out the conflicting arguments, Sheler concludes,

> The gospel portrait of Jesus of Nazareth appears far clearer, more consistent, and more credible than contentious scholarly discourse often makes it out to be. The Jesus of the gospels emerges as a bearer of hope, a doer and sayer of the unexpected. His message and miracle [*sic*] correspond. And the unknown man from Galilee becomes less of a stranger to our times. . . . The New Testament . . . bears strong and credible witness to two important pieces of historical data: an empty tomb and reports of post-resurrection appearances of the risen Christ. That, of course, falls far short of proving as incontestable objective fact the gospel claim that Jesus of Nazareth was raised from the dead. But it is no small thing. It establishes a credible historical foundation—a basis beyond mere fantasy or wishful thinking—upon which a resurrection faith can stand.

Unfortunately, Sheler then looks at the dubious "Bible Code" theory of Michael Drosnin and others, a part of the book that should have been omitted—though one can understand why a journalist would want to tackle it, for the theory has attracted a lot of attention. Certainly Sheler is to be thanked for his popular-level debunking of this nonsense.

For his concluding chapter, Sheler tries to answer the question, "Is the Bible true?" The last paragraphs break the tone of detached coolness that characterizes much of the book. He reminds his readers that something deeper still is going on in the Bible: "It is not merely to ancient history that the Bible directs our attention. It is to the God who is active in history, redeeming it and infusing it with meaning, that the Scriptures ultimately point."

For Christians, there are better light introductions to almost all of the topics Sheler discusses. On particular points, Sheler's volume can appear thin next to more rigorous treatments: on the Jesus Seminar, for instance, one might read *Jesus Under Fire: Modern Scholarship Reinvents the Historical Jesus* (1995), edited by Michael J. Wilkens and J. P. Moreland. Nor will this book satisfy the new wave of students whose view of history has been heavily influenced by postmodern epistemology: Sheler's book is an eminently "modern" approach.

Still, I would happily recommend this book—indeed, give it away as part of a responsible Christian witness—to the substantial numbers of people who know virtually nothing about Christianity or the Bible except for the esoteric and way-out things they have picked up from the more skeptical media. Wilkens and Moreland are far too technical for them, and a standard New Testament introduction would put them to sleep. This book might help them question the dogmatic agnosticism they have imbibed and leave them open for more serious conversations.

9

Review of Alan G. Padgett and Patrick R. Keifert, eds., *But Is It All True? The Bible and the Question of Truth*

Alan G. Padgett and Patrick R. Keifert, eds. *But Is It All True? The Bible and the Question of Truth*. Grand Rapids: Eerdmans, 2006. xii + 175 pp.

This book finds its origin in a 1999 colloquium at Luther Seminary. It is dedicated to Donald Juel *in memoriam* (d. 2003), since he helped to organize that colloquium. When he moved to Princeton, the project and the conversation partners "broadened and became more diverse" (p. 12).

The diversity of the book is both its strength and its weakness. The nine contributors include three systematicians, one Old Testament scholar, one professor of biblical theology, two professors of philosophy or philosophical theology, one professor of preaching, and one professor of religion. They lie across a sweep of theological stances as broad as a list of a mere nine essayists allows. The diversity makes for an interesting read if the subject itself is on one's radar screen, but the flip side is that this volume does not as a whole launch a new program or strike out in a new direction. Readers who are already familiar with many of the other contributions of these writers will not find anything very surprising or particularly innovative here (the blurbs on the back cover notwithstanding). The strength of the book is simply the way it brings together in one slim volume some of the diversity views (that we all know are out there) on how the Bible is "true."

Dennis T. Olson ("Truth and Torah: Reflections on Rationality and the Pentateuch" [pp. 16–33]) surveys the notion of truth in the Pentateuch. Hebrew אמת ('emet) "signifies both relational trust as well as a more objective testing for truth" (p. 20). This definition, in both its parts, strikes me as odd, focusing as it does on the mental/emotional processes connected with the word rather than on the meaning of the word itself. The word is bound up with reliability or faithfulness, and of course such reliability calls forth "relational trust"—but 'emet surely cannot be said to "signify" relational trust. When what is "reliable" is a report or a prophecy or the like, then surely if it is "reliable" we simply say, in English, that it is true or that it is telling the truth, not that it signifies "a more objective testing for truth." Inevitably we are warned that human beings in the Pentateuch "are given only partial glimpses of the truth of God's promises." Doubtless that statement is true, so true that I know of no one who would question it.

In the shortest contribution of the volume, Nicholas Wolterstorff ("True Words" [pp. 34–43]) offers the best opening sentence in the collection: "In the first part of this chapter I will argue that truth is *not* the main issue when we are dealing with Scripture; in the second part I will suggest that truth *is* the main issue" (p. 34). In substance, however, this chapter is very largely a convenient summary of his important book *Divine Discourse: Philosophical Reflections of the Claim that God Speaks* (Cambridge: Cambridge University Press, 1995). Instead of thinking of the Bible in terms of revelation, Wolterstorff proposes thinking of the Bible in terms of speech, that is, as discourse, with a variety of speech-acts possible, and on the assumption of "double-agency discourse" (p. 36). He acknowledges that this biblical speech includes assertions that are true or false, but because of the complexity and diversity of speech forms in the Bible he argues that we need a new and more complex definition of truth. "I suggest that the root notion of truth is that of something's measuring up—that is, measuring up in being or excellence" (p. 42). In this sense, he argues, truth is indeed "the fundamental issue to be raised concerning Scripture. Do the words of Scripture measure up?" (p. 43). The standard by which we measure such "measuring up" is not worked out. What is fairly clear, however, is that Wolterstorff loves to reflect on the many instances where "true" is used in Scripture of something *other* than propositions (e.g., "in the New Testament writings ascribed to John" [p. 42]) and offers almost no reflection on the many instances where "true" and cognates are used in Scripture of propositions.

Ben C. Ollenburger ("Pursing the Truth of Scripture: Reflections on Wolterstorff's *Divine Discourse*" [pp. 44–65]) is essentially a critical review. Among Ollenburger's "puzzlements" (his word) in reading *Divine Discourse* are Wolterstorff's "almost exclusive attention to sentences" (p. 50) with almost no reflection on discourse or diverse literary genres and his treatment of authorial intentions (Ollenburger follows Meir Sternberg's distinction between external and internal intentions). Ollenburger has serious reservations about the relationships between the first and second hermeneutics as Wolterstorff constructs them, and he details how none of Wolterstorff's examples of whether Scripture "measures up" is an assertion.

Mark I. Wallace ("The Rule of Love and the Testimony of the Spirit in Contemporary Hermeneutics" [pp. 66–85]) says that rule-governed approaches to biblical exegesis and criticism, such as the criterion of dissimilarity or the criterion of multiple attestation, have a certain limited use in making responsible decisions about what is authentic in the Gospels. (He seems unaware of the very substantial discussion on such criteria that has taken place since the work of Norman Perrin a quarter of a century ago.) But the results from such rule-governed approaches "fall short of actually construing the religious truth of the biblical witness—that is, what the Bible means in its fullness and integrity as a compelling theological witness to life's fundamental questions" (p. 69). He therefore promotes Augustine's hermeneutical principle: the aim must be to construe "the meaning of the biblical texts in a manner consistent with a life of charity and other respects" (p. 71). Following an example from Wolterstorff, Wallace asserts that in the light of Augustine's principle, the imprecatory psalms must be taken as negative examples: they are divine speech-acts only in the sense that they are "vivid (if sadly misguided) expressions of pent-up fury against those who make war against God's people" (p. 71). Wallace wants to make Augustine's thought so absolute that it enables us to take steps Augustine would never dream of, including discounting or marginalizing those parts of Scripture that do not contribute to this principle of love as Wallace understands it. With Stephen Davis (see below), Wallace agrees that the Gospel stories purport "to tell us what happened in the life and ministry of Jesus" (p. 75), but the point is surely not the conclusions drawn by "realist theologians" (p. 75) but the manner in which these accounts do or do not contribute to love. Wallace concludes his chapter with one or two examples of "how the love ideal works in an actual reading of the biblical texts," including homosexuality and violence. Regarding the former, he acknowledges "that the Bible is generally negative toward homosexuality" (p. 78) but argues that the love ideal drives us toward full acceptance.

More or less at the other end of the spectrum, Stephen T. Davis, "What Do We Mean When We Say, 'The Bible is True'?" [pp. 86–103]) operates out of a broadly confessional evangelical stance. Answers to the question raised by his title, he says, must accomplish three things: they must recognize that human beings are "verbivores," they must explain why Christians read the Bible as opposed to any other book (whether *The Iliad* or *The Koran* or *The Critique of Pure Reason*), and they "must explain why Christians take the Bible to be normative and authoritative" (p. 87). So what do we mean when we say that the Bible is true? Part of the answer, he argues, is that we commit ourselves to believe its statements, accepting their propositional content, and as a result "trust" them or "lay ourselves open" to them (p. 89). That is surely right, but still slightly shy of the heart of the issue for many Christians: they "accept the propositional content" and lay themselves open to it because they think that such content conforms to reality. Davis goes on to offer useful comments on what "inerrancy" might and might not mean and criticizes Wolterstorff at one or two crucial points (including how Wolterstorff handles the canonical Gospels [p. 97]). His criticism of Mark Wallace is more fundamental (pp. 96–101): Wallace's central difficulty is that by elevating an external principle such as Augustine's to absolute control, he has adopted "what is not a characteristic of the Bible but rather a result of an interaction between the Bible and a reader," and as a result this hermeneutic "does little to preserve any sense of the Bible's uniqueness" (p. 97).

Alan G. Padgett ("'I Am the Truth': An Understanding of Truth from Christology for Scripture" [pp. 104–14]) announces, "This chapter is about a confession, not a definition" (p. 104). Further:

> I do not seek a definition of truth, although I will mention some in passing. Rather, I want to stand under the truth and receive (understand) what light it brings. I do not seek to define, encompass, and regulate what truth is. Rather, I seek an understanding of truth that implies or suggests many working definitions, spread across many academic disciplines, in whatever art or science we find ourselves at work for the love of truth. I am forced to use the word "understanding" because I think it may be less confusing than other words; but my use of it here is idiosyncratic. By an "understanding of the truth" I mean something less than a theory of truth, less even than a definition of truth. In my work on epistemology I have come to the conclusion that the differing disciplines of academe serve different interests, arise out of different traditions of inquiry, and have different rationalities. (p. 106)

Although that sounds bracingly expansive and inclusive, I am not quite sure how a word such as "understanding" will prove "less confusing" if Padgett's use of it is "idiosyncratic." I would have thought that idiosyncratic usage of a term almost guarantees confusion. Nor am I quite certain why Padgett says he does not seek a definition of truth, when on the next page he proposes his own definition: "To begin with, I will simply propose that we understand truth as *the mediated disclosure of being* (or reality). Sometimes that truth will be mediated through everyday experience, or common sense, sometimes through the specifics of propositions" (p. 106; emphasis original). Padgett says there is a place for "true words"; he has been "impressed by" Alston's realist conception of truth. "We must not . . . wholly ignore true statements" (p. 109). But this "minimalist-realist" conception of truth must fit "into the larger understanding of truth" that he advances in the rest of this chapter, namely, that Christ is the truth and the Bible is the book of Christ. "This implies that the truth of Scripture is about our relationship with Christ, for a personal truth requires a personal relationship" (p. 111). Thus the Bible is "true when it mediates this personal truth to us" (p. 111). As for "the question of historical reference," the answer given by theologians as diverse as Ernst Troeltsch and N. T. Wright must be heeded: at least some "'symbols' or theological truth disclosed in the text demand a real historical event behind them" (p. 112)—although when the sweep runs from Troeltsch to Wright, I am not sure this is very clarifying. Even Bultmann hung on to his "das."

David Bartlett ("Preaching the Truth" [pp. 115–29]) begins well with a question asked by a character in one of Frederick Buechner's novels: "There's just one reason, you know, why I come dragging in there every Sunday. I want to find out if the whole thing's true. Just *true.* . . . That's all. Either it is, or it isn't, and that's the one question you avoid like death" (p. 115). The six brief sections that follow offer quasi-independent reflections that circle around the topic but are unlikely to satisfy this Buechner character. For instance, Bartlett tells us that to know truth is to know God, not to know about God (p. 116). Why the disjunction? The next section reminds us that Hans Frei suggests we read Scripture best "as a history-like narrative" (p. 118). Frei might well have believed the extratextual referentiality of this narrative, but "other interpreters of Frei and of Scripture" are happy to disown any extratextual referentiality in this "history-like narrative," finding it sufficient to rejoice over "its own internal coherence and power without worrying at all about its extratextual referents" (p. 118)—an astonishing elitist and intellectualist position that assumes the Bible tells us we are saved and find fullness of life by entertaining ideas, not by Christ himself. Isn't another word for a "history-like narrative" without any necessary extratextual referentiality a "novel"? Like Padgett, Bartlett prefers the path of open-endedness about these things: "My sense is that we neither ignore historical-critical issues nor harp on them" (p. 119). How that will help the preacher working on next Sunday's sermon, I have no idea. The remaining sections include some useful asides, while the eight-hundred-pound gorilla in the room is carefully left unaddressed.

From homiletics to education: Patrick R. Keifert ("Biblical Truth and Theological Education: A Rhetorical Strategy" [pp. 130–43]) is the most jargon-filled essay in the volume. A lot of his focus seems to be bound up with the interactions with the Bible that take place in the Christian community. At the heart of Keifert's essay is this: "My initial answer to the question 'When we say that the Bible is true, what do we mean?' is quite simply this: the Bible is true insofar as it makes possible the understanding of God truly" (p. 138). The methods "that appreciate its truthfulness are many. They include ascetic practices such as meditation and contemplation, singing, dancing, practices of social action on behalf of the vulnerable and poor, and the playful interaction of critical human understanding with text and tradition" (p. 138). The last line, of course, as Keifert acknowledges, owes a great deal to Gadamer.

The final essay, by Ellen Charry ("Walking in the Truth: On Knowing God" [pp. 144–69]), is perhaps the most creative contribution of the volume. In one sense, it does not belong in a volume with the title of this book, for Charry's focus is on how Scripture functions rather than on what it is. She begins with an overarching survey of two millennia of church history and its three "epistemological crises": the first was the West's recovery of Aristotle in the twelfth and thirteenth centuries and the move from sapiential theology to theory, the second was the rise of empiricism in the seventeenth century, and the third is the postmodern turn. Much of the rest of this chapter probes these developments in more detail, with reference to specific thinkers and with thoughtful reflection on the theological changes that have ensued. Something can be said for this schema, I am sure, but the exceptions that thoughtful readers will want to mention are so frequent and so powerful that the antithetical nature of Charry's exposition cries out to be challenged. Augustine, for instance, lies at the heart of the "sapiential" period in which, allegedly, all the focus was on the moral-psycho-social ends of truth, truth to make us happy and good, and not a matter of technical skills in the method of disputation, not truth versus error. Yet in his famous Letter 82 to Jerome, Augustine carefully lays out the "truthfulness" of Scripture *not* in sapiential/functional terms, but in terms that insist on its freedom from error, unlike the writings of any other, including Jerome (see 82.3–4). The example of Augustine is easily multiplied. Yet what is attractive about Charry's essay, despite its programmatic oversimplifications, is that because she focuses on what the Bible *can* do in changing people and on its proper functions and transformative power, she exposes the cultural/ecclesiological/spiritual/moral sterility of approaches to the Bible that are never more than intellectually exciting but that have neither divine authority nor the ring of conscience-binding truth. Unfortunately, because she does not tie her analysis to what the Bible is and thus to how she would herself address the controlling subject of this volume under review, she offers little guidance for the way ahead.

In short, this is a useful survey of some of the contemporary options. I cannot bring this review to an end without an amusing observation: without exception, these writers are embarrassed, to a greater or lesser degree, by assertions, by propositions. There are many statements of the sort, "Well, of course, we concede that there are some assertions in Scripture that are either true or untrue, but the really important element in Scripture is Christ as the truth (or the personal nature of truth, or the way Scripture functions to disclose the true God, or whatever)." There was not a single statement of the sort, "Well, of course, Christ is presented as the truth in the Gospel of John, but there are many propositions and assertions not only in John but throughout the Bible that must be thought of as true or false. We cannot long argue about what we mean by saying the Bible is 'true' unless we wrestle with the Bible's countless propositions." In other words, this book abounds in assertions about how unimportant assertions are.

10

Review of Roland Boer, *Rescuing the Bible*

Roland Boer. *Rescuing the Bible*. Oxford: Blackwell, 2007. vi + 177 pp.

Roland Boer, Reader in the Centre for Comparative Literature and Cultural Studies at Monash University in Australia, provides us with an argument in six theses, each of which then takes up one of the six substantive chapters of the book.

First thesis: "Since the old program of secularism has run aground, I propose a new secularism that sees the entwinement of religion and secularism as necessary and beneficial, that reads the Bible in light of theological suspicion, denounces the abuse of the Bible and fosters liberating readings and uses." Boer begins with a handful of definitions. He draws his understanding of what is secular from the Latin *saeculum*: "It designates a system of thought, indeed a way of living that draws its terms purely from this age and from this world" (p. 8). The problem, Boer asserts, is that such a notion of secularism easily slips into meaning that it is opposed to supernatural religion, at which point it becomes equivalent to atheism. But this antireligious overtone is "derivative and not crucial" to the understanding of secularism (p. 9). As for Boer's understanding of "biblical studies," the operative catchwords to adopt are "science" and "reason." "A discipline is 'scien-

Reprint of D. A. Carson, review of Roland Boer, *Rescuing the Bible*, *Review of Biblical Literature* (July 19, 2008), online: http://bookreviews.org/pdf/6394_6883.pdf. © Society of Biblical Literature. Roland Boer is research professor at the University of Newcastle, Australia.

tific' and operates according to principles of 'reason' if it makes use of evidence and develops its hypotheses and theories on the basis of such evidence, not on any divine revelation. As for the Bible, even theology and biblical studies must be scientific in order to be disciplines of any value" (p. 10). Boer insists that, if lecturers in biblical studies in a college preach from Scripture in a service, it only shows "how much the old program of secularism is flawed" (p. 11). These and other tensions, such as the rise and popularity of many "spiritualities," Boer lists to demonstrate the failure of the old secularism. "People hunger for spiritual realities, they say, for a deeper spiritual truth. As politely as possible, let me say that this is rubbish. Rather, the rise of spirituality is a major—I hesitate to write 'first'—sign of the tensions within secularism and the beginnings of post-secularism" (p. 18). The problems are compounded by the return of religion to prominence in the wake of 9/11: Boer does not hesitate to list a *bête-noir* or two whom he treats with exquisite scorn: Pat Robertson, Jerry Falwell, and, in his native Australia, Peter Costello. So what we need, he says, is a new secularism nicely summarized in five points: it recognizes that religion and secularism are inevitably entwined and asserts that this is to the benefit of both; it operates with a "theological suspicion" that treats the Bible neither as a sacred text nor "merely" as profane literature but is suspicious of both secular and religious (ab)uses of the Bible and denounces both, so as, wherever possible, to foster "emancipatory uses of the Bible," seeking a politics of alliance (p. 23). By "(ab)use" of texts Boer means "the use of texts in order to dominate, oppress and denigrate others" (p. 27)—not least in the cases where the text itself is denigrating others (as one of several examples, Boer offers "When to Stone Your Whole Family" [Deut. 13:6–10]). What Boer wants is an alliance between these new secularists, so committed, and believers of the left (as opposed to "reactionaries" and "fundamentalists"). Much of the rest of the book unpacks this agenda.

Second thesis:

> Since the religious left has been marginalized and has had the Bible stolen from it, and since the secular left is on the rise, in order to rescue the Bible we need a politics of alliance between the religious left and the old secular left. I call this alliance the "worldly left," one that is as wise as serpents and as innocent as doves.

The "religious left"—people in the past such as Wilberforce and those in synagogues and churches today who are passionate about social justice—are on the defensive. Boer claims that the religious right have "stolen the Bible" from the left, claiming that they alone are "Biblebased." Boer mentions those who are caught up in discussions of the "rapture index," along with the Hillsong crowd of Sydney and the Planetshakers of Melbourne; by contrast, he says, the religious left is small and weak. The secular left is experiencing a slight resurgence. These two forces of the left must combine their strengths. For those who are of the religious left, unlike Boer himself, inspiration can be found in the "groundbreaking work" (p. 43) of Norman Gottwald, who has "provided a road-map for the social and economic formation of ancient Israel" (p. 43), and the studies of Richard Horsley, who consistently attempts to interpret not only Jesus but nascent Christianity within the social matrix of a brutal Roman Empire. By combining the influence of the religious left and the secular left into one social force, Boer seeks to establish a powerful "worldly left"—"a way of thinking and living that draws its terms purely from this age and from this world" (p. 46), even while the word "world" simultaneously conjures up other connotations, "such as experience, maturity, and indeed worldly wisdom" (p. 46).

Third thesis: "Despite the best efforts to impose dominant viewpoints on the Bible, through canonization and interpretation, it remains an unruly and fractious collection of texts. For this reason it is a multi-valent collection, both folly to the rich and scandal to the poor." Following Ernst Bloch, Boer argues that the Bible "has an uncanny knack of undermining any position one might want to take" (p. 51). On the one hand, if the church sides with those who feel it necessary to go to war, it faces texts about loving enemies (Matt. 5:44) and turning the other cheek (Luke 6:29); on the other hand, if the church wishes to encourage peace, love, and understanding, it nevertheless reads that Jesus did not come to bring peace but a sword (Matt. 10:34). Bloch puzzled over the fact that the Bible is claimed by *both* sides of many of the conflicts he examined. His own solution was to assign the more reactionary texts, those that apparently support power and authority, to a later overlay. Boer prefers to learn from Antonio Gramsci, who argued that any hegemony is inherently unstable—a point picked up and developed by Jacques Derrida and other postmodern thinkers. Similarly, Boer argues, the very act of using the Bible to support any authority or hegemony is intrinsically unstable and calls forth countervailing voices. Boer appeals to what he judges to be later and domesticating additions to Ecclesiastes (so here he is closer to Bloch than he admits) or to ecclesiastical interpretations of the Song of Songs. His point is to assert the multivalence of Scripture and thus to undermine appeals to the Bible's authority by Christian Zionists, by those who reject homosexuality by appealing to the Bible, and so forth.

Fourth thesis:

The Bible is too important and too multi-valent a text to be left to the religious right. Thus it is necessary to take sides with the liberatory side of the
Bible, and in doing so we denounce the reactionary use and abuse of the
Bible, for imperial conquest, oppression of all types, and the support of
privilege and wealth.

Here Boer surveys a number of issues from an unyielding left position that heart-
ily avoids any nuance or suggestion that his opponents may occasionally have
a point—the war in Iraq, political visions articulated by a John Howard or a
Condoleeza Rice, (un)intelligent design, and so forth—laced with an array of
critical judgments (e.g., "no reputable biblical scholar believes that" Moses existed
[p. 83]). The right thing to do is to undermine all these stances by choosing those
options from Boer's multivalent Bible that agree with Boer—and, where necessary, simply by contradicting the Bible.

Fifth thesis: "Taking the side of liberation, we also need to recover the tradition
of revolutionary readings of the Bible." His personal favorites, Boer asserts, are
Thomas Müntzer, Gerrard Winstanley and the Diggers, and Camilo Torres.

Sixth thesis: "The Bible is one source for a political myth for the worldly left, a
political myth that, while keeping in mind the perpetual need for theological suspicion, condemns oppression, imagines a better society and draws deeply on the
mythic images of rebellious chaos." Boer acknowledges that in Marxist critiques
of oppression there is already "a deeply biblical current running" (p. 129). Boer
wants to strengthen this by fostering a hermeneutical, theological suspicion that
is analogous to the Marxist practice of ideological suspicion. Inevitably, then, he
wants to lean on Amos and some of the early chapters of Isaiah, on the exodus
call "let my people go" (Ex. 5:1), and on images of collective living in the early
chapters of Acts. Finally, since the Bible draws many links between chaos and
rebellion—and this rebellion is cast both "against God and against rulers who
claim to be appointed by God" (p. 146)—it is worth reappropriating the value
of chaos. Korah becomes a hero, and the attempt to squash chaos and produce
order is nothing other than "a desperate effort to overcome the threat of revolution" (p. 149).

This book, a fascinating mix of dogmatic left-wing self-righteousness com-
bined with rich and scathing condescension toward all who are even a tad less
left than the author, is rich in unintended irony. Boer cannot see how implausible
his arguments become. While nominally allowing "religious" people to believe in

the supernatural so long as they support his left-wing agenda and join forces with him in a "worldly" secularism, what he says about the Bible and about biblical scholarship is so blatantly committed to philosophical naturalism and historical minimalism that even the most mild supernaturalism is ridiculed: no allowance can be made for divine revelation, anyone who thinks Moses existed is not really a scholar, biblical studies can be called "scientific" only if the scholars themselves do not preach, and so forth. Boer consistently damns everyone on the right by ridiculing the obvious targets, but probably he would not appreciate it if a counterpart on the right ridiculed those on the left by skewering Joseph Stalin and Pol Pot. It turns out that Boer wants to "rescue" the Bible not only from what people on the right say that it means but from what the Bible itself says, for whenever the Bible, in all its multivalence, disagrees with Boer's vision of the *summum bonum*, it is to be undermined, set aside, and mocked—not even wrestled with. Readers are repeatedly told that those nasty right-wingers have "stolen" the Bible. Boer never considers the possibility that quite a few left-wingers have simply abandoned the Bible, leaving the terrain open for those who at least take it seriously. What will satisfy Boer, it seems, is not the liberation of the Bible but the liberation of the Bible from any agenda he considers right-wing, so that it can be locked in servitude to a left-wing agenda. Boer's dismissive arguments to prove the Bible is hopelessly multivalent—a commonplace among many modern and postmodern readers today—are spectacularly unconvincing because he does not interact with any serious literature (and there is two thousand years' worth of such literature) that argues, with various degrees of success, how the Bible *does* hang together. But perhaps this is not too surprising from an author who cherishes chaos precisely because chaos undermines *God's* authority—and all authority save Boer's must be overthrown. I think that many biblical writers would call that choice idolatry. At the end of the day, Boer is trying to rescue the Bible from God.

Permissions

Chapter 1 is taken from *The New Bible Commentary*, 4th ed., edited by Gordon J. Wenham, J. Alex Motyer, Donald A. Carson, and R. T. France. Copyright © 1994 by Inter-Varsity Press, UK. Used by permission of Inter-Varsity Press, Norton Street, Nottingham NG7 3HR, UK. And by permission of InterVarsity Press, PO Box 1400, Downers Grove, IL 60515, USA. www.ivpress.com.

Chapter 2 is taken from *Hermeneutics, Authority, and Canon*, edited by D. A. Carson and John D. Woodbridge. Copyright © 1983 D. A. Carson and John D. Woodbridge. Used by permission of Wipf & Stock Publishers, 199 West 8th Avenue, Suite 32, Eugene, OR 97401.

Chapter 3 is taken from *Scripture and Truth*, edited by D. A. Carson and John D. Woodbridge. Pages 65–95, 368–75. Copyright © 1983 D. A. Carson and John D. Woodbridge. Used by permission of Baker Publishing Group, P.O. Box 6287, Grand Rapids, MI 49516.

Chapter 4 is taken from *Scripture and Truth*, edited by D. A. Carson and John D. Woodbridge. Pages 115–42, 376–81. Copyright © 1983 D. A. Carson and John D. Woodbridge. Used by permission of Baker Publishing Group, P.O. Box 6287, Grand Rapids, MI 49516.

Chapter 5 is taken from *Dein Wort ist die Wahrheit: Beiträge zu einer schriftgemäßen Theologie* (Festschrift for Gerhard Maier), edited by Eberhard Hahn, Rolf Hille, Heinz-Werner Neudorfer. Pages 97–111. Copyright © 1997 SCM R. Brockhaus. Used by permission of SCM-Verlag GmbH & Co. KG, Bodenborn 43, 58452 Witten, Germany.

Chapter 6 is taken from *Journal of the Evangelical Theological Society* 26 (1983): 337–67. Copyright © 1983 D. A. Carson. Used by permission of the Evangelical Theological Society.

Chapter 7 is taken from *Trinity Journal* 27 (2006): 1–62. Copyright © 2006 *Trinity Journal*, Trinity Evangelical Divinity School, 2065 Half Day Road, Deerfield, IL 60015. Used by permission of *Trinity Journal.*

Chapter 8 is taken from *Christianity Today*, May 22, 2000, 87–88. Copyright © 2000 D. A. Carson. Used by permission of the author.

Chapter 9 is taken from *Review of Biblical Literature* 9 (2007): 44–49. Online: http://bookreviews.org/pdf/5224 5502.pdf. Copyright © 2007 Society of Biblical Literature.

Chapter 10 is taken from *Review of Biblical Literature,* July 19, 2008. Online: http://bookreviews.org/pdf/6394_6883.pdf. Copyright © 2008 Society of Biblical Literature.

Subject Index

Abraham, 20, 22, 25, 140, 214, 252, 259, 265, 279

accommodation. *See* Scripture: accommodation of

"analogy of the faith," 46, 144, 146–47, 182, 192

Bible. *See* Scripture

biblical theology, 19, 87, 114, 116–19, 144–47

Buddhism, 24

canon. *See* Scripture: canon

church history. *See* historical theology

common sense realism, 69–73

deduction, 80–81, 204–5

epistemology, 35–37, 96–105, 177–78, 179, 185–91, 219, 292, 306, 310

evangelicalism, 56–59, 61–63, 66, 70, 73–77, 108, 267

exegesis, 40–53, 76–77, 92, 99–100, 118–19, 144–47

faith and practice (as opposed to history and science), 62, 67–69, 203, 224, 234–35

God
   doctrine of, 19–21
   sovereignty of, 51
   See also Scripture: as the word of God

hermeneutics, 37–53. *See also* Scripture: genres in

"new hermeneutic," 35, 38–40, 97–105, 112
   history of, 37–40
   principles, 40–53
   propositions, 82, 92–97, 128, 201, 220, 226, 308, 310–11, 313

historical theology, 144–47
   early church, 112–14, 181
   importance of, 51, 73
   limitation of, 73
   See also Scripture: history of the doctrine of

Holy Spirit
   as the agent of God's revelation (inspiration), 21, 23, 31–32, 186, 198, 202, 219
   as the agent of illumination, 33, 35, 40, 52–53, 96, 105, 192–93, 242
   as the agent of regeneration, 45
   as the agent of sanctification, 240, 250–51
   interpreting references to the, 46

ICBI (International Council on Biblical Inerrancy), 58

induction, 80–81, 204–5

inerrancy. *See* Scripture: inerrancy of

inspiration. *See* Scripture: inspiration of

interpreting the Bible. *See* hermeneutics

Name Index

Abraham, William J., 57n6, 63n23, 80n78, 86–87, 197–209, 222

Achtemeier, Paul J., 75–76, 98–99

Ackerman, James S., 90–91

Allison, Gregg R., 180n

Augustine, 33, 181–82, 309–10, 312

Aune, David E., 94

Banks, R., 163–65

Barr, James, 76, 175, 199–200, 209–18

Barth, Karl, 34, 62–63, 82–83, 240, 241, 247

Bartlett, David L., 311–12

Basinger, David, 105–6

Basinger, Randall, 105–6

Bauer, Walter, 112–13, 120–21, 149

Beegle, Dewey M., 79–80, 220

Berthoud, Pierre, 277

Bloch, Ernst, 317

Blocher, Henri, 273

Bloesch, Donald G., 95–96, 148n127

Boer, Roland, 315–19

Briggs, Charles, 62

Bromiley, Geoffrey W., 95–96

Brown, Harold O. J., 103

Bruce, F. F., 139

Bultmann, Rudolf, 79, 153, 154–55, 161, 217

Burrows, Mark, 189

Cahill, P. Joseph, 99

Calvin, John, 63, 85, 104, 130–31, 184–86, 193, 242, 244–45, 254–55, 274

Charry, Ellen, 312–13

Childs, Brevard S., 103, 213

Clement of Alexandria, 181

Culpepper, R. Alan, 90

Davis, Stephen T., 310

Descartes, René, 191

Dibelius, M., 153

Dodd, C. H., 135

Drane, John W., 138–39

Dunn, James D. G., 57n5, 75, 116, 120–29, 149, 226

Enns, Peter, 255–83

Erasmus, 183

Fish, Stanley, 190

France, R. T., 123, 161

Frei, Hans, 90n105, 295, 311

Gabler, J., 114

Gaussen, Louis, 67, 86–87, 198, 203

Gerhardsson, B., 158

Grudem, Wayne, 95–96, 175

Gundry, Robert H., 93–94

Gunkel, Hermann, 153

Scripture Index